Producing Knowledge, Reproducing Gender

Power, Production and Practice
in Contemporary Ireland

Edited by

PAULINE CULLEN AND MARY P. CORCORAN

UNIVERSITY COLLEGE DUBLIN PRESS

PREAS CHOLÁISTE OLLSCOILE
BHAILE ÁTHA CLIATH
2020

First published 2020
by University College Dublin Press
UCD Humanities Institute
Belfield
Dublin 4
Ireland

www.ucdpress.ie

ISBN 978-1-910820-54-4 pb

Cataloguing in Publication data available from the British Library

*The right of Pauline Cullen and Mary P. Corcoran to be identified
as the editors of this work has been asserted by them*

Typeset in Scotland in Plantin and Fournier by Ryan Shiels
Text design by Lyn Davies
Printed on acid-free paper by CPI Antony Rowe,
Chippenham, Wilshire

Contents

PART II: THE POLITICS OF KNOWLEDGE PRODUCTION
Gender, the State and Civil Society

PART III: GENDER, KNOWLEDGE AND PUBLIC CULTURE

Acknowledgements

We acknowledge the support of the Department of Sociology, Maynooth University, in providing a publication grant towards the production costs of this book. The Irish artist, Eileen O'Sullivan, generously gave permission for the reproduction of her painting *Methods of Understanding* for the cover artwork. We think her image captures the sociological quest to illuminate and reflect on the forces that shape human and specifically women's experience.

The editorial staff at UCD Press, especially Noelle Moran, has been hugely supportive of the project from its inception to publication. We are also grateful to the anonymous referees who reviewed the manuscript. We thank all of our authors for their scholarship and collegiality, and for placing gender and knowledge at the centre of their contributions.

Finally, as this collection goes to press, unprecedented measures adopted to control the COVID-19 pandemic are challenging the very foundations of our social practices including how we care, work, act collectively and produce knowledge with deeply gendered effects. We hope for a post-virus context where gender understood in all its diversity informs analyses of this global crisis.

PAULINE CULLEN & MARY P. CORCORAN
May 2020

Abbreviations

ARC	Abortion Rights Campaign
ASN	Abortion Support Network
BPAS	British Pregnancy Advisory Services
CAO	Central Applications Office
CFA	Chartered Financial Analyst
CORI	Conference of Religious of Ireland
DRHE	Dublin Regional Housing Executive
ECCE	Early Childhood Care and Education
EEC	European Economic Community
EU	European Union
EWL	European Women's Lobby
FE	Further Education
GFC	Global Financial Crisis
GPA	Grade Point Average
HAP	Housing Assistance Payment
HEA	Higher Education Authority
HE	Higher Education
HEI	Higher Education Institution
HR	Human Relations
ICI	Immigrant Council of Ireland
ICT	Information and Communication Technology
IFPA	Irish Family Planning Association
IHREC	Irish Human Rights and Equality Commission
IMO	Irish Medical Organisation
INMO	Irish Nurses and Midwives Organisation
IT	Information Technology
ITC	Information Technology Companies
IWASG	Irish Women's Abortion Support Group
JCJDE	Joint Committee on Justice, Defence and Equality
KIF	Knowledge Intensive Firms
LC	Leaving Certificate
LGBT	Lesbian Gay Bisexual and Transgender (Community)
MEP	Member of the European Parliament
MERJ	Migrants and Ethnic-Minorities for Reproductive Justice
MLA	Member of the Legislative Assembly (Northern Ireland)

NI	Northern Ireland
NGO	Non-Governmental Organisation
NWCI	National Women's Council Ireland
OECD	Organisation for Economic Co-operation and Development
PAHRCA	Participatory Action Human Rights and Capability Approach
PAR	Participatory Action Research
PISA	Programme of International Students Assessment
PLDPA	Protection of Life in Pregnancy Act [2013]
ROSA	For Reproductive Rights, Against Oppression, Sexism and Austerity
RTÉ	Radio Telefis Eireann
RTÉ2	Radio Telefis Eireann (Channel 2)
SALI	Senior Academic Leadership Initiative
SJI	Social Justice Ireland
SPUC	Society for the Protection of Unborn Children
STEM	Science, Technology, Engineering and Mathematics
TALIS	Teaching and Learning International Survey
TG4	Irish language television channel
ToRL	Turn off the Red Light
TUSLA	The Child and Family Agency
UNAIDS	Joint United Nations Programme on HIV/AIDS
WHO	World Health Organisation
WLB	Work-Life Balance

List of Contributors

DR DELMA BYRNE is Assistant Professor at Maynooth University Departments of Sociology and Education. Her research interests focus on the sociology of education and social stratification, and the role of education in shaping life chances over the life-course, including labour market experiences. This body of work cross cuts issues of gender, social class, race/ethnicity/migrant status, and disability.

DR JOHN-PAUL BYRNE is a Postdoctoral researcher with the Hospital Doctor Retention and Motivation (HDRM) project based in the Royal College of Physicians of Ireland. He is a graduate of University College Dublin and Maynooth University. John-Paul is a recipient of the Government of Ireland Postgraduate Scholarship from the Irish Research Council (2012). His research interests lie primarily in the fields of sociology of work, psychosocial work conditions, and medical sociology.

MARY P. CORCORAN is Professor of Sociology in the Department of Sociology, Maynooth University. Her research interests include Irish migration, urban sociology, media, and public culture. Her published works include *A Sociology of Ireland* (co-authored, 2012) and the co-edited volume *Reflections on Crisis: The Role of Public Intellectuals* (2012) which examined the impact of expert knowledge on the framing of the 2008 crisis. As a member of Maynooth University's Academic Council and Governing Authority, she played a leading role in developing the institution's Equality, Diversity, and Intercultural policies.

CATRIONA CROWE is former Head of Special Projects at the National Archives of Ireland. She was Manager of the Census Online Project, which placed the Irish 1901 and 1911 censuses online free to access. She is editor of *Dublin 1911*, published by the Royal Irish Academy in late 2011. She presented the RTÉ documentaries, *Ireland before the Rising*, shown in February 2016, and *Life After the Rising*, shown in January 1919. She is a member of the Royal Irish Academy.

DR PAULINE CULLEN is Lecturer of Sociology and Politics in the Department of Sociology, Maynooth University. Her work examines civil society mobilisation on social justice and gender equality policy at national and European Union level, women's movements, and gender and political representation. She has also worked as a gender expert for advocacy organisations working on gender justice and equality issues. Her work has been published in the *Journal of Civil Society*, *Social Movement Studies*, *Gender Work and Organization*, *Politics & Gender* and *Policy & Society*.

DR RORY HEARNE is an Assistant Professor in Social Policy in the Department of Applied Social Studies at Maynooth University. He is author of *Housing Shock: The Irish Housing Crisis and how to solve it* (2020).

DR SINÉAD KENNEDY is a Marxist-feminist activist and teaches in the English Department at Maynooth University. She has written and commented widely on feminism, popular culture, Irish and European politics, and is currently completing a book on the Eighth Amendment. She is co-editor of *The Abortion Papers Ireland: Volume 2* (2015). She was the National Secretary and co-founder of the Coalition to Repeal the Eighth Amendment.

DR APHRA KERR is Associate Professor in the Department of Sociology at Maynooth University, where she teaches the sociology of media, technology, and digital communication. She is a collaborator of the ADAPT Centre for Digital Content Technology where she works on projects researching data governance and digital privacy and is co-PI on a project on *Gambling and its Social Impact in Ireland*. Aphra's books include *Global Games: Production, Circulation and Policy in the Networked Age* (2017), and she co-edited the games entries in *The International Encyclopaedia of Digital Communication and Society* (2015).

DR MARY P. MURPHY is Associate Professor in the Department of Sociology at Maynooth University. Her research interests include public policy, labour market and social security, power and civil society, and gender. A contributor to national debate, she was a member of the Irish Human Rights and Equality Commission 2013–17 and is currently a member of the Council of State. Recent co-edited books include T*he Irish Welfare state in the 21st Century: Challenges and Changes* (2016) and *Policy Analysis in Ireland* (forthcoming).

DR CLÍONA MURRAY is Lecturer in the School of Education at National University of Ireland Galway, where she teaches sociology of education. Her research interests include teacher identity and inclusive teaching, with a particular focus on educational inequalities. Her current research projects focus on alternative education provision.

DR ANNE O BRIEN is Lecturer in Media Studies at Maynooth University. She has published a number of articles on the representation of women in radio and television, on women workers in creative industries and examined why women leave careers in screen production. She has undertaken research on community media, examining its social benefit and governance needs in funded projects for the Broadcasting Authority of Ireland. She has written about how media produce content on mental ill health, suicide, intimate partner homicide, and domestic violence. Her most recent book *Women, Inequality and Media Work* explores Irish women's gendered experiences of film and television work (2019).

PROFESSOR PAT O CONNOR is Professor Emeritus of Sociology and Social Policy, University of Limerick and Visiting Professor, Geary Institute, UCD. Recent publications include: 'Micro-political practices in higher education: A challenge to excellence as a rationalizing myth?', in *Critical Studies in Education*; 'Creating gendered change in Irish higher education: Is managerial leadership up to the task?', in *Irish Educational Studies*; 'Leadership practices by senior position holders in Higher Educational Research Institutes: Stealth power in action?' in *Leadership*. With Kate White, she is currently editing a book on *Gender and Power in Higher Education in a Globalised World: Where to Now?*

DR CLARE O HAGAN is the Managing Director of The Equality Business, established in response to the growing demand for equality, diversity and inclusion consultancy and training in the Irish and European multinational and higher education sector. Clare holds a PhD from the University of Limerick and is the author of *Complex Inequalities and 'Working Mothers'* (2015).

JOSHUA D. SAVAGE is an Irish Research Council Postgraduate Scholar at Maynooth University, where his PhD work in Sociology focuses on queerness and inclusivity in digital games. He is also a research assistant for Ireland's Network in Play, which was founded as part of Canada's Re-Figuring Innovation in Games (ReFiG) Project. He received the Noma-Reischauer Prize in Japanese Studies from Harvard University in 2003 and has over a decade of teaching experience in Japan, Ireland, and the United States. Alongside his academic career, Joshua is a professional writer, editor, and designer, and his work appears in digital games worldwide.

DR CORINA SHEERIN is Lecturer in Finance at the National College of Ireland. Previously, Dr Sheerin worked as an Assistant Fund Manager at Pioneer Investment Management Ltd. Her research interests are located in the broad areas of gender and organisational studies, with recent studies with a particular focus on gendered spaces, leadership, and inequality led issues. Most recently, Corina won the Emerald Best Paper Award for the *Journal of European Training and Development* (2019) for her paper 'Gender segregated labour spaces and social capital: Does context matter?' as well the Emerald Highly Commended Award for *Gender in Management: An International Review Journal* (2019) for her paper 'Gender performativity and hegemonic masculinity'.

DR PAUL RYAN is an Assistant Professor in the Department of Sociology at Maynooth University. His research and teaching focuses on the intersection between family and personal life, sexuality, and the law. He has recently completed a project, funded by HIV Ireland (with Dr Kathryn McGarry) on 'Sex worker lives under the law: A community engaged study of access to health and justice in Ireland'. Paul's books include *Asking Angela: An Intimate History of Irish Lives* (2012), and *Male Sex Work in the Digital Age: Curated Lives* (2019).

Speaking Gendered Knowledge to Power

Pauline Cullen and Mary P. Corcoran

It is over 30 years since the first anthology providing a sociological inter-pretation of gender in Ireland was published, *Gender in Irish Society* (Curtin, Jackson, and O'Connor (eds) 1987). Much has changed since then, but there is still more to do. Gendered power relations have in recent times been placed centre-stage. Revelations of sexual misconduct have swept through Hollywood, the media more generally, boardrooms and the corridors of power. But while sexual misconduct has erupted into everyday conscious-ness demanding a response, it is business as usual elsewhere. The deep-structured gender divisions and forms of gender knowledge that almost imperceptibly frame our institutions, processes and practices remain largely intact.

In contemporary Ireland gender equality and claims for women's interests have featured in a series of public issues that have exercised the media, political elites, and public opinion. These include, waves of revelations about the fate of unwed mothers and babies subjected to state and church control; women's rights and access to reproductive health care; sexual harass-ment and assault specifically within cultural and creative industries; and the legal systems' approach to rape allegations. Women's political agency has also featured in important ways. A 2014 electoral gender quota delivered an increase in female political representation although women still make up just 22. 5 per cent of parliamentarians. The successful repeal of the ban on abortion in 2018 also indicated important undercurrents of gendered social change. Women from different generations and backgrounds, building on decades of activism, coalesced to secure a successful outcome. An increase in female candidates for local government and European elections in 2019 and the General Election in 2020 can be explained in part by an eagerness on the part of women politicised through campaigning to deepen their political engagement. However, a small increase at best in the percentage of women elected to local and national office indicates the complex ways in which progress on gender equality in politics and policy can advance, or be slowed by structures, cultures, and social practices. Slow progress has been made on reparations for women incarcerated in mother and baby home institutions. The continuing revelations of paternalism coupled with the clear gendered outcomes of marketising health and social care services, indicate the limits of policy responsiveness to women's interests in Ireland.

Women in Ireland have diverse and uneven experiences of gendered social change. Women's experiences are shaped by social class, geographical location, race, ethnicity, migration status, able-bodiedness and sexuality. Social location impacts significantly on opportunities for women in all their diversity to experience status equality, societal and cultural recognition. An intersectional perspective on women's social status is highly revealing. Lone parents, working-class women, Traveller women, racial and ethnic minority women, women in direct provision, women with disabilities and those subjected to violence and assault incur significant and systemic burdens and disadvantages.

Broader historical factors are key in making sense of the enduring and pervasive forms of gender inequality in Irish social, economic, political, and cultural contexts. These include the enduring influence of Catholic familial frameworks, a male breadwinner model, anti-intellectualism and a strong ideology of the market and charity in political culture and public policy (Lynch et al 2016:23). Women remain marginalised in media (O'Brien 2019) and politics (McGing 2018) and are significantly more likely than men to be in low-paid work (IHREC 2017). Despite the introduction of legal changes in support of marriage equality and access to abortion, as a low tax economy with a conservative gender regime, the state lacks capacity and political will to fund socially necessary reproductive and care work. As a result, such work remains feminised in the sphere of the private household (Russell et al 2019).

Austerity continues to haunt Irish social policy and has contributed to rising female and family homelessness, lone parent poverty and cuts to the wages of feminised, public sector workers (Social Justice Ireland 2019). The differentiated impact of austerity policies on ethnic minority and migrant women, female refugees, younger unemployed women, and older women has also raised challenges for women's organisations. Responding to different groups, organisations are forced to compete for scarce resources that constrain their capacity to attend to the intersectional realities at work in what is a permanent crisis for many (Bassel and Emejulu 2017; Murphy and Cullen 2018).

Irish society reflects the broader dynamics of late modernity and post crisis 'recovery' in a highly globalised neoliberal context. Social change is evidenced in the decline in social conservatism, a once potent force. Unlike other jurisdictions, hard right forms of populism in political party and civil society groups are largely absent. Demographic changes decimating other European countries have yet to take hold and despite austerity era emigration, a dynamic and diverse younger generation exercise their voice and vote in challenging ways. This has had implications for gender roles and patterns of family formation (Connolly et al 2015; Gray et al 2016). Increasing racial and ethnic diversity has in turn generated new forms of social identification, patterns of inclusion and exclusion (Fanning 2018; Gilmartin 2015) in gendered terms (Gilmartin and Migge 2016). From a sociological perspective, gender as a social practice, ideology and construct operates as a fundamental social divide and boundary-marker (Fuchs Epstein 2008) and is as such open to co-optation by macro political, economic, and social formations (Fraser 2016). A refocus on gender is also pertinent given how in other contexts gender ideologies have been used by authoritarian, nationalist and right-wing xenophobic forces to undermine liberal democracy, gender, and minority rights (Kantola and Lombardo 2017; Verloo et al 2018; Paternotte and Kuhar 2018).

Gender is an essential lens for understanding social change. Forces of social transformation can promote greater equality yet also deepen or produce new forms of stratification. Gender scholarship on Ireland has examined feminism and women's movements from a socio-historical perspective to better understand social change (Connolly 2003, Connolly and O'Toole 2005) and, in the more contemporaneous period, from the perspective of the economic boom known as the Celtic Tiger (Cullen 2008; DeWan 2010; Bracken 2016). Other work has focused on the role of women in the Northern Irish conflict (O'Keefe 2013). More recently there have been gendered analysis and feminist assessment of the implications of the economic crisis and austerity for public policy (Barry 2014; Murphy 2015) for women's organisations (Cullen and Fischer 2014; Cullen and Murphy 2017; Heffernan 2017) and for cultural production (Negra and Tasker 2014). Other assessments have drawn on academic and personal reflections to explore the past, present and future of Irish feminisms (Fischer and McAuliffe et al 2015) and the role of both nation and state in positioning women in Irish society in the last one hundred years (Hayes and Meagher et al 2016). Feminist political scientists have engaged with the issue of women's political agency in Ireland and their presence and representation in Parliament and Cabinet (Connolly 2013; Buckley and Galligan 2012). Gender representation in the Irish media (O'Brien 2019), and in higher education has also been explored (O'Connor 2015). Other scholars have mapped changing patterns of family formation, gender roles and attitudes in Ireland (O'Sullivan 2012; Fine-Davis 2016; O'Hagan 2015) and debates around reproductive rights (Schweppe 2008; Mullaly 2008; Quilty and Kennedy 2016; De Londras 2018).

This anthology builds on this work to document the continuing significance of gender as a marker of inequality, even as the discourse of gender equity gains greater currency in society. Here gender is referenced in ways that may suggest a binary understanding of women and men. However, this evocation of gender is used to draw attention to how such binary notions of 'masculine' and 'feminine', 'women' and 'men' are operationalised and put to work in the form of assumptions, categorisations and representations that pattern social structures and maintain diverse forms of gender inequality. In our analysis we reveal how understanding gender as a binary trope reinforces essentialist notions including that gender informs personality traits and behaviours that are specifically associated either with women or men (for example, women are caring; men are aggressive) (Richardson 2016: 9). Gender binaries have been used to make sense of the hierarchical nature of patriarchy, although this has been challenged by conceptualisations of gender as performance, understood as continuously produced through everyday practices and social interactions (Butler 2011). Aside from a recognition of gender as socially constructed, we align our analysis with the assertion that gender is connected to social, economic, and cultural status and power in society. In this sense, gender is theorised not as difference, but as a social division. To theorise gender as social division, therefore, is to examine how the social reproduction of gender difference in society is connected with the production of gender inequalities between women and men (Richardson 2016: 10–14). Gender is also recognised as multiple and context-specific and understood in materialist and embodied ways. Overall then we embrace the shift beyond modernist understandings of gender and by extension sexuality, as fixed, coherent, and stable, and endorse the challenges made by queer/feminist, post-modern and poststructuralist accounts that conceptualise these categories as plural, provisional, and situated (Richardson 2016: 20). In this way we acknowledge the non-binary nature of gender and an expansion of gender categories beyond a simple binary of 'male'/'female' to include, for example, people who identify as 'third gender' or genderqueer. When we reference women we also imply woman identified.

We recognise gaps in our attempts to encapsulate gender knowledge experience and acknowledge that an intersectional framework (Crenshaw 1991; Collins and Bilge 2016; Marx Ferree 2018) is essential to understand the experiences and realities women face (Richardson 2016). While indirectly many different categories of women are referenced here, this collection does not include comprehensive analysis of the experience of trans women, lesbian or non-binary women, Traveller or ethnic minority or migrant women. Moreover, our contributions do not offer a comprehensive account of the transnational and cross border influences that operate via migration and transnational feminist politics on gender knowledge production in Irish society. Gender knowledges produced by migrant women, in particular, feature here at best indirectly and deserve in future research to be a central component of analysis. We hope in a future volume to rectify this gap by including newer voices that can attest to the diversity of women and women-identified experiences as they relate to gender knowledge production in Irish society.

In what follows we draw attention to gendered structures, cultures, and processes of knowledge production as important but often neglected sites for examining gender inequality. This is a feminist perspective that seeks to add to feminist forms of analysis of how knowledge is gendered yet also draws attention to specific forms of knowledge about gender. In other words, the analysis here emphasises *how an underlying set of ideas about gender shapes the content of knowledge with gendered effects*. These include 'signification questions' (Verloo 2018: 21) in wider public debate such as 'what is gender' (e.g. A biological dichotomy? A social structure?) but also the normative positions on the 'right' ways of organising gender and the 'right' kind of evidence used to argue for it. These forms of gender knowledge underlie forms of knowledge production in implicit and explicit ways. A gender knowledge perspective includes a focus on specific forms of more implicit knowledge that is produced with intent to shape understanding and practices associated with gender. These include different forms of feminist knowledge and gender expertise. In this sense feminism(s) and the range of assessments of gender equality also constitute forms of gender knowledge. Knowledge about gender, therefore, underlines other knowledge claims. For instance, neoliberal economisation that ignores the gendered effects of economic processes while reinforcing ideas about gendered patterns of economic activity including the feminisation of unpaid work. Another example is gender expertise in gender and development policy that places ideas about women and girls at the centre of strategies to 'save' communities and improve market outcomes (Ferguson 2018). Feminism(s) and feminist knowledge play a role in intended and unintended ways in how these forms of gender knowledge operate and circulate in critical feminist analysis. Alternately, they may be co-opted in forms of state or market governmentality (Brown 2015), in popular cultural 'feminist' tropes (Rottenberg 2018), and alarmingly by radical and extreme right-wing social and political movements (Kovats 2018).

Borrowing from interpretative traditions and the sociology of knowledge, the gender knowledge concept assumes that every form of knowledge – everyday knowledge, expert knowledge, and popularised knowledge – is based upon a specific, often tacit, and unconscious, form of gender knowledge. As an analytical concept, tacit gender knowledge enables the examination and comparison of competing gendered meanings in processes and action (Young and Scherrer 2010; Cavaghan 2017).

[Gender knowledge is] knowledge . . . about the difference between the sexes, the reasoning of the self-evidence and evidence [of these differences], [and] the prevailing normative ideas about the 'correct' gender relations and divisions of labour between women and men (Andresen/Dölling 2005: 175).

For Cavaghan (2010: 19; 2017: 48):

The concept of gender knowledge not only captures implicit and explicit representations of, or beliefs about the sexes, and normative positions on the justification or appropriateness of relationships between the sexes; it also encompasses perceived evidence of these gender differences.

A focus on gender knowledge affords a critique of the apparent gender neutrality of knowledge allowing for the identification of specific sites and forms of gendered power relations. Applying such a concept especially helps to theorise the role of resistances and opposition in the dynamics, determinants and impacts of gender and sexual politics (Verloo 2018; Kuhar and Paternotte 2017). Several of the contributions to this anthology highlight just how actors, interests and institutions can work to block the diffusion of alternative gender knowledge and thus to maintain some specific rejection of, non-engagement with, or institutionalised ignorance of, gendered processes. Situating knowledge in networks of institutional power, recognising tacit knowledge as gendered, and approaching gendering knowledge as demanding organisational work, offers insight into the uneven progress of gendered social change (Cullen et al 2019).

The concept of gender knowledge also helps us understand perceptions of gender, how these perceptions are formed, and the attendant consequences. Cavaghan (2010: 19–21) drawing on Andresen/Dölling's (2005) work argues that at any point multiple competing gender knowledges can be present and available in a society. Andresen/Dölling distinguish between two 'levels' of gender knowledge: collectively held or 'objective' gender knowledge; and 'subjective' gender knowledge (2005: 50). These forms draw on existing classifications used in the sociology of knowledge (2005: 50) and can be summarised as follows:

(1) Practice, everyday knowledge. This knowledge is predominantly unreflexive and tacit. It may for instance, be dominated by cultural stereotypes.
(2) Institutionally produced knowledge including expert knowledge (such as that in religion, academic disciplines, or the law).
(3) Popular knowledge communicated by journalists, consultants, trades unions, social movements. This is an important intermediary between expert

and everyday knowledge (Andresen/Dölling 2005: 51 cited in Cavaghan 2010, p. 20).

Knowledge about gender underlines other knowledge claims and may define gender roles and what constitutes evidence of when and how gender matters in very different ways. Gender permeates all dimensions of social life. Everyone has their own particular 'gender knowledge', and their 'durable gendered assumptions are enmeshed in local understandings of "mainstream" issues and local practices' (Cavaghan 2017: 43).

Notably, Cavaghan (2010: 20) suggests that 'these levels and forms of gender knowledge may be complementary or in contest.' She continues to outline how in lived experience gender may be something we recognise only unreflectively 'in each other's appearance or attach to particular occupational statuses without noticing' (2010: 20). Academic disciplines and professional knowledge systems (such as law or medicine) may see gender simply as a dichotomous variable. This she contrasts with feminist knowledge that 'might construe gender as a socially constructed, hierarchical relationship which structures roles and outcomes' (2010: 20). In sum, she concludes that:

> Gender knowledge can be composed both then by subjective perceptions and individual knowledge concerning ourselves; by institutional interpretative frameworks which may operate locally within organisations or within disciplinary fields; as well as by interpretative frameworks circulating in popular and cultural frameworks (2010: 20).

Working from a gender knowledge perspective can help us to examine how ideas about gender underlie forms of expert knowledge (that can support forms of policy analysis) and by extension the rationales behind different professional and ideological projects. It can also help make sense of the distance between rhetorical commitments to gender equality and practical implementation that often falls short. Feminist theorisation within sociology (Connell 2011; Ridgeway 2011; Martin et al 2018; Ferree and Wade 2018; Messerschmidt et al 2018), work on gender and organisations (Acker 1990) and feminist critiques of development, policy-making and implementation more generally (Bustelo et al, 2016; Ferguson 2019), have all interrogated epistemic power as a site for the production and maintenance of gender relations, structures, practices and inequalities. These studies demonstrate how expert knowledges are gendered and reproduced in governance, social institutions, markets, and social practice. In these accounts knowledge that is inherently gendered and knowledge about gender are articulated, contested, co-opted, and resisted by different actors, interests, and institutions.

Feminist analysis has embraced the gender knowledge framework to explore the politics of feminist knowledge transfer and the role of gender expertise in international development, gender mainstreaming, higher education, and governance (Cavaghan 2017; Ferguson 2018). These assessments raise important issues long debated in feminist critiques of international financialisation, governance and development (Azocar and Ferree 2015; Prügl 2017; Hozić and True 2016). The fate of feminist knowledge and actors in these contests is key. It has been claimed that feminist ideas are combined with corporate logics and used to support the projects associated with what have been termed 'progressive neoliberal forces' (Fraser 2016). The broader relationship between feminism and neoliberalism has examined the role of gender ideologies and knowledge in sustaining yet also critiquing neoliberal institutions and practices (Griffin 2015; Walby 2011; McRobbie 2009; Gill 2016; Rottenberg 2018).

Other analysis has demonstrated how knowledge production is gendered with consequences for gender representation in higher education, corporations, and politics (Wajcman 1998; Childs and Krook 2009; O'Connor 2016; Marx Ferree and Zippel 2018; Cullen et al 2019). Studying the discursive constructions of gender also illustrates the ways that particular representations of subjects' roles and positions are offered, and others denied, while particular solutions to social problems are deemed legitimate and others marginalised. When combined with a focus on systems of governance and techniques of governmentality such accounts reveal the gendered norms and meanings that are at the core of gender inequality (Verloo 2007; Lorey 2012; Hemmings 2015; Kantola and Lombardo 2017: 7–8).

In this volume we investigate the role of gender knowledge in creating resistances to greater equality and diversity in sites of knowledge work, production, and dissemination. Approaching knowledge work, production and dissemination from a gendered perspective creates a deeper understanding of how gendered assumptions and meanings are locally constructed and negotiated in organisations, social practices, and everyday life. Such work indicates the durable and pervasive nature of gender as a social category and cognitive framework, in structuring who controls how we labour, what we know and how we know it (Connell 2002; Ridgeway 2011). Our contributors draw on a range of literature to recognise the ways in which actors including women resist, re-interpret and yet also re-inscribe gender constructs as they navigate care work, work outside the home, engage in education and social activism, participate in the public sphere, and are positioned as subjects of the state. Notably the contributions here also draw in different ways from this plurality of perspectives to address the hegemonies, resistances and marginalisations that shape forms of gender knowledge and knowledge production. Cognisant of calls to approach the study of gender and knowledge from an intersectional perspective (Bassel and Emejulu 2017) our contributions are sensitised to how gender intersects with other aspects of social experience and structure including class, race, and ethnicity. In sum, this collection aims to examine: What forms of knowledge are produced? Who produces such knowledge? How is it produced? And crucially, how does it serve or deny the interests of different women?

The volume is divided into three parts dealing broadly with the public domains of everyday life: the politics of work, institutional power dynamics and public cultures of exclusion. Each contribution is evidence-based and speaks to the central themes signalled earlier in this introduction: gender is socially constructed, and the analysis forwarded is aligned with the assertion that gender is connected to social, economic, and cultural status and power in society. In this sense, gender is theorised not as difference, but as a social division. As the reader will find the textured analyses presented by the authors produce rich gender knowledge that brings these different foci into sharp relief and demonstrate how gender inequality pervades all domains of public life.

PART I

Part I explores the impact of specific corporate ideologies and practices on the working conditions and career paths of knowledge workers in the IT sector, academia, investment banking and media production. Such high status, knowledge-intensive sectors appear to be a million miles away from the 'pink collar ghettos' of dead-end, poorly remunerated positions where women workers cluster. Yet, the contributors here clearly demonstrate the persistence of a power dynamic in the workplace that consistently benefits men at the expense of women. One of the key ways in which this dynamic is exercised is through social closure, whereby access to important opportunities and resources are not equally accessible to women and men. In each work setting women adapt to the prevailing culture but frequently do so in ways that do not disrupt the deeply inscribed work structures.

In Chapter 1, John-Paul Byrne uses data from working life interviews with Information Technology (IT) workers in Ireland and Denmark to explore the character of autonomy in IT and how it has – in practice – developed through the lens of male working lives. Autonomous working conditions bring flexibility, discretion, and de-regulated work environments. However, to forge a career in IT these conditions must be negotiated. Individuals must maximise work opportunities for technical experience, network development, and reputation management to enhance their prospects within a deeply insecure, volatile industry. But the reputational capital and networking capacity of women in IT is restricted due to the segregation of labour process tasks and the technical roles filled. Limited access to technical tasks, roles, and colleagues also narrows access to required upskilling experience and key networks, as both Irish and Danish women workers attest. De-regulated structures serve not to break down but conceal power and control within more ostensibly participatory systems. The demands of maintaining autonomous, interdependent, and insecure roles require occupationally defined logics that reinforce the patriarchy of IT work, producing a workplace that is subtly segregated.

The practices that inhibit gender equality in Science, Technology, Engineering and Mathematics (STEM) in the higher education sector is the focus of Pat O'Connor and Clare O'Hagan's analysis in Chapter 2. Drawing on the extensive literature in the field, they distinguish between the repertoire of actions and behaviours that society makes available for 'doing gender' ('gendering practices'), and the actual interactional doing of gender in real time and space ('practicing gender'). The authors are specifically concerned with illuminating the experiences of women and men involved in the creation and dissemination of knowledge in a case study Irish HEI. Drawing on data from qualitative interviews with 29 female and male respondents in STEM they identify five practices that perpetuate gender inequality. Three of these practices are at the micro-level and appear gender-neutral i.e. achieving professional visibility, cultivating local connections, and managing time appropriately. However, they tend to be more achievable, and more likely to be engaged in, by men. Focusing on what the individual can do 'to fix' their situation – how to literally play the 'career game' more successfully – ignores two further kinds of practices: gendered interactional practices and gendered stereotypical practices both of which explicitly reflect a meso-level gendered reality that affects women's opportunities and possibilities. The authors argue that in order to create change in male-dominated structures and masculinist cultures in STEM it is not sufficient to simply encourage women to adopt to what appear to be gender-neutral agentic practices. It is also necessary to challenge and reduce the impact of explicitly gendered practices.

Expectations of deep structural change in the investment banking sector post the 2008 financial crisis have not been fulfilled writes Corina Sheerin in Chapter 3. Rather, gendered segregation, gendered normative practices and social closure continue to prevail in the sector. Gender segregation on the one hand, and male hegemony, on the other, permeate the investment management workplace where men occupy positions of uncontested privilege such as fund management and trading, while women dominate back office support roles. While the financial services sector is relatively modest in Ireland, it nevertheless, shares the same overarching sectoral characteristics and norms as other global sites. Sheerin explores how and why occupational segregation by gender has prevailed in investment management and why men continue to disproportionally occupy positions of power and prestige. In the same vein as O'Connor and O'Hagan, Sheerin notes that 'doing of gender' supports social closure processes, whereby rewards are maximised by restricting access to resources and opportunities to a limited circle. Membership of the Old Boy's Club – mediated through elite school and university pedigrees – provides a justificatory basis of exclusion. Such social closure processes infiltrate all elements of the sector from recruitment to progression to retention. These mechanisms in turn underpin intransigent segregation.

Training her eye on media production professionals, Anne O'Brien, examines the gendering of work practices and their implications in the context of late capitalism and the increasing neo-liberalisation of creative labour. Chapter 4 draws on interviews with a sample of women working across the broadcasting sector. O'Brien demonstrates how gender processes that produce inequality are embedded in the everyday practices of media work. Women she suggests, work in a gendered and liminal space that involves co-existent and simultaneous practices of both engagement *and* exclusion. Role segregation, the gendered practices of production, the masculinist work culture, and the dearth of women in leadership positions in the sector, together serve to construct a liminal status for women workers. The pervasive and quotidian nature of this liminal positioning becomes semi-permanent for women over the life-course of their careers and is consequential in terms of their decision-making. Women in the media production sector adapt to their own gender-based exclusions from industry. They deploy techniques of self-conduct in order to self-exploit but in this practice lies the potential for alternative subjectivities and forms of resistance to the gendered norms of media production.

PART II

Part II moves the focus from work to politics, policymaking, advocacy, and movement mobilisation. The contributors here seek to uncover the gendered power dynamics that underpin the institutional structures of our political and civil society systems. In many respects women have made enormous strides in the public domain in terms of the broadening of their roles in the public sphere and their increased visibility. Yet, in many contexts the voices of women and the knowledge they produce – either grounded in experience or expertise – continues to be marginalised, side-lined, resisted or ignored. This is particularly consequential when dealing with public policymaking, the effect of which has a disproportionate impact on women's freedoms and capabilities. This part of the book situates knowledge in networks of institutional power, recognises tacit knowledge as gendered, and offers insight into the uneven progress of gendered social change (Cullen et al 2019). Chapters 5 and 6 show how gender intersects with other factors to shape how women's interests are understood and advanced in feminist organising in Ireland generally; and more specifically, how gender and other power dynamics are refracted through the prism of the Irish abortion debate. This raises important questions about who holds knowledge, and how that knowledge diffuses and impacts in wider society. Two further case studies of public policy-making – prostitution law and policy responses to homelessness – demonstrate how gendered knowledge about 'social problems' is constructed by expert knowledge holders within the system. Crucially, however, such expert systems may be challenged when the category of 'knowledge producers' is extended to include previously marginalised voices. This theme of giving voice in the public sphere links all four chapters.

Pauline Cullen notes, in Chapter 5, that the profile of women's organisations in Ireland is increasingly diverse ranging from grassroots women's community development groups, to young anarchist feminist collectives and bloggers. Some women's movements are distinctly feminist; others avoid the term even while consciously or unconsciously adopting feminist practices and attitudes. In this diverse range of mobilisations different forms of gender knowledge are constructed and communicated. Drawing on documentary and interview data, Cullen shows how a diversity of feminist and women's organisations employ gender ideologies and knowledge about gender to advocate for and about women's interests in Ireland. In two case studies – the 30% Club and the *Together for Yes* campaign that secured repeal of the constitutional ban on abortion – she illustrates different forms of gender knowledge including feminist knowledge and gender expertise operating in the Irish context. In the latter campaign a form of gender knowledge with feminist roots was made legible within women's lived experiences and suffering that served to secure positive gendered social change. In the former case neoliberal feminist ideas created gender knowledge that secured success for middle-class women but, at the same time, failed to address the challenges and difficulties of the vast majority of women who work.

Sinéad Kennedy further excavates questions of knowledge, power, and authority through the prism of the Irish abortion debate in Chapter 6. She asks: Whose knowledge is considered important? Who defines what is important to know? Who benefits from that knowledge and who does not? Who has access to knowledge and who does not? Abortion access in Ireland until recently had been highly restricted as a result of a constitutional prohibition – known as the eighth amendment – that equated the life of a pregnant woman with that of a foetus, permitting access to abortion only where a woman's life was at risk. The presence of the eighth amendment had far-reaching implications for knowledge production and distribution in Ireland in terms of science and research, healthcare, education, the law, and the media. Women's reproductive capacities had been highly controlled through the regulation of abortion information. Yet, women living in Ireland accessed abortion by travelling abroad to Britain and Europe, and illegally within Ireland by accessing the abortion pill online. Kennedy considers these issues in relation to the recent public debate around abortion, setting this against the backdrop of a history of social control exercised over women through the machinations of the state and the church. She concludes that knowledge can produce change, empower new actors from previously marginalised groups, and challenge traditional structures of power and authority.

The theme of sexuality and its control is re-visited in Chapter 7, where Paul Ryan explores the recent rise, and successful implementation, of a neo-abolitionist policy governing prostitution in Ireland, displacing the prohibitionist approach dominant since the establishment of the state. Ryan argues that this policy turn emerged from a knowledge vacuum in relation to the commercial sex sector and was facilitated by the rise of NGO-funded advocacy research committed to advancing an abolitionist position. Some of that research has subsequently been criticised as methodologically flawed. Central to this neo-abolitionist position is the belief that prostitution whether entered by coercion or consent, constitutes violence against women. Ryan traces the policy trajectory across time and analyses the currency of biographical survivor stories of women formerly involved in prostitution in advocacy campaigns. He finds that a clash of knowledge systems results: biographical accounts coupled with new knowledge about the sex industry displace traditional expert voices, particularly those of academics struggling to communicate both the nuances and complexities of the sex industry and the challenge of finding a single solution to end exploitation in the sector. Parliamentary committees find themselves sitting in judgement over competing knowledge claims from organisations representing both women formerly involved in the sex industry, those still working within it, and academic testimony that supports contrary positions.

In Chapter 8, Hearne and Murphy explicate the process of creating a gendered construction of, and new gendered knowledge about, the problem of family homelessness. A key objective is to explore the gendered construction of social problems through an innovative case study drawing on a Participatory Action Research approach that seeks to integrate the existing knowledge of female service users with the knowledge expertise of male policymakers. The framework that is operationalised brings together existing knowledge, methodologies and practices united by a focus on rights-based participation and deployed through participatory action research. This innovative approach generates new gendered knowledge about homelessness that was communicated directly by women service users to policymakers. The case study is contextualised through an exploration of Ireland's patriarchal and paternalistic Irish welfare regime that has historically tended to institutionalise poor women.

PART III

Part III moves beyond the worlds of work and politics to examine aspects of our public culture. We are interested in instances where cultural, social, and political differences (particularly in relation to gender) emerge as public phenomena and have a public resonance. In particular, we want to explore the ways in which aspects of public culture are organised, the value system that underpins them, and the social norms to which they give expression. Unless we truly know how cultural expectations and practices operate in the public sphere we cannot begin to instigate processes of change. A gender knowledge perspective allows us to identify and critically reflect upon the rationales behind different professional and ideological projects that form part of our public culture. It can also help make sense of the distance between rhetorical commitments to gender equality and practical implementation that often falls short. In this section, we explore the profession and changing culture of teaching, recreational aspects of technology and culture, and discursive public space all from a gender knowledge perspective. In each case study the authors demonstrate how appearances of gender neutrality or gender equity mask a much more troubling reality. The gendered regimes exposed persist because of deeply embedded structural exclusions that pervade our culture at-large.

The final contribution approaches the theme of public culture from a slightly different viewpoint. Archives constitute knowledge systems that are repositories of historical truth. As such they are a public good that should in principle be a resource accessible to all. Accessibility is particularly crucial for those seeking truth such as survivors of mother and baby homes and Magdalene laundries. Yet important historical records remain closed and effectively off limits. This has serious implications not only for survivors but also for scholarship generally, and the right in a democracy to speak truth to power.

Byrne and Murray critically examine the characteristics of new entrants to the field of teaching, a high demand third-level programme of study, in Chapter 9. The authors acknowledge the wide range of research that documents gender differences in entrance patterns and awards in initial teacher education in Ireland; gender differences in classroom interaction between teachers and male and female pupils/students; the impact of feminisation of the teaching profession; and the continued under representation of women in senior management positions in the sector. Feminist researchers, however, have challenged the rather one-sided debate about perceived gender imbalance within the profession and the lack of male teachers. The approach taken in this chapter is guided by more recent, international research that highlights the gendered social realities that accompany the decision to go into teaching and of early teaching experiences in other institutional contexts. Byrne and Murray bring a fresh focus to gender analysis in the teaching profession by foregrounding intersections of gender with social class, citizenship and country of origin, and disability. Their approach is quantitative drawing on national data on all applicants to publicly funded higher education institutions in the Republic of Ireland in 2012. The frame of analysis is located within a national context of increased ethnic diversity among the population, calls to diversify the teaching profession, and changes in teacher employment conditions. This new analysis of the teacher education sector integrates occupational sex-segregation perspectives, feminist scholarship on intersectionality, and quantitative research methodologies.

In Chapter 10, Kerr and Savage note that Ireland is home to global ICT companies like Facebook, Instagram, and Riot, and educates a high percentage of computer programmers by European standards. But the programming occupation and ICT workforce is still highly gender segregated, with the highest paying programming jobs dominated by men; women are more commonly to be found in business operations and 'below the line' community management jobs. Recruitment into the industry is reliant on a mix of cultural and social capital supplemented by a 'passion' for games. Over the past decade, policy and scientific initiatives have attempted to promote STEM in general and computer programming in particular through festivals, competitions, and media campaigns. Game jams are an example of such initiatives. They are mostly non-commercial and informal game development events organised by volunteers, academics, and the games industry. Groups or teams compete to develop the best game or project according to a general theme which is then judged by their peers. Kerr and Savage note that very little attention has been paid to the role of informal learning spaces and local technological cultures in reinforcing the gendered digital divide. Game jam attendees are mostly male, either studying or working in IT-related occupations, and are using these informal learning events to improve upon existing skills and to informally network with the games community. Despite their openness and attempts to embrace skill and knowledge diversity the reality is that these events are dominated by those with programming and computing skills and by those who can 'afford' to spend twelve hours at an informal skill and networking event. Gender inequality and discrimination conspire to structure and limit the access of women to game jams and may also play a role in reinforcing the gendered segregation of high-status game development jobs in Dublin (since they are informal pathway into such jobs). Kerr and Savage's response as scholar-activists was to develop a women-friendly game jam to challenge events that while 'open to all', in practice, are both implicitly and explicitly gendered.

In Chapter 11 Mary P. Corcoran focuses attention on the discursive public space available for women to contribute to knowledge production and critical review. Her analysis is set against the recent emergence of a powerful feminist voice disputing and challenging the under-representation of women as knowledge producers and disseminators within discursive public space. The broadsheet book review is a core element of cultural knowledge production, yet it has been largely overlooked by academics and movement activists in Ireland to date. Corcoran applies a gendered analytical framework to interrogate women's contributions to, and visibility in, the broadsheet book review. Her findings suggest that while a broadsheet newspaper may adapt a largely benign stance on gender issues (through for instance, its socially liberal ideology and provision of space to feminist columnists), it may simultaneously reproduce and legitimate forms of male gendered expertise. In the Book Review Section women are marginalised both as authors and as reviewers; books by and about men are privileged over those by and about women; and a high degree of gendered segregation of book genres prevails. There is, in other words, a clear disjuncture between a tacit commitment to gender equity in liberal broadsheet print media and the practice of gender equal representation. This case study illuminates the durability of the gender knowledge regime within what amounts to protected institutional practices.

Finally, Chapter 12 returns to the theme of Ireland's patriarchal culture (already referenced throughout this collection) as expressed in a repressive regime policed by the church with the complicity of the state. The historian and archivist Catriona Crowe explores guilt, shame, acknowledgment, and redress in the context of the institutional treatment of women and children. She offers a reflection on Ireland's recent history of unprecedented disclosures relating to the country's treatment of vulnerable women and children, across a unique archipelago of institutions – mother and baby homes, Magdalen asylums, industrial schools, and reformatories. These institutions were largely run by the Catholic Church and the Church of Ireland, with the State's full blessing. Disclosures in the public sphere about the treatment received by their inmates was shocking; physical, emotional, and sexual abuse were common, with consequential life-changing results for the victims. This

raises the question of how Ireland should now approach the questions acknowledgement and redress. More fundamentally, it raises question about the historical and contemporary nature of institutional knowledg creation, retention, and control. The chapter proposes that the only way t achieve a complete picture of what happened in these places is to have ful access to the archives relating to them. Crowe argues that both church anc state need to hugely improve access to their archives, for the sake of survivors who need personal information; for the sake of scholarship, which can help us to make sense of this extraordinary story; and to speak truth to the institutionalised power structures that produced and reproduced a culture of gender repression in Irish society.

REFERENCES

Acker, Joan 'Hierarchies, Jobs, bodies: A theory of gendered organizations', in *Gender and Society*, 4(2), 1990, pp 139–58. Retrieved from http://www.jstor.org/stable/189609

Andresen, Sünne/Dölling, Irene Umbau des Geschlechter-Wissens von Reformakteur 'Innen durch gender mainstreaming, in Ute Behning/ Birgit Sauer (Hrsg.), 'Was bewirkt gender main-streaming', in *Evaluierung durch Policy-Analysen* Ebook (Campus Verla, 2005).

Azocar, Maria J. and Myra Marx-Ferree, 'Gendered expertise', in *Gender & Society* 29(6), 2015, pp 841–62.

Barry Ursula, 'Gender perspective on the economic crisis: Ireland in an EU context', in *Gender, Sexuality & Feminism* 1(2), 2014, pp 82–103.

Bassel, Leah and Emejulu, Akwugo, *The Politics of Survival: Minority Women, Activism and Austerity in France and Britain* (Policy Press: Bristol, 2017).

Bracken, Claire, *Irish Feminist Futures* (Routledge: London, 2016).

Brown, Wendy, 'Undoing the demos: Neoliberalism's stealth revolution', in *European Journal of Cultural and Political Sociology*, 3(1) 2015, pp 129–37.

Buckley, Fiona, and Yvonne Galligan, 'Politics and gender on the island of Ireland: The Quest for Political Agency', in *Irish Political Studies* 28(3), 2013, pp 315–21.

Bustelo, Maria, Lisa Ferguson and Maxine Forest (eds), *The Politics of Feminist Knowledge Transfer: Gender Training and Gender Expertise* (Palgrave Macmillan: Basingstoke, 2016).

Cavaghan, Rosalind, 'Gender knowledge: A review of theory and practice', in Christoph Scherrer and Brigitte Young (Hrsg.), *Gender Knowledge and Knowledge Networks in International Political Economy*, Seite 2010, pp 18–35.

Cavaghan, Rosalind, 'Gender mainstreaming in the DGR as a knowledge process: Epistemic barriers to eradicating gender bias', in *Critical Policy Studies* 7(4), 2013, pp 407–21.

Cavaghan, Rosalind, *Making gender equality happen: Knowledge, change and resistance in EU gender mainstreaming* (Routledge: London, 2017).

Childs, Sarah, and Mona Lena Krook, 'Critical mass theory and women's political representation', in *Political Studies*, 56(3) 2018, pp 725–36.

Collins, Michael and Mary Murphy, 'Activation for what? Employment or a low pay economy', in M. P. Murphy and F. Dukelow (eds), *The Irish Welfare State in the 21st Century: Challenges and Changes* (Palgrave: Basingstoke, 2016), pp 67–92.

Collins-Hill, Patricia and Sirma Bilge, *Intersectionality: Key Concepts* (Polity Press: Cambridge, 2017).

Connell, Raewyn, *Gender* (John Wiley & Sons: UK, 2002) Malden, MA: Blackwell Publishers; Cambridge, UK: Polity Press, 2002.

Ibid., *Confronting equality: Gender, knowledge and global change* (Polity Press: Cambridge, 2011).

Connolly, Eileen, 'Parliaments as gendered institutions: The Irish Oireachtas', in *Irish Political Studies*, 28(3) 2013 pp 360–79.

Connolly, Linda, *The Irish Women's Movement: From Revolution to Devolution* (MacMillan/Palgrave: London and New York, 2003).

Connolly Linda and Tina O'Toole, *Documenting Irish Feminisms: The Second Wave* (Woodfield Press: Dublin, 2005).

Connolly, Linda (ed.), *The 'Irish' Family* (Routledge: London and New York, 2015).

Crenshaw, Kimberle, 'Mapping the margins: Intersectionality, identity politics, and violence against women of color', in *Stanford Law Review* 43(6), 1991, pp 1,241–99.

Cullen, Pauline, 'Irish women's organizations in an enlarged Europe', in S. Roth (ed.), *Gender Issues and Women's Movements in the Expanding European Union* (Berghahn Press: Oslo, 2008).

Cullen, Pauline and Clara Fischer, 'Conceptualising generational dynamics in feminist movements: Political generations, waves and affective economies', in *Sociology Compass*, 8(3), 2014, pp 282–93.

Cullen, Pauline, and Mary P. Murphy, 'Gendered mobilizations against austerity in Ireland', in *Gender, Work and Organization* 24(1), 2016, pp 83–97.

Ibid., 'Leading the debate for the business case for gender equality: Perilous for whom?', in *Gender, Work and Organization* 25(2), 2018, pp 110–26.

Cullen, Pauline, Myra Marx Ferree and Mieke Verloo, 'Introduction to special issue: Gender, knowledge, production and dissemination', in *Gender Work and Organization* 26(6), 2019, pp 765–71.

De Londras, Fiona and Mairead Enright, *Repealing the 8th: Reforming Abortion Law in Ireland* (Policy Press: Bristol, 2018).

DeWan, Jennifer K., 'The practice of politics: Feminism, activism and social change in Ireland', in J. Hogan, P. F. Donnelly and B. K. O'Rourke (eds), *Irish Business and Society: Governing, Participating and Transforming in the 21st Century* (Dublin: Gill & MacMillan, 2010), pp 520–36.

Fanning, Bryan, *Migration and the Making of Ireland* (UCD Press: Dublin, 2018).

Ferguson, Lisa, *Gender Training: A Transformative Tool for Gender Equality* (Palgrave Macmillan: Basingstoke, 2018).

Ferree, Marx Myra, '"Theories don't grow on trees": Contextualizing gender knowledge' in J. W. Messerschmidt and Patricia Yancey Martin, Michael A. Messner and Raewyn Connell (eds), *Gender Reckonings: New Social Theory and Research* (NYU Press: New York, 2018).

Ferree, Marx Myra and Zippel Kathrin, 'Gender equality in the age of academic capitalism: Cassandra and Pollyanna interpret university restructuring', in *Social Politics: International Studies in Gender, State and Society* 22(4), 2015, pp 561–84.

Fine-Davis, Margret, *Gender Role Attitudes in Ireland: Three Decades of Change* (Routledge: London, 2016).

Fischer, Clara, and Mary M. McAuliffe (eds), *Irish Feminisms: Past, Present, and Future* (Arlen House/Syracuse University Press: Syracuse, 2015).

Fraser, Nancy, 'Progressive neoliberalism versus reactionary populism: A choice that feminists should refuse', in *NORA: Nordic Journal of Feminist and Gender Research*, 24:4, 2016, pp 281–4.

Fuchs, Epstein, 'Cynthia great divides: The cultural, cognitive, and social bases of the global subordination of women', in *American Sociological Review*, 2007, 72(1), pp 1–22.

Gill, Rosalind, 'Post-feminism? New feminist visibilities in post-feminist times' in *Feminist Media Studies*, 16(4), 2016, pp 610–30.

Gilmartin, Mary, *Ireland and Migration in the 21st century* (Manchester University Press: Manchester, 2015).

Gilmartin, Mary and Bettina Migge, 'Migrant mothers and the geographies of belonging', in *Gender, Place, and Culture*, 23(2), 2016, pp 47–161.

Graff, Agnieszka, Ratna Kapur and Suzanna Danuta Walters, 'Introduction: Gender and the rise of the global right', in *Signs: Journal of Women in Culture and Society* 44(3), 2019, pp 541–60.

Gray, Jane, Ruth Geraghty, and David Ralph, *Family Rhythms: The changing Texture of Family Life in Ireland* (Manchester University Press: Manchester, 2016).

Griffin, Penny, 'Crisis, austerity and gendered governance: A feminist perspective', in *Feminist Review*, 10(9), 2015, pp 49–72.

Hayes, A., and M. Meagher (eds), A *Century of Progress? Irish Women Reflect* (Syracuse University Press/ Arlen House: Syracuse, 2016).

Hozić, Aida and Jacqui True, *Scandalous Economics: The Politics of Gender and Financial Crises* (Oxford University Press: New York 2016).

Heffernan, Emma 'Poverty and risk the impact of austerity on vulnerable females in Dublin's inner city', in E. Henderson, J. McHale and N. Moore Cherry (eds), *Debating Austerity in Ireland: Crisis Experience and Recovery (*Royal Irish Academy: Dublin, 2017).

Hemmings, Clare, 'Affective solidarity: Feminist reflexivity and political transformation', in Special Issue: 'Affecting feminism: Questions of feeling in feminist theory', in *Feminist Theory*, 13(2), 2012, pp 147–61.

Irish Human Rights and Equality Commission (IHREC) CEDAW Submission (IHREC: Dublin, 2017) https://www.ihrec.ie/documents/ireland-convention-elimination-forms-discrimination- women (2017).

Kantola, Johanna and Judith Squires (eds), 'From state feminism to market feminism?', in *International Political Science Review* 33(4), 2012, pp 382–400.

Kantola, Johanna and Emanuela Lombardo (eds), *Gender and the Economic Crisis in Europe: Politics, Institutions, and Intersectionality* (Palgrave MacMillan: Basingstoke, 2017).

Kovats, Eszter, 'Questioning consensus: Right-wing populism, anti-populism and the threat of gender ideology', in *Sociological Research Online* 23(2), 2018, pp 528–38.

Kuhar, Roman and David Paternotte, *Anti-Gender Campaigns in Europe: Mobilizing against Equality* (Rowman & Littlefield: London, 2017).

Lombardo, Emanuela, Pietra Meier and Mieke Verloo, 'Discursive dynamics in gender equality politics: What about "feminist taboos"?', in *European Journal of Women's Studies* 17(2), 2010, pp 105–23.

Lorey, Isabel, *State of Insecurity Government of the Precarious* (Verso Press: London and New York, 2015).

Lynch, Kathleen, Sara Cantillon and Margaret Crean, 'Inequality', in K. O. Roche, P. J. Connell and A. Prohtero (eds), *Austerity and Recovery in Ireland: Europe's Poster Child in Recession* (Oxford University Press: Oxford, 2016), pp 252–71.

McGing, Claire, 'The single transferable vote and women's representation in Ireland', in *Irish Political Studies*, 28(3), 2013, pp 322–40.

McRobbie, Angela, *The Aftermath of Feminism: Gender, Culture and Social Change* (Sage: London, 2008).

Messerschmidt, J. W., Patricia Yancey Martin, Michael A. Messner and Raewyn Connell (eds), *Gender Reckonings: New Social Theory and Research* (NYU Press: New York, 2018).

Mullaly, Siobhan, 'Migrant women destabilising borders: Citizenship debates in Ireland', in *Intersectionality and Beyond: Law, Power and the Politics of Location* (Routledge: London, 2008).

Murphy, Mary P., 'Gendering the narrative of the Irish crisis', in *Irish Political Studies*, 30(2) 2015, pp 220–37.

Ibid., 'Irish flex insecurity: The post crisis reality for vulnerable workers in Ireland', in *Social Policy & Administration*, 51(2), 2017, pp 223–403.

Murphy, Mary P. and Pauline Cullen, *Feminist Response to Austerity in Ireland: Country Case Study* (Rosa Luxembourg Foundation: Brussels, 2018).

Negra, Diane and Yvonne Tasker, *Gendering the Recession: Media and Culture in an Age of Austerity* (Duke University Press: Durham, 2014).

O'Brien, Anne, *Women, Inequality and Media Work* (Routledge: London, 2019).

O'Connor, Pat, 'Understanding success: A case study of gendered change in the professoriate', in *Journal of Higher Education Policy and Management* 36(2), 2014, pp 212–24.

O'Hagan, Clare, *Complex Inequality and Working Mothers* (Cork University Press: Cork, 2015).

O'Keefe, Theresa, *Feminist Identity: Development and Activism in Revolutionary Movements* (Palgrave Macmillan: London, 2013).

O'Sullivan, Sara, '"All changed, changed utterly?" Gender role attitudes and the feminisation of the Irish labour force', in *Women's Studies International Forum* 35(4), 2012, pp 223–32.

Paternotte, David and Roman Kuhar, 'Disentangling and locating the "global right": Anti-gender campaigns in Europe', *Politics and Governance* 6(3), 2018, pp 6–19.

Prügl, Elisabeth, 'Neoliberalising feminism', *New Political Economy* 20(4), 2015, pp 614–31.

Ibid., 'Neoliberalism with a feminist face: Crafting a new hegemony at the World Bank', in *Feminist Economics* 23(1), 2017, pp 30–53.

Quilty, Aideen, Sinéad Kennedy, and Catherine Conlon (eds), *The Abortion Papers Ireland: Volume II* (Cork University Press: Cork, 2015).

Richardson, Diane 'Conceptualising gender', in V. Robinson and D. Richardson (eds), *Introducing Gender and Women's Studies* (Palgrave Macmillan: Basingstoke, 2015), pp 3–22.

Ridgeway, Cecilia, *Framed by Gender: How Gender Inequality Persists in the Modern World* (Oxford University Press: Oxford, 2011).

Roberts, Adrienne, 'The political economy of "transnational business feminism"', in *International Feminist Journal of Politics* 17(2), 2015, pp 209–31.

Rottenberg, Catherine, 'Women who work: The limits of the neoliberal feminist *paradigm*', in *Gender Work and* Organization, 2018, pp 1–10.

Russell, Helen, Raffaele Grotti, Frances McGinnity, and Ivan Privalko, *Caring and Unpaid Work in Ireland* (Economic Social Research Institute: Dublin, 2019).

Schweppe, Jennifer, *Article 40.3.3° and Abortion in Ireland* (Liffey Press: Dublin, 2015).

Social Justice Ireland (SJI), 'Time to stop paying lip service to notions of gender equality, and start investing' (SJI, 2019) https://www.socialjustice.ie/content/policy-issues/time-stop-paying-lip-service-notions-gender-equality-and-start-investing

Wajcman, Judith, 'Feminist theories of technology', in *Cambridge Journal of Economics* 34(1), 2010, pp 143–52.

Walby, Sylvia, 'Is the knowledge society gendered?' in *Gender, Work and Organization,* 18(1), 2011, pp 1–29.

Williams, Christine, '"The glass escalator": Revisited gender inequality in neoliberal times', in *Gender & Society* 27(5), 2013, pp 609–29.

Young, B. and C. Scherrer (eds), 'Gender knowledge and knowledge networks', in *International Political Economy* (Nosmos: Dublin, 2010)

Verloo, Mieke (ed.), *Multiple Meanings of Gender Equality: A Critical Frame Analysis* (CPS Books: Budapest, 2007).

PART I

Gender, Knowledge and Work

The Segregating Structures of Information Technology: Gender and Autonomous Work

John-Paul Byrne

INTRODUCTION

One of the things that I really care a lot about personally . . . the lack of gender diversity in tech . . . It bothers me the number of women we have working in technical companies but not in technical roles. Because I think that skews the numbers a lot. People will look at this particular tech company and be like, oh well they have some percentage of women. But if you actually take all of the non-technical roles away . . . the numbers are still really, really bad . . . they are really bad here and they are really bad in a lot of companies (Helen, Technical Director, Denmark).

In an article in *The Atlantic* entitled 'Why is Silicon Valley so awful to women', Liza Mundy (2017) investigates the struggles faced by women forging careers in the heartland of Information Technology (IT). Summarising the experience of her interviewees Mundy highlights how relationships with colleagues and clients, career opportunities, and workplace cultures are rife with sexist behaviours and gendered practices. These women had learned to become comfortable with having their authority questioned and adept at extricating themselves from unwarranted male advances without damaging any egos. Low numbers of women in technical roles at Google, Twitter, Facebook, and Apple point to the interaction of these sexist practices working alongside gendered structures and exclusionary dynamics. Mundy's work raises a broader paradoxical feature of the IT sector. An ethos of diversity, flexibility, and boundary-breaking co-exists alongside a masculinist gender substructure (Acker 1990) which determines notions of professionalism (Ruiz Ben 2007) and work-life balance (Hari 2017), and privileges men through de-regulated informal rules (Williams 2013). The conditions of work and employment in IT represent an informative case for exploring the persistence of these flexible and unequal processes. ICT professionals represent the fastest growing job category in large-employing sectors with the number of women increasing, yet still only at 15 per cent (Eurofound 2017).

Relocating the work of Kanter (1977) and Acker (1990) in IT, the chapter illustrates how high levels of autonomy and flexibility in the IT sector rely upon, create, and reproduce gendered dynamics. As a form of knowledge production work, IT is underpinned by masculinist ideals which shape occupational and organisational practices that themselves rely on a gendered segregation of paid and unpaid work. Building on the author's doctoral research (Byrne 2016) the chapter is based on 34 semi-structured interviews with IT workers – 17 in both Ireland and Denmark. To focus on the experience of women the discussion draws primarily on data from in-depth working life interviews with ten women – five from each country. Interviews cover career histories and choices; the working conditions of key roles; and current conditions of working life (time, demands, work-life balance, pay, security). Accessing women in the IT industry through purposive and snowball sampling techniques proved difficult in both countries. However, as this study is part of a larger European Research Council funded project, *New Deals in the New Economy*, additional sources were available through triangulated methodology (e.g. surveys, expert interviews). Data analysis unpacked the composition of autonomous working lives in an industry at the leading edge of work organisation design and at the coalface of the marketised intensity of global capitalism (Ó Riain 2010).

Denmark and Ireland are small, open, export-oriented economies with populations of a relatively similar size. Yet they differ significantly in terms of socio-political structure. Denmark is identified as a social democratic welfare state, and Ireland as a liberal welfare state (Esping-Andersen 1990). Ireland has generally been typified by clientelism, social and economic non-interventionism, a deference to men and the Catholic Church, and a fragmented left politics (Adshead and Tonge 2009). Notions of welfare, the state, and democratic values have been largely built on an institutional context of patriarchy, clericalism, and conservatism (Coakley 2010, and Introduction to this volume). For Denmark, the social democratic ideals of equality, justice, representation, and redistribution are not just a political regime, they are the context of the country's affairs (Jenkins 2012). The state intervenes in the lives of individuals throughout the life-course. Denmark's high tax rates fund universal public services (healthcare, education, transport links, childcare) whereas Ireland's regime is based around more individually, and liberally, orientated monetary redistribution. In terms of gender regimes, Lewis (1992) classifies Denmark as a weak male breadwinner model (or dual earner) and Ireland as a strong male breadwinner model. Balancing the demands of work and family responsibilities is identified as a major stressor (Wajcman 2015; Moen et al. 2015), particularly for women working in institutional contexts where the male breadwinner model is still dominant (Ciccia and Verloo 2012).

Denmark is one of the European leaders in gender equality in employment, despite outranking Ireland on gendered differences in the flexibility of work and maintaining similarly high levels of horizontal gender segregation (European Institute for Gender Equality 2017). Ireland's labour market is also shaped by high rates of vertical segregation (Russell et al. 2009). In both Ireland and Denmark women account for approximately 30 per cent of workers in the Information and Communications sector (Central Statistics Office 2017; Statistics Denmark 2017). These countries represent different institutional contexts in which the capabilities of working lives – 'opportunities to be and do' (Sen 1999) – are embedded (Hobson 2014). However, different capacities for career advancement and balancing work-life responsibilities do not always surmount the gendered structures that underpin knowledge and opportunities in IT. The reputational capital and networking ability required to progress in the IT labour market is embedded within an archetypal neoliberal work bargain which exalts individual flexibility and discretion whilst segregating access to advantageous labour process tasks and technical roles. The chapter shows how the character of autonomy in IT – its norms, responsibilities, and interdependent work and employment demands – have developed through the lens of male working lives.

THE STRUCTURES OF AUTONOMY & KNOWLEDGE WORK

Autonomy, defined as 'regulation by the self' (Ryan and Deci 2006: 1557), links neoliberal notions of individualism and freedom with coveted job qualities such as job control and discretion. The opportunity to shape one's own occupational activities (Kohn 1976) is an increasingly prevalent feature of European working life (Eurofound 2015). However, the transition from alienating organisational hierarchies of Fordism to globally networked production and participative post-industrial labour processes has fragmented occupational structures and complicated work autonomy (Blauner 1964; Braverman 1974; Edwards 1979; Sennett 1998). The conditions of work *and* employment have become more flexible and more insecure leading to a merging of firm and worker interests, and a normative form of employer control which elicits worker commitment (Kunda 2006; Walton 1986).

Responsible autonomy (Friedman 1977) offers flexibility and discretion, but it also brings increased intensity of work and a required investment of more of the 'whole person' (Thompson 2003) in line with organisational goals.

Autonomy is now embedded within a complex web of interdependencies and indeterminacies (Berardi 2009). As such, it is not free of structural forces. It is a relational and interdependent phenomenon that can present counter-intuitive conditions which challenge the experience of self-regulation and discretion at work, especially in knowledge-intensive industries (Byrne 2016). These include boundaryless and unpredictable temporal demands (Allvin 2008; O'Carroll 2015); required strategies to define when and where work does and does not occur (Moen et al. 2013); balancing required interactive time with interruptions from de-synchronised autonomous colleagues (Perlow 1999; Lund et al. 2011); labour processes that rely on people in a different physical and temporal space (Ó Riain 2006); and, managerial authority and responsibilities that increase work-life conflict (Schieman et al. 2009). Finding employment security in a volatile and market-sensitive knowledge industry like IT is an increasingly individual and intensive endeavour (Benner 2002). These conditions form the occupational norms and knowledge which determine the demands of work and employment in IT (Cushen and Thompson 2002). They also expose the gendered structures which have emerged within a male dominated industry. Constant availability, unpredictability, work-home boundary-crossing, individually sourced upskilling and peer-network cultivation represent role demands underpinned by a complex masculinist gendered substructure (Acker 1990). The IT industry mirrors the gendered nature of corporate bureaucracies first identified by Kanter (1977). 'Neutral', marketised role requirements are incompatible with perceptions of femininity and social reproduction roles. Walby (2011) highlights three specific ways in which knowledge society is gendered: temporalities, spatialities, and contractualities. In the IT case, implicit gendered norms are reproduced through: boundarylessness, interdependence, and employability (Byrne 2016).

Boundaryless Temporality

The task of balancing the temporal imperatives of the organisation and a private life, represents *the* characteristic condition of knowledge workers lives (Allvin 2008). Boundaryless demands are built on a reinforced gender division between work (public) and non-work (private) roles (Acker 1990; Hochschild and Machung 1990). Access to the resource of unlimited time to dedicate to organisational imperatives becomes a differentiating feature which favours men (Rutherford 2001; Williams 2013). Responding to intensive and unbounded temporal demands Moen et al. (2013: 79) highlight how knowledge workers consent to the 'temporal organisation of professional work' through the use of individual 'time-work' strategies, or what Allvin (2008: 36) calls 'regulative work'. Women in traditional domestic contexts found leaving the job as the only strategy of 'scaling back' work obligations. The inability to contain work and allocate time to the family was viewed as a personal failing (Moen et al. 2013). These female professionals working in a high-tech organisation in the US found themselves in between the expectations of marketised project time (Shih 2004) and their role as caregiver (Hochschild and Machung 1990). The key bargain here places privately negotiated working autonomy in direct competition with publicly defined (and unchallenged) organisational goals and deadlines, leaving two competing temporal structures; 'a corporate one of boundary crossing and a private one of boundary maintenance' (O'Carroll 2015: 92). Similarly, Hari's (2017) study of Canadian tech companies highlights the implicit gender norms underpinning work-life balance (WLB practices) as HR deliberately separated care from WLB initiatives. Noting the 'semi-permeable boundary between work and home' (2017: 108) these practices meant work could impede home, but home could not impede work. For these IT companies, social reproductive roles were beyond the remit of their WLB practices, thus reinforcing the assumption that their workers are individuals who have few temporal obligations beyond work

For O'Carroll (2015), the unpredictability of 'market time' in the high-tech sector is a pervasive force shaping these temporal logics and tensions. These competing temporal orders serve to preserve the gendering of roles (Acker 1990), creating a 'new temporal regime' (Kamp et al.'s 2011: 231) where constant availability becomes a symbol of commitment. The temporal and autonomous demands of knowledge work often belie its flexibility; 'Flexibility . . . can also be a trap, as it makes non-working time available to the company' (O'Carroll 2015: 145) and doesn't always translate into increased capacity to manage work-life balance (Hari 2017). The impact of flexibility stigma – more common among men – on career opportunities can influence the take-up of flexi-time policies (Chung 2017). So-called gender-neutral flexible policies at the state and workplace level, do not always reflect implementation or take-up due to the potential repercussions for employment security. The role of available, committed IT worker who can meet the demands of unpredictable and boundaryless temporalities is not gender neutral (Acker 1990; Hari 2017; Mundy 2017).

The Interdependence of Internal Relations

Benson and Brown (2007) identify three inter-related facets of knowledge work practices: autonomy, task interdependence, and variety. Task interdependence refers to a division of labour shaped by inter-team and intra-team co-dependency with tasks and processes occurring simultaneously.

The working rhythms (Hvid et al. 2008) of colleagues and clients represent an interdependent working condition which impinges on the forming of individual re-regulatory strategies (Allvin 2008). Perlow (1999) notes the 'time famine' of software engineers which arises out of a complex interplay of required individual and interactive demands leading to positive interactions or negative interruptions. A multitude of autonomous but interdependent workers can lead to a de-synchronisation and unpredictability of task-flow (Lund et al. 2011), further fuelling boundaryless temporal regimes. The combination of individual and interactive work can lead to other colleagues becoming a controlling presence (O'Carroll 2015) or a concertive form of control (Barker 1993) which is less apparent and more restrictive because it is legitimized by the workers themselves. When some workers are women, their capabilities (Hobson 2014) for re-regulation may differ from male colleagues – especially in traditional gender ideology contexts (Hochschild and Machung 1989). Even where this is not the case, the informal dynamics of team work in IT, populated primarily by men, can lead to an entrenchment of gendered roles based on perceived abilities to meet interdependent demands – themselves underpinned by competing temporal structures of work and home (Acker 1990; Hari 2017; Hochschild and Machung 1989).

Variety refers to the range of tasks which need to be addressed, and often contain uncertain or unpredictable outcomes and processes (Benson and Brown 2007; O'Carroll 2015). Task variety is perceived as one of the most attractive and beneficial aspects of knowledge work, though it can also be stifled. Holt and Lewis's (2011) study of Danish workplace practices identifies the process of 'gliding gender segregation' where women with similar levels of education and experience to men end up in more routine positions within the organisation. The authors find that competence and commitment – required to get 'interesting' jobs – were wrapped up in ideals of visibility (making yourself heard, not making use of work-family policies) and the ability to meet non-standard hours at short notice. The women in the study were aware that getting these roles meant 'playing male games' (see also O'Connor and O'Hagan this volume). Where women did change their behaviour to compete, this legitimised masculine regimes. Grosen et al. (2012) find similar gender naturalisation processes whereby the temporal logics and boundary maintenance required of knowledge workers leads to a gendering of typical work conditions. These spatial divergences (Walby 2011) impinge not only on the technical and temporal expectations of women in autonomous positions, but also on their opportunities for up-skilling and career progression. Women face different bundles of opportunities, controls, and demands when compared to men (Crowley 2013). As high autonomy at work does not always ensure job security, these different bundles lead to an uneven gendered distribution of human and social capital (Walby 2011) required to upskill and compete as an 'entrepreneurial self' (Scharff 2016, 112) in the knowledge economy.

Individualised Employability

The institutionalisation of numerical and functional flexibility has altered the quality of working life autonomy, tying workers, and working conditions closer to market fluctuations while absolving employers of responsibility for the security of employees (O'Carroll 2015). Autonomous knowledge work is embedded within an unequal neoliberal employment bargain which requires unconditional investment of time and effort from workers, for rewards from employers which are wholly dependent on performance in the market (Thompson 2003). Organisational flexibility and networked production bind job security to firm competitiveness. Post-industrial occupations are rife with 'low status control' (Siegrist 1996: 27) i.e. threats to the continuity of occupational roles and career sustainability. Consequently, employment security has become individualised (Sennett 1998) as workers seek security in the upskilling efforts and the networks and reputations of external labour markets. Shih (2006) notes how networks are used by women and Asian immigrants in Silicon Valley to rival traditional 'old white boys' networks' and enable job-hopping around firms perceived as discriminatory. Cushen and Thompson (2012) reveal how angry knowledge workers in a global, leading-edge technology company in Ireland completely rejected the organisational brand narrative as they perceived it as an attempt to conceal the tenuous nature of their employment. Yet they maintained high performance levels due to a commitment to the work, professional knowledge, and skills. The attachment here was to occupational prestige and norms. Firms provide learning opportunities rather than security, and individually managed informal networks are crucial to future employment prospects (Benner 2002). Forging a career in IT adds employment management work (Halpin and Smith 2017) to the boundaryless and temporal demands previously discussed. This consists of a range of 'individual and relational' strategies of maximising *current* work opportunities for *future* employment security.

Knowledge workers have internalised responsibility for their own careers and consent to demanding, erratic working conditions to strengthen their own career prospects (Shih 2004). The combination of high autonomy and low security enables limitless labour through the neoliberal ideology of 'entrepreneurial selves' who relate to themselves as a business which must constantly self-improve, compete with others, and repudiate those who are not entrepreneurial (Scharff 2016). This entrepreneurial subjectivity (Scharff

2016) captures the links between boundaryless, interdependent and employ-ability structures of autonomy in knowledge work which establish gendered boundaries based on who cannot, or are perceived unable, to meet these implicit demands. Thus, professionalism in IT and gendered meanings become mutually constitutive as women remain in communicative roles, separated from technical tasks and opportunities (Ruiz Ben 2007).

Truss et al's (2012) study of 'knowledge intensive firms' (KIFs) in Ireland and the UK analysed the experience of women in the software and pharmaceutical industry. Although women had similar levels of education to men, they earned significantly less, were less represented in senior roles, had lower levels of job autonomy and security, limited 'innovative work behaviour', a more negative view of career prospects, and equal levels of task interdependence. The segregation into more routine roles (Holt and Lewis 2011) meant that they were not able to convert newfound skills into innovative work behaviours on the job, subsequently leading to a decrease in career prospects. The result is a 'cycle of disadvantage' for women where segregation within teams and firms reinforces unequal career opportunities and forms of employment (Truss et al. 2012). This study illustrates the close links between the gendering of knowledge accumulation, and deviating employment types, or 'contractualities' (Walby 2011) in IT. Within de-regulated employment management work (Halpin and Smith 2017) the opportunities to acquire the necessary human and social capital to compete in the IT labour market diverge into gendered paths, with women at risk of falling through the 'trap door' (Williams 2013) of the IT industry. I now turn to an examination of how these gendered structures are experienced by IT workers in Ireland and Denmark.

THE GENDERING OF TASKS: WORDS, VISIBILITY AND JUGGLING

Words & Visibility

It is not that equal . . . if you have got a male dominated job or a female dominated job, and they have had the same amount of years studying, then it wouldn't be paid the same . . . we have three female developers and the rest are male, and we have about twenty of those I would say. And in our department, which is the business consultants, it is vice versa. We have seventeen and two of them are men, because it is a more, I don't know if you would call it a touchy-feely job, but it is a communicative job. You have got to please one part and please the other part, so we do that well . . . talk this language with this person and talk that language with that person so they understand because beforehand it was developers speaking directly with the clients and they had no idea. So that is basically through words, written or spoken . . . (Karen, IT Consultant, Denmark).

Seven of the ten women were in a position where the primary duties are communication and management, rather than technical or developmental. Titles include project manager, HR consultant, IT business consultant, and a head of IT which essentially involved managing various project leaders. The disparity between the roles taken up by men and women in her employment was not lost on Karen whose role involves linking customers and developers to solve system bugs. In common with Helen who introduced this chapter, Karen is acutely aware of the links between gender, role type, skills, and pay. The women in her department inhabit a world of communication rather than development. Explicitly linking gendered ideas and jurisdictional competence (Ruiz Ben 2007), she depicts the development world as male and the world of 'words' (written or spoken) as female. Linking this segregation of tasks to pay, Karen indicates that ability with 'words' is worth less than technical ability, reinforcing gender inequality in pay. Lisa, a Senior Compliance Officer from Ireland, also noted the importance of communication skills throughout her career: 'the roles I put myself into I am dealing with so many different personalities'. Like Karen, her responsibilities revolve around colleagues and customers rather than technical processes.

Emily describes how the designation of women into communicative roles plays out at the level of the team labour process. She described a major element of her job as 'asking people to do things'. This is a skill for which she feels she has a natural inclination whereas the males in her team are better at the technical aspects of the job:

> So, we have done this job, we have to write it up . . . document it. The guys wouldn't document anything . . . let's say we [interviewee and interviewer] worked on something very technical and you came up with a great solution . . . I would be like, that is brilliant, let's write that down, I would not have come up with that . . . that would be so useful for everybody else . . . but you wouldn't be bothered because you could come up with it again in a second whereas I could see the value in what you have done because maybe I wouldn't have done that . . . am I saying the guys are more technical? Maybe. (Emily, Project Manager, Ireland).

Here, Emily portrays a simple but revealing everyday labour process where gendered distinctions in positions, tasks, skills, and priorities serve to solidify the gender essentialism of roles and interactions in the workplace (Acker 1990). When a solution has been found to a technical problem, she is often the person who will document this solution. The male developers who came up with the solution have no interest in documenting it because they 'could come up with it again in a second'. Emily links her weaker technical skills to the gendered segregation of project tasks. Her willingness to document it, and her male colleagues' disinterest, is perpetuated by the gendered distinction of skills. This, in turn, preserves the gendered designation of tasks. Elaborating further, she noted that within the scrum teams in her company, the scrum-master (i.e. the communicator) was often the woman. Compartmentalisation into communicative tasks – and roles – not only limits technical development, it also has implications for internal relations as respect often accompanies technical expertise. 'For better or for worse I think engineers tend to respect managers and they respect leaders who are also technical people. . . . I am the same way . . . I have more respect for them if they have a technical background' (Helen, Technical Director, Denmark).

Even where technical ability is acknowledged, patriarchal structures can fill the vacuum of de-regulated working conditions. Irina (UX Product Manager, Denmark) felt that she had hit 'a glass ceiling' when debating a project team's make-up and strategy with senior male colleagues, who were not as skilled in UX design. For Irina it was the physicality, confidence, and bravado of these men that convinced their director of the way forward, and thus undermined her superior technical competence and knowledge of her team:

> I was personally hurt . . . they were saying we need someone who is really experienced . . . we have hired some very senior designers . . . both of them are men and both of them are very confident and tall and masculine and very good public speakers, all of that . . . I think they kind of saw me as, because they don't understand the field, they don't know design. So, what do I look like? Do I look like someone who is very experienced and competent? I am aware that I am a soft-spoken small woman who doesn't necessarily look very old, but this is just what is going through my head. I really felt like I hit the glass ceiling. I felt like they were using that against me (Irina, UX Product Manager, Denmark).

Irina felt her physical appearance meant she could not play the masculine game of being visible and heard (Holt and Lewis 2011). This experience points to the barriers inherent in the interplay of gender essentialism, team autonomy, and occupational norms. The link between everyday tasks and roles within labour processes, temporal demands, technical competence, and acquired knowledge become entwined and act as gendered structures differentiating opportunities for men and women in IT in both countries. Divergent occupational paths are not reined in by an institutional context which provides enhanced capabilities (Hobson 2014) for women to be visible in the workplace and 'juggle' boundaryless and interdependent demands with caring responsibilities. It is to the latter that I now turn.

Juggling Expectations

Probably one night a week I do a proper logon and clear out my email, maybe two or three hours . . . all through the week I am watching what is happening and whatever happens might cause me to logon for half an hour and deal with something time sensitive . . . If I am in the middle of dinner or if I am doing something with one of the kids . . . I am not going to take your call . . . I might listen to your voice mail on the way home. So, feel free to call me whenever you want . . . I am taking responsibility for whether it is a good time to call (Laura, Head of IT, Ireland).

Describing how she reacts to work demands that regularly breach the work-home boundary, Laura outlines a temporal rhythm which is almost entirely aligned with the needs of her employer, though her kids have a legitimate right to interrupt. She is on the lookout for anything 'time sensitive', notes that being able to 'pre-empt' is beneficial and asserts that she takes 'responsibility for whether it is a good time to call', not her employer. These strategies require a constant juggling of temporal demands based on the expectations of traditional caregiver roles, and the requirements of current – and future – work tasks. Discussing the barriers for women advancing to senior technical positions in IT, Emily and Mary pointed to the occupationally legitimated but self-imposed incompatibility of caregiver and senior role expectations:

you have a smart phone, Wi-Fi everywhere . . . for other people it would just be normal for them to check their emails all of the time. You don't get any break from it then . . . I have two kids; I don't really want to be getting phone calls in the evening and . . . It just seems to be the culture that has crept in . . . (Mary, Project Manager, Ireland)

it is a barrier to women . . . a manager position . . . maybe it is perceived that you have to work nine hours a day. You are thinking my kids deserve more than that . . . it is that kind of juggling that might be a barrier as well . . . I was probably thinking I am not putting myself forward for management because I would have to work more . . . and my kids are more important than that. So that might be a decision that a lot of women are making in their heads, my kids are more important than my career . . . I had four babysitters last week . . . It is a lot of juggling yes . . . It can be a little bit stressful . . . It is ok, but it is ok because you have made it ok because you have juggled and you have got all this plan A, plan B, you have got a plan C sometimes. . . (Emily, Project Manager, Ireland)

Mary notes the combined impact of ICT capacities and colleagues' behaviours in legitimating a culture of boundaryless time and space for work activities thus restricting the enactment of a family role (Hari 2017). For Emily, the theme is 'juggling'. This is required to meet the expectations of a management role and avoid threatening the boundaries of family time. Women may be hesitant to apply for these roles unless they are certain they can incorporate them into suitable temporal rhythms. As it stands, Emily must constantly negotiate the demands of childminding at an individual level as plans A, B, and C are required to ensure her children are cared for when she is at work. Career progression means complicating this further. The consequent self-restriction is a symptom of interlacing structural barriers; the occupational norms of constant re-regulation and traditional care-giver contexts. Emily's strategies represent the re-regulative tasks inherent in the flexible, post-industrial 'second-shift' (Hochschild and Machung 1990) where the maintenance of work time and space is complicated by the temporal demands of non-work roles, underpinned by structures of gendered norms. These incompatible role expectations have implications for the career decisions of women in IT. In terms of balancing childcare and work in Denmark, Karen provides a striking contrast:

> That is made much easier over here. First of all, I had maternity leave for a year with nearly full pay . . . after that there was day care facilities which were easy. So not a problem really . . . if somebody calls you to a meeting at 3:00 but you have put into your calendar that I need to leave at 3:00 because I need to fetch my children before the day care closes, that is an accepted excuse . . . (Karen, IT Consultant, Denmark).

Institutional contexts that provide generous maternity leave, subsidised childcare and family friendly working arrangements clearly influence the experience of autonomy in working life. Karen's autonomy is enhanced by an institutional context defined by collective regulation (e.g. high taxes, large welfare state, subsidised childcare, and a linked, bounded worktime). For Emily, a more de-regulated institutional context demands strategies of 'juggling' which must be sourced and sustained at the individual level. Whilst coping with the demands of work and family seems easier in the Danish context, these capabilities do not mitigate the structural, cultural, and practice-based dynamics that gender IT work, as depicted by Karen and Helen previously. The gendering of tasks and roles within these labour processes has a knock-on effect on the accumulation of knowledge required to sustain careers in the IT labour market.

DIVERGING KNOWLEDGE: INSECURE EMPLOYABILITY AND
PROFESSIONAL CAPITAL

The notion of security was a complex topic for participants. Derek (Head of Professional Services, Ireland) described it as an industry in which there is a 'lack of future'. However, only 29 per cent of Irish participants agreed that they might lose their job in the next six months and only one Danish participant agreed with this statement. Additionally, most participants agreed that they felt secure in their job. Exploring the experience of security further it emerged that participants linked the feeling of security to their own ability to gain further employment elsewhere, rather than traditional job security with one employer:

> permanent doesn't mean a whole tonne anymore . . . there was this constant possibility, like I don't think my job was particularly at risk but there were two or three rounds of redundancies . . . So, you never think that you are secure in anything . . . I think I am just doing my own forward planning (Rebecca, IT HR Consultant, Ireland).

> I am not going to lose sleep over that [job insecurity], I am sure I can find something else (Irina, UX Product Manager, Denmark).

> Is it a contradiction to say I felt secure in the job but also thought I could lose it? . . . I still feel I could lose my job in the next six months because of what is going on . . . but I still feel secure in my job . . . I fitted into the team . . . but that is not to say that at another higher level someone will come in and say, sorry we have to let you go. So, within my job I might feel secure, but in this industry . . . (Emily, Project Manager, Ireland).

Security is de-linked from both the present and the employer. Feeling secure becomes linked with job-fit rather than employment contract. The feeling of job insecurity seemed to be offset by a belief in employment security. Rebecca notes that 'permanent' doesn't mean what it used to, so she must do her 'own forward planning', legitimating the volatile rhythms of the industry. Emily, while discussing the contradiction of feeling secure and thinking she could lose her job, implies that individual performance has become de-linked from organisational strategies. Even working well with your team does not protect from potential redundancy. The participants, particularly those who had experience with redundancy rounds, acknowledged that takeovers, outsourcing, and restructuring were always lurking around the corner and they had no influence over organisational strategies. Individual performance therefore is linked to future employment prospects rather than current job security. Mary (Project Manager, Ireland) notes how 'organisational jockeying' for projects can lead to under-resourced teams and leave workers uncertain of what's around the corner, having 'to kind of ride the wave' of the industry. Security exists in the future but requires constant attention to work upskilling and networking opportunities in the present:

> am I advancing . . . is my job security, well not looking necessarily at your job security as within a single company, it is across the industry . . . You have to keep up skills absolutely (Peter, Software Development Engineer, Ireland).

> The first port of call would always be your personal network and your personal connections . . . The most likely way you are going to get in or get a job or get started in a new place is going to be through referral or a connection . . . (Luke, Consultant, Ireland).

> it is personal stuff and personal contacts. It is important what people think of you. That is very important . . . (Lars, Senior Developer, Denmark).

Peter describes an employment bargain where security is located within the industry rather than a firm. Keeping skills up to date becomes a prerogative of individual employability as technological developments are key to 'progression' for firms *and* workers. These comments illustrate how employability demands can lead to an intensification of the experience of work and feed into an erratic, boundaryless working time as not only jobs, but careers, are being earned. Luke and Lars also highlight the importance of networks and reputation to their future employment. Over 40 per cent of Danish participants acquired their current job via a personal contact while 53 per cent of the Irish participants did. Networks matter in work and in the labour market to maintain currency, capital, and future prospects. Networks are inherently gendered. They are fuelled by reputational capital (innovation, visibility, and reliability) that may also be easier to maintain for workers with fewer caring responsibilities in more technically skilled and evolving areas. Network visibility is also secured via the social life around IT work:

> I think to be really, really good . . . like I was doing coding . . . that was the only job that I had ever done . . . I kind of just thought, I can't keep upskilling. Because I was working on a team of guys, there was probably about 20 guys and I was the only girl and I just thought, oh if this is the life that I am going to have ahead of me, just working on massive teams of guys all the time, it probably wasn't what I wanted to do (Lisa, Senior Compliance Officer, Ireland).

Lisa describes this world of competition and upskilling as a male one. Her unwillingness to 'keep upskilling' is tied to a disinterest in working and socialising with large teams of men for the rest of her career. These feelings of being in a minority status illustrate once more the role of visibility in IT working conditions, adding to Irina's previous comments on the role of her physical appearance. Helen also notes the importance of the social scene around IT networks and its masculine character:

> they don't like the idea necessarily of a woman disrupting the boy's club and I really think that is true. I have seen off site where they are going out for whiskey and cigars and stuff like that and I have to wonder is part of it like they wonder how would a woman impact my whiskey and cigar boy's club thing. . . (Helen, Technical Director, Denmark).

Employability in IT requires access to 'interesting' positions which, as discussed previously, is not always equal. Women's ability to exploit these conditions may be impeded by maternity leave, school hours, or an inability to move for other jobs. This is especially the case in male-breadwinner contexts where access to the resource of boundaryless time for work (Rutherford 2001) is gendered. Throughout the previous two sections female interviewees have described the masculine substructure of IT work as one shaped by: male dominance of developmental roles and technical competence; boundaryless availability for work, learning and network cultivation; visibility as commitment; and constant competition (see also Sheerin this volume). The normative and linked structures of boundaryless temporalities, interdependent demands, and individualised employability, fill the de-regulated space of high autonomy – and implicitly advantage men. For Helen, the patriarchal nature of IT work was evident as progressing to the role of Technical Director meant fighting the 'boys' club':

> Going from the mid-level role to the more senior role, that was actually really hard. And I don't think that [firm] is unique in this. I really believe that in development organisations in general, the senior management . . . it tends to be like a boy's club . . . I really had to fight for the better part of a year . . . it was a struggle . . . if I hadn't been motivated and determined to do it I think it wouldn't have happened (Helen, Technical Director, Denmark).

The character of autonomy in IT has developed through the lens of male working lives. Consequently, the form and demands of de-regulated working conditions and insecure networked employment have become interdependent. It is this interdependence of work and employment trajectories which serve to reinforce gender segregation in IT. The reputational capital and networking ability of women in IT is restricted due to the segregation of labour process tasks and technical roles. Colleagues may also limit access to required upskilling experience *and* key networks. The individualised and insecure nature of the IT labour market interlaces with the normative forces re-regulating autonomous IT work to gender professional knowledge. The following section maps these structures of segregation.

THE INTERLOCKING & SEGREGATING STRUCTURES OF AUTONOMOUS IT WORK

The character of autonomy in IT has legitimised demands of boundary-lessness, interdependence, visibility, insecure employability, reputational capital, and peer networks. These have emerged through – and reproduce – an industry shaped by a hegemonic masculine substructure (Acker 1990; Hari 2017; Ruiz Ben 2007). The close reciprocal relationship between advantageous work opportunities, boundaryless time, and career prospects is perceived as incompatible with perceptions of femininity and traditional social reproduction ideologies. Figure 1 illustrates how the homosocial reproduction of men in technical and senior positions in IT (Kanter 1977) is linked to the gendered meanings (Acker 1990) of autonomous work (boundarylessness, visibility, interdependence) – via interlocking and diverging paths in task, training, experience and employability opportunities. These convoluted power structures within working conditions and employ-ment practices intersect (Smith 1997; Sennett 1998) and act as a form of social closure (Rutherford 2001) which re-inscribes gendered structures within autonomous IT work.

Interviewees encountered labour processes and working conditions characterised by the ideals of a masculinist gender substructure (Acker 1990; Hari 2017). These practices impact capabilities for technical knowledge accumulation through gendered ascriptions of competence (Ruiz Ben 2007) and result in gliding gender segregation (Holt and Lewis 2011) into communicative roles. Subsequently the type of knowledge gained within IT work becomes gendered. Due to the competitive and volatile nature of the IT industry, insecure employability requires a negotiation and maximisation of upskilling, networking, and reputation-enhancing oppor-tunities whilst in work. This requires access to tasks, roles, and social spaces which are not always open to women – especially in male breadwinner contexts where boundaryless work time is impeded by private temporal regimes. Here, the capabilities diverge for attaining the human and social

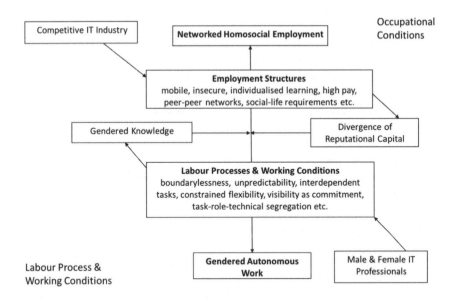

Figure 1: The Segregating Structures of Autonomy in IT

capital (Walby 2011) required to ensure employability in IT by gender. These de-regulated structures serve not to break down but conceal power and control within more participatory systems. Gliding gender segregation (Holt and Lewis 2011) and cycles of disadvantage (Truss et al. 2012) become mutually constitutive precisely because the opportunities available in work are so important to employment security in IT. The gendering of autonomy in IT is reproduced by the intersection of these working conditions and employment practices (Acker 1990; Smith 1997).

The pervasiveness of these structures is evident in their strength across two different socio-political contexts offering different capabilities for managing work and family roles. Even in the Danish context, where participants spoke of institutional resources which aided the balancing of work and childcare demands, these 'capabilities' (Hobson 2014) did not surmount the segregating structures linking work and employment in IT. Interestingly, Helen notes that the Danish context of high levels of societal equality and traditional gender ideologies may actually reinforce horizontal gender segregation in Danish education, feeding limited numbers of women into the IT labour market. The importance of on-the-job experience, upskilling, and networking intensifies this segregation. Helen describes how knowledge about gender at societal level can impact on the gendering of knowledge within an apparently diverse industry:

> I would be interested to know if there is an equivalent number of women in lower level technical roles and they are just less likely to move up or whether there is just less of them in general. I think one of the big things is there is a lot of equality in society . . . if you look at toys for kids, in Denmark everything is super heavily gendered, you can have this blue thing with trucks or you can have this pink thing with dolls and that is it . . . I would venture to guess that actually there are just less women studying these areas to even go into the work force in the first place because in Denmark we don't believe that you are better if you are a programmer or work in construction . . . Maybe that is part of it (Helen, Technical Director, Denmark).

Gendered structures are wrought and sustained by the quality of autonomous work in IT. De-regulated environments of work and employment provide flexibility, discretion, and a whole host of temporal, relational, and employment demands which must be negotiated on a consistent basis and embody the requirements of an IT worker (Acker 1990). Where time and visibility become symbols of commitment, competing temporal structures (O'Carroll 2015) place different pressures and opportunities on male and female IT workers. The female participants' experience highlights how the structures of autonomy – conserved by a gendering of relations and practices at the labour process level – stunt technical development, restrict opportunities for technical roles, and consequently limit employability activities. This intersection of controls genders the knowledge required to earn and sustain a technical career in this knowledge industry. I have demonstrated the continued relevance of the work of Acker (1990) and Kanter (1977) on organisational dynamics. Progressive industries and organisations remain shaped by the interlinked and gendered structures of autonomous working conditions and networked employment opportunities in IT. A masculine substructure is legitimised and reproduced within a neutral, inclusive industry through the gendered requirements of boundarylessness, visibility, upskilling, networking, and reputational capital which serve to reinforce the patriarchy of IT work.

CONCLUSION

Autonomy in IT work is embodied by masculine ideals. These autonomous conditions provide high levels of individual flexibility and discretion whilst also concealing more implicit and interconnected structures which segregate opportunities for men and women. The endurance of segregated opportunities within an industry lauded for its diversity and innovation represents an informative case of how new forms of knowledge work – despite their flexibility – are still underpinned by gendered structures. Drawing on in-depth working life interviews with IT workers in Ireland and Denmark, I have depicted the restriction on opportunities for women across tasks, teams, roles, and professional knowledge, thus facilitating the re-inscription of gendered norms (Connell 2002) in IT work.

A particular feature of autonomy in IT is the interdependence of work opportunities and employability prospects. The gendering of tasks and roles thus facilitates a gendered divergence of the technical and social capital (Walby 2011) required to compete as an entrepreneurial self (Scharff 2016) within this neoliberal work bargain. The result is an interlocking of structures which legitimate and reproduce masculine regimes in IT (Figure 1). Here, the homosocial reproduction (Kanter 1977) of men in technical and senior positions intertwines with the gendered meanings (Acker 1990) of boundarylessness, visibility, interdependence, and employability. This is evident across both Irish and Danish institutional contexts despite the fact that each offer different capabilities for managing work and caregiver roles. Autonomy in IT offers de-regulated work and employment environments in which gendered knowledge practices reinforce knowledge about gender, coercing women down a path of gliding task segregation (Holt and Lewis 2011), cycles of disadvantage in the labour market (Truss et al. 2012) and potentially the 'trap door' (Williams 2013) of a technical career.

Acknowledgement

This research was funded by the European Research Council via the *New Deals in the Economy* project led by Professor Seán Ó Riain at Maynooth University (Grant ID: 283778), and the Irish Research Council via a Postgraduate Scholarship awarded to the author.

REFERENCES

Acker, Joan, 'Hierarchies, jobs, bodies: A theory of gendered organizations', in *Gender and Society*, 4(2), 1990, pp 139–58.

Adshead, Maura and Jonathan Tonge, *Politics in Ireland: Convergence and Divergence in a Two-Polity Island* (Palgrave Macmillan: New York, 2009).

Allvin, Michael, 'New rules of work: Exploring the boundaryless job', in Katharina Naswall, Johnny Hellgren and Magnus Sverke (eds), *The Individual in the Changing Working Life* (Cambridge University Press: Cambridge, 2008).

Barker, James R, 'Tightening the Iron Cage: Concertive control in self-managing teams', in *Administrative Science Quarterly*, 38(3), 1993, pp 408-37.

Benner, Chris, *Work in the New Economy: Flexible Labor Markets in Silicon Valley* (Blackwell Publishers Ltd: Oxford, 2002).

Benson, John, and Michelle Brown, 'Knowledge workers: What keeps them committed; what turns them away', in *Work, Employment & Society*, 21(1), 2007, pp 121–41.

Berardi, Franco, *The Soul at Work. From Alienation to Autonomy* (Semiotext(e): California, 2009).

Blauner, Robert, *Alienation and Freedom: The Factory Worker and His Industry* (University of Chicago Press: Chicago, 1964).

Braverman, Harry, *Labor and Monopoly Capital: The Degradation of Work in the Twentieth Century* (Monthly Review Press: New York, 1974).

Byrne, John-Paul, *The Antinomies of Autonomy: The Social Structure of Stressors in Ireland and Denmark* (Maynooth, 2016), Maynooth University EThesis Repository http://eprints.maynoothuniversity.ie/8149/

Central Statistics Office, *Women and Men in Ireland 2016* (Cork, 2017), CSO: https://www.cso.ie/en/releasesandpublications/ep/pwamii/womenandmeninireland2016/

Chung, Heejung, *Work Autonomy, Flexibility, and Work-Life Balance* (University of Kent Work Autonomy and Flexibility Project: Kent, 2017).

Ciccia, Rossella and Mieke Verloo, 'Parental leave regulations and the persistence of the male breadwinner model: Using fuzzy-set ideal type analysis to assess gender equality in an enlarged Europe', in *Journal of European Social Policy*, 22(5), 2012, pp 507–28.

Coakley, John, 'Society and political culture', in John Coakley and Michael Gallagher (eds), *Politics in the Republic of Ireland 5th edition* (Routledge: New York, 2010).

Connell, Raewyn W., *Gender* (John Wiley & Sons: UK, 2002).

Crowley, Martha, 'Gender, the labor process and dignity at work', in *Social Forces*, 91(4), 2013, pp 1,209–38.

Cushen, Jean, and Paul Thompson, 'Doing the right thing? HRM and the angry knowledge worker', in *New Technology, Work and Employment*, 27(2), 2012, pp 79–92.

Edwards, Richard, *Contested Terrain: The Transformation of the Workplace in the Twentieth Century* (Basic Books: New York, 1979).

Esping Andersen, Gøsta, *The Three Worlds of Welfare Capitalism* (Princeton University Press: Princeton, 1990).

Eurofound, *First Findings from the 6th European Working Conditions Survey* (European Foundation for the Improvement of Living and Working Conditions: Dublin, 2015).

Ibid., *Occupational Change and Wage Inequality: European Jobs Monitor 2017* (Publications Office of the European Union: Luxembourg, 2017).

European Institute for Gender Equality, *Gender Equality Index 2017: Measuring Gender Equality in the European Union 2005–2015* (Publications Office of the European Union: Luxembourg, 2017).

Friedman, Andrew. L., *Industry and Labour* (Macmillan: London, 1977).

Grosen, Sidsel Lond, Helle Holt, and Henrik Lambrecht Lund, 'The naturalization of gender segregation in a Danish bank', in *Nordic Journal of Working Life Studies*, 2(1), 2012, pp 61–79.

Halpin, Brian W. and Vicki Smith, 'Employment management work: A case study and theoretical framework', in *Work and Occupations*, 44(4), 2017, pp 339–75.

Hari, Amrita, 'Who gets to "work hard, play hard"? Gendering the work-life balance rhetoric in Canadian tech companies', in *Gender, Work & Organisation*, 24(2), 2017, pp 99–114.

Hobson, Barbara (ed.), *Worklife Balance: The Agency & Capabilities Gap* (Oxford University Press: Oxford, 2014).

Hochschild, Arlie and Anne Machung, *The Second Shift: Working Families and the Revolution at Home* (Penguin Publishing Group: New York, 1989).

Holt, Helle and Suzan Lewis, 'You can stand on your head and still end up with lower pay': Gliding segregation and gendered work practices in Danish "family-friendly" workplaces', in *Gender, Work & Organization*, 18, 2011, pp e202–21.

Hvid, Helge, Henrik Lambrecht Lund and Jan Pejtersen, 'Control, flexibility and rhythms', in *Scandinavian Journal of Work, Environment and Health*, 6, 2008, pp 83–90.

Jenkins, Richard, *Being Danish: Paradoxes of Identity in Everyday Life* (Museum Tusculanum Press: Copenhagen, 2012).

Kamp, Annette, Henrik Lambrecht Lund, and Helge Søndergaard Hvid, 'Negotiating time, meaning and identity in boundaryless work', in *Journal of Workplace Learning*, 23(4), 2011, pp 229–42.

Kanter, Rosabeth Moss, *Men and Women of the Corporation* (Basic Books: New York, 1977).

Kohn, Melvin L., 'Occupational structure and alienation', in *American Journal of Sociology*, 82(1), 1976, pp 111–30.

Kunda, Gideon, *Engineering Culture: Control and Commitment in a High-Tech Corporation* (Temple University Press: Philadelphia, 2006).

Lewis, Jane, 'Gender and the development of welfare regimes', in *Journal of European Social Policy*, 2(3), 1992, pp 159–73.

Lund, Henrik Lambrecht, Helge Hvid and Annette Kamp, 'Perceived time, temporal order and control in boundaryless work' in Peter Vink and Jussi Kantola (eds), *Advances in Occupational, Social, and Organizational Ergonomics* (Taylor and Francis: Boca Raton, 2011).

Moen, Phyllis, Anne Kaduk, Ellen Ernst Kossek, Leslie Hammer, Orfeu M. Buxton, Emily O'Donnell, David Almeida, Kimberly Fox, Eric Tranby, J. Michael Oakes, and Lynne Casper, 'Is work-family conflict a multilevel stressor linking job conditions to mental health? Evidence from the work, family and health network', in Samantha K. Ammons and Erin L. Kelly (eds), *Research in the Sociology of Work: Work and Family in the New Economy*, 26, 2015, pp 177–217.

Moen, Phyllis, Jack Lam, Samantha Ammons, and Erin L. Kelly, 'Time work by overworked professionals: Strategies in response to the stress of higher status', in *Work and Occupations*, 40(2), 2013, pp 79–114.

Mundy, Liza, 'Why is Silicon Valley so awful to women' in *The Atlantic*, 319(3), 2017, pp 37–61.

O'Carroll, Aileen, *Working Time, Knowledge Work and Post-Industrial Society: Unpredictable Work* (Palgrave MacMillan: New York, 2015).

Ó Riain, Seán, 'The missing customer and the ever-present market: Software work in the service economy', in *Work and Occupations*, 37, 2010, pp 320–48.

Ibid., 'Time space intensification: Karl Polanyi, the double movement and global informational capitalism', in *Theory and Society*, 35, 2006, pp 507–28.

Perlow, Leslie A., 'The time famine: Toward a sociology of work time', in *Administrative Science Quarterly*, 44(1), 1999, pp 57–81.

Ruiz Ben, Esther, 'Defining expertise in software development while doing gender' in *Gender, Work & Organization*, 14(4), 2007, pp 312–32.

Russell, Helen, Frances McGinnity and Gillian Kingston, *Gender and the Quality of Work: From Boom to Recession* (ESRI and The Equality Authority: Dublin, 2014).

Rutherford, Sarah, 'Are you going home already? The long hours culture, women managers, and patriarchal closure', in *Time and Society*, 10(2–3), 2001, pp 259–76.

Ryan, Richard M., and Edward L. Deci, 'Self-regulation and the problem of human autonomy: Does psychology need choice, self-determination, and will?' in *Journal of Personality*, 74(6), 2006, pp 1,55–85.

Scharff, Christina, 'The psychic life of Neoliberalism: Mapping the contours of entrepreneurial subjectivity' in *Theory, Culture and Society*, 33(6), 2016, pp 107–22.

Schieman, Scott, Melissa A. Milkie and Paul Glavin, 'When work interferes with life: Work-nonwork interference and the influence of work-related demands and resources', in *American Sociological Review*, 74(6), 2009, pp 966–88.

Sen, Amartya, *Development as Freedom* (Alfred A. Knopf Inc.: New York, 1999).

Sennett, Richard, *The Corrosion of Character: The Personal Consequences of Work in the New Capitalism* (W. W. Norton & Company: New York, 1998).

Shih, Johanna, 'Circumventing discrimination: Gender and ethnic strategies in Silicon Valley', in *Gender and Society*, 20(2), 2004, pp 177–206.

Ibid., 'Project time in Silicon Valley', in *Qualitative Sociology*, 27(2), 2004, pp 223–45.

Siegrist, Johannes, 'Adverse health effects of high-effort/low-reward conditions', in *Journal of Occupational Health Psychology*, 1(1), 1996, pp 27–41.

Smith, Vicki, 'New forms of work organization', in *Annual Review of Sociology*, 23, 1997, pp 315–39.

Statistics Denmark, *Statistical Yearbook 2017* (Statistics Denmark: Copenhagen, 2017).

Thompson, Paul, 'Disconnected capitalism: Or why employers can't keep their side of the bargain', in *Work, Employment and Society*, 17(2), 2003, pp 359–78.

Truss, Catherine, Edel Conway, Alessia d'Amato, Gráinne Kelly, Kathy Monks, Enda Hannon, and Patrick C. Flood, 'Knowledge work: Gender-blind or gender-biased?', in *Work, Employment & Society*, 26(5), 2012, pp 735–54.

Wajcman, Judy, *Pressed for Time: The Acceleration of Life in Digital Capitalism* (University of Chicago Press: Chicago, 2015).

Walby, Sylvia, 'Is the knowledge society gendered', in *Gender, Work & Organization*, 18(1), 2011, pp 1–29.

Walton, Richard E., 'From control to commitment in the workplace', in *Harvard Business Review*, 63(2), 1986, pp 76–84.

Williams, Christine L., 'The glass escalator, revisited: Gender inequality in neoliberal times', in *Gender & Society*, 27(5), 2013, pp 609–29.

TWO

The Academic Career Game and Gender Related Practices in STEM in Higher Education

Pat O'Connor and Clare O'Hagan

INTRODUCTION

The production, evaluation and dissemination of knowledge is a core element in Higher Education Institutions (HEIs). It is also one of the ways through which gender inequality is perpetuated. In HEIs, as indeed in the wider society, Science, Technology, Engineering and Mathematics (STEM) is particularly valued and its development and dissemination is perceived by the State as being core to the national interest (O'Connor 2014). STEM has been depicted as a highly masculinist area (Hekman 2004), one which is unreflective about the 'relationships of vassalage' (Etzkowitz et al. 2007: 405) in which knowledge is created. It is also a male dominated area in the sense that women are underrepresented in it both horizontally and vertically (Husu 2000 and 2013; O'Connor 2014; White 2014). In 2016, women made up only 24 per cent of the top-level academic staff in all disciplines in the European Union (Grade A: full professoriate), and only 15 per cent of those in science and engineering (EU 2019). It has been suggested that:

> Western science and technology are culturally masculinised. This is not just a question of personnel . . . The guiding metaphors of scientific research, the impersonality of its discourse, the structures of power and communication in science, the reproduction of its internal culture, all stem from the social position of dominant men in a gendered world (Connell 2005: 6).

In this chapter we illuminate the experiences of men and women involved in the creation and dissemination of knowledge in STEM in a case study Irish HEI.

Morley (2011: 224) argues that despite fears about the feminisation of the academy, gender inequity in universities remains remarkably intractable, with gender inequalities being obscured or ignored (David 2011). Women continue to be benchmarked in relation to male norms, entering a matrix of declared and hidden rules (Lynch et al., 2012; Morley 2013a and b). Structural, cultural and attitudinal barriers continue to reinforce gender differences, placing expectations on women to assimilate into a male-dominated organisational structure and culture, with gender inequality perpetuated through masculinised forms of control and the devaluation of teaching and pastoral care (Danowitz-Sagaria and Agans 2006; Bagilhole and White 2011; Thornton 2013; Hey 2011). Thus, those involved in the creation and dissemination of knowledge are themselves embedded in a male-dominated masculinist structure and culture, which in the case of STEM is portrayed as gender neutral (Britton 2017).

The concept of career traditionally implies an organisational career, defined as a 'sequence of promotions and other upward moves in a work-related hierarchy during the course of a person's work-life' (Hall 1976: 2). As such, it involves education and training in the context of a linear organisational career path with at least the possibility of upward progression. According to Raddon (2002: 391) the 'successful academic' has a linear career path; devotes all of their time and energy to the university; networks both in and out of work hours; builds a reputation through research; is 'career-oriented', 'productive', 'hardworking' and 'enthusiastic'; publishes in the right journals; gains the majority of their experience within a 'prestigious' faculty or field and focuses on research rather than teaching, administration or pastoral activities. This denotes a particular construction of academia and of gender and, by extension, of gendered knowledge.

At any moment in time HEIs play several games with different goals and rules: 'the research game, the income-generation game, the quality game, the teaching game' (Trowler and Bamber 2005: 188). The players within the HEIs are individual academics and researchers, whose participation in these games can collectively be called the 'career game'. Implicit in the concept of the career game is the idea of a strategic approach to career development within the context of male-dominated structural and cultural political agendas (Morley 2013a). It has been suggested that: 'Understanding how power and relationships within these neo-liberal circumstances operate in the university context is necessary . . . [to] navigate a way forward and to provide possibilities for change' (McKay and Monk 2017: 1,251). The potentially masculine metaphor of the 'career game' is explored in this article because it emerged in the data. Career games can be thought of as forms of gendered knowledge. The 'games' that individuals chose to play may be more/less congruent with those favoured by their institution at any one point in time, with implications for their own individual careers. Thus, factors related to the perceived purpose of higher education as well as constructions of and the enactment of gender shape the kinds of individual 'career games' that are most likely to be successfully enacted and rewarded.

Research on the under-representation of women in STEM has focused on women's preferences and biology; the leaky pipeline; the organisational culture and structure, etc. Here we focus on practices which inhibit gender equality in STEM in one case study HEI. Practices and practicing refer to 'arrays of human activity centrally organised around shared practical understanding' (Schatzki 2001: 11). Practices are embodied and a skilled and appropriate body is essential to their accomplishment (Martin 2003: 361). Such practices are frequently depicted as gender neutral, but they are differentially available to men and women, and differentially evaluated when enacted by men and women. They are thus crucially important in perpetuating gendered knowledge and gender inequality. The practices selected are exemplars of those that are 'internalised as a regulatory mechanism' (Morley 2014: 457). Thus, they operate internally as well as externally in maintaining a gender order which differentially evaluates men and women, and which perpetuates the under-representation of women in STEM.

Three purportedly gender-neutral practices are identified i.e. achieving professional visibility, cultivating local connections, and managing time appropriately (O'Hagan et al. 2016). These practices implicitly see the solution to women's under-representation in STEM in individual agentic terms. They focus on the micro-level in what purport to be gender-neutral structures and cultures. Enacting them is depicted as key to success in the career game. The first of these practices is professional visibility which involves recognition within the field and brings material and symbolic benefits, because it is instrumental in increasing opportunities to collaborate on grant applications, to increase research output, obtain professional invitations, and positions the academic for employment elsewhere. Although ostensibly gender neutral, Bagilhole and Goode (2001) found that self-promotion is itself gendered, while Lynch and Ivancheva (2015) found that those who are well known internationally in academia are disproportionately men.

The second practice identified is cultivating local connections. Powerful allies can allocate resources, including funding and appointments, impart insider information, and make introductions to powerful others. Again, although purportedly gender neutral, in predominantly male-dominated contexts, such as STEM, men have an advantage because careers are progressed through homosociability (i.e. the tendency to select people like oneself: Grummell et al. 2009) and networking, and men benefit from such relationships with other men (Morley 2008). Indeed, Bagilhole and Goode (2001) found that in terms of academic careers, individualism is the myth while male support systems are the reality.

The third practice identified was managing time appropriately. Time must be managed and invested in valued activities, as defined by the priorities of the specific university. The appropriate management of time is depicted as an individual responsibility (Urry 2004), with a long hours' culture being presented as gender neutral (O'Connor 2015). However, it disproportionately disadvantages those with familial and caring responsibilities, and these are most likely to be women (Lynch and Ivancheva 2015; Devine et al. 2011).

In addition to these purportedly gender-neutral practices, two explicitly gendered practices are identified at the meso-level. They make explicit the underlying gendered structures and culture and highlight the ways in which women's success in the career game is inhibited. These practices draw on Martin's (2003) differentiation between the interactional doing of gender in real time and space (here referred to as gendered interactional practices) and the repertoire of actions and behaviours that society makes available for doing gender (here referred to as gendered stereotypical practices) reflecting underlying gendered cultural stereotypes involving women and science. Both of these gendered practices reflect an underlying institutional gendered reality which the first three micro-level practices ignore. We argue that in order to create change in gendered masculinist knowledge producing and disseminating structures it is not sufficient to simply encourage women to adopt what appear to be gender-neutral agentic practices. It is also necessary to challenge and reduce the impact of explicitly gendered practices, whether these are interactional or stereotypical (see Van den Brink and Benschop 2012; Peterson and Jordansson 2017).

METHODOLOGY

The study was undertaken as part of a wider European research project investigating structural and cultural barriers to women's careers in STEM. The Irish Higher Education Institution is a relatively new, government-funded, independent university which provides research and teaching from undergraduate to postdoctoral levels. At the end of 2012, when the project started, the organisation had 13,000+ students and 1,300 staff. STEM academics were in one of its four faculties.

A constructivist-interpretative paradigm was adopted which assumes a relativist ontology (Denzin and Lincoln 2013: 26–27). A qualitative methodology was employed in the grounded theory tradition (Padgett 2008). The

28

research sample included both women and men, selected on the basis of their gender and their positions (at early-, mid- and senior levels). The majority were selected by random sampling, with purposive sampling where there were few available participants. The data in this chapter draws on qualitative interviews with 29 respondents (18 men and 11 women) at different levels in STEM in the case study university.[1] All interviews were recorded and transcribed. Respondents signed consent forms and received transcripts post interview. They are identified by their gender (M/F) and a unique identifier number. Since the number of women in senior positions is very small, in the interests of confidentiality, the respondents' positions are not indicated.

Manual content analysis was used, because it is a systematic, replicable technique for compressing many words of text into fewer content categories based on explicit rules of coding (Krippendorff 1980; Weber 1990). Analysis of the qualitative data involved extrapolating conceptual categories from the codes, followed by cycles of further coding, categorisation and theory building through the emergence of categories in the data (Charmaz 2006: 188). Career practices in general, and the career game in particular, were not an explicit focus of the research but emerged from successive readings of the transcripts.

THE ACADEMIC CAREER GAME

All games have rules, therefore everyone who plays the game should know the rules. The academic career game has been seen as a stereotypically masculinist game: developed by men for men or women acting as pseudo males (Morley 2013a). In the present study, without exception, when men were asked if gender affected their careers, they said it had not, and were puzzled by the question, with many saying it was not something they had ever considered. Thus, as in the case of other dimensions (such as whiteness), men were typically unaware of privileging (Connell 1987).

Women and men referred to 'the game' (although men were more likely to do so): implicitly suggesting that they were aware of the underlying politics of the HEI and located career advancement in that context. An understanding of the rules of the game and of the power and politics within the organisation was seen as essential:

> Because an organisation is made up of people, [it] gets captured by people with their own agendas. Whether that's the President sort of saying well I'm going to push Medicine and Education and Health sciences and this and that or whether it's the perceived or real rivalries between different departments. In our faculty for

instance, there's a sort of on-going battle you know for resources and supremacy and whatever you know. Yeah so that's, that's the problem always with organisations really. It's all politics (F/40).

It was seen as important to find out the rules of the game: 'Sometimes that becomes a matter of playing the game. How many marks are you going to get for being an editor? How many marks are you going to get for writing another paper?' (M/35). The game is seen as a tough one and one that requires knowledge about power and the experience of dealing with it:

> I feel that I'm not in the game long enough and I do think it is a bit of a game, it's a bit of a political game as well you know. And I think anyone who says it isn't I think are lying to themselves. So I'm kind of learning the politics. So that's a major thing for me and I think I've developed a much thicker skin than when I first started here. And I don't think it's anything [to do with] because I'm female. I had to develop [one] I think anyone who starts out in academia has to develop a very thick skin . . . I used to take things really personally and I realised you know that a lot of this is a political game. If you learn to play the game right you have a better chance of reaching the finish line (F/41).

The ability to play the game successfully is not perceived as gendered. It requires all players to develop 'a very thick skin', one that can handle rejection and failure and not take reversals personally. The fact that this game is a political game in a context where power is overwhelmingly held by men is effectively ignored. In such a context, not being 'one of the boys' positions women as deficient, as needing to change in order to 'play the game' – a fact ignored by this respondent (see also Britton 2017). Attitudes to playing the game varied. Some women and men distanced themselves from it 'I purposely don't get involved in the politics of it' (M/42). Other respondents were even more critical: 'politics is for politicians. I, I no, I don't enjoy it, I don't enjoy it in the workplace' (M/33).

Some respondents were opposed to managerialist processes which they saw as creating a context where the passionate, totally committed concept of the (implicitly male) scientist doing 'good work' was replaced by a more bureaucratic managerialist one: one who was, for example, more concerned with producing the required number of articles a year, rather than holding off on publications until a genuine research breakthrough had been achieved:

> Quite often of course people play the game, they are often more successful, no doubt about it. Yeah, just tick the boxes, you know, rather than doing good work, tick the boxes and get your promotion . . . (M/43).

For others playing the game was not a cynical exercise since they located it in the context of 'being passionate' about what they do:

> I think you need to be passionate about what you do first of all, if you're in a job that you're not passionate about, you're not going to advance your career, that's the first thing I'd say and the second thing I'd say is to find out what are the driving forces for promotion, that's just play the game . . . but be passionate about what you're doing and if you're passionate about what you do then you will publish, and you can target the right publications (M/21).

Clearly, this respondent sees the career game as a competition. There is an implicit assumption that passion will be sufficient to enable one to enact appropriate practices such as 'targeting the right publications'. For him there is no contradiction between passion and playing the (implicitly male) game.

One of the features of academic life is that the culture relies on individuals to be self-motivated, and to want to 'play the career game'. Academic freedom, and a lack of sanction, effectively allowed some academics to refuse to do tasks if they did not want to play the game: 'you can do as little or as much as you want. That seems to be how it is . . . you go so far . . . I can go further but do I really want to go further? And other people just love the drive and the cut and thrust' (M/42). This suggests there are those who play the career game in expectation of promotion to higher levels, and there are those who have opted out. This is not surprising in the context of a promotion round in the HEI where many candidates had been unsuccessful and in a context where an individualist culture creates competition among colleagues:

> [You] try and keep ahead of the game . . . You're very isolated . . . I think it's very, I find it very lonesome. Here, you have to be, like if I wasn't self-motivated. Even though some days to be honest, I do find it hard . . . and a lot of the time I say to myself, 'this can't be good for a lot of people' (M/31).

In summary, although both women and men referred to career games, men were more likely to do so. When we look in more detail at the academic practices involved in playing that game, it is clear that directly and indirectly, gender affected the conditions under which those involved in the creation and dissemination of knowledge worked in STEM. Thus, the very conditions involved in the production of knowledge were gendered. We now look at those academic practices that are seen as relevant to career advancement in the context of the academic career game.

We focus on five key career practices: three purportedly gender neutral ones at the micro-level i.e. achieving professional visibility, acquiring local political connections and managing time appropriately; and two explicitly gendered ones at the meso-level i.e. gendered interactional practices and gendered stereotypical practices, both of which explicitly highlight the existence of an underlying gendered structure and culture, with implications for women's careers.

Achieving Professional Visibility

Both women and men agreed that visibility was important although they disagreed as regards which activities would bring most visibility. Many academics in the case study HEI felt that there was an implicit message that research was much more important in the 'career game':

> it's in everybody's interest now to be getting published . . . Exactly for their own careers as much as anything else, but also for their internal self-esteem . . . I'm sure there's probably a game part to it as well but I'm sure that's part and parcel of everything (M/21).

Research production appears to be the only thing that seems to be valued and rewarded, with 'stars' frequently being recruited by HEIs specifically to enhance research output:

> high profile professors are parachuted in. I suppose they're parachuted in to beef up the research profile . . . they won't be doing the teaching and people give out about that. So, the research seems to be a profile, a profile builder . . . something that you need to have for success at the high levels (M/42).

The focus on research at the expense of focusing on students and teaching was also noted:

> Well yeah, and in terms of research excellence, publishing in top journals that's it – the high impact journals. You know that's, peer review journals, that's research excellence . . . they talk about you know, the number of PhD [students] and Masters [students], but nobody gives a damn [about them] (M/25).

A significant contributor to professional visibility is the opportunity to develop relationships that lead to professional collaborations and an appropriate network of contacts. Access to such networks has been shown to be gendered in male-dominated contexts, reflecting the existence of male gatekeepers (Husu 2004) and homosociability (Grummell et al. 2009; Blackmore et al. 2006). Women were more likely than men to see visibility as difficult to achieve. For example, the male-dominated social locations in which networking takes place are not easily accessed by women:

> It shouldn't be any harder [for women] but it does seem to be. But I think in terms of networking as a woman, because most of the networking is done in a social environment . . . If I was at a conference on my own and I didn't know anybody, then I'd be very reluctant to go into the bar and network on my own (F/19).

No man mentioned gender as a potential barrier to building contacts and networks in a professional context, suggesting that gender is invisible to men in the male-dominated STEM area.

Professional visibility is facilitated by international mobility. To achieve visibility, one must have time to do the promotional work that internationalising one's work requires, not only writing and research time, but also travelling, networking, attending conferences and engaging in self-promotion. Family responsibilities (including childcare and other caring responsibilities) are still regarded as primarily women's responsibilities. Women were more likely to speak of the impact of domestic and caring responsibilities on their ability to network at conferences:

> I'd go to a conference and I wouldn't stay the whole time. I would just go and do my papers, stay a day or two and come back. 1 wouldn't, you know, 1 wouldn't do all the networking, I'd come home to sort of be with the kids (F/40).

In summary, while both men and women regarded such visibility as a key career-related practice, it was seen as more accessible to men. Thus, the practice of achieving professional visibility in the area of knowledge production, although purportedly neutral, was in fact gendered.

Cultivating Local Political Connections

Women tend to be more ambivalent about 'playing the game' (Davey 2008) possibly because they are less clear about the 'rules' in male-dominated structures or see themselves as less culturally valued and hence less able to leverage support in such contexts. They prefer the 'honest work', reflecting an acceptance of individual merit, and seeing achievements gained through political connections as unacceptable (O'Connor et al. 2017). Only men perceived the practice of cultivating local powerful others as important. 'Paying forward' and creating bonds of indebtedness is normalised for them in the academic environment:

It's a promotion competition. If you've nobody on the other side of the table fighting your case, you've no chance . . . You arrange [that] through [favours], you know . . . Because when they pick up the phone and ask you to do something you do it. And you do it not just once you might do it fifty times. So, when your application goes in you'd expect them to support you (M/23).

Other male respondents suggested that acquiring power by taking a management position was also a way to develop relationships with powerful others. 'Managing' those in powerful positions was seen as essential: 'how I manage the Dean and the President will probably have, will affect . . . how I'm seen performing in this office. If I manage upstairs well enough to keep my guys happy, that would be a success' (M/23). Only male respondents recognised the significance of cultivating local political connections, reflecting a gendering of informal knowledge and an acceptance of sources of (male) power. In a Spanish university context such ties were described as 'inbreeding' and were seen as extremely important (Cruz-Castro and Sanz-Menéndez 2010; Vázquez-Cupero and Elston 2006; Montez -Lopez and O'Connor 2018).

The practice of developing coalitions of support within their own institutions, including acquiring connections with those in management positions, being loyal to them and doing favours for them was only practiced by men although women noticed their male colleagues engaging in this practice. It can be seen as expressing and reflected a 'patriarchal support system' (Bagilhole and Goode 2001). It is possible that the absence of an infrastructure of women in senior positions in STEM was associated with women's failure to contemplate that strategy. In 2012 there was no woman at all at full professorial level in STEM in the case study HEI. By 2016 it had increased to ten per cent (very close to the EU average of 13 per cent, now 15 per cent: EU, 2019). The initiation by the Minister for Higher Education of the Senior Academic Leadership Initiative (SALI), involving 45 posts (less than ten per cent of the total number of professorial posts) is a way of targeting posts at those areas where women are particularly under-represented (O'Connor, 2020). In a societal context where there are very few women in senior positions in any institution (implicitly reflecting and reinforcing a devaluation of women), women have bought into the idea of individual objectively assessed merit. This affects their willingness to cultivate local connections, particularly in a context such as STEM, where scientific objectivity and an unproblematised concept of merit is valorised.

In summary, the practice of cultivating local connections, which can be seen as an essentially gendered practice, perpetuates male advantage and women's disadvantage: underlining its gendered character. It is a key element in the production and maintenance of gendered knowledge – indeed of what counts as valued knowledge – in HEIs.

Managing Time Appropriately

Time must be used not only efficiently but also morally (Walker 2009) in the pursuit of those activities which the organisation values (O'Connor and O'Hagan 2016). Efficiency in terms of the generation of publications was of paramount concern albeit there was some debate as to whether quantity or quality was most important. Securing funding was also seen as important. The experience of 'no time' arises from the need for competing priorities to be juggled in the context of intensification of work and compression of time (O'Carroll 2015). It was occasionally recognised that managing time can exact a high personal cost, for both women and men:

> The very successful (academics) are generally obsessed. And they don't really have anything else going on in their lives. And they are, as a result, bad fathers and bad parents and bad husbands and bad friends because they don't have the time for anything else. And that's the sacrifice that they make, to be the best in their field. So being the best in your field doesn't always equate with being the best person in your life or for yourself, so it's something, that you either decide to go with or not (M/36).

A male academic suggested that in the competitive environment of the university, the expectation to work long hours has been normalised:

> Be industrial, you know, work hard. Be productive and . . . do a fifty, sixty-hour week . . . You know, I don't think – there's no real short cuts, there's no real short cuts to that . . . Yea, and I think maybe fifty, sixty hours is too much, but I, I think that's reality, it's competitive (M/23).

The expectations as regards the normality of a long hours' culture and its impact on behaviour was also noted by a female academic:

> I rarely leave here before six or seven . . . And I bring work home with me, or I go home and have dinner and come back in here. I work all weekends as well (F/41).

A long hours' culture was perceived to exist by both men and women. In a gender audit in the case study university, Richardson (2008) found that on average women in STEM worked longer hours per week than men (51 versus 47 respectively). They also spent significantly fewer hours during weekdays than their male counterparts on research (9 versus 19 hours), and significantly more on teaching (21 versus 15 hours) and administration (14 versus 11 hours). In addition, they spent more time preparing teaching and on administration at the weekends. A similar trend was identified in another Irish university (Coate and Kandiko Howson 2014). Such patterns are not a peculiarly Irish phenomenon. Britton (2017) noted that workloads were one area where women were more likely to see gender inequality as visible (although even there it was not seen as intentional). Typically, women carry higher teaching loads. Powerful others allocate resources and tasks and cultivating local political connections can help to influence the distribution of the load. This can disproportionately disadvantage those without such allies: 'my teaching load is by far the biggest in the department . . . You see, that's the thing, you can't ask me to increase my research profile if . . . I'm going to be teaching twenty hours a week' (F/41). The unequal and disproportionate allocation of teaching loads to women ensures that they cannot manage their time as effectively as their male colleagues in terms of achieving university priorities around research output. There was also some evidence that teaching was seen as less critical than research as an evaluative criterion for promotion (O'Connor and O'Hagan 2016). Such patterns raise issues about the impact of stereotypes on the allocation of workloads, and ultimately reflect the gendered structures within which such 'normal' allocation occurs (Britton 2017).

In summary, although the individually agentic career practice was depicted as gender neutral, it was in fact gendered and reflected and reinforced the wider gendered structures within which knowledge was created in STEM environments in HEIs.

Gendered Interactional Practices

Women tend not to notice gender inequality or its consequences, particularly in male-dominated areas where they are undertaking stereotypical male tasks. Fleeting interactional incidents are one context in which they may recognise gendered interactional practices (Martin 2006; Britton 2017). Such interactional 'practicing' of gender may not only involve perceived explicit discrimination, but also more subtle manifestations such as Othering. Frequently such incidents are seen as atypical events, rather than as reflections of the underlying patterns of structural and cultural gendered inequality in knowledge production.

There is a good deal of evidence of the undervaluing of women in higher educational contexts, reflected in, for example, the existence of double standards in evaluating women's competence. Moss-Racusin et al (2012) showed that both men and women in research-intensive universities favoured a CV with a male name over an identical female one. Similar patterns have appeared in other studies (for exampleNielsen 2016), reflecting an underlying cognitive bias against women, one that is particularly likely to be evoked in male-dominated contexts (Ridgeway, 2011). Fraser (2008) has referred to it as misrecognition, while Bourdieu (2001) has described it as a negative symbolic co-efficient. Such a cognitive bias has been tracked in the negative evaluation of characteristics in women that would be positively evaluated in men (Eagly and Carli 2007). Subtle misrecognition (Fraser, 2008) and informal sexism and bias (Flood and Pease 2005) were occasionally recognised by women. As one woman who was chronologically older than her career stage noted:

> I find that if you are in a group discussion, they listen to you – but the man in the group will be listened to more . . . They will listen to you of course but they won't say 'oh that's a good idea (.)' Then 'anyone else?' and then suddenly the guy who says something . . . he will be listened to. Young or old (F/24).

Awareness of the existence of an underlying gendered culture was also occasionally provoked by gendered interaction practices in recruitment fora. For one respondent the experience eroded her confidence and stimulated an awareness that there was a gendered dynamic present in recruitment boards:

> And you just feel like this young one, particularly a girl in the room with all these men . . . You're definitely still an outsider, and you are. I definitely have felt the female thing there. Definitely. Just like this young girl that can't say a word (F/32).

Only one man recognised the routine 'Othering' of women in STEM in the HEI. He was in a marginal position himself (based on his lower educational level) and this may account for his awareness:

> The one female colleague I have in this department who works in my area, I see her struggling big-time because she doesn't have those relationships; she's been effectively, she's been excluded. A clique has developed within the department . . . . I don't know if it's gender or if it it's just personal to her. I don't know, I'd be making assumptions about the value systems of the people who have excluded her if I was to say it's gendered but it's hard not to recognise that she's the only female and she's the one excluded, you know. For her, I see it as being a really significant issue (M/17).

Gendered ideologies are internalised and reflected in different forms of gender knowledge. They include the gendering of a sense of felt entitlement i.e. a feeling or belief that you deserve special privileges (Lewis and Smithson 2001) which is reflected in and shaped by gendered interaction (Ridgeway 2011; Flood and Pease 2005). Low levels of entitlement were mainly evident among the women as in other studies (Valian 2005; Rafnsdóttir and Heijstra 2011). For example, one woman (F/41) felt that any attempt to negotiate working from home would reflect an inadequate appreciation of her place in the hierarchy (i.e. it would be 'cheeky') although she recognised that this arrangement had been successfully negotiated by two male colleagues who were at the same level:

> I know one academic here works from home two days a week. I don't know if I'd be able to get away with that . . . even though my head of department probably would be aware I would be working, whereas . . . there's a couple of [male] members of staff here who have no problem, maybe they have more of a neck on them than I do to say 'look we're working from home and you know don't be knocking at my door'. . . [The] two of them are junior faculty members, until they were promoted recently. So I'm here the exact same amount of time and I wouldn't say that you know. I think it's cheeky (F/41).

As she perceives it, her male colleagues feel entitled to ask for privileges, such as flexible working, whereas she does not. Furthermore, it would be 'cheeky' for her to ask for it, suggesting that it would breach implicit gendered hierarchical considerations.

In summary, in this as in Britton's (2017) study, only a minority of women referred to gendered interactional practices in the case study organisation. We cannot say for sure to what extent they have affected other women, but it seems possible that they may have done so.

Gendered Stereotypical Practices

Martin (2003) differentiates between the interactional practicing of gender and the gendered cultural scripts or stereotypes which are drawn on to legitimate gendered organisational structural and cultural arrangements. These are practices that at least potentially limit women's opportunities and possibilities, and even their perception of these. Britton (2017) referred to such stereotypes underpinning expectations regarding the provision of emotional support, and the connection between masculinity and leadership in the minds of staff. In the STEM area, such stereotypes underpin depictions of scientists and STEM arenas as male, and family responsibilities as largely female. More specifically, they include stereotypes about science and women's place in the discipline as well as stereotypes about the bearing and rearing of children. Such gendered stereotypical practices legitimate the exclusion of women from particular areas and/or their subordinate position within those areas.

One of the respondents highlighted the contradictory patterns that emerged during women's educational careers in terms of STEM:

> Women – or well – girls in [2nd level] schools perform better in maths and science than the boys, but when they get to college [Higher Education] suddenly they perform poorly, and the men excel, so what's happening there? . . . Something's happening there and it's cultural (F/28).

As she sees it, women's under-representation in STEM reflects cultural factors in HEIs since girls perform better than boys at second level. Women referred to a culture in STEM that expected 'a different type of girl', one who was stereotypically masculine:

> I am a girl and I don't deny it and I am a real girly girl . . . But I think society and maybe this environment expects that if you are going be a girl in this position you have to be a different type of girl. You have to be [single minded] Nothing else comes in your way and you have to fight harder, you do, if you want to get places as a woman (F/18).

Stereotypes reflect and reinforce underlying power relations between men and women: 'The most undesirable traits in women are those like domineering and arrogant that violate the cultural presumption of women's subordinate status' (Ridgeway 2011: 59). Harris et al. (1998: 140) found that both women and men perceived the need for academics to be 'ruthless and aggressive' to succeed. Such characteristics appear to conflict with constructions of femininity and women's role as the 'good citizens' in HEIs (Bagilhole 1993).

Maternity has been shown to have a considerable direct and indirect impact on women's careers in STEM (Herman et al. 2013). This is partly because they are then no longer seen as 'one of the boys' (Ranson 2005: 145). There is a widespread stereotype that women's principal role is to bear and rear children (Coate and Kandiko Howson 2016; Valian 2005). A male supervisor highlighted the problems [as he saw them] created by a post-doctoral student who became pregnant less than a year into an industry-based project: He 'had to fight with the agency to get the maternity leave allowed, so they gave us a small extension on the project, but the industry wasn't happy . . . the project never recovered'. This experience affected his future hiring intentions, and ultimately reinforced his belief that STEM and maternity are incompatible: 'if I have another project, do I go for a woman who is not child-bearing? Forty-five and upwards? Or a guy or a girl who's in the early twenties, single, do you know what I mean?' (M/23).

As noted earlier, the long hours' culture with its 'care-less' structures (Lynch et al. 2012) is widely accepted in STEM (Beraud 2009). This has

39

implications for women. A discourse of choice (ultimately reflecting a de-gendered individualised stereotype) was referred to by several women:

> the decision to go part-time was my own . . . I wanted to be able to spend time with him [son] . . . I mean it's my own decision. So, I can't really complain about it . . . I think any kind of ambition, career ambition, is kind of down the line until I can get back in full-time (F/19).

The decision to work part-time meant that this respondent could have no expectation for career progression, despite her strong commitment to research. Like many of Britton's (2017) and Rhoton's (2011) respondents she showed no awareness of the structural impediments to her career progression, focusing instead on her own agentic decision making and depicted herself as making a personal choice in a gender-neutral knowledge producing context.

In summary, gendered stereotypical practices reflect stereotypes about science and women. In the STEM context they implicitly and explicitly affect women's careers. In many cases women were neither conscious nor accepting of these stereotypes. However, they were aware of the perceived incompatibility of maternity with the (implicitly monastic) stereotype of the scientist. In that context there was a reliance on a discourse of individual choice the implicit suggestion being that women had only themselves to blame if they decided to work part-time. The internalisation of norms of individual responsibilisation and a related failure to recognise the systemic reality of gender in the structure and culture of male-dominated STEM organisations, has implications for the gendered production of knowledge.

CONCLUSION

HEIs in general, and the STEM area in particular, is located in gendered organisations with bureaucratically organised career structures. Implicit in the concept of the career game is the idea of a strategic approach to career development within the context of political agendas. These agendas are created in and by male-dominated structures and masculinist cultures. Thus, as noted by Britton (2017: 8) 'Masculinity is invisibly embedded in the mindset and career path of the ideal-typical scientist, and yet at the same time science supports notions of value-free inquiry and purely meritocratic standards of achievement'.

We have identified five practices involved in the career game. Practices are embodied and a skilled and appropriate body is basic to their accomplishment (Martin 2003). Implicitly, these practices are differentially available to and achievable by women. This is concealed by an agentic micro-level focus on what purport to be gender-neutral practices such as achieving professional visibility, cultivating local connections, and managing time. The practices of professional visibility and cultivating political connections advantage men and disadvantage women, while managing time particularly disadvantages women. Their deleterious impact is further exacerbated by the meso-level gendered interactional and gendered stereotypical practices. These affect women's opportunities and possibilities, although in many cases this was not recognised, and these practices were implicitly or explicitly accepted.

If women advert to the systemic structural and cultural reality of gender, they effectively reinforce their Outsider status since there is a 'pervasive and systemic institutional order' (Prentice 2000: 196) in which women and their work is devalued. Thus, many men and women depict the STEM environment as gender neutral. Without exception, when men were asked if gender affected their careers, they said it had not. For the most part, only when women found themselves unable to engage in activities to the same extent as their male colleagues did they recognise the gendering of the practices involved in the career game, both those that purported to be gender neutral as well as those that were explicitly gendered, involving a matrix of declared and hidden (gendered) rules (Lynch et al. 2012). These rules reflect gendered knowledge, but paradoxically this knowledge is not perceived as such.

It is not sufficient to simply encourage women to adopt what appear to be gender-neutral, agentic practices implicit in the idea of the career game. It is also necessary to challenge and reduce the impact of gendered interactional practices as well as tackling gendered stereotypical practices. Together these five practices – achieving professional visibility; cultivating local political connections; managing time appropriately; gendered interactional practices; and gendered stereotypical practices – are the mechanism through which the position of women in STEM is maintained.

Note

Interview guides were developed which contained questions such as: *What personal competences and/or characteristics do you think are necessary for a successful career in this University? Do you engage in any activities designed to develop these competences? Specify.* Respondents spoke about career practices in response to these questions. Questions related to gender included: *Has gender affected your career progression in a positive or negative way? Specify. Have personal or domestic issues influenced your career decisions?*

Acknowledgement

Supported by European Commission Grant number 287526

REFERENCES

Acker, Joan, 'Hierarchies, jobs, bodies: A theory of gendered organizations', in *Gender and Society*, 4, 1990, pp 139–58.

Adcroft, Andy and David Taylor, 'Support for new career academics: An integrated model for research intensive university business and management schools', in *Studies in Higher Education*, 38(6), 2013, pp 827–40.

Bagilhole, Barbara, 'Survivors in a male preserve: A study of British women academics experiences and perceptions of discrimination in a UK university', in *Higher Education* 26 (4), 1993, pp 431–47.

Bagilhole, Barbara and Jackie Goode, 'The contradiction of the myth of individual merit, and the reality of a patriarchal support system in academic careers: A feminist investigation', in *European Journal of Women's Studies*, 8, 2001, pp 161–80.

Bagilhole, Barbara and Kate White (eds), *Gender, Power and Management: A Cross Cultural Analysis of Higher Education* (Palgrave Macmillan: Basingstoke, 2011).

Beraud, Andre, 'Women in the rat race: Women's careers in technological higher education', in Anke Lipinsky (ed.), *Encouragement to Advance: Supporting Women in European Science Careers* (Kleine Verlag: Bielefield, Germany, 2009), pp 154–83.

Blackmore, Jill, Pat Thomson and Karin Barty, 'Principal selection: Homosociability, the search for security and the production of normalised principal identities', in *Educational Management, Administration and Leadership*, 34(3), 2006, pp 297–317.

Britton, Dana M., 'Beyond the chilly climate: The salience of gender in women's academic careers', in *Gender and Society*, 31(1), 2017, pp 5–27.

Coate, Kelly and Camille Kandiko Howson, 'Indicators of esteem: Gender prestige in academic work', in *British Journal of Sociology of Education*, 37(4), 2016, pp 567–85.

Connell, R. W., *Gender, Power and Society* (Polity Press: Cambridge, 1987).

Ibid., *Masculinities*, 2nd edn (Polity Press: Cambridge, 2005).

Charmaz, Kathy, *Constructing Grounded Theory* (Sage: London, 2006).

Cruz-Castro Laura and Luis Sanz-Menéndez, 'Mobility versus job stability: Assessing tenure and productivity outcomes', in *Research Policy*, 39(1), 2010, pp 27–38.

Danowitz-Sagaria, Mary Ann and L. J Agans, 'Gender equality in US higher education: Inter/National framing and institutional realities', in K. Yokoyama (ed.), *Gender and Higher Education: Australia, Japan, the UK and USA* (Higher Education Institute Press: Hiroshima, 2006), pp 47–68.

Davey, Kate Mackenzie, 'Women's accounts of organizational politics as a gendering process', in *Gender, Work & Organization*, 15(6), 2008, pp 650–71.

David, Miriam E., 'Overview of researching global higher education: Challenge, change or crisis?', in *Contemporary Social Science*, 2011, p. 6, pp 147–63.

Denzin, Norman. K. and Yvonna S. Lincoln (eds), 'Introduction: The discipline and practice of qualitative research', in *The Landscape of Qualitative Research* 4th edn (Sage: California, 2013) pp 1–42.

Devine, Dympna, Bernie Grummell, and Kathleen Lynch, 'Crafting the elastic self? Gender and identities in senior appointments in Irish education', in *Gender Work and Organization*, 18, 2011, pp 631–49.

Eagly, Alice H. and Linda L. Carli, 'Women and the labyrinth of leadership', in *Harvard Business Review*, Sept. 2007 https://hbr.org/2007/09/women-and-the-labyrinth-of-leadership

Etzkowitz Henry, S. Fuchs, N. Gupta, et al. (eds), 'The coming revolution in science', in E. J. Hackett, O. Amsterdamska, M. Lynch et al. (eds), *The Handbook of Science and Technology Studies*, 3rd edn (MA: Society for Social Studies of Science: Cambridge, 2007) pp 403–29.

European Union. (2019). *She Figures, 2018: Gender in Research and Innovation, Statistics, and Indicators*. https://ec.europa.eu/info/publications/she-figures-2018_en

Faulkner, Wendy, *Genders in/of Engineering* (University of Edinburgh, Research report: Edinburgh, 2006) http://www.sps.ed.ac.uk/__data/assets/pdf_file/0020/4862/FaulknerGendersinEngineeringreport.pdf

Flood, Michael and Bob Pease, 'Undoing men's privilege and advancing gender equality in public sector institutions', in *Policy and Society*, Special Issue 24(4), 2005, pp 119–38.

Fraser, Nancy, *Adding Insult to Injury: Nancy Fraser Debates her Critics*, in K. Olson ed. (Verso: London, 2008).

Grummell, Bernie, Dympna Devine and Kathleen Lynch, 'The care-less manager: Gender, care and new managerialism in higher education', *Gender and Education*, 2009, 21, pp 191–208.

Hall, Douglas T., *Careers in Organisations* (Scott Foresman and Co.: Santa Monica, California, 1976).

Harris, Patricia, Bev Thiele, and Jan Currie, 'Success, gender and academic voices: Consuming passion or selling the soul?', in *Gender and Education*, 10, 1998, pp 133–48.

Hekman, Susanne, 'Truth and method: Feminist standpoint revised', in Sandra Harding (ed.), *Feminist Standpoint Theory and Reader: Intellectual and Political Controversies* (Routledge: London, 2004), pp 225–42.

Herman, Clem, Suzan Lewis, and Anne Laurie Humbert, 'Women scientists and engineers in European companies: Putting motherhood under the microscope', *Gender, Work and Organization*, 20(5), 2013, pp 116–31.

Hey, Valerie, 'Affective asymmetries: Academics, austerity and the mis/recognition of emotion', in *Contemporary Social Science*, 6, 2011, pp 207–22.

Holton, Judith A., 'The coding process and its challenges', in Anthony Bryant and Kathy Charmaz (eds), *The Sage Handbook of Grounded Theory* (Sage: London, 2007), pp 265–89.

Husu, Liisa, 'Gender discrimination in the promised land of gender equality', in *Higher Education in Europe*, 25, 2000, pp 221–28.

Ibid., 'Gate-keeping, gender equality and scientific excellence', in Margo Brouns and Elizabetta Addis (eds), *Gender and Excellence in the Making* (European Commission: Brussels, 2004), pp 69–76.

Ibid., 'Recognize hidden roadblocks; Laboratory life: Scientists of the world speak up for equality', *Nature*, 495, 2013, pp 35–8.

Krippendorff, Klaus, *Content Analysis: An Introduction to its Methodology* (Sage: California, 1980).

Lewis, Suzan, and Janet Smithson, 'Sense of entitlement for the reconciliation of employment and family life', in *Human Relations*, 54(11), 2001, pp 1,455–81.

Lynch, Kathleen, Bernie Grummell and Dympna Devine, *New Managerialism in Education: Commercialisation, Carelessness and Gender* (Palgrave: London, 2012).

Lynch, Kathleen and Mariya Ivancheva, 'Academic freedom and commercialisation of universities: A critical ethical analysis', in *Ethics in Science and Environmental Politics*, 15, 2015, pp 71–85.

Martin, Patricia Yancey, '"Mobilizing masculinities": Women's experiences of men at work', in *Organization*, 8(4), 2001, pp 587–618.

Ibid., "Said and done" versus "saying and doing": Gendering practices, practicing gender at work', in *Gender and Society*, 17, 2003, pp 342–66.

Ibid., 'Practicing gender at work: Further thoughts on reflexivity', in *Gender Work and Organization*, 13(3), 2006, pp 254–76.

McKay, Lorraine, and Sue Monk, 'Early career academics learning the game in whackademia', in *Higher Education Research and Development*, 36(6), 2017, pp 1,251–63.

Montes Lopez, Estrella, and Pat O'Connor, 'Micropolitics and meritocracy: Improbable bedfellows?', in *Educational Management Administration and Leadership*, 2018, DOI: 10.1177/1741143218759090

Morley, Louise, *The Micropolitics of Professionalism: Power and Collective Identities in Higher Education. Exploring Professionalism* (Bedford Way Papers: London, 2008).

Ibid., 'Misogyny posing as measurement: Disrupting the feminisation crisis discourse', in *Contemporary Social Science*, 6, 2011, pp 223–35.

Ibid., 'The rules of the game: Women and the leaderist turn in higher education', in *Gender and Education*, 25(1), 2013a, pp 116–31.

Ibid., *Women and Higher Education Leadership: Absences and Aspirations* (Leadership Foundation for Higher Education: London, 2013b).

Ibid., 'Education and neo-liberal globalization', in *British Journal of Sociology of Education*, 3, 2014, pp 457–68.

Moss-Racusin, A. Corinne, John F. Dovidio, Victoria L. Brescoll, Mark J. Graham, and Jo Handelsman, 'Science faculty's subtle gender biases favour male students', in *PNAS* 9 Oct. 2012, 109(41), pp 16,474–9.

Nielsen, Mathias Wullum, 'Limits to meritocracy? Gender in academic recruitment and promotion processes', *Science and Public Policy*, 43(3), 2016, pp 386–99.

O'Carroll, Aileen, *Working Time, Knowledge Work and Post-Industrial Society: Unpredictable Work* (Palgrave MacMillan: New York, 2015).

O'Connor, Pat, *Management and Gender in Higher Education* (Manchester University Press: Manchester, 2014).

Ibid., 'Good jobs but places for women?', in *Gender and Education*, 2015, p 27, pp 304–19.

Ibid.,'Are universities still male dominated? What can be done?' *Publicpolicy.ie* file:///C:/Users/patoc/OneDrive/Documents/PDF%20AND%20PRE-PUBLICATION%20VERSIONS%20for%20repositories/2020%20Publicpolicypiece%204th%20March%202020.pdf

O'Connor, Pat, Clare O'Hagan, and Julia Brannen, 'Exploration of masculinities in academic organisations: A tentative typology using career and relationship commitment', in *Current Sociology*, 63(4), 2015, pp 528–46.

O'Connor, Pat, and Anita Goransson, 'Constructing or rejecting the notion of the Other in university management: The cases of Ireland and Sweden', in *Educational Management Administration and Leadership*, 43(2), 2015, pp 323–40.

O'Connor, Pat, and Clare O'Hagan, 'Excellence in university academic staff evaluation: A problematic reality?', in *Studies in Higher Education*, 41(11), 2016, pp 1,943–57.

O'Hagan, Clare, Pat O'Connor, Eva Sophia Myers et al., 'Perpetuating academic capitalism and maintaining gender orders through career practices in STEM in universities', in *Critical Studies in Education*, 2016, DOI 10.1080/17508487.2016. 1238403.

Padgett, Deborah K, *Qualitative Methods in Social Work* 2nd edn (Sage: New York, 2008).

Peterson, Helen and Birgitta Jordansson, 'Gender equality as a core academic value: Undoing gender in a 'non-traditional' Swedish university', in Kate White and Pat O'Connor (eds), *Gendered Success in Higher Education: Global Perspectives* (Palgrave Macmillan: London, 2017), pp 27–48.

Prentice, Susan, 'The conceptual politics of chilly climate controversies', in *Gender and Education*, 12(2), 2000, pp 195–207.

Raddon, Arwen, 'Mothers in the academy: Positioned and positioning within discourses of the "successful academic" and the "good mother"', in *Studies in Higher Education*, 27(4), 2002, pp 387–403.

Rafnsdóttir, Gudbjörg Linda and Thamar.M. Heijstra, 'Balancing work–family life in academia: The power of time', in *Gender, Work and Organization*, 20 (3), 2011, pp 283–96.

Ranson, Gillian, '"No longer one of the boys": Negotiations with motherhood as prospect or reality among women in engineering', in *Canadian Review of Sociology*, 42(2), 2005, pp 145–66.

Rhoton, Laura A., 'Distancing as a gendered barrier: Understanding women scientists gender practices', in *Gender and Society*, 25(6), 2011, pp 696–716.

Richardson, Ita, *Gender Audit of Science, Engineering and Technology Staff and researchers at the University of Limerick*, Final Report (University of Limerick: Limerick, 2008).

Ridgeway, Cecilia, *Framed by Gender: How Gender Inequality Persists in the Modern World* (Oxford University Press: Oxford, 2011).

Schatzki, Theodore R., 'Introduction: Practice theory,' in Theodore R. Schatzki, Karin Knorr Cetina and Eike Von Savigny (eds), *The Practice Turn in Contemporary Theory* (Routledge: New York, 2001), pp 10–23.

Thornton, Margaret, 'The mirage of merit', in *Australian Feminist Studies*, 28, 2013, pp 127–43.

Trowler, Paul and Roni Bamber, 'Compulsory higher education teacher training: Joined up policies, institutional architectures and enhancement cultures', in *International Journal for Academic Development*, 10(2), 2005, pp 79–93.

Urry, John, 'Small worlds and the new "social physics"', in *Global Networks*, 4, 2004, pp 109–30.

Van den Brink, Marieke, and Yvonne Benschop, 'Slaying the seven-headed dragon: The quest for gender change in academia', in *Gender, Work & Organization*, 19, 2012, pp 71–92.

Valian, Virginia, 'Beyond gender schemas: Improving the advancement of women in academia', in *Hypatia*, 20(3), 2005, pp 198–213.

Vázquez-Cupeiro Susana and Mary Ann Elston, 'Gender and academic career trajectories in Spain: From gendered passion to consecration in a sistema endogámico?' in *Employee Relations*, 28(6), 2006, pp 588–603.

Walker, Judith, 'Time as the fourth dimension in the globalization of higher education', in *The Journal of Higher Education*, 80, 2009, pp 483–509.

Weber, Robert Philip, *Basic Content Analysis* 2nd edn (Sage: Newbury Park, California, 1990).

White, Kate, *Keeping Women in Science* (Melbourne University Press: Melbourne, 2014).

THREE

Banking on Masculinity: Social Closure in the Irish Investment Management Sector

Corina Sheerin

In the aftermath of the global financial crisis (GFC) discussion abounded on the significance of 'group think', asymmetric gender relations and hyper-masculinity as contributory factors to poor financial decision-making (Hearit 2017; Prügl 2012; MacLean 2016). This put a spotlight on the 'truths' concerning men and women and their gender roles and identities within finance. Historically the sector is characterised by an embodied masculine culture, described as 'a gendered arena where a particular masculinised set of performances is more highly valorized than other ways of being in the workplace' (McDowell 2010: 653). Drawing on original empirical data collected from women working in the sector, I demonstrate that not much has changed in the post-crisis period: the landscape of investment management remains a male preserve despite equality legislation and sectoral gender initiatives. Daily 'norms' and behaviour are situated within hegemonic masculinist structures of knowledge production that significantly influence how social realities are constructed and, more particularly, how gender is defined and performed in this workplace.

THE IRISH INVESTMENT MANAGEMENT LANDSCAPE

The investment management sector is an essential element of international financial services that has been growing rapidly (PwC 2017). It provides financial intermediation ensuring that capital can move between those who wish to invest and those who require investment. The investment management sector plays an important role in Irish economic growth. Currently, more than 50 per cent of the world's leading financial services firms have a base in Ireland and in 2016, assets under management were €4.1 trillion with over 14,000 people employed in the sector (Irish Funds 2017: 2).

Despite the ubiquitous use of the term investment management, no universal agreement has been reached on what exactly the term constitutes with 'investment banking', 'asset management', and 'fund management' used interchangeably to describe the sector. Here I use the typology as set out by Forfás[1] (2014; 2007) wherein investment management is comprised of two sub-sectors of employment: 'front office' (investment management) and 'back office' (fund servicing). Front office usually refers to those elite, high-earning roles associated with the management of funds and revenue generation. Examples of such elite positions include trader, fund manager, and equity analyst. Those in front office roles usually hold a postgraduate qualification and/or a professional qualification such as that of the Chartered Financial Analyst (CFA). Back office refers to those working in fund administration and fund servicing. These positions are usually administrative and operational in nature and are concerned with the processing of trades and financial transactions.

A major international survey undertaken in 2015 by Morningstar, across 56 countries covering the period 2008–15 estimated that four in every five fund managers were male. In Ireland, it is approximately eight in every nine. In 2015, the highest percentage of female fund managers was in Portugal (27 per cent), followed closely by Hong Kong at 25.6 per cent. The lowest proportion of female fund managers was in Poland at 6.7 per cent. Compared to the situation in 2008, very little had changed. In 2015, 11.5 per cent of all fund managers in Ireland were female down from 13.1 per cent in 2008; in the UK, the figure was 13.4 per cent in 2015, relatively unchanged from 13.1 per cent five years earlier. The USA recorded a decline in women fund managers from 11.4 per cent in 2008 to 9.7 per cent in 2015 (Morningstar 2015). When compared to other professional occupations across the labour market, such as law and medicine, women in investment management remain disproportionally under-represented. This is the case despite widespread acceptance that more diverse senior teams could have reduced the 'group think' that contributed to the crisis (Cullen and Murphy 2017; Prügl 2012). While both Ireland and Iceland reviewed and reformed banking regulation, corporate governance regimes and policy tools post GFC, only Iceland made decisive efforts to address the gender dimension of the crisis. In Ireland, there has been limited commitment to embed gender diversity explicitly within governance structures.

EXPLAINING OCCUPATIONAL GENDER SEGREGATION IN INVESTMENT MANAGEMENT

A plethora of explanations exist as to why gender segregation has persisted in the labour market generally. Obstacles such as lack of mentors and role models, difficulties in accessing networks as well as organisational practices, norms and structures, all influences how gender knowledge and relations are produced and maintained in the workforce. The main explanatory models are briefly summarised here. All of them to one degree or another contribute to a form of social closure, a meta-concept that helps us to interpret the experiences of women working in the sector.

Sourcing Role Models and Mentors

Role models and mentors play an essential role in female career development, and in particular within male domains (Burke 2017; Kossek, Su, and Wu 2017; Ramaswami, Carter and Dreher 2016). Having the opportunity to refer to and engage with appropriate female role models and mentors plays an essential role in providing an intangible yet vital signal of the 'proof of possibility' (Sealy 2009: 6). Mentoring provides an important support for career success and advancement to roles such as those in the front office where women are in a minority (Hughes and Sheerin 2016). When women are present in such roles, it signals visibility and has symbolic consequences for the mentee by creating new knowledge about who fits within the leadership elite of the sector. However, the persistence of the old boys' network coupled with the inherent sectoral stereotypes present women as not quite the right 'fit' for elite positions of power. This, in turn, creates difficulties for women in securing mentors and further amplifies the ongoing homosociability in the sector (Groysberg 2008). While women are cognisant of the importance of mentoring from senior male 'gatekeepers,' equally they are apprehensive about how they should behave in a culture permeated by sexism and homosocial behaviours (Van den Brink and Benschop 2014; Broadbridge 2010). For instance, within investment banking women seeking senior male mentors express concern about how such a relationship might be misconstrued resulting in reputational risk for both parties (Pryce and Sealy 2013).

The Old Boys' Network and Leaning In

The ability to network and thus accumulate social capital is essential to career success. Networks provide access to privileged information about the 'rules of the game' including job opportunities and informal norms, technical expertise, and increased levels of visibility (Lewchuk 2013; Chivers

2011; Kumra and Vinnicombe 2010). For women, the process of accessing support in the form of networks is a challenging task, characterised by barriers from the outset (see also O'Connor and O'Hagan, this collection). Research suggests that such networks may take on the characteristics of a 'male mafia' closing ranks both in and outside of work to exclude women (Aitchison 1995: 30; Prügl, 2012). As observed by Schilt and Connell (2007: 597) the 'strength of these enlistments, and the lack of viable alternative interactional scripts in the context of the workplace' exemplify both the gendered workplace hierarchy and the challenges facing women in their negotiation of gender identity.

The 'school tie' plays a pivotal role in the preservation of the old boys' network and influencing career progression (Kennedy and Power, 2010: Palmer, 2000). Courtois (2018) has demonstrated how elite private boys' schools in Ireland constitute a specific site for networking, purposive selective isolation, and the reproduction of social inequality. Such environments facilitate lifelong relationships and connections that extend beyond the school gates and into the workplace. Elite jobs in professions such as banking are allocated to candidates who have the relevant individual 'merit' as measured by 'polish' and 'pedigree', (Rivera 2016). Merit reflects access to economic, social, and cultural capital. In investment management, the school/college attended, sport played, and associated connections all determine 'merit'. The intersectionality of class, gender and race ultimately has a significant role in the maintenance and reproduction of male privilege and masculinist-led knowledge about gender.

Sandberg (2014) argued that women's lack of progression is a consequence of an ambition gap and a lack of willingness to put themselves forward and 'lean in' to prove their competence. As a philosophy, the lean in movement is fundamentally flawed and has little relevance for the majority of women who lack privilege. It ignores the pervasive and ongoing social and structural inequalities in the workplace. Equally, it is futile to present women's absence from front office roles as simply a woman's issue rather than a complex problem underpinned by patriarchy and homosocial reproduction in both the public and the private sphere.

Organisational Norms, Practices, and Structures

Pullen, Rhodes, and Thanem (2017) and Acker (1990) posit that the structure of an organisation impacts the experiences of the individual where that organisation and/or occupation is itself considered 'gendered'. Researchers contend that within the investment management sector 'organisations are blind to gender through a perpetuation of the unstated male norm and suppression of gender differences' (North-Samardzic and Taksa 2011: 201). While investment firms develop policies and criteria in line with equality legislation, once implemented, they merely serve a figurative function and have limited influence on day-to-day actions, behaviours, and understandings of gender (Hearit 2017; Roth 2006). Until the underlying values regarding patriarchy and gendered knowledge are resisted and a regime of gender equality and transformational interventions are put in place, women will continue to be represented as differentiated others. For instance, one tactic that privileges men and disadvantages women in the UK banking sector is widespread presenteeism (Weber 2013; Sealy 2010; Granleese 2004). Granleese (2004: 224), claimed that presenteeism was more evident among men in the sector and this was in part due to a 'new behavioural pattern of resistance by men when women encroach on male territory'. Success is associated with 'being present' as opposed to being productive.

Wombs in Waiting

Many firms claim to have gender-neutral policies, flexible working arrangements, and an awareness of family life and work-life balance. In practice, supports are not always readily available. Maternity leave, for example, remains a contentious issue. Many women fear that taking maternity leave implies that they are not as committed to the organisation, especially when compared to male peers. High profile figures such as Marissa Mayer, CEO of Yahoo, who took three weeks maternity leave and restricted flexible work arrangements for employees, increases the pressure on women in terms of combining work and motherhood (Tajlili 2014). England (2017) and Roth (2006) claim that the gender segregation of men and women commences, not when women have a family, but because of their potential to have one. Labelled as 'wombs in waiting'- women are disadvantaged because of their potential to have a family (Sylvia Ann Hewlett quoted in Mills 2010).

Life and Language of the Boys' Club

An investigation into the culture of the investment banking sector highlighted the gendered context of the sector and the sexist behaviour faced by women daily (The Equality and Human Rights Commission 2009: 51). Front office is in essence a heterosexual machismo space, where homosocial behaviour and sexist language constitutes a daily ritual (McDowell 2010; Greenfield et al. 2002; Rutherford 2014). Women have difficulty challenging this behaviour as they risk being branded as whingers and/or having their careers negatively impacted as a result (MacLean 2016; North-Samardzic and Taksa 2011). Desk and department heads very often tolerated the outrageous and improper behaviour of '"eccentrics (or childish pissheads) as some may call them" so long as they were making money' (Anderson 2009:43). Direct exclusion of women from networks or male-dominated events is often perpetrated through social activities and/or client entertainment that is 'commonly set in masculinized arenas, including golf clubs or hospitality suites at major football clubs as well as the lap dancing clubs' (McDowell 2010: 653). Regardless of how women 'do gender' they are invariably cast as the 'outsider', purposefully differentiated from those who 'belong' in the club (Fisher and Kinsey 2014).

Doing Gender on the Inside

A social constructionist approach posits that gender is not a given but rather accomplished in social interactions (West and Zimmerman 1987). Gender is theorised as 'doing' rather than 'being' (Butler 1990), and as flexible and only 'fixed in place by culturally constituted gendered practices' (Gherardi 2005:222). The context of where one performs gender has become increasingly important in the discussion of gender as a social construct (see also O'Connor and O'Hagan, this volume). Women in investment banking struggle daily over how best to behave and 'do' gender based on prevailing expectations and perceptions. More often than not women face double standards and regardless of their behaviour are treated differently to male peers. For those men who are considered confident, aggressive, and well networked, promotion to front office is a forgone conclusion. Conversely, women who adopt such attributes, are labelled as aggressive or overly emotional (Wajcman 1998; Bevan and Learmonth 2013; Britton 2017). The investment banking environment is predicated on an understanding of the status and importance of certain roles and their corresponding 'ideal' gender. Informal social interactions provide knowledge about how to behave, act and perform with peers in this space. Women are identified as not the appropriate 'fit' for front office roles. Gender is understood and realised through the language used, sexist behaviours and sexual harassment. Such hegemonic 'norms' are used to control and shape organisations, and the literature suggests they face very little resistance. For most, there is an acceptance of the hierarchical patriarchal structures, and a widespread understanding of its salience in all aspects of the investment banking culture (Gregory 2016; MacLean 2016). Challenges are rare because of the fear of further marginalisation and a reinforcement of outsider status (McDowell 2011).

SOCIAL CLOSURE THEORY

Given the recurrent theme of exclusion evident in the literature reviewed above, I believe it is useful to explore the concept of closure more comprehensively as an overarching explanatory framework for interpreting gender inequality in investment management. 'Closure', according to Weber, denotes 'the more or less intentional process of groups drawing boundaries against outsiders, driven not only by economic interests but also by a tradition of affectual bonds' (Cardona 2013: 2). 'Closure' has been defined by Parkin (1974: 3) as 'the process by which social collectives seek to maximize rewards by restricting access to rewards and opportunities to a limited circle of eligibles.' The theory has been used to demonstrate the extensive variety of exclusion strategies and tactics underpinning gendered occupational segregation (Powell and Sang 2015; Lutter 2015; Lefevre et al. 2010; Teljeur and O'Dowd 2009; Bolton and Muzio 2007). Closure regimes have been shown to facilitate 'boundary drawing' within elite professions such as investment management, ensuring that women are excluded from senior high earning positions (Costen et al. 2012: 3). By erecting barriers and drawing boundaries in a 'hostile' environment, women are excluded from the investment floor, thus ensuring that men maintain their power, and status and keep women 'outside the club'.

I now turn to an examination of the experiences of women in Ireland working in investment management. I consider those experiences in light of social closure theory as a meta-theoretical framework that best explains gender segregation and inequality in the Irish investment management sector.

THE FIELDWORK

Sample and Method

Sixteen women, who were currently working, or had worked in investment management in Ireland in the previous two years, were interviewed using a snowball sampling technique. Care was taken to ensure that initial interviewees were not known to each other, thus ensuring a broad sample. The interviewees selected were working in different companies and all at differing stages and levels in their organisations. Each interviewee was asked to recount their experiences of day-to-day life in the sector, as well as their experience in recruitment and progression. Retention was also discussed and was a particularly emotive issue for the six interviewees who had left investment management at the time of the interviews. Table 1 contains a profile of the interviewees.

Table 1: *Investment Management Employee Profile*

Participant	Age 18-25	Age 25-35	Age 35-45	Job Title	Length of Service in Sector	Dependent Children	Back/ Middle Office	Front Office
1			✓	Head of Global Consumer Research	15 years	Yes, one dependent child		✓
2			✓	Senior Credit Analyst	18 years	No	✓	
3 Leaver		✓		Trading Systems Analyst	5 years	Yes, two dependent children	✓	
4 Leaver			✓	Accounts Director	14 years	No	✓	
5		✓		Private Client Executive	9 years	Yes, one dependent child	✓	✓
6			✓	Debt Investor Relations	13 years	Yes, one dependent child	✓	
7 Leaver		✓		Private Pensions Manager	13 years	No	✓	
8			✓	Investment Manager	12 years	No		✓
9		✓		Senior Credit Analyst	11 years	No		✓
10		✓		Client Relationship Executive	2.5 years	No	✓	
11 Leaver	✓			Junior Analyst Support	18 months	No	✓	
12			✓	Equity Analyst	13 years	No		✓
13 Leaver	✓			Fixed Income Analyst	1.5 years	No		✓
14		✓		Quantitative Analyst	2 years	No	✓	
15			✓	Financial Analyst	7 years	Yes, two dependent children	✓	
16 Leaver			✓	Back Office Manager	7 years	No	✓	

Given the feminist lens of the research coupled with the interpretivist philosophical stance, the constant comparative method of data analysis was used to examine the data. This theory-building approach was non-linear and iterative and allowed the data guide the findings (Miles and Huberman 1994; Lincoln and Guba 1985).

DISCUSSION OF FINDINGS

The findings indicate that women face a complex range of obstacles in both 'doing gender' and navigating their careers within the sector. Such impediments are particularly to the fore in the promotion track to front office roles. Figure 1 sets out a framework of the barriers women face in

Figure 1: Framework of Barriers

negotiating their gender and surviving in the boys' club. Among the participants, there is evidence of three main clusters of barriers that mutually interact. I classify them broadly as individual, organisational and cultural barriers. Overwhelmingly, participants report that the inherent culture of the sector – where women are closed out and represented as the 'other', 'different' and 'not the right fit' – is the most challenging and pervasive barrier faced.

Cultural Factors

The overwhelming influence on female experience in investment management is the culture of the sector. In particular, the extreme performance-driven atmosphere and the embedded old boys' network emerge as significant obstacles that lead women to be cast as 'different' or 'outsiders'. The women describe the sector as a 'very macho sort of environment [where] you were judged by your results' (Participant 1). Their experience resonates with McDowell's observation that an 'an aggressive, hetero-sexualized masculine confidence' and 'atmosphere of suppressed panic and macho culture' characterises the investment floor (2010: 653). Quotidien cultural norms are underpinned by overstated forms of masculinity and a stressful working environment that is continuously hostile to women, and maintains that only those careers that are linear and uninterrupted can be successful. Such heteronormative assumptions produce and reproduce social relations that sustain the 'male as manager' as the norm. Derogations from that norm are not entertained as one participant illustrated: 'There was a woman in the Back Office who asked to go on a three day week and they were looking at her like she had two heads, there was no way, it was all or nothing' (Participant 7). The existence of the boys' club is seen as a 'cultural thing that has remained within the industry for years'. Its existence testifies to the fact that knowledge is rooted in power relations. Those in powerful positions are almost exclusively men. Most respondents were of the view that the sector would be 'very slow to lose this – you see no women in management positions or very few' (Participant 1). Because gendered culture is normalised, it masks the embodied nature of work (Acker, 1990). The boys' club mentality is considered an accepted norm, in particular, in front office:

> Yeah, it's tough, on the trading floors, the environment is very different, it's not very female-friendly, you have to be willing to put up with a lot of things that men would be much more comfortable with than women probably. (Participant 5)

Stereotypical assumptions and biases are embedded to the degree that women are likelier to comply (rather than resist).

All of the respondents agree that the old boys' network is characterised by subtle discrimination and exclusion:

> You couldn't put your finger on it and say strategically they don't choose women, but yet if you looked at the statistics there were no senior women . . . so really it is an invisible layer, it's a barrier. It will all be denied if they were questions . . . it would be completely denied but . . . it exists. (Participant 2).

The culture is underpinned by the informal nature of the network formation process and the difficulties for women gaining access to the club. As noted earlier class and gender intersect in the drive for career success. Elite school and sports connections – which are exclusively male orientated – are highlighted as key to bonding, making connections, sharing information, and contributing to decision-making:

> In Ireland, a lot of the guys would have gone to school together or played rugby together . . . it [boys' club mentality] is definitely still there. (Participant 6)

> If you could have gone to Gonzaga or Blackrock, gone to UCD, studied Commerce or Economics, and then gone into Davy Stockbrokers, and that was literally the demographic and profile of pretty much everyone in there. If you were anything other than that, you weren't part of the club essentially. (Participant 15)

People in elite positions within Irish business and politics are disproportionately drawn from among those who attended elite private schools. These men think of each other as members of a closed club who are 'homogeneous socially and culturally, have similar interests and experiences and adhere to the same values' (Courtois 2018: 126).

Sexualised and homosocial behaviours form an intrinsic part of the bonding capital within the old boys' network. One interviewee who has left the investment banking sector outlines the regular outings to strip clubs:

> The major thing you are up against is networking and the culture in investment banks to go to strip clubs – that's a major problem. I know if you are in the business side it's difficult, the IT side – the IT geeks, are not that interested in going to strip clubs, they are all nice people, but when you are with the traders. . . (Participant 3)

Such behaviours places women firmly in the outsider role and reinforces the perspective that 'the financial industry is very much a man's space . . . it's a fact that the important places are more or less for men.' (Participant 9).

Women accept that gaining entry to networks is a challenge and social events are commonly used as a mechanism for men to 'close ranks' so when invited, it is a must to be 'seen':

> There'd be always the Friday night drinking. In the beginning, we wouldn't have been invited, and then eventually, we got some invites, and I would make sure that I went along, even if I had other plans or I just did not want to go, because it was so important, even just for one or two drinks. You weren't part of that network. You weren't part of that club. You just had to try and do everything to try and be there. (Participant 11)

A number of the women highlight the difficulties not just in negotiating entry to the boys' club, but in how to perform their gender once inside, in a space which was a 'very boy's kind of culture, a lot of jokes, pies down the pub'. (Participant 2). Some women reference the double-bind faced when trying to both fit in and remain true to themselves. For example, it is considered important at social events to be able to 'keep up' in the drinking stakes to be accepted by the men, but in doing so, they are pigeon-holed as non-feminine (Participant 5). Another participant observes:

> It's funny because I think if you were able to socialize with the men you were seen as a very hard woman. The women that were traders were hard and vicious. (Participant 4)

These findings clearly indicate that the sector is characterised by a masculinist culture rife with gender and occupational stereotypes.

Organisational Factors

Organisational norms and structures emerge as significant impediments to career progression and advancement. Respondents note that organisational practices are such that often women are inadvertently placed into certain roles due to sectoral stereotyping and, in particular, this is evident within front office roles. Alongside this, women report that the absence of a clear progression path is a disadvantage in relation to advancement. Most are of the view that access to gendered networks and a nepotism-based promotion ladder of 'who you know' rather than 'what you know' is the guiding force in career success:

> They're very impermeable [glass ceilings], it's not anything that's going to be blatantly against legislation and equality laws, it's very subtle, it's the 'we go out for golf and we do the deal' [mentality]. (Participant 4)

The implicit association of men with front office roles and women as deficient in terms of their qualification for such roles, is further evidence of the discrimination the latter face.

Most respondents believed that having a role model and/or mentor is a significant advantage in learning about their role professionally as well as gaining understanding about social norms and how to 'do gender' on the job:

> Being mentored is really positive, being part of somebody's successful team, being in with the right people, that's all hugely positive particularly in terms of getting you to be able to express your initial ideas and knowing. (Participant 10)

> ... to have more women within these [Front Office] roles for a start would give a very good message to other women that are coming up in lower positions. (Participant 14)

Women recognise male mentors as particularly powerful. For front office staff, the pragmatism of male bosses is cited as a specific advantage, as is their ability to separate personal issues from professional ones. However, women also recognise that deficiencies exist in male mentorship. For instance, most women believe that men cannot provide guidance regarding how best to manage one's gender in a male space and how to navigate a successful career without becoming one of the boys. The participants did, however, agree that a senior male mentor or sponsor, albeit imperfect, is more advantageous to their career progression than a senior woman. Those few senior women who are present are perceived to be overly protective of their own position:

Male bosses are just a bit more pragmatic and they see that by helping people under them, that makes them look good, whereas women immediately feel the threat and see it as you're against me, men are a bit more sensible and think, well, if you're doing well, I look good, because ultimately I'm secure in my role. (Participant 8)

The respondents accept that it is the sectoral culture that to some degree forces behaviours of self-preservation upon senior women. They recognise that at all levels within the organisation women have to assimilate to the male-dominated cultural norms and adjust their gender in order to avoid being excluded.

The way in which work is organised and the attendant expectations is incompatible with family commitments. The work process is characterised by long hours, both inside and outside the office and an assumption that a successful career is one which is linear, uninterrupted, and where one is always available.

There is a pervasive acceptance of long hours and a presenteeism ethos where 'it doesn't matter if you're playing Solitaire, you need to be at the desk'. (Participant 4). Many women perceive this as a closure tactic. Women with families are unable to be present to the same degree and are, therefore, considered less committed:

The long hours certainly applies because it's seen – if you're seen to be working around the clock you are obviously viewed upon as being very dedicated and very into your job . . . you've a better chance of progression. If you have a family then you can't be there after five o'clock in the evening. (Participant 14)

Presenteeism becomes a proxy for firm loyalty, ambition and, in some instances, performance. As a consequence, women are closed out of pro-motion opportunities:

Sometimes people remember this at bonus time . . . at promotion time, I saw X at their desk at seven o'clock at night, Y had gone home even though Y could've done much more work during the day than X. (Participant 13)

For all of the women, there is collective dismay at the conflict between raising a family and career advancement in the sector. Most felt that: 'it is much more difficult for women than for men' (Participant 3) and 'the trade-off for women is greater than that for men because of family responsibly.' (Participant 13). Participants indicate the difficulties in developing a viable career strategy or progression path. Women with and without children recognise the challenge of balancing family and work. All acknowledge that beyond a certain point on the career trajectory women often opt out of the progression track or indeed the sector. While this is perceived as an individual decision, crucially it is influenced significantly by the sectoral culture and organisational structures and practices including lack of work-life balance, lack of role models, mentors, etc. 'I didn't apply for any [promotions]. There wasn't evidence or prospects for females with a family that you can see for moving up the ladder.' (Participant 14)

Individual Level Barriers

Finally, the respondents reflected on the person-environment interaction and specifically the level of compatibility or perceived compatibility between the individual and the organisation. Ambition, confidence, aggression, and flexibility are character traits traditionally associated with men and are regarded as a *sine qua non* for successfully navigating a career path in the sector. Respondents reported that differences – both perceived and real – are highlighted continuously to reinforce men's dominant positions. Women are not the right 'fit' for front office. However, in practice 'fit' constitutes an intangible set of qualities determined largely by senior male gatekeepers (Rivera 2016). My evidence suggests that women internalise stereotypes about gender appropriate traits and concomitantly, exhibit little resistance to such gendered stereotypes. When asked about why fewer women are in front office, participants note that:

> women are sometimes not attracted to it [front office] because they don't have self-confidence and belief . . . men are better risk takers, and maybe that means that they're more suited to those [front office] jobs. (Participant 9)

> It is assumed that the men are more suited to going out and getting the business. Men are so much more aggressive. (Participant 2).

All respondents agreed that front office required individuals who are confident and have high levels of self-belief. There is widespread agreement that male confidence is a consequence of the culture of privilege that men enjoy within the sector. This is particularly evident when examining pay and progression:

> I think that men have more confidence and more belief in themselves than we [women] would. Men think, OK Yes, I'm underpaid and they're lucky to get me . . . I'd be more, well maybe I'm lucky to be here. . . (Participant 16)

> You can see it first-hand when people go in for a pay rise – women ask for it, men demand it (Participant 1).

A number of respondents believe that cultural constructs of so called valuable personal qualities rather than proven abilities impact promotional decisions. This is articulated clearly by Participant 3, who left the sector as a consequence of the culture:

> it takes an awful lot of courage . . . to push against the closed door to get the promotion. I was sidestepped for promotion and they brought a guy in above me.

This respondent was subsequently informed that management did not consider her as a potential candidate, nor did they expect her to consider herself as such. For many women, there is a perception that regardless of ability, merely being female would adversely impact progression to front office. This was in part due to the widely held beliefs among men and women that there is a higher level of organisational commitment evident among men because they have fewer caring responsibilities. As a consequence of these stereotypes, many are of the view that to succeed, women must undertake a daily performance of undoing their gender. Only those women who conform to the stereotyped image of a single, power-driven employee with no children could make it to the front office.

CONCLUSION

The investment management sector has its own set of dominant masculine characteristics which influence every facet of the business and shape the organisational culture as well as understandings about gender roles and identities. The performance-driven and hostile culture of the sector underpins organisational processes and practices. Moreover, it normalises men's privilege and presents women as outsiders. The privilege men enjoy alongside the embedded cultural norms facilitates knowledge production about gender, which is hegemonic in nature, and reflective of a 'turbo-masculine embodiment' (Gregory 2016: 151). Women are regularly reminded in their daily interactions and doing of gender that they are 'different' to men and that difference is equated with not being the right fit and, ultimately, with subordination (West and Zimmerman 1987). Even for those women who attempt to undo gender, closure is experienced. Sectoral norms such as a macho performance and competitive-led culture, highly sexualised language, and social interactions imbued with male traits set out an understanding about gendered relations and, in particular, the presumed 'normative' gender representations of men as the only right fit for front office roles (McDowell 2011; Roth 2006).

Sustaining and reinforcing the male-dominated culture are organisational structures, processes, and norms, all of which are themselves borne out of the predominant patriarchal culture. Within the sector, women are closed out in terms of both gaining knowledge about their own role as well as being a part of the production of knowledge about gender in the sector (Pullen, Rhodes, and Thanem 2017; North-Samardzic and Taksa 2011; Acker 1990). Women lack appropriate role models and mentors and are excluded from networks, which in turn disadvantages them in comparison with their male peers (Hughes and Sheerin 2016; Pryce and Sealy 2013). Often exclusion and discrimination are enacted through men's networks based on shared sport, school ties, 'pedigree' or other connections (Rowe and Crafford 2003; Prügl, 2012; Rivera 2016; Courtois 2018). Exclusionary recruitment practices, opaque and 'male-merit' led promotion practices, as well as presenteeism, serve to support the ongoing masculinist construction of an appropriate fit with a front office role. Senior male gatekeepers occupy power positions and hold vital information about the 'rules of the game'. Women indicate that such individuals close ranks, both overtly and covertly, in order to withhold knowledge and close them out (Wilson 2017).

Knowledge production about gender within investment management is itself highly gendered. My findings reinforce the case that young women at the early career-building stage are excluded because they are perceived to lack appropriate (male) personality traits to fit within the sector (Hearit 2017). Evidence of ongoing knowledge production of 'norms' that maintain gender distinctions and difference is ever present and reinforces the perspective that women do not belong. In line with the literature, my findings further suggest that there are few challenges to the ongoing gender inequality in the sector (Gregory 2016; MacLean 2016). Most respondents indicate that much of the discrimination they face is covert. Some fear that challenging male privilege and discriminatory practices may backfire. They may be seen as disruptive (MacDowell 2011) or they may be labelled troublemakers who either can't perform adequately or simply do not fit within the sector. HR structures and procedures, while well intentioned, are not seen as efficacious in tackling sexist behaviour and addressing gender segregation and inequality.

The sector is characterised by a high degree of social closure. Insiders set and use boundaries to protect their own interests and opportunities and restrict access to those they do not consider to be the right fit. Senior male elites create and maintain a cultural script, which is dominated by patriarchal ideology and serves to close women out. Through cultural norms, constructs and organisational structures and processes, an ongoing reproduction of masculinist beliefs and forms of understanding about gender relations and gender roles occurs. This conceptualisation of gender has at its core the message that women and men are different, and that this difference serves as a legitimate basis for the exercise of asymmetrical power. Closure tactics ensure that the elite aspects of a profession, such as front office investment management, remain occupied predominantly by men (Costen et al. 2012; Ashley 2010).

Investment management is a setting of extreme gender segregation within the banking sector. It embodies a masculinist culture, characterised by the old boys' network and elite senior male gatekeepers. It is kept in place by conscious and unconscious gender biases. Within the sector, gender is produced, reproduced, and performed in every aspect of the workplace. The consequence of this is far reaching in terms of maintenance of gendered hierarchies and marginalisation of women. Such a culture promotes and mobilises heteronormative masculinities, supporting an ongoing masculinist discourse of gender and gender relations.

Notes

1 Forfás was the national agency responsible for providing policy advice to the Irish government on enterprise, trade, employment, and innovation. It was dissolved in August 2014 and its policy functions and role integrated into the Department of Jobs, Enterprise, and Innovation.

REFERENCES

Acker, J., 'Hierarchies, jobs, bodies: A theory of gendered organisations', in *Gender & Society*, 4(2), 1990, pp 139–58.

Aitchison, C., 'She's not one of the boys', in *The Independent*, 16 February 1995.

Anderson, G., *Cityboy: Beer and Loathing in the Square Mile* (Headline: London, 2009).

Ashley, L., '"They're not all bastards": Prospects for gender equality in the UK's elite law firms', 23 Dec. 2010, Cass Centre for Professional Service Firms Working Paper.

Bevan, V. and M. Learmonth, '"I wouldn't say it's sexism, except that . . . it's all these little subtle things": Healthcare scientists' accounts of gender in healthcare science laboratories', in *Social Studies of Science*, 43(1), 2013, pp 136–58.

Bolton, S. C. and D. Muzio, D., '"Can't live with 'em; can't live without 'em": Gendered segmentation in the legal profession', in *Sociology*, 41(1), 2007, pp 47–64.

Britton, D. M., 'Beyond the chilly climate: The salience of gender in women's academic careers', in *Gender & Society*, 31(1), 2017, pp 5–27.

Broadbridge, A. and J. Hearn, 'Gender and management: New directions in research and continuing patterns in practice', in *British Journal of Management*, 19, 2008, pp S38–49.

Broadbridge, A. M., '"Window dressing?" Women, careers and retail management' (DPhil thesis, University of Stirling, 2010).

Burke, W. W., *Organisation Change: Theory and Practice* (Sage: New York, 2017).

Butler, J., *Gender trouble: Feminism and the Subversion of Identity* (Routledge: New York, 1990).

Cardona, A., 'Closing the group or the market? The two sides of Weber's concept of closure and their relevance for the study of intergroup inequality', SFB 882 Working Paper Series No. 15 (DFG Research Centre: University of Bielefeld, Germany, 2013).

Chang, S. A., 'Outsiders and outperformers: Women in fund management', in *Finance Professionals Post* [online], 2010. Available from: <http://post.nyssa.org/nyssa-news/2010/04/outsiders-and-outperformers-women-in-fund-management.html>, accessed 31 Oct. 2018.

Chivers, G., 'Supporting informal learning by traders in investment banks' in *Journal of European Industrial Training*, 35, 2011, pp 154–75.

Costen, W. M., C. E. Hardigree, and M. A. Testagrossa, 'Glass ceiling or saran wrap™? Women in gaming management', *UNLV Gaming Research and Review Journal*, 7(2), 2012, pp 1–12.

Courtois, A., 'Conclusion', in *Elite Schooling and Social Inequality* (Palgrave Macmillan: London, 2018, pp 191–203).

Cullen, P., and M. P. Murphy, 'Gendered mobilizations against austerity in Ireland', in *Gender, Work & Organisation*, 24(1), 2017 pp 83–97.

England, P., *Comparable Worth: Theories and Evidence* (Routledge: New York, 2017).

Equality and Human Rights Commission, *Financial Services Inquiry: Sex Discrimination and Gender Pay Gap Report of the Equality and Human Rights Commission* (Equality and Human Rights Commission: Manchester, 2009).

Fisher, V., and S. Kinsey, 'Behind closed doors!: Homosocial desire and the academic boys' club', in *Gender in Management: An International Journal*, 29(1), 2014, pp 44–64.

Forfás, *Assessing the Demand for Big Data and Analytics Skills, 2013–2020*. Report of the Expert Group on Future Skills Needs (Dublin, 2014).

Ibid., *Future Skills and Research Needs of the International Financial Services Industry*. Report of the Expert Group on Future Skills Needs (Dublin, Dec. 2007).

Gherardi, S., 'Feminist theory and organisation theory: A dialogue on new bases, in *The Oxford Handbook of Organisation Theory* (Oxford University Press: Oxford, 2005).

Granleese, J., 'Occupational pressures in banking: Gender differences', in *Women in Management Review*, 19(4), 2004, pp 219–26.

Greenfield, S., J. Peters, N. Lane, T. Rees, and G. Samuels, *Set Fair: A Report on Women in Science, Engineering, and Technology from the Baroness Greenfield CBE to the Secretary of State for Trade and Industry* (Greenfield Report). (Department of Trade and Industry: London, 2002).

Gregory, M. R., *The Face of the Firm: Corporate Hegemonic Masculinity at Work* (Routledge, 2016).

Groysberg, B., 'How star women build portable skills', *Harvard Business Review* (February 2008).

Hearit, L. B., 'Women on Wall Street', in *The Handbook of Financial Communication and Investor Relations* (Wiley-Blackwell: New Jersey, US, 2017), pp 137–44.

Hughes, C., and C. Sheerin, 'Reflections on the relationship between mentoring, female development and career progression: Investment management versus Human

Resource management', in *International Journal of HRD Practice Policy and Research*, 1(2), 2016, pp 41–54.

Irish Funds, 'Why Ireland', 2017, available from https://files.irishfunds.ie/1489525513-IF_WhyIreland_Brochure_euro_03-2017.pdf>, accessed 31 October 2018.

Kelan, E., *Performing Gender at Work* (Palgrave: Basingstoke, 2009).

Kennedy, M. and M. J. Power, 'The ssmokescreen of meritocracy: Elite education in Ireland and the reproduction of class privilege', in *Journal for Critical Education Policy Studies*, 8(2), 2010, pp 222–48.

Kossek, E. E., R. Su, and L. Wu, '"Opting out" or "pushed out?" Integrating perspectives on women's career equality for gender inclusion and interventions', in *Journal of Management*, 43(1), 2017, pp 228–54.

Kumra, S. and S.Vinnecombe, 'Impressing for success: A gendered analysis of a key social capital accumulation strategy', in *Gender, Work & Organisation*, 17(5), 2010, pp 521–46.

Lefevre, J. H., M. Roupret., S. Kerneis, and L. Karila, 'Career choices of medical students: A national survey of 1780 students', in *Medical Education*, 44(6), 2010, pp 603–12.

Lewchuk, D. K., 'Collateral consequences: The effects of decriminalizing prostitution on women's equality in business', in *Appeal*, 18(1), 2013, pp 105–63.

Lincoln, Y. S. and E. G. Guba, *Naturalistic Inquiry* (Sage Publications: Newbury Park, CA, 1985).

Lutter, M., 'Do women suffer from network closure? The moderating effect of social capital on gender inequality in a project-based labor market, 1929 to 2010' in *American Sociological Review*, 80(2), 2015, pp 329–58.

McDowell, L., *Capital Culture: Gender at Work in the City* (Wiley-Blackwell: Oxford, 2011).

Ibid., 'Capital culture revisited: Sex, testosterone and the city', in *International Journal of Urban and Regional Research*, 34(3), 2010, pp 652–8.

MacLean, K., 'Gender, risk and the Wall Street alpha male', in *Journal of Gender Studies*, 25(4), 2016, pp 427–44.

Miles, M. B. and A. M Huberman, *Qualitative Data Analysis: An Expanded Sourcebook* (Sage: Thousand Oaks, CA; London, 1994)..

Mills, E., 'Sisterhood costs us jobs', in *Sunday Times*, 7 Feb. 2010.

Morningstar, 'Morningstar: Fund managers by gender', [online] June 2015, available from https://corporate.morningstar.com/US/documents/ResearchPapers/Fund-Managers-by-Gender.pdf>, accessed 31 Oct. 2018.

North-Samardzic, A. and L. Taksa, 'The impact of gender culture on women's career trajectories: An Australian case study', in *Equality, Diversity and Inclusion: An International Journal*, 30(3), 2011, pp 196–216.

Palmer, C., 'A job, old boy? The school ties that still bind', in *The Observer* [online], 11 June 2000, available from www.guardian.co.uk/money/2000/jun/11/workandcareers.madeleinebunting2>, accessed 31 October 2018.

Parkin, F., *The Social Analysis of Class Structure* (Routledge: London, 1974).

Powell, A. and K. J. Sang, 'Everyday experiences of sexism in male-dominated professions: A Bourdieusian perspective' *Sociology*, 49(5), 2015, pp 919–36.

Prügl, E., '"If Lehman brothers had been Lehman sisters. . .": Gender and myth in the aftermath of the financial crisis', in *International Political Sociology*, 6(1), 2012, pp 21–35.

Rivera, L. A., *Pedigree: How Elite Students get Elite Jobs* (Princeton University Press: Princeton, NJ, 2016).

Pryce, P. and R. Sealy, 'Promoting women to MD in investment banking: Multi-level influences', in *Gender in Management: An International Journal*, 28(8), 2013, pp 448–67.

Pullen, A., C. Rhodes, and T. Thanem, 'Affective politics in gendered organisations: Affirmative notes on becoming-woman', *Organisation*, 24(1), 2017, pp 105–23.

PwC, 'Global assets under management set to rise to $145.4 trillion by 2025', 2017, available from: <https://press.pwc.com/News-releases/global-assets-under-management-set-to-rise-to--145.4-trillion-by-2025/s/e236a113-5115-4421-9c75-77191733f15f>, accessed 31 Oct. 2018.

Ramaswami, A. N., M. Carter, and G. F. Dreher, 'Expatriation and career success: A human capital perspective', in *Human Relations*, 69(10), 2016, pp 1,959–87.

Roth, L. M., *Selling Women Short: Gender and Money on Wall Street* (Princeton University Press: Princeton, NJ, 2006)

Rowe, T. and A. Crafford, 'A study of barriers to career advancement for professional women in investment banking', in *South African Journal of Human Resource Management*, 1(2), 2003, pp 21–7.

Rutherford, S., 'Gendered organisational cultures, structures and processes: The cultural exclusion of women in organisations', in *Gender in Organizations: Are Men Allies or Adversaries to Women's Career Advancement* (Edward Elgar: US, 2014), pp 193–216.

Sandberg, S., *Lean in: Women, Work, and the Will to Lead* (Random House: NY, 2013).

Schilt, K., & C. Connell, C., 'Do workplace gender transitions make gender trouble?', in *Gender, Work, & Organisation*, 14(6), 2007, pp 596–618.

Sealy, R. 'Changing perceptions of meritocracy in senior women's careers', in *Gender in Management: An International Journal*, 25(3), 2010, pp 184–97.

Ibid., 'A qualitative examination of the importance of female role models in investment banks', PhD thesis (Cranfield University: UK, 2009).

Tajlili, M. H., 'A framework for promoting women's career intentionality and work-life integration' in *The Career Development Quarterly*, 62(3), 2014, pp 254–67.

Tannen, D., 'The double bind', in S. Morrison (ed.), *Thirty Ways of Looking at Hillary* (Harper Collins: New York, NY 2008), pp 126–39.

Teljeur, C. and T. O'Dowd, 'The feminisation of general practice: Crisis or business as usual', in *The Lancet*, 374(9,696), 2009, p. 1,147.

Van den Brink, M., and Y. Benschop, 'Gender in academic networking: The role of gatekeepers in professorial recruitment', in *Journal of Management Studies*, 51(3), 2014, pp 460–92.

Wajcman, J., *Managing Like a Man: Women and Men in Corporate Management* (Polity Press in association with Blackwell Publishers Ltd.: Cambridge, 1998).

Weber, L., 'Go ahead, Hit the Snooze Button', in *Wall Street Journal* [online], 23 Jan. 2013, available from www.wsj.com/articles/SB10001424127887323301104578257894191502654>, accessed 31 Oct. 2018.

West, C. and D. H. Zimmerman, 'Doing gender', in *Gender & Society*, 1(2), 1987, pp 125–51.

Wilson, F. M., *Organisational Behaviour and Gender* (Routledge: London, 2017).

FOUR

Film, Television and Gendered Work in Ireland

Anne O'Brien

INTRODUCTION

In October 2017 over 75 women in the Hollywood film industry accused Harvey Weinstein of rape, sexual assault and sexual abuse spanning a timeframe of 30 years, (*Time Magazine*, 2 July 2018). These accusations subsequently led to the viral spread of #MeToo, as women from all over the globe documented, through social media, the widespread prevalence of sexual harassment in the workplace. What began as a Hollywood scandal has finally served to lift the lid on the global problem not just of sexual harassment but also of gender inequality in screen production work.

Women in the Irish film and television industries are not immune to experiences of gender inequality which are embedded in their everyday practices of production. This study, based on over 40 interviews with women working in all areas of film and television production, shows that women experience structural inequality in terms of their segregation into particular roles, how they encounter the gendering of everyday routines of film and television production, and a work culture that is masculinist. While it is important to examine and understand the structural and cultural inequalities that women face in Ireland it is also necessary to explore what women do with that experience of inequality. Respondents were clear that they were doing the work and participating whole-heartedly in the industry, but nonetheless, they believed themselves, as well as their work, to be peripheralised. Women respond to gender inequality in their work by understanding themselves as liminal entities: they are constantly in 'a position of ambiguity and uncertainty' because they occupy a status of being simultaneously both insider in terms of expertise and outsider in terms of their gender identity (Chreim 2002). In the analysis that follows the processes, practices, and culture that gender film and television production are connected with women's accounts of their subjective identities as liminal. Women may comply with or repudiate these structuring practices and processes.

There is a connection between the inequality contained in women's creative labour practices and their subjectivity or agentic interpretations of their own lived realities of film and television work. This formulation of the problem of gender inequality in screen production work goes beyond describing where women are situated 'objectively' with regards to inequality in the Irish industries. Instead I interrogate how gender 'gets inside' women to shape their participation in and experience of their working lives. I examine how work shapes women's knowledge of themselves as workers. Finally, I ask how the processes that shape women's subjectivities might act to reproduce or perhaps even eventually repudiate the inequalities that underpin gendered labour. Women, I argue, operationalise techniques of self-conduct that self-exploit but also offer the potential for alternative subjectivities or forms of repudiation of the gendered norms of film and television production. Their liminal 'betwixt and between' position excludes women but also creates opportunity. Women may repudiate the normative conditions that confront them. They can use liminality in various ways to reconstruct a more empowered sense of themselves and their place in Irish screen production. This they do by refusing to compromise their caring roles for work, by acknowledging that all of life is not merely a pitch for work and by valuing the relationships and trust that they enact in their creative work practices in film and television.

WOMEN IN MEDIA PRODUCTION IN IRELAND

The structural inequalities that are experienced by women in film and television production in the global context map fairly precisely onto the Irish context. Women media workers in the UK experience horizontal segregation at entry level between technical and production roles and ongoing vertical segregation between low status administration work and high-status decision-making positions (Gill 2002). Irish research similarly suggests that the gendered production process is continually reproduced through channelling women and men into different areas of production with different rewards accruing for different types of work (O'Brien 2015). Men consequently experience an invisible glass escalator of upward career progression based on the masculine privilege of presumed potential (Steiner 2015). Meanwhile women constantly have to prove their ability with a resultant slower career progression (McCracken 2000). Gender impacts in additional negative ways on the everyday routines of media production. Gender shapes the point of view applied to content as well as the behaviour expected of women workers (O'Brien 2015). Women workers in the Irish context are allocated different types of assignments to men, and they note that a masculinist world view generally prevails in terms of the angles or perspective applied to stories in Irish film and television content (O'Brien 2015: 263). Women also experience the qualitative nature of production work differently to their male colleagues insofar as they are expected to take on the 'emotional labour' role (Hochschild 1983) of programme-making. Traditional gender divisions around women's supposed 'natural' affinity with this type of affective work are very evident in the Irish case. These feminised work tasks, however, are not explicitly valued in Ireland as part of the production process (O'Brien 2019: 10).

Irish women share the experiences of their global colleagues in terms of the structural inequalities that shape film and television work. Gender inequality is embedded in the work culture that underpins the Irish industries. The prevailing work culture is experienced as both gendered and problematic for Irish women. It requires that they subscribe to traditionally masculine work practices of long working hours, a rigid separation of career and life, and a lack of workplace flexibility. Deviations from the masculinist norms of maintaining long hours and complete availability are made explicitly unacceptable within the Irish film and television production industries (O'Brien 2014). In addition, there is also considerable evidence internationally 'that gendered identities at work are being constructed in traditional ways, drawing in particular on women's perceived "soft skills"' (Geurrier et al. 2009: 494). Irish women experience bias in terms of perception of their skills. For instance, they sense that their approach to narrative, directing and budgets are questioned, purely because of the gendering of those skills as predominantly masculine (O'Brien, 2018). Women also experience outright gender-based discrimination in terms of a pay gap as well as through the promotion system, where they are slower to progress into senior roles in production than their male equivalents. For many, production work demands a level of availability that is more difficult for women because they are engaged in a disproportionate amount of care work relative to men. In Ireland, this is all the more problematic because of the dearth of state support for childcare. In this specific context Irish media organisations largely fail to consider this additional burden faced by women nor do they offer any alternative ways of working within media production. For mothers in the Irish industry the demanding masculinist work culture, which means childcare is often needed sporadically or at anti-social times, culminates in them feeling forced out of their media careers (O'Brien 2014).

As a reaction to the increasing informalisation of media production, workers in Europe, the UK and also in Ireland have adapted by intensifying their use of networks to secure contracts or 'gigs' on a freelance basis (Ursell

2000). Media industries are highly networked for men and women but additional gendered challenges exist for women around self-promotion, accruing social or reputational capital, and engaging in a work culture that is biased and discriminates against them (Blair 2001; Conor et al. 2015, O'Connor and O'Hagan in this volume). The key problem for women is that while the networks mediating employment are a source of stability for some, they are simultaneously a source of exclusion for others (Walby 2011). This dynamic maps more or less seamlessly onto the Irish film and television production context where a relatively small number of independent production companies and commissioning bodies are easily identifiable to each other and relatively enmeshed. In Ireland media production networks tend to reinforce the status of workers who already have high levels of social and cultural capital and those who have a capacity to mediate the allocation of work. In the UK, Smith and McKinlay note 'Even for those with established credentials, breaking through the barrier of established male networks is difficult . . . creativity and willingness to take risks is not enough' (2009: 87). Male subcultures in the UK can thus act as old boys' networks that create barriers to women a situation that resonates for Irish women workers in this and other sectors (see Sheerin in this volume).

In summary, Irish research generally confirms findings from the UK and elsewhere that film and television production work is characterised by structural and cultural inequalities that are based on gendered identities. A number of scholars have explored the question of how women internalise experiences of neoliberalism and how those shape their identity. For instance, Gill and Scharff place an emphasis on the ways in which neoliberal governing practices quite literally 'get inside us' to materialise or constitute women's subjectivities (2011: 8). Gill and Scharff's work focuses on the ways in which neoliberal workers are self-entrepreneurial, constantly strategising, with power operating through technologies of the self and through the worker's own subjectivity. Indeed, they argue that women constitute the 'perfect neoliberal subjects' (2011: 8). However, these assessments do not examine women's agentic position within those structures and cultures of inequality or within those gendered identities. Relatively little research examines how gender inequality, rather than neoliberalism, can shape subjectivity. Further analysis is required to better understand what it is that women do with their experiences of gender inequality. How does being a gendered and unequal worker shape how women understand themselves and their work?; what gendered knowledge does it offer them?; and what possibilities might a gendered subjectivity open up for them and their work?

SUBJECTIVITIES AND LIMINALITY

Creative Work Subjectivities

Mayer is amongst the few scholars who thoroughly addresses creative labour practices and female subjectivity. She argues that the act of work implicitly constructs identities in and through labour. Female-identified work supports labour relations, but this work 'appears otherwise' as a natural form of production, with capitalism profiting from these 'invisible' inputs (2011: 18–19). Mayer describes the conjuncture of invisible labours and identity constructions and advances a number of claims. Firstly, she suggests that new relationships emerge between the material and symbolic dimensions of labour, opening new possibilities for identities. Secondly, the emergent subjectivities that capitalism now demands from its labourers continue to draw on the residual identities that have corresponded to invisible labour in the past. And thirdly, Mayor notes that the role of worker's agency is relevant to how labour is articulated along gender lines (2011: 19–21). Whereas Mayer addresses some of the links between gendered labour and identity, there remains still a question about how gender identity and work are connected, beyond the category of invisible labour. In particular this raises the question of what other technologies of self might contribute to creating gendered experiences of labour and how might gendered subjectivities impact to reproduce or to resist the experience of labour?

Neoliberalism and Subjectivities

In her discussion of neoliberalism and insecurity and not gender per se, Lorey makes the argument that 'Techniques of self-conduct comprise active modes of self-exploitation. . .', (2015: 106). She further proposes that inherent in these modes of self-exploitation are 'new modes of subjectivation, or the internalisation of identity, which are able to elude neoliberal forms of domination and enable new practices of resistive composition and constituent power' (2015: 106). Just as Lorey argues that modes of subjectivity can evade neoliberal domination, I propose here that the same process is at work with regards to gendered exploitation in that women adapt to their own gender-based exclusions from industry. They operationalise techniques of self-conduct in order to self-exploit but in this operationalisation also lies the potential for alternative subjectivities and repudiation of the gendered norms of media production. I argue that the technique they operationalise is one of liminal positionality within media work. Women both participate in media industries but keep a psychological and social distance from an industry that is unequal in terms of gender. Women are permanently in but not of the industry. Through liminality women can 'breach existing relations of domination, a breach that signifies a certain affirmation in which something new can emerge' (Lorey 2015: 107). Liminal modes of subjectivity are not always subsumed into normative practices of gendering in the labour force. Crucially, Lorey argues that 'In uncertain, flexibilised and discontinuous working and living conditions, subjectivations arise that do not entirely correspond to the neoliberal logic of valorization, and which may resist and refute it' (2015: 103). In the same vein, I argue that where there exists unequal gendered labour, subjectivations arise that can challenge and repudiate the normativity or valorisation of gendering and may ultimately refute it.

Internalising Liminality

Liminality describes threshold situations that are part of a rite of passage or 'betwixt and between' positions amongst small cultural groups (Van Gennep 1960; Turner 1982). The concept of liminality has been used in organisational studies to describe employees in organisational threshold situations where there is an absence of a long-term ongoing relationship with the organisation for which they work (Sturdy et al. 2009; Borg and Söderlund 2014). Garsten has described these 'liminal workers' as constantly betwixt and between, lacking the 'structural bond created by a regular employment position, yet drawn into extended circles of loyalty' (1999: 603). Beech (2011) has claimed that liminality can describe a longitudinal experience of ambiguity or a permanent form of identity. Liminality denotes subjects that are 'neither "in" nor "out"' but are 'separated from familiar space, routine temporal order or hegemonic social structures' (Sweeney, 2009). Liminality is used here as a metaphor to describe women's understanding of their gendered condition in media work as one of being in 'a position of ambiguity and uncertainty' (Chreim 2002). That position of liminality enables women to reflexively critique or even resist their full incorporation or assimilation into creative industries. It is in the meanings that women give to their work, as liminal subjects, that accounts of the creation of gendered subjectivities and explanations of compliance or rejection of subjectivities and broader structural processes of gender inequality are to be found. In the analysis that follows the processes, practices, and culture that are central to the gendering of screen production in Ireland are linked to the articulation of female workers' subjective identities as liminal, and to their consequent compliance with and/or refusals of these processes and practices.

METHODOLOGY

The data for this research were gathered through semi-structured interviews with a snowball sample of 40 women film and television workers, conducted from 2012–18. This category included executives, creative producers and directors, middle-ranking producer-directors, production managers and technical operatives as well as low status administrative, support and entry level technical workers working in both film and television production. Respondents worked as freelancers or on temporary or on permanent contracts. Some worked for one or more of Ireland's two dual-funded, public service broadcasters, RTÉ and the Irish language station TG4, or with the commercial broadcaster Virgin Media or with one of the 150 small to medium-sized independent screen production companies that are active in the industry. The women worked across various genres of content production such as news, current affairs, drama, factual and documentary. All interviews were audio recorded, transcribed, and anonymised.

The Irish media industry is small and highly networked and many of the respondents did not want to be identifiable within the industry, nor did they want to be perceived within the sector to be 'causing trouble' over gender inequality. One published interview with a filmmaker was also used as a source of data on women's experiences of that industry (Canty 2017). Details of respondents' work roles were occasionally changed to prevent their identification. The women interviewed were reluctant to essentialise gender as a category and did not see it in terms of a strict binary. The researcher's interpretation of how they viewed gender in the context of interview answers was that they saw it as about 'practices that are perceived, interpreted and or intended as (being) about gender' (Martin Yancey 2003: 342). Findings from a small snowball sample that focus on subjective experiences of workers within a single jurisdiction are not generalisable beyond those terms. Nonetheless, although the findings relate to the specifics of the Irish case, they offer insights into the nature of work in film, television and media production more broadly, as perceived by women employed in the sector, and are perhaps applicable also to creative or knowledge production workers more generally (see chapters by J. P. Byrne, C. Sheerin, A. Kerr and J. Savage in this volume).

LIMINAL WOMEN

Women in this study are aware of how they are positioned as liminal within media industries in a number of ways that are structural. They are liminal because of the roles and assignments that they do not get. They are defined as liminal through the masculinist world view applied to content that they are expected to create. Their liminal position is reinforced through the gendered behaviour expected of them. Women are insiders and outsiders because they participate in production but are constantly questioned while doing so. Similarly, women are clear that they are not treated equally within the culture of film and television production. They experience a veto on women self-promoting. They have a disproportionate amount of emotional work allocated to them. Women experience an ongoing pay gap. All of this inequality is underpinned by demands that women remain 'likeable' throughout rather than becoming 'difficult' about gender equality issues. The appearance of consensus rather than the acknowledgement of conflict is important to the everyday functioning of the industry.

With regard to role allocation, on entry to the industry as film or television interns or runners, women noted that they were often overlooked for technical roles in ways that were gendered. This practice existed right from the outset of their careers. One respondent observed:

> I watched very young men come into the office and be given opportunities before me. It did feel like they were trusted because they were male. I knew for a fact they weren't as experienced as me and I'd be sitting there available to do whatever it might be and they'd get given the job. (E)

This bias continued when men were 'nurtured in a way around technical things' (E) while women were challenged in the same work. As an Emmy nominated producer notes 'when working with a crew you aren't familiar with, you get people challenging you in ways that I'm positive they don't challenge guys. For instance, they think you never shot an interview before' (Morfoot 2016). The flip side of this gendering of roles was that 'women are assumed to be better in the production or office side' (H). Production roles, however, are seen as less risky and less visible and so offer a slower route to progression within the industry where less mentorship or sponsorship can occur.

Women also experienced routine aspects of production work such as the allocation of assignments amongst available staff, the traditional expectations around the angles that would be applied to content and the dynamics of teamwork in ways that were gendered and that made women structurally ambiguous. Gender inequalities in society were reproduced in media workers' perspectives on content and so 'Men are more likely to be correspondents covering politics, business, or economics . . . and women cover topics considered "soft", like health and education.' (H) The problem with this routine practice of allocating hard stories to men was that they were 'rated more highly in terms of news value, and that gives the impression that stories covered by men are more prestigious.' (H) In a similar way, a drama director noted that

> There's a whole area of storytelling that doesn't seem to be accessible to female directors, because they don't seem to be seen to have access to their full humanity because of how women are seen. The big expensive movies . . . have never had a female writer or director, because these are male worlds, and there's a fear that you're not going to get full humanity if you're a female director. (Q)

The message women get from these routine practices is that men should cover the (masculine) normative point of view on 'important' content. Women simply are not sufficiently capable or skilled to apply a human perspective to the same hard news or male blockbuster worlds.

The gendering of the production team was also enacted in terms of appearance by punishing non-traditional cultural notions of particular types of femininities. Women were expected in some cases to conform to certain stereotypical behaviours most notably around the question of workplace self-promotion and with taking on the emotional labour of production. Women agreed that they tended to have to do 'more cajoling and encouraging to get people to do their bit to get the programme to air.' (D) They were also clear that because of the invisibility of this emotional work, much of it was undervalued by the industry. The veto on self-promotion that women experienced meant that they could not highlight these aspects of their work publicly and so women did the additional work while it remained invisible, serving to render them less valuable than male workers and therefore more liminal in status. In addition, women's practices of directing and constructing narrative were constantly undermined. As one director observed 'Mainstream funding bodies say that my stuff isn't "narrative" enough.' (T) She also proposed that women direct differently because of their social experience of gender identity and as such tended to see women when they looked through the lens. However, this difference was interpreted by crew and funders not as a 'creative' asset but rather as suspect, or not adequately normative/masculine.

Women experienced a significant and pervasive imperative to be 'likeable' and not to not be seen as 'difficult'. This was an issue that women experienced in ways that were not just a norm of neoliberal self-entrepreneurialism but in ways that were gendered as well. 'Reputational terrorism' or profound fear of sustaining reputational damage, was not something that interviewees believed their male peers experienced. The women worked on their likeability in minor ways, like rewording emails, or appearing to be friendly in ways they observed their male colleagues did not have to. 'I've heard my male colleagues on the phone to producers and if I spoke to them like that then I'd worry that I'd never get a job again.' (E) This gendered pressure to conform with notions of being 'nice' and not 'causing trouble' impacted in major ways such as with unequal pay. As one director noted 'When it came to invoicing I got a call complaining about my rate saying "I've never paid this rate before" and it was lower than my male counterparts. I knew one of the male directors . . . and he got no phone calls about the same rate.' (E) For men in media production this emotional work of gendered peer recognition and highly conditional acceptability of the female subject simply did not seem to exist. In summary, women were aware of how they were rendered liminal through assignment and role allocations, perspectives applied to content, expectations of their behaviour, questioning of their practice, and vetoing self-promotion all the while demanding that they are compliant with gender inequalities.

SELF-IDENTITY: INTERNALISING LIMINALITY

Similar processes also acted to shape women's subjectivity and create an internal narrative about women's place in media production. Respondents acknowledged that they felt they were neither fully incorporated into the industry nor entirely excluded from it. Respondents experienced their place in media production as structurally ambiguous, as 'betwixt and between', neither fully normative nor entirely excluded and they described how that had impacted on their self-identity as media workers. The internal narrative that formed around experiences of exclusion were articulated in a number of ways: in terms of how they were different and unequal to men; how they had less status or could go unseen; how they experienced contingency in their work by being judged more harshly or questioned more than male colleagues.

Women were clear that their experience was not equivalent to that of their male colleagues 'I don't think it's very equal' (R) and 'going onto a very male set is intimidating.' (A) 'As a woman you need to be able to get on with men. . .' (P) They acknowledged that gender as a dimension of their work lives was difficult to see clearly at times and to articulate in terms of specific incidents. Nonetheless women offered evidence that they were highly aware of gender-based divisions, and that this had impacted on their sense of self as workers in the industry:

It's hard to describe the gender thing sometimes because it's your day to day reality. It's only when you start opening up the topic and look at men your age and see how things are going for them then you think 'Hang on a minute!' (E)

Some women self-identified in terms of a deficit of status in relation to men. They were aware of this and believed that it had impacted negatively on their confidence. One producer observed 'There's an automatic higher reverence for men.' (B) This higher status placed women in a more peripheral position, of which they were cognisant: 'He had a macho attitude, when I worked with him he dismissed me.' (C) Women directors spoke frequently about being undermined by more junior camera operators: 'The male cameraman kept trying to direct all of the scenes' (L); and highlighted the impact this could have on confidence and self-belief: 'The male cameraman took over and the male presenter listened to him, not me . . . I've never seen it happen to male directors that they're questioned.' (E) That particular director had stalled on starting her own company despite having extensive credits for directing because of a dearth of confidence which arose from a gendered erosion of her status as a director, which was very much an everyday experience. 'Having the confidence to make that leap, it's hard to imagine . . . but why can't I do it? There's a block, if I was a guy I would be doing this, because I wouldn't have to fight for my rate, argue for my credit, all that stuff.' (E)

Women had internalised a point of view in which their status in the industry was more contingent than their male colleagues. One series producer commented 'I think men's mistakes are forgiven more easily. Women's career progression is damaged if they are part of a programme that is not a success.' (D) Another producer noted 'Men make mistakes and cover up and there's no payback' (B); whereas another director noted that in the case of women: 'You really do have to prove yourself again and again.' (C) Yet another director knew she had been marginalised relative to her male peers because 'I've been fobbed off more than once with a credit that didn't mean much, that said I only had a tangential role, when I did all the work.' (E) Another director recounts being questioned so profoundly that she 'came off the phone shaking . . . I felt so ridiculous . . . It was so traumatic.' (Q) In various ways women respondents explicitly acknowledged their own erasure from the masculine normativity of production. 'I think that there's men who give each other jobs and they don't particularly see women at all. . .' (N2).

Women were clear that the gendering of their work identities was a position that was held not just at an individual level but by the industry as a community of practitioners: 'It's not a man–woman thing per se . . . it's a community of people who don't perceive women to be trustworthy, or a safe bet.' (M) The gendered view of women as liminal in production, present but not normative, was the position that women had internalised as 'normal'. While women took the industry seriously and engaged fully, their gender status rendered them peripheral, marginal, more contingent, which made them simultaneously both insiders and outsiders. One director described how difficult it was to name this liminal positionality:

> It's hard to put your finger on it and say I did not get hired because I am a woman . . . But you can't make that phone call and ask is that why you didn't get hired . . . And then you think you're being paranoid that it's about gender, that it's because you're a woman . . . But I know what I'm saying is true, based on my own experiences . . . I know it, but I just can't say it. (E)

While women's liminal status is problematic for them in terms of the inequalities they face within film and television production, nonetheless many women do adapt to this ongoing negotiation of status. They do this in a variety of ways either by complying, in pragmatic ways, with the masculinist normativity of the sector or alternatively by resisting their liminal positioning and redefining their relationship with work more on their own terms.

RESPONDING TO LIMINALITY: COMPLIANCE OR RESISTANCE

With regard to compliance with expectations that surround them as workers, one of the ways in which women adapt is, for instance, by not seeking any accommodation from industry to their status as caregivers. They adapt to a care work burden by trying to reorganise their workdays and weeks, by making their work seasonal, by taking leaves of absence, or even by changing direction within film and television so that they can do care work while also 'staying' in the industry. Changing career paths through lateral moves within production helped some women to sustain a viable work-life, but it made no demand on the industry itself to change gender inequalities that saw women struggle more than men with balancing care and work requirements. As one director recounted different jobs make different demands and produce different logics depending on your priorities:

> There are certain jobs that are all or nothing, and series producer or exec producer are all or nothing jobs. There are other jobs that are more flexible and family friendly; [studio] directing is one of them. (I)

Rather than ask to job share or work part-time this executive producer took the normativity of the role's demands as a fixed given and instead she became a freelance studio director. A number of years later freelance contracts dried up and she ended up leaving the industry entirely, a departure that was framed as a personal 'decision' rather than a failure of a sector to retain proven talent.

Women's compliant response to their liminal subjectivities disallowed any public claim that the challenges they faced in terms of being rendered liminal in production work were gender specific. Even in situations of outright discrimination, interviewees oftentimes adapted their own behaviours rather than directly challenging bias in a confrontational manner. This was particularly in play in relation to issues arising from motherhood. One freelancer with a large independent production company stated 'When they found out I was expecting they tried to replace me with another presenter.' (O) That didn't happen, mainly because of statutory protections, but the presenter nonetheless took a shortened maternity leave and juggled breast-feeding around the usual, 12–14 hour, shoot-days. It was not only freelance workers who experienced this discrimination. Large companies and broad-casters were also perceived to be guilty of discriminating against pregnant employees when they should have been observing legislation protecting women's status. But none of the women pursued their legislative rights. Their reluctance to insist on rights was due to a desire not to be 'seen as trouble' (C) and to retain their reputations, an issue that is undoubtedly relevant to male employees too but which is more salient for women in all sorts of additional and gendered ways over the life-course of their careers.

Women complied with the status quo of gender-based inequality by trying to 'fit in' with the masculinist norms of industry and 'getting on' with the work. They seemed to see no alternative to the industry as it was structured and practiced. As one producer put it:

> You just had to put up and shut up, because you knew that if you made a 'fuss' it would backfire on you, you would be the problem. I worked for a large company, they knew the law but they didn't act and I couldn't pay the price of forcing them to act, it would literally cost me work. (P)

Another series producer commented on her adaption to gender bias by 'hardening' to it:

> I did run into problems with camera or sound operators giving me a bit of lip, and they probably wouldn't have said those things to men. I do think men get away with a bit more, but you learn very quickly to be hardened to that, and the only way to answer that is to do a really good job, and then you don't get lip from anyone. (I)

Alternatively, other women did respond to their liminal positioning by resisting the masculinist normativity of production work. They in effect practiced an alternative subjectivity within the industry, articulated in terms of an insistence on doing things their own way. For instance, some women adopt an alternative, more creative and fulfilling space within but also somewhat outside of normative expectations of the film and television industries. Women adopted a perspective that all of life was not simply a 'pitch' for work (Gill 2011). As one respondent put it 'It's important to have a life beyond work, otherwise what are we making programmes about?' (F) Another director described how the content of her work became more important to her than her position within the industry:

> As a filmmaker . . . you have to have your own artistic statement and be your own PR machine, and I don't want that. So, I make my films from an activist place, I realise there are limits to that but I'm more interested in that than in cinema as an industry. (T)

Another way in which women created alternative self-identities and ways of being in film and television production was to place emphasis on connectedness and to value the importance of social relationships at work. One director was clear that she valued the work intimacy of shooting programmes, as she observed of her co-workers 'they're like a friend for life because you spend hours and hours and days and days with another person and you're both really invested in the process . . . You really feel like you're shaping it together. . .' (M). Another producer commented 'there's a big relationship of trust between me and my collaborators . . . it tends to be amongst the women, there's a friendship that forms' (A).

Women were proactively creating relations of trust in a homosocial fashion, but the women were also explicitly bypassing the gendered questioning of their status and ability and using their liminal position to impose a new order and emphasis on collaboration within production work. Many of the women interviewed were interested in facilitating what other people brought to production. As a film director puts it:

> I have a huge passion for working with performers. Because my work is so personal, I focus a lot on backstory – not just my own but that of the performer . . . it's important for me to create a connection between my experience and theirs. (Canty 2016)

An Irish-based producer noted that she had a different perspective and a different way of working: 'I think that women can collaborate properly, I don't want to generalise but with many men there's an inherent ego thing and it's hard to overcome.' (J) Respondents used liminal competencies to create alternative approaches to production that emphasised shared relations and social connection in their work. They resisted the normative priorities of the workplace from a liminal vantage point.

Gendering in Irish film and television industries is in evidence in the structural segregation of media workers and in the masculinist work culture that characterise the sector. Women's responses to these inequalities can result in them operationalising techniques of self-conduct in order to self-exploit in a gendered manner, but also offers the potential to refuse that identity. Women occupy a liminal position, neither fully in nor out of industry, which is operationalised through processes of questioning them, excluding them, lowering their status, and applying a double standard. This liminal status can, however, be appropriated by women to their own subjective ends and can constitute a refusal to internalise masculinist norms. Many of the women interviewed here adopted a perspective on work that prioritises life beyond work, sees them work outside of industry structures, results in them changing industry priorities and insists on social relationality and collaboration as central to the process of production.

There is no reason to think that the responses that are articulated by Irish women here would not also be offered by women working in most liberal democratic contexts. Many of the women interviewed participate in film and television as globally networked industries. They interact with production in Ireland but also in international co-productions in Europe and in Hollywood. Their experiences, though articulated here in terms of their experiences of Irish industries, cannot be understood as entirely or only Irish because of the global nature of much film and television production. The gender inequality documented here is not the only inequality that women face in media production, nor can it be understood in isolation from other intersectional inequalities such as race, sexuality, and class divisions. Women, in all the complexities of their multiple identities, still face unique processes of liminalisation that set them apart from other workers because of gender. The structural barriers that women face in media industries still need to be addressed through processes of unionisation and corporatist bargaining. It is equally important to understand the mechanisms through which gender, as a dimension of the self-identity of workers, can become internalised in ways that limit but also potentially liberate women to participate more fully and to challenge the status quo of the production of culture and the production of knowledge.

REFERENCES

Beech, Nic, 'Liminality and the practices of identity reconstruction', in *Human Relations*, 64(2), 2011, pp 285–302.

Blair, Helen, 'You're only as good as your last job: The labour process and labour market in the British film industry', in *Work, Employment and Society*, 15(1), 2001, pp 149–69.

Borg, Elisabeth, and Jonas Söderlund, 'Liminality competence: An interpretative study of mobile project workers' conception of liminality at work', in *Management Learning*, 46, 2014, pp 260–79.

Canty, Katherine, 'Evolving a patient filmmaking practice', Source http://www.directedbywomen.com, accessed Sept. 2017.

Chreim, Samia, 'Influencing organisational identification during a major change: A communication-based perspective', in *Human Relations*, 55(9), 2002, pp 1,117–37.

Conor, Bridget, Rosalind Gill and Stephanie Taylor, *Gender and Creative Labour* (Wiley Blackwell: Malden MA & Oxford, 2015).

Garsten, Christina, 'Betwixt and between: Temporary employees as liminal subjects in flexible organisations', in *Organisation Studies*, 1999, 20(4), pp 601–17.

Gill, Rosalind, 'Cool, creative and egalitarian? Exploring gender in project-based new media work in Europe', in *Information, Communication & Society*, 5(1), 2002, pp 70–89.

Ibid., '"Life is a pitch": Managing the self in new media work', in Mark Deuze (ed.), *Managing Media Work* (Sage: California, London, New Delhi & Singapore, 2011), pp 249–62.

Gill, Rosalind, and Christina Scharff, *New Femininities: Postfeminism, Neoliberalism and Subjectivity* (Palgrave Macmillan: Basingstoke, 2011).

Guerrier, Yvonne, Christina Evans, Judith Glover, and Cornelia Wilson, '"Technical, but not very. . .": Constructing gendered identities in IT-related employment', in *Work, Employment and Society*, 23(3), 2009, pp 494–511.

Hochschild, Arlie, *The Managed Heart* (University of California Press: Berkeley, 1983).

Lorey, Isabelle, *State of Insecurity: Government of the Precarious* (Verso Futures: London & New York, 2015).

Martin Yancey, Patricia, '"Said and Done" versus "Saying and Doing": Gendering Practices. Practicing gender at work', in *Gender & Society*, 17(3), 2011, pp 342–66.

Martinez, Gina, "Harvey Weinstein Indicted on New Sexual Assault Charges After 3rd Accuser Comes Forward" *Time Magazine*, 2 July 2018. https://time.com/5328315/harvey-weinstein-indictment-new-charges/ Accessed 8 September 2018.

Mayer, Vicki, *Below the Line: Producers and Production Studies in the New Television Economy* (Duke University Press: Durham, 2011).

McCracken, Douglas, 'Winning the talent war for women: Sometimes it takes a revolution', in *Harvard Business Review*, 78(6), 2000, pp 159–60, 162, 164–67.

Morfoot, Addie, 'Oscars: Examining gender bias in the documentary categories'. Source http://variety.com/2016/film/news/gender-bias-documentary-industry-1201708404/

O'Brien, Anne, '"Men own television": Why women leave media work', in *Media, Culture & Society*, 36(8), 2014, pp 1,207–18.

Ibid., 'Producing television and reproducing gender', in *Television & New Media* 16(3), 2015, pp 259–74.

Ibid., '(Not) getting the credit: Women, liminal subjectivity and resisting neoliberalism in documentary production', in *Media, Culture & Society*, 40(5), 2018, pp 673–88.

Ibid., *Women, Inequality and Media Work* (Routledge: London & New York, 2019).

Smith, Chris and Alan McKinlay, *Creative Labour: Working in the Creative Industries* (Palgrave Macmillan: Basingstoke, 2009).

Steiner, Linda, 'Glassy architectures in journalism', in Cynthia Carter (ed.), *The Routledge Companion to Media and Gender* (Routledge: London & New York, 2015) pp 620–31.

Sturdy, Andrew, Timothy Clark, Robin Fincham, & Karen Handley, 'Between innovation and legitimation-boundaries and knowledge flow in management consultancy', in *Organisation*, 16(5), 2009, pp 627–53.

Sweeney, Brendan, 'Producing liminal space: Gender, age and class in Northern Ontario's tree planting industry', in *Gender, Pace and Culture*, 16(5), 2009, pp 569–86.

Turner, Victor W., *From Ritual to Theatre: The Human Seriousness at Play* (Performing Arts Journal: New York, 1982).

Ursell, Gillian, 'Television production: Issues of exploitation, commodification and subjectivity in UK television labour markets', in *Media, Culture & Society*, 22(6), 2000, pp 805–25.

Van Gennep, Arnold, *The Rites of Passage* (University of Chicago Press: Chicago, 1960).

Walby, Sylvia, 'Is the knowledge society gendered?', in *Gender, Work and Organisation*, 18(1), 2011, pp 1–29.

PART II

The Politics of Knowledge Production

Gender, the State and Civil Society

From Self-Entrepreneurs to Rights-Bearers: Varieties of Gender Knowledge Production in Activisms for Women in Ireland

Pauline Cullen

INTRODUCTION

This chapter examines how feminist and women's organisations employ different forms of gender knowledge to advocate for and about women's interests in Ireland. The objective is to outline the context within which women's organisations and mobilisations on women's interests[1] occur and the forms of knowledge about gender they articulate. I examine the forms of gender knowledge that can be identified in (a) the 30% Club, an organisation that engages in activism for women to access decision-making roles in corporate contexts and (b) the Together for Yes campaign for reproductive rights. Comparing these different forms of activism and their different conceptualisations of gender knowledge illustrates divergences in how women's interests are conceived, articulated, and communicated. The comparative logic underlining the choice of cases lies in the contrast between gender knowledge practices constructed in corporate and often business led contexts, and those emerging from a range of feminism(s) located in civil society and articulated through grassroot and established feminist organisations.

Analysis at national and EU level suggests that gender equality has been depoliticised and narrowed to human capital and corporatised constructs of women in leadership and decision-making (Elomäki 2017). Reproductive rights remain a significant site of opposition and contest, often linked to extreme right and populist right-wing politics (Graff et al 2019). Analysis of both cases through a gender knowledge framework provides insights into how feminism(s) and feminist politics draw on different or overlapping forms of gender knowledge to mobilise, and the limits and/or potential of feminist knowledge(s) to underline or disrupt ideas about gender and women's rights in society.

The role of gender knowledge production is key in shaping access to policymakers, resources, and the public sphere (Cavaghan 2015; Verloo et al. 2018). Gender knowledge claims also underline patterns of contest and collaboration across women's organisations and movements in differentiating membership, the strategic orientations of organisations and competing claims of 'feminist competency' and/or intersectional credibility. The questions I pose include: To what extent does feminist knowledge feature in mobilisations for women? What role does organisational, generational and other dynamics of class, race and ethnicity play in the forms of gender knowledge produced? What forms of gender knowledge advanced by women's organisations hold most purchase with state bodies and within public discourse?

While different constituencies of women pursue different strategies and employ different forms of gender knowledge, feminist gender knowledge when it features, does so in implicit ways. Both forms of activism offer different conceptualisations of gender relations, the public/private divide, and what constitutes gender expertise and evidence of gendered experiences. Activism on women in decision-making and leadership, in the form of the 30% Club draws on largely neo-liberalised ideas and the business case for gender equality. The focus on women in leadership is often most palatable to capital and state interests especially when it provides opportunities for 'credit' claiming on advancing gender equality in the absence of commitments to more radical strategies such as gender quotas (Better Boards 2019). Activism on reproductive rights, in the form of the Together for Yes campaign for Repeal of the Eighth Amendment, was rooted in feminist frameworks, and relied on gender knowledge derived from the personal testimony of women. Class dynamics shape both forms of activism. Poor and ethnic minority women are either invisible or find less space and support for their gender knowledge claims. Overall, a hierarchy of gender knowledge claims is evident, with forms of gender knowledge that align with aspects of progressive neoliberalism (Fraser 2017) gaining traction in both political and public contexts.

Gender knowledge refers, in the broadest sense, to how gender relations are perceived, and the grounds for that perception (Connell 2011; Prügl 2017). Ideas about gender roles are deeply inscribed in knowledge systems and play a shaping role in claims-making, role-taking, forms of validation of expertise, and gender relations (Kantola and Lombardo 2017). These ideas are communicated in discourse and practice and in the context of mobilisation on women's interests reflecting the interpretative frameworks operating in organisations. In other words, collective action on women's interests indicate a set of frameworks, with variable levels of consistency, used to define women, understand gender relations, and frame the issue of gender equality in society. In what follows I outline the theoretical frameworks used to assess activism on women's interests in Ireland through a gender knowledge perspective. I then detail the ideologies, institutions, and societal context within which such activism occurs focusing on two cases – women in decision-making and the campaign to repeal the Eighth Amendment prohibition on abortion. I conclude with an assessment of the forms of gender knowledge communicated by these forms of mobilisation, and the implications more broadly for feminism(s) and activism on gender equality in Ireland and beyond.

THEORISING GENDER KNOWLEDGE IN WOMEN'S ORGANISATIONS

Scholars working in interpretative traditions and the sociology of knowledge suggest that every form of practical knowing – be it everyday knowledge, expert knowledge or popularised knowledge – is based upon a specific, often tacit and unconscious, form of gender knowledge (Young and Scherrer 2010; Cavaghan 2017). As an analytical concept, tacit gender knowledge enables the examination and comparison of competing gendered meanings in processes and action. It is at its core a critique of the apparent gender neutrality of knowledge and it allows for the identification of specific sites and forms of gendered power relations. It also allows for analysis of where resistances and backlash to gender expertise occurs, and how gender ideologies can be used to undermine advances towards gender equality (Verloo 2018; Kuhar and Paternotte 2017). In this chapter, gender knowledge(s) implicit and those explicit known as gender expertise and those constituted as feminist knowledge are examined as forms of knowledge production within women's organisations (Cavaghan 2017). In the former case, gender slips silently into organisational practices. In the latter, gender relations are brought to the surface of organisational knowledge work. Here, contestations over expertise engage ideas about gender inequality and interpretations of women's presence (and by extension men's), roles, action, interests, needs, rights, and capacity for voice. As gender knowledge becomes more explicit women's authority over naming, describing and interpreting evidences of inequality is itself articulated, contested, co-opted and resisted (Cullen, Ferree and Verloo 2019).

Applying a gender knowledge analysis can help researchers to gain a deeper understanding of the normative and epistemic barriers to the successful application of gender equality policies, as well as the mechanisms through which gender inequality is maintained in practice (Cavaghan 2017).

In this context epistemic norms and values regarding the perception of evidence, come together to influence the way gender can be perceived and practiced. Here I examine the underlying forms of gender knowledge operating in activism on women's interests that, in specific contexts, may be constructed as forms of *gender expertise*, and in others, as forms of *feminist knowledge*. I suggest that the version of gender knowledge employed has direct implications for the kinds of mobilisations that occur and the potential and limits of advancing different forms of feminist and gender knowledge in Irish society.

Gender knowledge informs the strategies and tactics used by movements and organisations that take on different approaches at different times in light of opportunities presented, in response to spaces opened up for activism, and in assessing the efficacy of past strategies. Gender knowledge is revealed in how women's groups make specific claims to understand issues that affect women and often detail the specific social, economic, political, and cultural changes required to secure greater equality. While distinctions between feminist and gender knowledge can be less than satisfactory, definitions of feminist knowledge indicate that gender inequality is understood in structural and systematic terms, and in some formulations is committed to the transformation of intersectionally unequal power relations (Stachowitsch 2019). In gender knowledge terms, feminism itself changes in engagements with different governance structures. At the core of this process is the development of a particular kind of feminist knowledge: co-opted, governance-friendly expert knowledge that fits with the prevailing logics of neoliberal governance (Prügl 2017; Griffin 2015). Feminist expertise is also often positioned as 'non-knowledge' that can be ignored or obscured in organisational contexts in what has been termed strategic ignorance (McGoey 2012). Knowledge produced by feminist and gender scholars is as such often viewed as flawed or partial (Pereira 2012) or ideological and therefore without merit. The term gender ideology is routinely used by faith-based and extreme right-wing political movements to oppose women's and LGBT rights' activism, and to characterise scholarship deconstructing essentialist and naturalistic assumptions about gender and sexuality (Paternotte and Kuhar 2018: 8). Both cases examined here include campaigns and frameworks aligned to different degrees with political and economic elites. Paradoxically, the potential for co-optation rises as feminists' access authority within institutions, but insider access and alliances are also invaluable assets in securing, using and validating feminist knowledge (Cullen et al. 2019).

FEMINISMS AND GENDER KNOWLEDGE

In gender knowledge terms, women's organisations increasingly meet the state and private sector demands for evidence-based gender expertise. The provision of such expertise requires funding stability that can orient women's groups away from more radical forms of activism. Analysis indicates that at times narrow and instrumentalised ideas about gender are reproduced in the forms of gender expertise and training provided to private sector actors in areas such as higher education, corporations, and international development (Bustelo et al. 2016). In broader terms new forms of financialisation and economic governance operating internationally (especially at EU-level) but embedded in national contexts have worked to depoliticise and instrumentalise approaches to gender equality leaving less space for feminist activism (Walby 2015; Guerrina 2017; Murphy and Cullen 2018). Feminist responses to these developments are complicated by the distortion and exploitation of feminist ideas and discourse and the rise of corporatised expert knowledge that reproduce gender equality in political debates in ways that take it far from feminist aims (Kantola and Lombardo 2017: 9).

Feminism(s) that operates close to the market and the state often termed market or governance feminism understood as complicit in capitalist and austerity processes (Kantola and Squires 2012; Griffin 2015; Fraser 2017). Post-feminism (McRobbie 2009) has also been identified as a form of gender knowledge that emphasises empowerment and choice, underplays structural constraints, and promotes psychological sets of 'competitive' dispositions seen as essential for surviving and thriving in neoliberal society. Gender knowledge, in this context, relies on forms of political rationality, subjectivation and governmentalities that encourage an entrepreneurial approach to gender equality. This in turn conceals new forms of gender regulation and in the process displaces radical feminist ideas (Gill 2017). Neoliberalised feminism (Gill 2016; Fraser 2017) in similar terms is theorised as the collusion of feminist ideas with forms of neoliberal rationality that promote constant affective and physical investment from women as they pursue contemporary norms of female and 'feminist' self-improvement (Rottenberg 2018). Here forms of gender knowledge supported by popular feminism (Banet-Weiser 2018) reproduces a neoliberal feminist subject that erases the private and public divide, responsibilising women to participate in forms of constant self-investment to increase their 'stock' and achieve their best 'self' professionally and personally (Rottenberg 2018).

Women's organisations participate in the dissemination of this form of gender knowledge when they support corporate 'lean in' approaches to improve gender representation and programmes that capacity build poor women to compete in the labour market. Such neo-liberal feminist perspectives advanced by individuals including Ivanka Trump construct the aspirational woman as one who succeeds in all areas of care and work. Such (middle-class) women achieve the 'magic balance' as they assume responsibility for, if not the actual labour of, social reproduction and paid work (Rottenberg 2018).

Analysis of how women's organisations reproduce these versions of gender knowledge have involved accusations of co-optation and fears about the appropriation, dilution and reinterpretation of feminist discourses and practices by non-feminist actors for their purposes (Prügl 2017; Stachowitsch, 2019). Indeed, it is difficult to sustain the idea of feminism or its ideas as completely autonomous since it has been argued that feminism has always been attached to some form of institution or organisation, be that the state, the empire or the market (Emejulu 2018). Feminist projects that originate in different forms of feminism are best understood as power-infused fields, which produce their own inclusions and exclusions and seek various alliances (de Jong and Kimm 2017: 189–91; Eschle and Maiguashca 2018). In this process, feminist practices, priorities, discourses and associated forms of gender knowledge may become contained (Prügl 2017; Griffin 2015) or may remain critically engaged and self-reflexive as they are included in the very political projects that are resisted (Newman 2013; Halley et al 2018).

IRISH POLITICAL CULTURE, CIVIL SOCIETY AND WOMEN'S
MOVEMENTS

Women's organisations operate in the context of Irish political culture, ideology, and institutions. Ireland is a highly globalised economic regime with a hybrid welfare system that combines strong liberal characteristics with conservative and Catholic features and a strong variant of the male breadwinner regime (Murphy and Cullen 2018). Gender distinctiveness is coded in Constitutional protections for women in the home, which sit in tension with neo-liberal activation of women in labour markets. As a relatively low tax economy, Ireland also lacks capacity to fund socially necessary reproductive and care work, and as a result such work remains feminised in the sphere of the private household (and even more so after austerity). Social disinvestment in the wider care infrastructure, exacerbated by forms of permanent austerity, also leaves women responsible for unpaid care work while many work in low-paid care work (Murphy and Cullen 2018).

Despite the introduction in 2016 of a gender quota for national electoral candidates, Ireland occupies 80th place in the global league of parliamentary inequality. Women comprise 22 per cent of the national parliament and 23 per cent of local level politicians. In business, women comprise just 13 per cent of the boards of listed Irish companies – well below the EU average of 23 per cent. The deficit in gender representation combines with other gendered penalties – including high cost childcare and until recently restrictive access to reproductive rights – to create a patriarchal dividend. Austerity era cuts in funding (in the order of 40 per cent) for some women's groups have also meant the overall gender equality architecture is under resourced. Competitive tendering for community organisations and the austerity-related dismantling of equality infrastructure has also narrowed options for activism on gender equality (Harvey 2014).

Broader factors shaping civil society are also pertinent. These include a 'weak infrastructure of dissent and leftist political organisation', shaped by postcolonial forms of hierarchy and authority embedded in strong church/ state relations (Murphy 2011: 173). Key organisations have participated in a corporatist arrangement with the state (social partnership) which has left a legacy of interdependence between the state and civil society. Over decades, organisations have grown comfortable and skilled in populist and single-issue forms of campaigning and enjoyed a significant level of access, even if that access sits alongside declining influence (Kirby and Murphy 2011). Research suggests that activism on women's interests have adapted to this context drawing on defensive and reactive styles of protest that lack a more strategic and long-term offensive orientation. In effect, for many women's organisations that are dependent on state funds, a politics of adaptation and survival has predominated. Service provision has been prioritised over advocacy (Cullen and Murphy 2017). In this context, the role of gender knowledge is central to how women's organisations interact with state sponsored strong discourses of 'economic recovery' and state and societal claims of progress on gender equality.

State projects to deal with gender inequality, in higher education, corporations, cultural and sport industries have involved mapping, scoping, and measuring female under-representation (Murphy and Cullen 2018). The forms of gender knowledge produced by these exercises include statistical evidence and/or survey data to establish the existence of gender inequality. The development of an evidence base is significant, especially in the absence of gender disaggregated data. However, it can also under-emphasise the power dimension of gender struggles and/or leave prevailing gender constructs untouched (Hoskyns and Rai 2007). Technicalisation of gender also makes it easier for gender advocates to sell their agenda to policy makers. However, these forms of gender knowledge and the aspirational commitments to tackle gender inequality that accompany them are at risk of being defined as evidence of change in the absence of concrete and resourced actions. Organisations and movements may also assemble personal testimony to raise issues of gender inequality (see Ryan and Kennedy in this volume). However, the deployment of these forms of gender knowledge is risky. Not only can they result in victim-blaming, they can also contribute to instrumentalising female suffering. Working from a gender knowledge perspective to uncover the implications of the *forms* of knowledge produced by state and women's organisations reveals the need to re-politicise gender and create spaces that empower the most marginalised to express themselves and offer alternative gender knowledge as a form of critique and contest.

I now draw on participant observation, documentary and interview data to chart how women's organisations define gender roles and construct and communicate forms of gender knowledge.[2] A key aspect of the analysis involves identifying underlying forms of gender knowledge informing the strategies and tactics employed. Given the small scale of the study, the aim is to offer an indicative assessment of different forms of gender knowledge that circulate within different forms of activism on women's issues in Ireland. In particular, I evaluate the implications of the forms of knowledge produced, strategies adopted and outcomes for progress on gender equality.

WOMEN IN DECISION MAKING: BETTER BALANCE FOR BETTER BUSINESS

A wide range of gender knowledge production is associated with the economic crisis of 2008. In the United Kingdom women's organisations, working specifically with minority and poor women, have drawn on feminist economic analysis to illustrate the disproportionate effects of austerity on such women (Women's Budget Group 2017). Other women's organisations that operate forms of market feminism responded to the financial crisis by using statistical data on levels of gender representation to argue for in-stitutional measures to enhance women's participation (Griffin 2015: 66). In the Irish context, groups such as the 30% Club are indicative of this form of mobilisation focusing on capacity-building initiatives for entrepreneurial women to advance in senior decision-making roles, while opposing the use of gender quotas. Here ideas about gender equality are tied to business case rationales and essentialist arguments about the specific gendered qualities that women bring to governance and decision-making. Such gender equality initiatives rely on ideas that women can act as change agents set in play to clean up and create more diverse institutions. These business case models are underpinned by specific forms of gender knowledge that social change can be managed like a business plan, and that women possess inherent qualities that can be used to better balance the books (Cullen and

Murphy 2017). An underling premise of this form of activism is that when a critical mass of women are placed in senior decision-making roles in corporations, government, the state and higher education they can act to promote gender knowledge supportive of greater gender equality.

The 30% Club was first launched in the UK in 2010 with a goal of achieving a minimum of 30 per cent of women on FTSE-100 boards by the end of 2015. It describes itself as 'an international, business-led approach focused on developing a pipeline of senior female talent' (30% Club Handbook 2018). In Ireland, the 30% Club (subtitled Growth through Diversity) was established in 2015, with the vision that:

> gender balance on boards and executive leadership not only encourages better leadership and governance, but further contributes to better all-round board performance, and ultimately increased corporate performance for both companies and their shareholders (30% Club Handbook 2018).

Senior business leaders, predominantly men, are specific targets and 'champions' of this approach. Listed within the organisation's central objectives are:

> Providing a platform for business leaders to share information on building a stronger and sustainable pipeline of female talent and engaging men as champions of better gender balance (2017b: 12).

The organisation claims that in excess of 200 Irish Chairs and CEOs of leading businesses are supporters. That support, the organisation believes, will obviate the need for gender quotas:

> Leaders are committed to accelerating gender balance in their organisations through voluntary actions. The 30% Club Ireland does not believe mandatory quotas are the right approach in the private sector at this time (2017a: 3).

The 30% Club forms alliances with or sponsors a variety of Women in Leadership events, with entities such as the Bank of New York Mellon, Accenture, PwC and KPMG. For instance, the 'Women Driving Economic Progress' event held in October 2018 followed a typical formula that includes a speaker list of high-profile, high-achieving women including celebrities, such as Martha Stewart, former ambassadors, and women from political contexts including Cherie Blair. Speakers draw from their personal testimonials to 'inspire women to achieve'. Male champions and allies are featured alongside these prominent successful women as well as diversity specialists who provide data to evidence the profit-making potential of increasing diversity among leadership teams. Male champions in particular frequently detail their cutting edge and exemplary forms of gender and diversity management in rhetoric inflected with forms of paternalism alongside self-congratulation. The 30% Club also runs networking and mentoring schemes and events that provide 'high potential' women with opportunities for human capital formation and capacity-building.[2]

In addition, the 30% Club makes submissions on public policy issues including state commitments to gender equality and proposed legislation on the gender pay gap. In their submission to a public consultation on the Irish National Women's Strategy they state:

> Business leadership is key: this takes the issue beyond a specialist diversity effort and into mainstream talent management (Public Consultation on the New National Women's Strategy 30% Club Ireland Response 2017a: 3).

Equality, fairness and diversity arguments are eschewed in favour of human capital rationales in the form of talent management for individual ends. A strong discourse of talent is evident, supporting a discourse of meritocracy and human capital formation, and a basic business case rationale:

> The government has acknowledged that the advancement of women in leadership is a key issue to be addressed. There is a strong business case that better gender balance leads to better decisions and therefore to better business performance (2017a: 4).

However, the state is not expected to regulate or legislate for change, with voluntary and collaborative approaches from private sector actors viewed as essential:

> [Internal targets rather than] strict quotas . . . could allow businesses to take actions suited to their particular challenges, recognising that creating better gender balance makes good business sense (2017a: 5).

While women are understood as the actors that need particular forms of encouragement and support, change is understood to require action from society and the state more generally:

> One challenge with the gender debate is that it is often seen as a women's issue as opposed to a society and business issue. We believe that leadership from government and employers is key to achieving meaningful and sustainable change (2017a: 5).

The gender debate referenced here suggests a dismissal of specific feminist argumentation, while remedies for low-levels of women in leadership are sought from business and state leaders (both disproportionately men). This formulation seems to reject approaches that solely responsibilise women to achieve gender parity in representation. However, it also reinforces other arguments, made by those opposing positive actions including gender quotas that real change on gender equality has to happen in society rather than in specific organisations who are powerless to confront broader forces of gender socialisation.

'Hard' data including statistical data, league tables from the OECD that rank levels of gender representation in decision-making and assessments from 'prestigious' publications such as *The Economist* are invoked to establish the need to take action. Surveys of 'Women in Management' are deployed to reject the 'glass-ceiling' metaphor in favour of highlighting women's advancement to middle management:

> It is evident that women's participation in management is inversely related to the leadership hierarchy, reflecting the 'sticky floor', rather than the glass ceiling, that women encounter as they get stuck in the bottleneck of middle management (2017a: 6).

Here the 'sticky floor' metaphor implies more individual-level and self-imposed limitations regarding advancement, including 'women's own reluctance to invest in social capital' (2017a: 5).

In a submission on a legislative proposal requiring companies to publish data on gender pay gaps the organisation extended its qualified support suggesting:

> appropriate narrative disclosure for organisations over certain size criteria – while transparency and granularity of data is important, we must protect firms where gaps exist and allow them to explain the justifications for same (2017b: 6).

Vertical gender segregation in the labour market is also recognised:

> Where women have found seniority, they are more likely to be found in traditionally female-dominated functions such as HR and marketing and less likely to occupy leadership positions in Finance, Sales, Operations and IT (2017b: 5).

The 'pipeline' metaphor is ubiquitous in 30% Club materials, underlining an assumption that gender parity will increase once there are sufficient numbers of qualified women in the hiring pool. This simplistic metaphor has been critiqued for its lack of emphasis on discriminatory factors that *block* female advancement, its overall linearity and its reductive approach to organisational culture and the complexity of work-life conflict for women (Soe and Yakura 2008). The talent pool argument is amplified by the assertion that 'talent management processes are not typically gender-intelligent' (2018: 10). Drawing on the work of behavioural psychology, the 30% Club nuances the general claim that women lack confidence and eschews explanations that call out sexist and discriminatory practices:

> Women express confidence and claim ownership of performance outcomes in a way that talent management and appraisal processes may not be alive to. . .
> . . . Talented women may go 'unseen' or be described as 'not ready' much earlier in the career path than is traditionally assumed (2018: 10–12)

And so, the 30% Club requests that:

> a gender lens to be applied to policies around recruitment, promotion, and retention, in order to remove what are referred to as inherent biases (2017b: 12).

Inherent biases are to be addressed through continuous unconscious-bias training to be promoted at all levels in business. Research suggests that unconscious bias and diversity training have minimal long-term effects on changing workforce behaviour and may promote a backlash or even give those who discriminate a 'moral license' to continue in their behaviour.[3]

The 30% Club recognises care and social reproduction commitments on the part of women but in a depoliticised way:

> One of the challenges for women in their career can be that in dual-working parent families, the mother still takes on a lot more of the home responsibilities (2017a: 6).

This is to be resolved by businesses supporting the capacity to:

> work flexibly and from home, especially with the advancement in technology tools to help us work from anywhere (2017a: 6).

Here public private distinctions are erased as home becomes available as a context for work, and workers are 'always potentially on' to produce (Rottenberg 2018). Public policies are also indicted as essential in 'harnessing female talent'. In this context, structural barriers to gender equality and feminist knowledge are drawn upon in calls to improve access to affordable and quality childcare and stronger initiatives to encourage take-up of shared parental leave. This invocation of work-life balance suggests popularised neoliberal feminist ideas that require women to 'have it all' through constant self-management affording a seamless and agile transition between working and private life. Although there are calls for more even sharing of such work, social reproduction and care work are maintained as part of middle-class aspirational women's normative trajectory (Rottenberg 2018: 5). Other aspects of feminist knowledge are invoked including references to gender socialisation in education and low take up of STEM education. These problems should be confronted by the creation of:

> a learning environment free from gender stereotyping and with real focus on full development of potential and employability (2017a: 10–12).

The potential of young women and girls can thus be unlocked as they aspire towards entrepreneurial self-advancement and career excellence. Women are also characterised as unaware of their potential and in need of role models to activate their pursuit of leadership:

> If a woman cannot see a woman at the Board level of her organisation it is harder for her to see herself striving for that position (2017a:12).

Men's role in gender inequality is characterised simply as a lack of awareness:

> As men have been the beneficiaries in business, they often do not notice the privilege that they have and therefore often struggle to understand the debate or feel the need to be actively participating (2017b: 3)

Broader suggestions to create more 'buy in' from men include:

> to continue to have a male Minister championing the gender issue. This will promote an understanding that gender balance is good for education, business, and society. It will also highlight that this is something that affects both men and women (2017 :12).

Harnessing the power of symbolic representation of women in society is also recommended:

> Many countries are looking to redress gender imbalances in street names, naming of bridges, buildings, relooking at the people recognised in public monuments, art, portraits, currency, etc. (2017a: 12).

Analysis of women in business networks suggests that they are sites that espouse feminist claims but reproduce neo-liberal, individualist approaches (Avdelidou-Fischer and Kirton 2015; Mickey 2018; Jones et al 2019).

However, it is important to note how feminist knowledge intrudes here. The frameworks used to promote women in leadership *also* make specific claims on the state with regards to the gender equality agenda, and more opaquely, on society-at-large. While the discourse deployed does not solely rest on 'fixing women' in order to achieve individual change, nevertheless, capacity-building, marketised and metric-led initiatives predominate. While structural analysis of gender inequality is loosely tied to broader issues of work-life balance or gender socialisation, unsurprisingly, discrimination and patriarchal power systems are largely left untroubled.

TOGETHER FOR YES: PRIVATE ISSUES AND PUBLIC SUPPORT

I now explore the successful campaign that secured a repeal of a constitutional ban on abortion in Ireland in May 2018 (for more on Abortion Reform see Sinéad Kennedy in this volume). Ireland has a poor record on intimate citizenship rights for women. Denied access to safe, legal, and affordable termination of pregnancy in Ireland, Irish women had continually mobilised for a constitutional amendment to repeal the 1983 Eighth Amendment that effectively banned abortion in the state. In a break from past political consensus, a May 2017 Citizens' Assembly recommended legislative and constitutional reforms to government that if enacted, would amount to safe legal abortion in Ireland. A parliamentary committee began deliberation in September 2017 and made recommendations in December 2017 that called for a repeal of the amendment. The government duly accepted the recommendation and scheduled a referendum for 25 May 2018.

Repeal of the Eighth Amendment garnered governmental support, although polling in advance of the referendum indicated a close margin between both those supporting and opposing repeal (Leahy 2018a). A decline in the moral authority held by the Catholic Church has played a role in an increased support for repeal and is, in part, a function of revelations of historic institutionalised child abuse and cruelty towards pregnant women, and the reluctance of the church authorities to provide for victims through reparations. At the same time, broader cultural shifts associated with the emergence of new feminist organisations encouraged women to speak out about their experiences of crisis pregnancy and abortion. Analysis also suggests that the return of Irish emigrants from more liberal countries had driven change (McKay 2018).

The campaign to repeal the Eighth amendment had a long genesis in decades of feminist campaigning by a variety of different feminist groups. The coalition that delivered the successful outcome included second-wave women, liberal and radical feminists and young student-led organisations. The most prominent included the National Women's Council of Ireland (the NWCI, the state feminist organisation); the Abortion Rights Campaign (ARC): an anarchist, radical feminist grassroots collective; and the long standing organisation, Action for Choice. Coalition between these organisations was not a given, as ideological, and strategic differences meant that previous collaboration was episodic and symbolic at best. However, when the referendum was announced, a period of communication and cooperation between the organisations led to a commitment to launch a common campaign as the Coalition to Repeal the Eighth.

A key challenge for the repeal campaign lay in countering forms of gender 'expertise' and gender knowledge promoted by pro-life exponents which included warnings of selective abortion particularly of foetuses with disabilities and the potential use of abortion as a form of contraception. These often medicalised forms of claims-making, drew on older gender knowledge rooted in forms of state and church-sanctioned social control that constructed the state as the guardian of unborn life and women as in need of protection from this potential 'choice'. ARC and Action for Choice communicated feminist bodily autonomy arguments, with ARC in particular adopting intersectional frameworks seeking free, legal, and safe abortion. ARC had successfully mobilised a grass-roots network of activists across the country and staged annual 'March for Choice' events drawing thousands of supporters. Other organisations focused on insider tactics, gauging party political sentiment. Activists from all contexts reported a series of 'tough conversations' in the process of forming the coalition (Trapped in Time Event, Repeal the Eighth October 2017). Veteran activists recognised that the ARC had organised successfully, if less strategically. If incorporated into a broader alliance ARC offered the human capital of younger activists and a regional infrastructure that could be exploited. This act of coalition marked a shift in the campaign towards message discipline and by extension an effort to reconcile tensions between radical and liberal-feminist knowledge frameworks on abortion.

The NWCI, whose membership included organisations ambivalent on the issue, had historically maintained their own forms of ambiguity on abortion. However, more recently, the organisation evolved its own stance rooted in a recognition of a political and societal context where past contests over abortion were deeply contentious and polarising. As such the NWCI had launched its own campaign in late 2017 entitled 'Every Woman' that downplayed the focus on abortion arguing for better access to a new model for reproductive healthcare. Abortion was referred to as 'a necessary element of obstetric care'. NWCI materials stated:

> Our hope is to build a sensitive and inclusive consensus that acknowledges
> people's experience of pregnancy and family life in all its diversity and complexity
> (NWCI 2018: 3).

Countering efforts of the pro-life campaign to medicalise female reproductive behaviour according to a pro-life agenda, here messaging drew on
forms of gender knowledge that underlined the deficits in all forms of
reproductive health care in Ireland and the complexities of family formation.

Initially, the ARC maintained its demand for 'free, safe, and legal'
including late-term abortion while the NWCI, supported a 12-week limit for
most cases, adopting a 'safe, rare and legal' message. As the referendum
neared, however, the coalition shifted tack to create a universalising message
that de-emphasised specific provisions to replace the repealed amendment,
focusing instead solely on the removal of the constitutional article. This was
deemed essential to convince those undecided or middle-ground voters
(Interview with NWCI leader of the Coalition to Repeal the Eighth December
2017). The Coalition to Repeal the Eighth launched its official campaign in
March 2018, entitled 'Together for Yes'. The launch statement read:

> Together for Yes is the National Civil Society Campaign to remove the Eighth
> Amendment from the Constitution. Together we are campaigning for a more
> compassionate Ireland that allows abortion care for women who need it (Together
> for Yes Campaign 2018).

Emphasising care, compassion, and change, showcasing women's experiential knowledge and testimony rather than pro-abortion language of bodily
autonomy or choice marked a significant break from past repeal campaigns.
A combination of constituent support groups supported the campaign,
including representatives of the healthcare professions such as Doctors for
Choice and Midwives for Choice. As such, some of the most prominent
campaigning came from medical professionals arguing that the constitutional
ban limited their capacity to provide the best care for patients. This was
supported by several cases of maternal death, including that of Dr Savita
Halappanavar who was denied a termination of her pregnancy (Quilty and
Kennedy 2016). Medicalised knowledge was linked to feminist argumentation
around women's rights to access excellent and appropriate health care
befitting a modern medical system. This focus on safety, supervision and
regulation was contrasted with the use of abortion pills secured from online
vendors and consumed in private without medical support due to fears of
criminalisation.

A central slogan of the campaign became '*Sometimes a private matter
needs public support*'. Under this rubric countless women relayed through

social and traditional media formats their personal experiences of abortion, notably involving travelling to the United Kingdom to obtain the procedure. While younger women's stories were recounted, efforts were made to highlight the stories of parents experiencing a pregnancy with a fatal foetal abnormality, or the predicaments of rape or incest victims (Interview with leaders of Together for Yes campaign). Repealing the restriction on abortion was framed as a merciful solution for those parents seeking a termination of an unviable pregnancy. This was deemed particularly effective in:

> putting a face to the argument and pulling people towards the idea of mothers and families requiring better health care (Interview with Leader of the National Conversation May 2018).

Couples were often featured, maternal bereavement was highlighted, and feminist knowledge focusing on individual female choice was de-emphasised. Overall a strong universalising strategy was put in place aimed at cementing a winnable campaign (Trapped in Time Event, Repeal the Eighth October 2017).

Although minority women were featured in a minor way in published campaign materials, they were not visible in the regional campaigning. In the final weeks of the campaign, the Together for Yes did use a twitter hashtag whoneedsyouryes# which elicited a significant response from those claiming to be migrant women without the right to vote asking for support from the majority population for their specific circumstances. In April 2018, a small group of ethnic minority women formed Migrants and Ethnic-Minorities for Reproductive Justice (MERJ). Citing statistics that '25 per cent of women having babies in Ireland are migrants and 40 per cent of all maternal deaths happen to ethnic minority women', MERJ activists made a link between racial stereotyping and the perceived discriminatory experience of women of colour in the Irish health services (MERJ 2018). Here a new form of intersectional gender knowledge was offered to nuance the more general campaign messaging.

The Together for Yes campaign is acknowledged to have played a major role in delivering the sizeable margin by which the referendum passed, alongside broader attitudinal change on the issue, than neither polling or political elites predicted (Leahy 2018b).[4] In the context of a center-right and gendered political party culture nominally in favour of repeal yet reliant on rural and older voting blocs, post-referendum campaigns then worked to gain the most liberal and elaborated version of abortion regime possible. Together for Yes, as a campaign to remove a constitutional ban on abortion, had deep roots in feminist knowledge and frameworks, yet in working to reach a broad constituency, it eschewed a radical feminist framing, potentially marginalising at times the perspectives of many young, working-class and minority women. This framework aimed to cultivate a form of gender knowledge that could demobilise morality-based arguments of anti-choice actors and interests while recruiting 'middle Ireland' and retaining centrist party political support. While strategically astute, these forms of engagement offered little direct challenge to broader forms of intersectional disadvantage that underline gender inequality in Ireland.[5]

GENDER KNOWLEDGE, FEMINIST KNOWLEDGE AND GENDER EQUALITY

I have made the argument for a gender knowledge approach to understanding activism on women's interests in Ireland. In the cases examined here, I outlined two contrasting forms of activism on two distinctly different issues of interest to women. In the first case, a corporate-led organisation drawing on a business case rationale works to advance women in commercial contexts. Gender knowledge claims rest on the unique qualities that women bring to decision-making and more broadly how diversity supports corporate growth.

Gender knowledge produced by the 30% Club includes a focus on gender difference, with women possessing invaluable characteristics required to deliver better economic outcomes and men essential in other respects as actors, that when sufficiently enlightened, will agree to open opportunities for female advancement. Women are constituted 'not as rights-bearing liberal subjects who must fight discrimination in order to gain access to the market place to sell their labour' (Rottenberg 2018 : 5), but rather as self-entrepreneurs who must agitate to acquire the appropriate assets to succeed. Personal testimony of successful women underlines their entrepreneurial skills including negotiating and networking. Such skills, offered in workshops and touted at leadership events, are constructed as essential assets for aspirational women. Structural obstacles that create care and social reproductive burdens on women are acknowledged. But neoliberal rationalities that eschew a division between public and private sphere promote the notion of technologically agile workers who can astutely achieve work-life balance and minimise gendered care penalties. Successful women require support, mentorship, and recognition by powerful men, but must also labour ceaselessly in private and public spheres. As Rottenberg (2018: 7) argues, neoliberal feminist knowledge claims ensure that gender parity is understood through benchmarks, targets, competition, and success, not the liberal feminist formulations of *equal rights, autonomy,* and *emancipation.* Male power and privilege in corporate domains are acknowledged, while enlightened and progressive male champions are celebrated for their courage and foresight.

In the Together for Yes Campaign a diverse coalition of feminist and women's organisations mobilised a successful grass-roots campaign to deliver repeal of the constitutional ban on abortion. While activists and campaigners worked from a range of perspectives, a common 'middle ground' message was produced to secure support from the broadest range of voters. While technical and medical knowledge featured in some aspects of the campaign especially in warnings regarding risks posed particularly to young women using abortion pills without medical supervision, personal experiential knowledge of crisis pregnancy and fatal foetal abnormality predominated. Gender knowledge in this messaging rendered women and parents as rights-bearing individuals deserving freedoms, and sensitive and compassionate forms of health care. Women's reproductive lives were defined as complex, and in cases of unplanned pregnancy and fatal foetal diagnosis were constrained in damaging ways by outmoded legal and societal conventions. In the slogan – *'Sometimes a private matter needs public support'* – the private sphere, long constructed by feminists as a prison of sexism and patriarchy, was politicised in subtle ways as 'the personal is political' and requiring the intervention of a caring and empathetic 'public'. Radical feminist knowledge was de-emphasised in favour of gender knowledge rooted in familial and maternal frameworks emphasising compassion, care, and empathy, in particular for bereaved parents. While women's subjectivities were privileged, men also featured as bereaved fathers, supportive partners, and/or empathetic medical professionals. This form of evidence base, highly emotive and affective in content, worked to de-stigmatise abortion for many, empowering some to share deeply marginalising experiences. In a broader sense, the form of gender knowledge produced here confronted ideologies of social conservatism, that are in many respects already in decline in Irish society while aligning with forms of progressive neoliberalism (Fraser 2016) embraced by centrist political parties and in particular international corporate actors.

In the Repeal case a form of gender knowledge with feminist roots was made legible within women's lived experiences and suffering, serving to secure positive gendered social change. In the 30% Club case, neoliberal feminist ideas create gender knowledge that may secure success for middle-class women but fail to address the challenges and difficulties of the vast majority of women who work. Gender knowledge, in this regard, is partial and excludes women in low-paid precarious work that leads to a reification of white, class privilege (Rottenberg 2018: 7). The latter form of gender knowledge is silent on a large class of women classified as 'non-aspirational' whom neoliberal feminism forsakes as expendable on the one hand, yet essential in performing outsourced service and care work, on the other (Rottenberg 2018: 8).

Fraser (2016) argues that feminism has formed a perverse political alignment with progressive neoliberal forces. Progressive ideals, including diversity, women's rights and sexual minority rights lend charisma and gloss to destructive dynamics of financialisation inherent within neoliberal capitalism (2017: 282). The veneer of an emancipatory charisma borrowed from feminism has allowed progress and emancipation to be identified with meritocracy as opposed to equality as evidenced in the rise of talented women and minorities in the 'winner take all' corporate hierarchy (2017: 282).

The form of gender knowledge that gains most traction in Ireland is a function of a neoliberalism where political culture largely resists redistributive claims and responds most positively to populist and single-issue demands. In this context, despite significant austerity era pay cuts for feminised public sector workers, the discussion of gender pay gaps relate to higher-paid women. At the same time calls for better support to reconcile work-life conflict and incentivising men to take more care work, neglect the roll out of activation policies that target lone-parents, and the overall systematic and long-term state led social disinvestment. While abortion services involve resource commitments, contests continue around church control of maternity hospitals, and transparency and accountability in screening programmes for women's reproductive health care. It is imperative to better understand how gender knowledge produced by women activists and women's organisations support or undermine different women's interests. Such an understanding may equip us to confront the complexities and complicities that arise in feminism (s) and women's organising while offering the possibility that different types of women can articulate their often conflicting interests and take collective action to secure gender justice for all.

Notes

1 Understanding women as a social category and class of political agents must account for their diversity and at the same time their shared connections that can ground a shared commitment to address inequalities yet that does not assume a common interest. Feminism(s) are also assumed here to reflect the diversity in feminist frameworks and models of mobilisation.

2 Source: www.30percentclub.org/initiatives/leadership-courses

3 Source: www.irishtimes.com/business/work/workplace-inequality-its-days-are-numbered-1.3670730

4 In the end, grass-roots mobilization, largely delivered by ARC, tactical learning gleaned from moderate feminists, including middle-ground messaging, alongside an

emigrant home to vote campaign and the support of relevant political party elites all contributed to deliver the successful outcome.

5   This said, networks constructed to mobilise repeal activists have endured and may engender progressive forms of political organising in the future.

REFERENCES

Adshead, Maura, 'An advocacy coalition framework approach to the rise and fall of social partnership', in *Irish Political Studies*, 26(1), 2011, pp 73–93.

Avdelidou-Fischer, Nicole, and Gail Kirton, 'Beyond burned bras and purple dungarees: Feminist orientations within working women's networks', *European Journal of Women's Studies*, 23(2), 2016. pp 124–39.

Banet-Weiser, Sarah, *Empowered: Popular Feminism and popular Misogyny* (Duke University Press: Durham, 2018).

Bustelo, Maria., Lisa Ferguson, and Maxine Forest (eds), *The Politics of Feminist Knowledge Transfer: Gender Training and Gender Expertise* (Palgrave Macmillan: Basingstoke, 2016).

Cavaghan, Rosalind, *Making Gender Equality Happen: Knowledge, Change and Resistance in EU Gender Mainstreaming* (Routledge: London, 2017).

Coalition to Repeal the Eighth, 'Trapped in time 1983–2017: Round table discussion with '83 anti-amendment campaigners' (Dublin, 5 Oct. 2017) Source: www.repealeight.ie/ 1983-2017-trapped-in-time/

Coalition to Repeal the Eighth, Campaign Launch Statement (Dublin, 2017).

Connell, Raewyn, *Confronting Equality: Gender, Knowledge and Global Change* (Polity Press: Cambridge, 2011).

Cullen, Pauline and Mary P. Murphy, 'Gendered mobilisations against austerity In Ireland', in *Gender, Work and Organisation,* 24(1), 2016, pp 83–97.

Ibid., 'Leading the debate for the business case for gender equality: Perilous for whom?' in *Gender, Work and Organisation*, 25(2), 2018, pp 110–26.

Cullen, Pauline, Myra Marx Ferree and Mieke Verloo, 'Introduction to special issue: Gender, knowledge production and dissemination', in *Gender Work and Organisation*, 26(6), 2019, pp 765–71.

De Jong, Sara, and Sara Kimm, 'The co-optation of feminisms: A research agenda', in *International Feminist Journal of Politics*, 19(2), 2017, pp 185–200.

Elomäki, Anna, 'Gender quotas for corporate boards: Depoliticizing gender and the economy', in *Nora: Nordic Journal of Feminist and Gender Research*, 26(1), 2018, pp 53–68.

Emejulu, Akwugo, 'Crisis politics and the challenge of intersectional solidarity' (London School of Economics and Political Science (LSE): London, 2018). Source: www.youtube.com/watch?v=tVL_8497-co

Eschle, Catherine, and Bice Maiguashca, 'Theorising feminist organising in and against neoliberalism: Beyond co-optation and resistance?', in *European Journal of Politics and Gender*, 1(2), 2018, pp 223–39.

Fraser Nancy, 'Progressive neoliberalism versus reactionary populism: A choice that feminists should refuse', in *NORA: Nordic Journal of Feminist and Gender Research*, 24(4), 2016, pp 281–4.

Gill, Rosalind, 'Post-postfeminism?: New feminist visibilities in postfeminist times', in *Feminist Media Studies*, 16(4), 2016, pp 610–30.

Graff, Agnieszka, Ratna Kapur, and Suzanna Danuta Walters, 'Introduction: Gender and the rise of the global right', in *Signs: Journal of Women in Culture and Society*, 44(3), 2019, pp 541–60.

Griffin, Penny, 'Crisis, austerity and gendered governance: A feminist perspective', in *Feminist Review*, 10(9), 2015, pp 49–72.

Guerrina, Roberta, 'Gender and the economic crisis', in J. Kantola and E. Lombardo (eds), *Gender and the Economic Crisis in Europe: Politics, Institutions and Intersectionality* (Palgrave MacMillan: Basingstoke, 2017), pp 95–115.

Halley, Janet, Prabha Kotiswaran, Rachel Rebouché, and Hila Shamir, *Governance Feminism: An Introduction* (Minnesota University Press: Minnesota, 2018).

Harvey, Brian, 'Are we paying for that?: Government funding and social justice advocacy (The Advocacy Initiative: Dublin, 2014).

Hoskyns, Catherine and Shirin M. Rai, 'Recasting the global political economy: Counting women's unpaid work', in *New Political Economy*, 12(3), 2007, pp 297–317.

Jones. S. A., A. Dy, and N. Vershinia, '"We were fighting for our place": Resisting gender knowledge regimes through feminist knowledge network formation', in *Gender, Work and Organisation*, 26(6), 2019, pp 789–804.

Kantola Johanna and Judith Squires, 'From state feminism to market feminism?' in *International Political Science Review*, 33(4), 2012, pp 382–400.

Kantola, Johanna and Emanuela Lombardo (eds), *Gender and the Economic Crisis in Europe; Politics, Institutions, and Intersectionality* (Palgrave MacMillan: Basingstoke, 2017).

Kirby Peadar and Mary P. Murphy, *Towards a Second Republic Ireland: Politics after the Celtic Tiger* (Pluto Press: London, 2011).

Kuhar, Roman and David Paternotte, *Anti-Gender Campaigns in Europe: Mobilizing against Equality* (Rowman & Littlefield: London, 2017).

Leahy, Pat, 'Yes campaign's outreach to middle ground delivered the landslide Undecideds swung in huge numbers to Yes, as politicians struggled to keep up with pace of change', in *The Irish Times*, Sunday, May 27 2018.

McGoey, Linsey, 'The logic of strategic ignorance', in *British Journal of Sociology*, 63(3), 2012, pp 533–76.

McKay, Susan, 'Ireland's feminists lost the abortion argument in '83; This time we can win', in *The New York Times*, 5 May, 2018.

McRobbie, Angela, *The Aftermath of Feminism: Gender, Culture and Social Change* (Sage: London, 2008).

MERJ, Migrants and Ethnic minorities for Reproductive Justice, 2018. Source: www.togetherforyes.ie/together-for-yes-supports-migrants-rights-groups-calling-for-the-removal-of-the-8th-amendment/

Murphy, Mary P., and Pauline Cullen, *Feminist Response to Austerity in Ireland: Country Case Study* (Rosa Luxembourg Foundation: Brussels, 2018).

Murphy Mary P., 'Civil society in the shadow of the Irish State', in *Irish Journal of Sociology*, 19(2), 2011, pp 170–87.

Newman, Janet, 'Spaces of power: Feminism, neoliberalism and gendered labor', in *Social Politics Social Politics: International Studies in Gender, State & Society*, 20(2), 2013, pp 200–21.

National Women's Council of Ireland (NWCI), 'Every woman: Affordable, accessible healthcare options for women and girls in Ireland' (NWCI: Dublin, November, 2018).

Oireachtas bill to establish the referendum on the Eight Amendment. Source: www.oireachtas.ie/en/debates/debate/dail/2018-03-20/10/ (2017).

Pereira, Maria do Mar, *Power, knowledge and feminist scholarship: An ethnography of academia* (Routledge: London, 2017).

Prügl, Elisabeth, 'Neoliberalism with a feminist face: Crafting a new hegemony at the world bank'. in *Feminist Economics*, 23(1), 2017, pp 30–53.

Quilty, Aideen, Sinead Kennedy, and Catherine Conlon (eds), *The Abortion Papers Ireland: Volume II* (Cork University Press: Cork, 2015).

Repeal the Eighth (October 2017) Source: www.repealeight.ie/1983-2017-trapped-in-time/ 2017.

Rottenberg, Catherine, 'Women who work: The limits of the neoliberal feminist paradigm', in *Gender Work and Organisation Journal* (Wiley Online Library: 2018), pp 1,073–82.

Soe, Louise and Elaine Yakura, 'What's wrong with the pipeline?: Assumptions about gender and culture in IT work', in *Women's Studies*, 37(3), 2008, pp 176–201.

Stachowitsch, Saskia, 'Beyond "market" and "state" feminism: Gender knowledge at the intersections of marketization and securitization', in *Politics & Gender*, 15(1), 2019, pp 151–73.

The 30% Club, National Women's Strategy Submission, 2017a.

The 30% Club, Gender Pay Gap Submission, 2017b. https://30percentclub.org/assets/uploads/Ireland/PDFs/30__Club_Ireland_Gender_Paygap_Submission__FINAL.pdf
The 30% Club, Information Booklet, 2018. https://30percentclub.org/about/chapters/ireland

Together for Yes: The National Campaign to Remove the Eighth Amendment. Source: www.togetherforyes.ie/about-us/who-we-are/ 2018

Verloo, M., *Varieties of Opposition to Gender Equality in Europe* (Routledge: London, 2018), just a book

Walby, S., 'Is the knowledge society gendered?' in *Gender, Work and Organisation*, 18(1), 2011, pp 1–29.

Women's Budget Group Intersecting Inequalities, 2017. https://wbg.org.uk/analysis/intersecting-inequalities/

Young, B., and C. Scherrer (eds), *Gender Knowledge and Knowledge Networks in International Political Economy* (Nosmos: Baden-Baden, 2010).

SIX

The Right to Know: Gender, Power, Reproduction and Knowledge Regulation in Ireland

Sinéad Kennedy

'We lived, as usual, by ignoring.
Ignoring isn't the same as ignorance, you have to work at it,'
(Margaret Atwood, *The Handmaid's Tale*, 1996: 89)

It has become a truism to say that knowledge is power. For Michel Foucault, one of the key theoreticians of the knowledge-power nexus, power and knowledge are insidiously related, because the exercise of power is largely determined by knowledge. Thus, the manner in which a society produces and regulates knowledge will reveal significant insights into the nature of that society and how power operates: Who has access to knowledge and who does not? Whose knowledge is considered important? Who defines what is important to know? Who benefits from that knowledge and who does not? Mary Beard in her treatise on women and power argues that too often 'women are not perceived to be fully within the structures of power' (Beard 2017: 83). Indeed, it is arguably that gender may be understood as the subject that makes power visible, so that exploring a society through the prism of gender will reveal important insights into knowledge, power, and authority. In order to investigate the intimate relationship that exists between knowledge and gender in Irish society I explore women's reproductive lives in Ireland; a country where the 'right to know' has been as tightly controlled as the 'right to choose'.[1]

Until recently abortion access in Ireland was highly restricted as a result of a constitutional prohibition introduced in 1983 – known as the Eighth Amendment – that equated, in legal terms at least, the life of a pregnant woman with that of a foetus or embryo. Abortion was only permitted when a woman faced 'a real and substantial' risk to her life. Historically, one of the key ways that abortion access was controlled was through the regulation of information about abortion. Nevertheless, women living in Ireland did access abortion; legally by travelling to Britain and Europe; and illegally within Ireland, by accessing medical abortions via the 'abortion pill' online. Ireland's constitutional ban on abortion was removed by referendum in May 2018, but until abortion services were introduced in January 2019 on average, every day, nine women and girls living in Ireland travelled to England for an abortion.[2] The majority of these women were aged between 20 and 34, and more than half were already mothers.[3] Reasons for terminating pregnancies vary but the reason all women travelled is the same; they could not access safe and legal abortion services in Ireland, as procuring an abortion there was a criminal offence that carried a 14-year prison sentence. Furthermore, abortion access in Ireland was highly mediated by race, class, and migration status. Women who cannot afford to travel abroad, and who do not possess the necessary visa or travel documents are either forced to continue with the pregnancy or to access an illegal abortion online, risking both their health and possible criminalisation.

By focusing on a number of key public debates around abortion and reproduction in Ireland I explore the gendered nature of the discursive devices employed to both uphold and challenge the status quo on reproductive choices The illegal nature of abortion in Ireland and the continued restrictions have resulted in women challenging traditional and gendered dichotomies constructed between public and private forms of knowledge, often producing their own alternative forms of expertise. As Foucault argues 'where there is power there is resistance' (1998: 95). In this chapter I argue that the gendered relationship between public and private knowledge is more accurately understood as dynamic in nature, where private activities and conversations can be understood as an alternative form of knowledge that exists in the public domain: a form of radical knowledge that would eventually contribute to changing public policy on abortion in Ireland (see also Cullen in this volume). I conclude by examining the central role that women's private knowledge played in the 2018 campaign to remove Ireland's constitutional ban on abortion by empowering new actors from previously marginalised groups to challenge traditional structures of power and authority.

HISTORY

Ireland's abortion ban pre-dates the foundation of the state, with the introduction in 1861 of the Offences Against the Person Act, which specifically criminalised a woman who attempted to procure her own abortion (see Farrell 2013: 82–3). This 1861 Act, Pauline Jackson observed, should be understood in the context of a whole series of laws passed in the nineteenth century that were concerned with regulating bodies and sexual behaviour (1987: 6). The abortion ban was incorporated into Irish law following independence from Britain in 1922 and was further extended to a constitutional prohibition in 1983 when a referendum amended the constitution to include a specific right to life for the 'unborn' (Article 40.3.3°). Abortion, Rosalind Petchesky argues, is the 'fulcrum of a much broader ideological struggle in which the very meanings of the family, the state, motherhood, and young women's sexuality are contested' (1990: xi). It is therefore no surprise that given the post-colonial Irish state's struggle for recognition and self-identity, that sexuality, and women's reproductive capacities in particular, would become such a site of ideological contestation. In order to understand how Ireland came to have such strictly regulated abortion laws, it is necessary to consider how the regulation and control of sexuality, and by extension knowledge, came to be woven into the structures of the Irish state. This regulatory framework was certainly not unique to Ireland. Its origins can be located within the 'wider context of Victorian attitudes to women, marriage and the family'. However, what was unique was 'how long this Victorian regime lasted and how deeply it seeped into the minds and bodies of the Irish' (Inglis 2005: 11).

The Irish Free State emerged from the detritus of the War of Independence with Britain and a short but vicious post-colonial civil war. Almost immediately the newly partitioned state, created in 1922, adopted Catholicism as one of its principle regulating ideologies. The Catholic Church conferred on the new fledgling state a powerful sense of the legitimacy it sought as a new post-colonial state, and secured the delivery of ideologically driven education, health, and welfare systems. It also allowed the post-colonial state to disassociate itself from revolutionary struggles that had been central to its foundation, including significant socialist and feminist movements (see Ward 1996). Furthermore, Michael G. Cronin argues that for a newly formed state born out of counter-revolutionary struggle, the regulation and control of sexual behaviour created a sense of social stability for a state in flux. This regulatory ideal of sexuality also became a way of extending the hegemony of the newly empowered Catholic middle classes who emerged as the bearers of stability and morality (2012: 52). The alliance between church and state culminated with the 1937 Irish Constitution, a deeply conservative document, produced through an intimate collaboration between the Catholic Church and the political establishment. The 1937 Constitution was the culmination of a whole series of legal measures introduced by the Free State that were designed to erase women from public life. With its enactment 'women's political, economic and reproductive rights had been so severely curtailed so as to make it clear and explicit that women were indeed barred from claiming for themselves a political subjectivity, a public identity' (Valilius 1992: 43). Within the Constitution, the institutions of marriage and family enjoy privileged positions. The 'imagined' family is highly gendered where the 'special' role of women within the private home is elevated as an ideal. In Article 41 on the family, the words 'State', 'Family' and 'Nation' are all capitalised, as if 'patriarchally synonymous', while the terms 'woman' and 'mother' remain in lower case, suggesting that they exist 'as an object problematically situated within constitutional discourse', (Collins and Hanafin 2001: 64). Furthermore, 'woman' and 'mother' are understood here to be interchangeable terms, (Riddick cited in Conrad 2004: 73). This family, so cherished in the text of the constitution, would become the instrument through which regulatory ideals about gender and sexuality would be exercised, and, by extension, through which power and social cohesion were maintained. We now know that this vision of the stable traditional family so cherished by Catholic Ireland rested upon a particularly brutal system of containment where women and their children were considered 'little more than a commodity for trade amongst religious orders' with the knowledge and complicity of the state (O'Fátharta 2015).

In the years following independence, the post-colonial state utilised reproduction, as a 'medium through which competing national origin stories that focus on Irish national identity and cultural self-determination . . . [were] imagined and expressed' (Oaks 1997: 133). As a result, Eithne Luibhéid (2013: 127) argues that women's commitment to reproducing the next generation of the Irish nation became 'elevated to a symbol of Ireland's moral and cultural distinctiveness' over Britain, a position consistent with the constitution's reproductive logic that all children born on the island of Ireland were automatically granted citizenship at birth (until 2004).[4] Here we can locate an unspoken determination to characterise Ireland as 'not-England' by creating a coherent national identity that defined 'Irishness' as Catholic and white (see Fletcher 2005; Lentin 2013). As we will see these ideologies were reflected in struggles around knowledge and reproduction as women's sexuality was directed into marriage and motherhood.

KNOWLEDGE PRODUCTION AND CONTAINMENT

The production and containment of knowledge of women's sexual and reproductive capacities would become a central component in the project of Irish national identity formation. Clodagh Corcoran has noted how Irish society has never, either in its social standards nor its legislations, 'embodied principles and behaviours that respect the sexual rights of women' (Ryan 2010: 10). The infamous 'Mother and Child Scheme' introduced by Minister for Health, Dr Noël Browne, in the early 1950s, is particularly noteworthy in this regard. The bill provided for free medical care for all mothers and their children up to the age of 16. The Irish bishops objected on the basis that it represented state interference in the private domain of the family. However, as Chrystel Hug notes, one of the key concerns of the Catholic hierarchy that was never explicitly stated was the fear that doctors would provide sexual education under the guise of gynaecological advice to their female patients, including advice on family planning (1999: 84–5). As the Bishop of Ferns stated:

> Education in regard to motherhood includes instruction in regard to sex relations, chastity, and marriage. The State has no competence to give instructions in such matters. We regard with the greatest apprehension the proposal to give to local medical officers the right to tell Catholic girls and women how they should behave in regard to this sphere of conduct at once so delicate and sacred. Gynaecological care may be, and in some other countries is, interpreted to include provision for birth limitation and abortion. We have no guarantee that State officials will respect Catholic principles in regard to these matters (Hug 1995: ibid).

The defeat of the 'Mother and Child Scheme' demonstrated that the regulation of knowledge particularly in relation to female sexuality was a key strategy in maintaining the Church's control over reproduction and the integrity of the family in its traditional form.

The contemporaneous use of symphysiotomy[5] in state-funded maternity hospitals with religious enthuses that promoted Catholic social teaching reveals how women's reproductive bodies in Ireland have been subjected to abuse and mutilation, often without consent and knowledge. The practice of symphysiotomy was largely abandoned in obstetric practice in other Western countries when the development of antibiotics resulted in caesarean sections became safer. However, in Ireland from the 1940s until the 1960s, and in the case of Our Lady of Lourdes Hospital in Drogheda up to the 1980s, symphysiotomy continued to be practiced as an alternative to a caesarean section. Maternity hospitals with a Catholic ethos were reluctant to perform caesarean sections which would limit the number of children that a woman could safely deliver. Symphysiotomy, which widens the birth canal thereby facilitating future multiple births, was a response to:

> a particular set of state and religious structures which facilitated harmful medical practice. There was not the same reliance on symphysiotomy in the same types of

case in any other country, precisely because that set of state and religious structures did not exist (Enright, no date or page given).

The United Nation Human Rights Committee estimated in 2014 that 1,500 women and girls, some as young as 14 years old, underwent symphysiotomies between 1944 and 1987 (UN Human Rights Committee 2014). The procedure was largely performed without women's knowledge and for many survivors that 'knowledge came belatedly' several decades after the fact through media reports. Survivors of the procedure struggled to be heard and to have their experiences recognised as knowledge by both medical and legal professions. An investigation into the practice in Ireland conducted by Judge Maureen Harding Clarke, produced a report that was informed largely by male medical experts, giving scant attention to the perspectives of the women who underwent the procedure. The report, Linda Connolly argues, essentially 'reflects a view that women give birth because men help them and intervene to save their lives' (*The Irish Examiner*, 29 Nov. 2016). The experiential knowledge of women was largely ignored or side-lined with women who campaigned against the findings of the official investigations dismissed in the words of journalist Paul Cullen as a 'vociferous lobby group' (*The Irish Times*, 23 Nov. 2016). It was not until the emergence of the Repeal campaign with its emphasis on women's experience as knowledge that this strict dichotomy between public and private forms of gendered knowledge would begin to dissolve.

EIGHTH AMENDMENT

Countries in North America and Europe began liberalising their abortion laws in the 1970s and 1980s as a result of the struggles of the women's liberation movements. Ireland however remained an outlier, holding a referendum in 1983 to introduce a constitutional ban on abortion. The Eighth Amendment, which became article 40.3.3 of the Constitution, was designed to copper-fasten the prohibition on abortion by equating, in legal terms at least, the life of a pregnant woman with that of a foetus. It reads: 'The State acknowledges the right to life of the unborn and, with due regard to the equal right to life of the mother, guarantees in its laws to respect, and, as far as practicable, by its laws to defend and vindicate that right.' These 43 words clearly subordinated the life of a pregnant woman to that of the foetus, and rendered abortion illegal in Ireland in all circumstances, except where there was a 'real and substantial risk' to the life, as distinct from the health, of the pregnant woman.[6] The Eighth Amendment Ivana Bacik argued was 'uniquely misogynistic, in that it expressly sets up the right to life of both the pregnant woman and the foetus that she carries in conflict – anticipating that a time would come when somebody would have to decide between them' (2013: 22). As we will see, legal and medical hegemonic knowledge systems wield power and coincide with a liberal famialist state creating significant gendered effects, albeit unevenly experienced. The Eighth Amendment can thus be understood as a form of gendered social control articulated through legal and medical knowledge systems that were largely hostile to the lived experiences and knowledge of women.

The origins of the campaign to introduce this amendment may be located in the 1970s when a number of very small conservative Catholic groups fearing the potential legalisation of abortion in the future sought to enshrine Catholic teaching on abortion in the Constitution (O'Reilly 1992). Their anxiety had a number of sources: firstly, throughout the 1960s and 1970s Irish society feared that the growing support for the great social liberalisation of Irish society could led to abortion becoming legal in Ireland at some point in the future and thereby ensure a 'backlash' against what they viewed was the increasing advance of a liberal social agenda. In particular the emergence of women's movement in the 1970s began to challenge many of the paternalistic and unequal aspects of the famialist state. Secondly, Ireland had joined the European Economic Community (EEC), now the European Union (EU), in 1973 and began to change a number of laws. Following the introduction of equal pay legislation in Ireland, Irish conservatives began to argue that Europe was attempting to force a liberal social regime onto Ireland and that it would soon force Ireland to adopt a liberal 'abortion on demand' regime. Thirdly, in 1973 the United States Supreme Court legalised abortion in the *Roe v Wade* case (Sanger 2017). That judgement had a profound effective on conservative forces in Ireland, who began to fear that at some point a similar case would arise in Ireland, and that the Irish Supreme Court would decide that the right to privacy in marital affairs not only included a right to contraception (as the Supreme Court ruled in the *1978 McGee* case[7]), but the right to abortion as well. As far as these forces were concerned, a constitutional provision explicitly banning abortion outright was required in order to protect against possible future judicial activism. This led to an intensified campaign to change the Constitution; a debate characterised by historian Diarmaid Ferriter as 'one of the most poisonous witnessed in twentieth-century Ireland' (2005: 716). The amendment was passed by referendum with a two to one majority on 7 September 1983.

Knowledge construction and control have always reflected wider dynamics at play in Irish society, and this was clearly the care in relation to abortion. Conservative forces found by the end of the 1980s that they were unable to hold back the tide of secularisation. The collapse of Catholic hegemony, long in the making, was accelerated by the revelations around sexual abuse, the Magdalene and religious institutions, and the mother and baby homes (see Crowe in this volume). The blame for this painful, abusive aspect of Irish history cannot be solely located at the gates of the Catholic Church. Rather, the wider ideas and assumptions that contributed to and facilitated this abuse are intimately woven into the structure of the Irish state.

Support for the anti-abortion position had also began to erode during this period. There were two important turning points in this breakdown, both involving tragic cases where people were forced to confront the complexity of Irish abortion laws not as theoretical or abstract ethical questions but to recognise the effect Irish law had on women. The first was the 1992 X Case which involved a 14-year-old rape victim known only as Miss X. In February 1992, the parents of Miss X attempted to take her to Britain for an abortion because their child said that she would rather end her own life than give birth. The response of the Irish State was to issue a High Court injunction preventing her from leaving the country. When the story broke in the Irish media some days later, there was a public outcry with thousands protesting at her treatment. The parents of Miss X lodged an appeal with the Supreme Court who eventually reversed the High Court decision, concluding that a woman had a right to abortion in Ireland if her life is at risk, including at risk by suicide. The consequence of that Supreme Court ruling meant that abortion was now legal in Ireland, albeit in highly restrictive circumstances. Yet, the following November, the government, under pressure from the Catholic right, held a three-part referenda hoping to reverse the Supreme Court decision. They failed. This time the electorate voted in favour of a maintaining the X Case judgement; they also supported a constitutional amendment guaranteeing the right to travel abroad for an abortion and an amendment giving women the right to access abortion information. However, six successive governments then failed to introduce the necessary legislate to give effect to the Supreme Court judgement. Therefore, without legislation there was no legal clarity on the issue, which would become a contributing factor in the death of a pregnant woman in 2012.

The consequences of Ireland's abortion laws for pregnant women living in Ireland were profound. In October 2012, Savita Halappanavar, an Indian woman living in Ireland, presented to University College Galway Hospital with a miscarriage. Following a medical examination, the miscarriage was confirmed but the doctor treating her felt that due to presence of a foetal heartbeat they could not act, citing the Eighth Amendment. The delay proved fatal and she died of septicaemia (Holland 2013). The death of Ms Halappanavar provoked another wave of national horror at Ireland's punitive abortion regime and 'X-Case' legislation. The Protection of Life During Pregnancy Act (PLDPA) 2013 permitting abortions where a woman's life is at risk – including the risk of suicide – was finally introduced. Yet despite the introduction of the highly restrictive PLDPA, the presence of the Eighth Amendment meant that it was effectively meaningless. In the summer of 2014, a young migrant woman Ms Y, suicidal and pregnant as a result of rape, was refused access to an abortion. Out of desperation, the vulnerable woman went on hunger strike but, instead of acceding to her request for the abortion she was legally entitled to under the PLDPA, an order to force-feed her was obtained from the High Court, and she was coerced into continuing her pregnancy until the foetus was viable (see Holland 2014). What both the case of Ms Halappanavar and that of Ms Y reveal is not just that the women's own wishes and knowledge were ignored or side-lined but that these had no place within the formal structures of medical-judicial knowledge and power.

CENSORSHIP AND DENIAL OF KNOWLEDGE

Central to the maintenance and enforcement of Ireland's punitive abortion regime is the regulation and control of knowledge. The state's determination to regulate information reflects specific gender ideologies about women's competence and capacity to adjudicate information, and as a result, challenging this regulation has been central to feminist activism in Ireland for decades. Between 1992 and 2017, 17 separate reports have been commissioned by various apparatuses of the state under the auspices of legislative, executive or judicial powers.[8] With the exception of the 2017 Citizens' Assembly Report the voices and experiences of women who have had abortions are completely absent from these reports. Lynn Freedman in her study of the human rights' implications of restricting access to knowledge about reproductive healthcare has argued that censorship, manipulation and control of information concerning reproduction and sexuality 'involves a fundamental assault on the personhood, on the physical integrity and emotional well-being of people' and involves 'state control over some of the most basic elements of what it means to be human' (1995: 1). In Ireland, for most of the twentieth century women were not only prevented from accessing contraception and abortion but, even in terms of their proscribed reproduction functions of pregnancy and childbirth, were denied knowledge and decision-making capacities.

One of the key ways in which knowledge was regulated and controlled by the early Irish State was through censorship (Carson 1990). The *Report of the Committee on Evil Literature* (1926) – on which the 1929 Censorship of Publications Act would be based – found that birth control was widely practiced in Ireland in both urban and rural area. The report denounced the increase of births outside of marriage, the growth of contraceptive use and the proliferation of sexual offences, concluding that there was a 'widespread dissemination of knowledge propagated to free vice of its most powerful restraints' (Hug 1999: 79). The 1929 Act 'reflected the moral concerns and principles' of the new Irish State, prohibiting literature on three key grounds: that it is 'in . . . general tendency indecent or obscene'; that it gives 'an unduly large proportion of space to the publication of matter relating to crime'; and that it encourages 'the unnatural prevention of conception or the procurement of an abortion or miscarriage'. The Censorship Board – appointed by the Minister for Justice and accountable only to the Minister, not the wider public – was required to take into consideration 'the literary, artistic, scientific or historic merit or importance and the general tenor of the book' before making a decision to ban. The Boards is also, the Act states, expected to consider 'the class of reader . . . which may reasonably be expected to read such a book' (Carson, 1990: 9). The determination of obscenity based on the class of reader has a long history and was certainly not unique to the Irish Free State, revealing how the regulation of knowledge is intimately connected to the legitimisation of particular forms of power (Kendrick 1996).

The Act was amended in 1945 and again in 1967 permitted the banning of books for two further reasons: for being indecent or obscene, or for advocating the procurement of abortion or miscarriage. It limited the ban to twelve years for a book that was obscene but publications that advocated abortion were considered an exception, and thus banned indefinitely. As of 2018 only one book was banned for being indecent or obscene (Barry 2016) while eight books were banned for providing information on how to procure an abortion.[9] Three of the books were explicitly about abortion: *Abortion Internationally* (banned since 1983); *Abortion: Our Struggle for Control* (banned since 1983); and *Abortion: Right or Wrong* (banned since 1942). Four of the banned books are sex guides: *How to Drive Your Man Wild in Bed* (banned since 1985); and *The Complete Guide to Sex* (banned since 1990); *Make it Happy: What Sex is All About*, *The Book of Love*; and the slightly more medical *The Love Diseases*. These texts have all been banned since the early 1980s because they appear to contain information about the procurement of abortion.

Censorship of material around abortion was not confined to literature. In March 1994 '*50,000 Secret Journeys*', a documentary commissioned by the Irish national broadcaster RTÉ featured interviews with three Irish women speaking on camera about their personal experience of abortion for the first time on Irish television. The documentary was pulled from its prime-time transmission slot the day before broadcast. RTÉ management deemed the documentary 'unbalanced' and were concerned that women in the film 'did not show enough remorse' (Siggins 2016). The documentary was eventually shown later in the year, albeit renamed with a less provocative title: '*The Abortion Debate*'. More problematically, however, it was screened as part of late-night current affairs package that 'included a separate filmed item about unmarried mothers, with contributions from an academic, two co-ordinators of support groups for lone parents, a senior social worker and a barrister – but no actual single parents were interviewed' (Siggins ibid). The filmmaker Hilary Duffy, interviewed by Siggins, noted how the accompanying film about lone parents excluded the subjects, focusing instead on expert analysis, a practice of excluding the subject that her film had deliberately set out to avoid.

As a result of the strict regulation and control of knowledge around abortion, one of the key ways in which feminists and activists have challenged abortion laws in Ireland is by creating alternative sources of knowledge. In the aftermath of the 1983 Referendum anti-abortion groups, in particular the Society for the Protection of Unborn Children Ireland (SPUC), began to focus their efforts on closing abortion referral clinics. The abortion referral agencies in question were offering non-directive counselling and giving women who choose abortion the contact details of clinics in Britain. In June 1985 SPUC initiated legal action against two of the main providers of pregnancy counselling in Ireland – Open Door Counselling and the Well Woman Centre. The Attorney-General subsequently joined the action and in December 1986 the High Court issued an injunction prohibiting both organisations from offering pregnancy counselling services, with Justice Hamilton arguing that it was illegal to provide information in Ireland about abortion clinics in Britain. The centres stopped providing the information but appealed the decision to the Supreme Court. The Court denied the appeal on 16 March 1988.

The injunction was clarified to prohibit the communication of the names, addresses, and contact numbers of all abortion clinics outside the State. In September 1988, on the strength of the Hamilton judgement, SPUC obtained an injunction against three students' unions for including abortion information in their student handbooks. The handbooks contained detailed information about contraception, issues to consider when deciding whether or not to have an abortion, and the names and addresses of abortion clinics in Britain, (Coliver 1995: 167–8). Restrictions on abortion information became so tightly controlled that in 1990 the women's magazine *Cosmopolitan*, following complaints from the Offices of Censorship of Publications, began publishing a separate Irish Edition that substituted a blank page for the page where ads for abortion services would normally be printed with a 'Publisher's Notice' explaining why. In May 1992 Easons, Ireland's largest distributor to retail newsagents, refused to sell and distribute imported copies of *The Guardian* newspaper when they arrived at Dublin Airport because the issue included a full page advertisement for Marie Stopes Clinics, which is a provider of abortion services in Britain (RTE Archives). As Hug noted:

> The SPUC cases proved that an ordinary citizen can enforce the law as in Article 40.3.3 and deprive women in distress of the necessary information relative to their decision to terminate their pregnancy. As long as the right to 'travel', as it became euphemistically known, and the right to information were not explicitly recognised by Irish law, Irish women would not be in a position to take moral and responsible decisions in an honest manner (1999: 160).

Access to abortion information was finally legislated for in 1995 following the 1992 referenda with the introduction of The Regulation of Information (Services outside the State for the Termination of Pregnancies) Act.

In response campaigners shifted tactics and began to concentrate on providing abortion information instead of counselling in defiance of the injunction, creating a different form of knowledge. The Director of Open Door Counselling, Ruth Riddick, established an emergency telephone hotline 'Open Line Helpline' so that women living in Ireland could continue to access abortion information. The number of the helpline was distributed through fliers, stickers, and graffiti on toilet doors in pubs and nightclubs. Activists would frequently gather outside the GPO in Dublin at weekends chanting the number of the helpline: '*6794700 Women have the right to know!*' Ensuring that women living in Ireland had access to accurate information about abortion and how to access abortion services became one of the key strategies of Irish feminist activists throughout the 1980s and early 1990s (Rossiter 2009). However, even when abortion information was legal in 1995, the information was highly mediated and controlled. The 1995 Act which remained the law until 2019 only allowed doctors (as well as advisory agencies and individual counsellors) to give information on abortion services available outside of the State. However, the Act required any information on abortion services be provided along with information on parenting and adoption and only given in the context of one-to-one counselling. Doctors and clinics offering crisis pregnancy counselling were obliged to give women information on parenting and adoption but could refuse to give information on abortion. This led to a proliferation of so called 'rogue pregnancy agencies'[10] and created barriers to women, particularly those who are young and vulnerable, gaining access to accurate and safe information. These agencies advertised themselves as offering advice on all options available to pregnant women but focused on misinformation or anti-abortion information (Barton 2017). The Act also prohibited a doctor from making an appointment for an abortion in another state on behalf of their patient, even if the woman was experiencing serious medical problems. With the proliferation of the internet, social media and smart phones, abortion information certainly became more easily available; but not for everyone, so it would be a mistake to underestimate how vital activist work was and continues to be. One important source of knowledge particularly for marginalised and vulnerable women who found that Ireland's harsh abortion laws left them with few options was the British-based Abortion Support Network (ASN). Founded in 2009 by Mara Clarke and supported by over 90 volunteers, ASN provides information, financial assistance, and accommodation in volunteer homes to those forced to travel from Ireland and Northern Ireland (as well as the Isle of Man, Malta, and Gibraltar). The ASN continued the work of the Irish Women's Abortion Support Group (IWASG), which supported women from 1980 onwards, often drawing ire from the Irish community in Britain (Rossiter 2009). The work of the IWASG and ASN highlights the important transnational aspect of the struggle for reproductive rights: an often-invisible aspect of feminist activism that is essential to the creation of new forms of knowledge.

Increasingly women were accessing abortion in early pregnancy using abortion pills. These are purchased online, unregulated, and taken at home in a clandestine manner and are currently illegal. While no one knows exactly how many women and girls take medical abortion pills, at least 1,748 women and girls living in Ireland ordered abortion pills from just one online provider – Women on Web – in 2016 (Aiken, Gomperts and Trussell 2017). A second online provider – Women Help Women – reported that 878 women used its service in 2017, an increase of 190 per cent on 2016. In the first quarter of 2018, 323 women accessed a medical abortion, a 90 per cent increase on the same period last year (Women Help Women, 2018). While the option of medical abortion is generally safe and effective, it cannot be considered acceptable healthcare as it does not reflect an active preference, but the lack of safe options and alternatives. Expert testimony to the Oireachtas in 2017 noted that those using abortion pills do so without medical guidance and are less likely to seek medical help if they experience any complications in part due to fear of legal prosecution and a potential 14-year prison sentence for accessing illegal abortion (Aiken 2017). Nevertheless, for women who could not afford to or were unable to travel abroad, the abortion pill was, in general, a safe and affordable alternative. Abortion rights' activists did important work in raising awareness about these services (See ROSA http://rosa.ie and Need Abortion Ireland https://needabortion ireland.org). The illegal nature of abortion meant that women, unlike men, had their access to accurate knowledge about reproductive healthcare determined not as matter healthcare, but as a matter of criminal law: a form of subversive knowledge.

REPEAL

On 25 May 2018 the Irish electorate voted by an extraordinary two-to-one majority to legalise abortion in an historic referendum outcome. The result, with a powerful note of symmetry, reversed the result of the original referendum. The most notable and, arguably, the most important feature of the referendum was the role that women's storytelling played in the campaign. If, as Sanger argues, citizens are not just subjects of the law but 'are also supposed to make law, directly or indirectly' then 'we cannot advance how we and our representatives think about something – and certainly not how it should be regulated – until we start talking about it' (2017: xiii). In 2000 the Irish Family Planning Association published a collection of stories, entitled *The Irish Journey*. The stories were authored anonymously. The most notable feature of the discussion around the publication was how rare it was for women to have a space to articulate their experiences of abortion in their own words and for people to hear these stories unmediated by 'experts'.

One of the key breakthroughs in the repeal campaign was when women began to publicly recount their experiences of abortion. Journalists and writers such as Roisin Ingle, Tara Flynn and Kitty Holland used their public platforms to tell their own abortion stories. They were certainly met with abuse – much of it on social media platforms – but they also received huge support and gratitude from thousands of women who felt their acts of bravery had given permission for others to tell their own stories. In January 2018, five months before the repeal referendum, a Facebook page was established called 'In Her Shoes' whose sole purpose was to offer women the space to tell their abortion stories. It quickly became a phenomenon received over 100,000 'likes' in a matter of weeks. The stories were published anonymously but, as the referendum approached, women began linking the page to their personal Facebook pages, adding their own stories. Across the print and broadcast media women came forward to tell their own stories and experiences. Women's stories were also a central pillar in the Together for Yes: the National Campaign to Remove the Eighth Amendment (see also Cullen in this volume). An exit poll conducted by RTÉ on the day of the referendum revealed that 43 per cent of voters said that the 'personal stories' covered in the media were the 'sources of information' most important in making the decision on how to vote in the referendum (RTÉ and Behaviour & Attitudes 2018). Through storytelling the dichotomy between public and private knowledge began to disappear with women's stories becoming a type of unarchived knowledge. Rebecca Ann Barr writes of the important contribution of storytelling to alternative forms of public knowledge:

To speak these stories was activism and legal fictions had for so long made these narratives impossible: but narrative was necessary to make change happen . . . These stories expanded the public sphere's capacity for distributing empathy amongst all citizens, a political prerequisite to allowing women fuller participation in civil life. This astonishing permutation allowed women to speak of their bodies and fertility in new and significant ways (2019 no page given).

This knowledge would prove central to the referendum victory liberating the abortion debate from the hierarchical and gendered legal-medical structure of knowledge.

The ramifications of this new form of gendered knowledge continue to be felt within Irish society, particularly at an institutional level. In April 2018, in the midst of the referendum campaign, it was revealed that at least 221 women who developed cervical cancer had had their test results audited by CervicalCheck, but only one in five of the women affected was informed at the time the information about the smear test audits became available. The government ordered an immediate inquiry. The report produced in October 2018 by Dr Gabriel Scally, in direct contrast to the report on symphysiotomy, put women and their experiences at the centre of the official document. Scally (2018) repeatedly refers in the report to knowing things 'from the women and their families'. As Susan McKay notes:

Scally brings a feminist sensibility to his task . . . The victims of the catastrophe are placed at the heart of the work and presented as a pre-eminent source of vital information. They are given support in the process, enabled to participate . . . There is a high degree of sensitivity. Some women came to meetings but not to make submissions. Scally notes that their participation as listeners was also a contribution (2018 no page given).

The report also noted that current legal remedies are not capable of resolving the deep hurt, anguish and resentment felt by many of the women and families as this, he rightly contends, would require something 'very different' (Scally 2018). What that is remains to be determined but it is clear from the history of the Irish State that it will involve a confrontation with structures of knowledge and power, particularly, in relation to gender.

CONCLUSIONS

For the first time ever in an Irish public debate about abortion regulation the voices and experiences of women who had had abortions were heard. One of the key challenges of drafting abortion law is to ensure that it will allow women to gain access to the information and services that they need. Achieving this means that the state respects a woman's ability to make and implement decisions about her reproduction body. As Freedman and Isaacs note this requires a focus not only on the content of women's choices, but on the relationship between a woman's ability to make and carry out those choices, and her ability to maintain a sense of control over what happens in her life (1993: 27–8).

Access to information is largely understood to be peripheral to the wider debates about abortion and healthcare. But, as Freedman has argued, too often we fail to recognise that censorship of reproductive healthcare information as a human rights' violation. This, she argues, is telling about the manner in which we have been conditioned to think about healthcare, and women's reproduction in particular (1995: 1–2). Health and healthcare knowledge are powerful political categories that must themselves be subject to careful analyses. As we have seen in this chapter, discourses and women's health have too often in Ireland served historically to reinforce dominant ideological constructs about the role of women in the family and society. The rhetoric of women's healthcare is used by anti-abortion activists and the political right to promote and obscure their political and religious agendas which have very little to do with health. At the core of these debates about abortion and knowledge is the nature of women's lives and the conditions under which they struggle for freedom and dignity.

Notes

1   In this chapter I use the word 'woman' in reference to people who need to access abortion because the particular debate addressed is connected to very specific historical debates about women, state, and nation in Ireland. However, I fully acknowledge that not everyone who needs an abortion is, or identifies, as a woman.

2   Provisional figures from the British Pregnancy Advisory Services (BPAS), one of the main abortion providers in England for women living in Ireland, suggest a decrease in the first three months of 2019 of 85 per cent in the numbers travelling from the Republic. See Joyce Fegan 'Imperfect system and cruel barriers still stopping women accessing abortion' in *Irish Examiner*, 3 June 2019.

3   These statistics, based on data collected by the UK Department of Health Statistics, refer to women resident in the Republic of Ireland who travelled to both England and Wales to access safe abortion services. These figures are widely acknowledged to be underestimation as they do not include women who travel to Scotland or to other countries in Europe. The figures also fail to account for women who do not provide their Irish address to clinics or hospitals often to protect their anonymity.

4   The automatic right to citizenship was removed by referendum in June 2004 that followed a racially charged moral panic about pregnant migrant women. The 27th

amendment of the Constitution provided that children born on the island of Ireland to parents who were both foreign nationals would no longer have a constitutional right to citizenship of the Republic of Ireland.

5   Symphysiotomy is a procedure that involves the slicing through of the cartilage and ligaments of a pelvic joint (or in extreme cases, called pubiotomy, sawing through the bone of the pelvis itself) in order to widen it and allow a baby to be delivered unobstructed.

6   In the 1992 X Case Judgement the majority opinion of the Irish Supreme Court held that a woman had a right to an abortion under Article 40.3.3 if there was 'a real and substantial risk' to her life. This right did not exist if there was a risk to her health but not her life; however, it did exist if the risk was the possibility of suicide. See *Attorney General v X*, [1992] IESC 1; [1992] 1 IR 1. For discussion see Jennifer Schweppe, 'Introduction', in Jennifer Schweppe (ed.), *The Unborn Child, Article 40.3.3 and Abortion in Ireland: 25 Years of Protection?* (Dublin 2008) and Ruadhán Mac Cormaic, *The Supreme Court* (Dublin 2017).

7   *McGee v. The Attorney General* [1974] IR 284. The Supreme Court ruled by a four to one majority in favour of Mary McGee, determining that married couples have the constitutional right to make private decisions on family planning and lay the ground to the eventual legalisation of the sale of contraceptives in Ireland.

8   Reports on Abortion in the public domain: Sunniva McDonagh, *The Attorney General v. X and Others* (Dublin, 1992); *Report of the Constitution Review Group* (Dublin 1996); Department of the Taoiseach, *Green Paper on Abortion* (Dublin, 1999); All Party Oireachtas Committee on Constitution, *Fifth Progress Report* (Dublin 2002); K. Rundle, C. Leigh, H. McGee, and R. Layte, *Irish Contraception and Crisis Pregnancy* (Dublin, 2004.); S. Clements and R. Ingham, *Improving Knowledge Regarding Abortions Performed on Irish Women in the UK* (Dublin, 2007); Crisis Pregnancy Agency, *Strategy: Leading an Integrated Approach to Reducing Crisis Pregnancy* (Dublin, 2007); H. P. McGee, K, Rundle, R. D. Layte, and C. D. Donnelly, *The Irish Study of Sexual Health and Relationships Sub-Report 2: Sexual Health Challenges and Related Service Provision (*Dublin, 2008); Government Submission of Action Plan to Council of Europe in relation to the Execution of the European Court of Human Rights Judgment in the case of A, B and C v Ireland. 25579/05 [2010] ECHR 2032 (16 December 2010); Report of the Expert Group on the A, B and C v. Ireland Cases (2012); Orla McBride, Karen Morgan and Hannah McGee, *Irish Contraception and Crisis Pregnancy Study* (Dublin, 2012); Health Services Executive Crisis Pregnancy Programme (ICCP-2010); *A Survey of the General Population*, Royal College of Surgeons of Ireland; Houses of the Oireachtas Joint Committee on Health and Children, Report on Protection of Life during Pregnancy Bill 2013 (Heads of) Volume 1 May 2013 31/HHCN/012 900, Department of Health, *Implementation of the Protection of Life During Pregnancy Act 2013 – Guidance Document for Health Professionals* (2014); Department of Health, *First Report on the Protection of Life during Pregnancy Act. 2* (2015); Justice Mary Laffoy, *First Report and Recommendations of the Citizens' Assembly: The Eighth Amendment to the Constitution* (June 2017); *All Party Oireachtas Committee on the Recommendations of the Citizens' Assembly: The Eighth Amendment to the Constitution* (December 2017). Not in the public domain: *A Memorandum of Government Preparatory to the Protocol 17 of the European Treaties of February 1992.* This list does not include court

cases and legal advice in Ireland, press releases, private studies, and academic research. I am very grateful to Pauline Cullen who compiled this list and shared it with me.

9 Following the repeal of the Eighth Amendment in 2018 the Health (Regulation of Termination of Pregnancy) Act 2018 which legalised abortion in certain circumstances also repealed the relevant sections of the Censorship of Publication Acts that banned books for advocating the procurement of abortion.

10 The sole purpose of what have come to be termed 'Rogue Crisis pregnancy Agencies' is to prevent women from having abortions. In many instances, they misinform and intimidate women to achieve their aim. Women describe being harassed, bullied, and given blatantly false information. While they may present themselves as offering medical advice or counselling services, most rogue agency volunteers who work directly with women are not counsellors or healthcare professionals.

REFERENCES

Aiken, Abigail, 'Opening statement to the Joint Oireachtas Committee on the Eighth Amendment to the Constitution', 11 Oct. 2017.

www.oireachtas.ie/parliament/media/committees/eighthamendmentoftheconstiution/Opening-Statement-by-Professor-Abigail-Aiken,-University-of-Texas.pdf Accessed 27 July 2018.

Aiken Abigail, Rebecca Gomperts, J. Trussell, 'Experiences and characteristics of women seeking and completing at-home medical termination of pregnancy through online telemedicine in Ireland and Northern Ireland: A population-based analysis' in *British Journal of Obstetrics Gynaecology*, 124(8), 2017, pp 1,208–15.

Atwood, Margaret, *The Handmaid's Tale* (Vintage: London, 1996).

Bacik, Ivana, 'Legislating for Article 40.3.3°', in *Irish Journal of Legal Studies*, 3(3), 2013, pp 18–35.

Barry, Michael, 'Censorship board bans book for the first time since 1998', in *Irish Times*, 12 Mar 2016. www.irishtimes.com/news/ireland/irish-news/censorship-board-bans-book-for-the-first-time-since-1998-1.2571029 Accessed 27 July 2018.

Barton, Sarah, 'HSE: Tackling rogue pregnancy agencies is constant battle', in *Irish Times* 17 Nov. 2017. www.irishtimes.com/news/politics/hse-tackling-rogue-pregnancy-agencies-is-constant-battle-1.3293342 Accessed 30 July 2018.

Beard, Mary, *Women & Power: A Manifesto* (Profile Books: London, 2017).

Carson, Julie (ed.), *Banned in Ireland: Censorship and the Irish Writer* (Routledge: London, 1990).

Coliver, Sandra, '"Ireland" in Article 19, International Centre against Censorship', in *The Right to Know: Human Rights and Access to Reproductive Health Information* (University of Pennsylvania Press: Philadelphia, 1995), pp 159–80.

Collins, Barry & Patrick Hanafin, 'Mothers, maidens and the myth of origins in the Irish Constitution', in *Law and Critique*, 12, 2001, pp 53–73.

Connolly, Linda, 'Symphysiotomy report begets more questions', in *Irish Examiner*, 29 Nov. 2016 www.irishexaminer.com/viewpoints/analysis/symphysiotomy-report-begets-more-questions-432728.html Accessed 27 July 2018.

Conrad, Kathryn, *Locked in the Family Cell: Gender, Sexuality, and Political Agency in Irish National Discourse* (University of Wisconsin Press: Madison, 2004).

Cronin, Michael, *Impure Thoughts: Sexuality, Catholicism and Literature in Twentieth Century Ireland* (Manchester University Press: Manchester, 2012).

Cullen, Paul, 'Symphysiotomy: The whitewash that never was', in *Irish Times*, 23 Nov. 2016 www.irishtimes.com/opinion/symphysiotomy-the-whitewash-that-never-was-1.2878271 Accessed 27 July 2018.

Enright, Mairéad, 'Notes on Judge Harding-Clark's report on the symphysiotomy payment scheme', in *Human Rights in Ireland Blog* http://humanrights.ie/law-culture-and-religion/notes-on-judge-harding- clarks-report-on-the-symphysiotomy-payment-scheme/ Accessed 30 March 2018.

Farrell, Elaine, '*A Most Diabolical Deed': Infanticide and Irish Society, 1850–1900* (Manchester University Press: Manchester, 2013).

Fegan, Joyce, 'Imperfect system and cruel barriers still stopping women accessing abortion', in *Irish Examiner*, 3 June 2019. www.irishexaminer.com/breakingnews/specialreports/imperfect-system-and-cruel-barriers-still-stopping-women-access-abortion-928382.html Accessed 20 June 2019.

Ferriter, Diarmaid, *The Transformation of Ireland 1900–2000* (Profile Books: London, 2005).

Fletcher, Ruth, 'Reproducing Irishness: Race, Gender, and abortion law', in *Canadian Journal of Women and Law*, 17(2), 2005, pp 356–404.

Foucault, Michel, *The History of Sexuality: Volume 1* (Penguin: London, 1998).

Freedman, Lynn P., 'Censorship and manipulation of reproductive health information: An issue of human rights and women's health', in Article 19, International Centre Against Censorship, *The Right to Know: Human Rights and Access to Reproductive Health Information* (University of Pennsylvania Press: Philadelphia, 1995), pp 1–37.

Freedman, Lynn P. & Stephen L. Isaacs, 'Human rights and reproductive choice', in *Studies in Family Planning*, 24(1), 1993, pp 18–30.

Holland, Kitty, *Savita: A Tragedy that Shook a Nation* (Transworld: Dublin, 2013).

Ibid., 'Timeline of Ms Y Case', in *The Irish Times*, 04 Oct. 2014. www.irishtimes.com/news/social-affairs/timeline-of-ms-y-case-1.1951699 Accessed 6 June 2018.

Hug, Chrystel, *The Politics of Sexual Morality in Ireland* (Macmillan: London, 1999).

Inglis, Tom, 'Origins and legacies of Irish prudery: Sexuality and social control in modern Ireland, in *Eire Ireland*, 40(3–4), 2005, pp 9–37.

Irish Family Planning Association, *The Irish Journey: Women's Stories of Abortion* (IFPA,: Dublin, 2000).

Jackson, Pauline, *Abortion Trials and Tribulations* (University College Dublin: Dublin, 1987).

Kendrick, Walter, *The Secret Museum: Pornography in Modern Culture* (University of California Press: Berkeley CA., 1996).

Lentin, Ronit, 'A woman died: Abortion and the politics of birth in Ireland', in *Feminist Review*, 105, 2013, pp 130–6.

Luibhéid, Eithne, *Pregnant on Arrival: Making the Illegal Immigrant* (University of Minnesota Press: London & Minneapolis, 2013).

Mac Cormaic, Ruadhán, *The Supreme Court* (Penguin: Dublin, 2017).

Oaks, Laury, 'Irishness, Eurocitizens, and reproductive rights', in *Reproducing Reproduction*(University of Pennsylvania Press: Philadelphia, 1997).

Ó Fátharta, Conall, 'Bessborough death record concerns were raised in 2012' in *The Irish Examiner*, 02 Jun. 2015.

O'Reilly, Emily, *Masterminds of the Right* (Attic Press: Dublin, 1992).

Petchesky, Rosalind Pollack, *Abortion and Woman's Choice: The State, Sexuality, and Reproductive Freedom* (Northeastern University Press: Boston, 1990).

Rossiter, Ann, *Ireland's Hidden Diaspora; The 'Abortion Trail' and the Making of the London-Irish Underground, 1980–2000* (IASC Publishing: London, 2009).

RTÉ Archives, 'Newspaper pulled over abortion services ad 1992'. www.rte.ie/archives/2017/0518/876228-guardian-newspaper-withheld-from-sale/ Accessed 24 Jun. 2019.

RTE & Behaviour & Attitudes Exit Poll, 'Thirty-Sixth Amendment to the Constitution Exit

Poll 25 May 2018.' Available at https://static.rasset.ie/documents/news/2018/05/rte-exit-poll-final-11pm.pdf Accessed 17 Oct. 2018.

Ryan, Mary, 'A feminism of their own?: Irish women's history and contemporary Irishwomen's writing', in *Estudios Irlandeses*, 5, 2010, pp 92–101.

Sanger, Carol, *About Abortion: Terminating Pregnancy in Twenty-First Century America* (Harvard University Press: Cambridge Mass., 2017).

Scally, Gabriel, *Scoping Inquiry into the Cervical Check Screening Programme.* Final Report Sept. 2018. Available at http://scallyreview.ie/wp-content/uploads/2018/09/Scoping-Inquiry-into-CervicalCheck-Final-Report.pdf Accessed 18 Oct. 2018.

Schweppe, Jennifer, 'Introduction', in Jennifer Schweppe (ed.), *The Unborn Child, Article 40.3.3 and Abortion in Ireland: 25 Years of Protection?* (Liffey Press: Dublin, 2008).

Siggins, Lorna, 'RTÉ told us our abortion film lacked balance', in *The Irish Times*, 11 Apr. 2016. www.irishtimes.com/life-and-style/people/rté-told-us-our-abortion-film-lacked-balance-1.2602308. Accessed 27 July 2018.

UN Human Rights Committee 'Concluding observations on the Fourth Periodic Report of Ireland', CCPR//C/IRL/CO/4, para 11 (19 Aug. 2014).

Valiulis, Maryann Gialanella, 'Defining their role in the new state: Irishwomen's protestagainst the Juries Act of 1927, in *Canadian Journal of Irish Studies*, 18(1), 1992, pp 43–60.

Ward, Margaret, *Unmanageable Revolutionaries: Women and Irish Nationalism* (Pluto Press: London, 1996).

Women Help Women, 'In solidarity with repeal the 8th! Referendum in Ireland on May 25th!', on Women Help Women blog, 10 April 2018. https://womenhelp.org/en/page/900/in-solidarity-with-repeal-the-8th-referendum-in-ireland-on-may-25th Accessed 27 July 2018.

SEVEN

Contested Knowledge: Victim Narratives, Autobiography, and the Rise of Neo-Abolitionist Prostitution Policy in Ireland

Paul Ryan

INTRODUCTION

The purchase of sex became a criminal offence with the passage of the Criminal Law (Sexual Offences) Act 2017. This marked the successful culmination of a long civil society campaign that convinced policy makers that the law was the solution to the exploitation and abuse perpetrated against women within the sex industry. The stories of women who had experienced abuse formed part of the evidence presented to politicians engaged in legislative review. In this chapter I explore how such stories become forms of gender knowledge. Stories were deployed by competing feminist advocacy groups during the political campaigns to introduce (or oppose) the sex-purchase ban. The campaigns provide a lens to examine how a particular form of gender knowledge emerged as *the* dominant narrative to depict/represent and understand the experience of women within the sex industry. This narrative had the effect of silencing and marginalising alternative stories that had a different take on the regularisation and/or prohibition of sex work in Ireland. This dominant narrative relied upon a carceral feminism that seeks the protection of the rights of women in prostitution through criminalisation and surveillance rather than welfare reform (Jackson 2016: 28, 30).[1] Carceral feminism has been closely associated with the work of Elizabeth Bernstein (2010, 2012). Bernstein documents the shift from neo-liberal strategies criminalising poor women to versions of feminist activism that embrace the carceral state particularly in the areas of rape, sexual violence and more recently, human trafficking.

Drawing from the work of Hesford (2011) and Plummer (1995, 2017) I argue that the framing of these stories created narratives that became part of a political and symbolic strategy. They sought to validate and institutionalise certain truth claims about sex work centring upon a portrayal of women as lacking agency, often duped, and deceived into the exploitative world of prostitution. These truth claims followed a modernist sexual storytelling arc. The storyteller is on a journey of suffering and redemption, where 'personal, secretive, shameful worlds get remoulded into stories that are public, participatory and proud' (Plummer 1995: 108). These stories frame the social 'problem' of prostitution and, crucially, reflect forms of gender knowledge that construct sex workers solely as victims.

I explore the rise of autobiographical survivor stories, most notably Rachel Moran's book *Paid For* (2013), which saw her become a leading figure in the campaign to introduce the Nordic-style sex purchase ban in Ireland and abroad.[2] Central to Moran's story is the documentation of certain 'universal' truths about prostitution that transcend her individual experience. Stories like Moran's tell us not just *what* is being told but contribute to narratives telling us *how* stories are told (Plummer 2017: 281). The gender knowledge that is produced creates a narrative power. It elevates individual stories into wider public discourse that may support carceral responses while regulating how other stories are received. As a result, alternative stories of sex work that are more nuanced, discontinuous, or 'messy' become increasingly difficult to communicate either by the storytellers themselves or by the researchers who have collected them. Most commonly the latter are told within a 'rights-based' frame that offers a counter-narrative where the criminalisation, violence and stigma surrounding sex work become the social problem, as opposed to prostitution itself (Jackson 2016: 28). Moreover, counter-narratives that are much less dependent on a unitary or universal *truth* rely upon a diversity of late-modern formats to communicate to the wider public. For example, Irish sex worker Kate McGrew recounted her story not through a published book but through performing art and appearing on the RTÉ2 reality television show *Connected* (2013)[3]. The expanding genre of digital sexual storytelling takes places in a global context that is mediated through online communities, enabling a cheaper, more accessible, and less regulated means to reach the public. Online fora like YouTube facilitate the dissemination of McGrew's performances that show case her sexual politics and challenge dominant narratives about sex work.

In this chapter I will compare Moran and McGrew's storytelling through Plummer's (2017: 283) critical 'moments' interpretive framework which focuses on the birth, institutionalisation and negotiation of life stories. Both narratives communicated specific forms of gender knowledge, constituting women in the sex industry as either passive, duped victims, or willing participants with agency. Ultimately, as the prospective legislation on prostitution entered the political domain it fell to Oireachtas (parliamentary) committees to adjudicate the credibility of the competing knowledge claims. The gender knowledge claims that carceral feminism produced, and that most closely aligned with the narrative preference of key state actors, at both national and transnational level, would ultimately win out ensuring the passage of the sex purchase ban into Irish law.

THE RISE OF NEO-ABOLITIONISM

Since gaining independence in 1922, the Irish State had maintained the British policy of containment of prostitution, displaying a reluctance to legislate and acting only when it was deemed a public nuisance (Ryan & Ward 2017: 48). Prostitution played a symbolic role during political and cultural nationalist campaigns for independence, as an unsavoury symptom of the English colonial presence in Ireland. The claims that prostitution was an English vice, alien to the Irish character, were of course fanciful. Prostitution was widespread throughout Ireland not just in garrison towns with a large military presence (Luddy 2007: 13). The passage of the *Criminal Law Amendment Act* (1935) recognised the reality of the extent of prostitution. This Act was fuelled by a moral panic following claims about sexual immorality revealed through the Carrigan Report (1931): the work of an extra-parliamentary committee of investigation (Smith 2007: 1–20; Ward 2010: 49). The Minister for Justice James Kenney established the committee which was shrouded in secrecy – even members of the Oireachtas did not know who its members were – ostensibly to review the Criminal Law Amendment Act 1880 and 1885[4] and to tackle juvenile prostitution. However, its remit remained wide and ambiguous with 29 expert witnesses giving evidence in private on 'sexual immorality'. Recommendations that issued on regulating public dance halls, banning contraceptives, and tackling prostitution became law under the new Fianna Fáil government led by Éamon de Valera.

The Act accelerated the closure of brothels by giving the police new powers to search premises and impose stronger penalties on the owners. Prostitution policy remained prohibitionist in character with women also targeted by the *Police Clauses Act* 1847 that outlawed loitering and causing public nuisance while the term 'common law prostitute' was retained, allowing Gardaí sweeping powers to criminalise any woman they deemed suspect (Ward 2010: 51). The term 'common law prostitute' was removed by the *Criminal Law (Sexual Offences) Act 1993* after a Supreme Court ruling deemed it unconstitutional. The aim of the 1993 Act was to address the emergence of massage parlours and the impact of the heroin epidemic on the social organisation of prostitution. The Second Commission for the Status of Women, which reported in 1993, debated both the regulation and abolition of prostitution. However, their final recommendation to government was greater collaboration between NGOs and women working within prostitution, to develop a range of exit strategies (Ward 2010: 54). The 1993 Act was considered regressive in some quarters. Senator David Norris described it as an attack on the most vulnerable in society by making provision for increased fines for solicitation and the creation of new crimes such as curb crawling.[5] The Minister of Justice made clear, however, that the state sought not to criminalise the prostitute and had no role in policing consensual commercial sex (Ryan and Ward 2017: 48–9). Notwithstanding the law's intention, in practice there was an increase in prosecutions for prostitution-related offences (Ward 2010: 53).

A turning point in the institutionalisation of neo-abolitionism in civic and political life came with the founding of the non-governmental organisation the Immigrant Council of Ireland (ICI) in 2001 with funding from the Religious Sisters of Ireland. ICI embarked upon a campaign to introduce a law, similar to one passed in Sweden in 1999 that criminalised the purchase of sex (Levy 2015). The campaign had three objectives: alliance building, evidence gathering and parliamentary engagement. Firstly, ICI lobbied a wide range of organisations, including political parties, state feminist organisations, trade unions and professional organisations to support their call for a change in the law that would see the introduction of a sex purchase ban. This strategy was undertaken in conjunction with Ruhama – an organisation founded by the Good Shepherd Sisters and the Sisters of Our Lady of Charity – that helps women who are victims of exploitation and trafficking within prostitution. This broad alliance which was called *Turn off the Red Light* (ToRL) promoted a carceral feminism that sought to leverage the institutions of the state, including the criminal justice system to provide legal protections for women to achieve equality between cis-gendered men and women (Bernstein 2012: 235).

Such an approach rested upon a belief that *all* women would benefit from an extension of the penal state and increased police surveillance powers, a contention that has been heavily criticised for solely promoting the interests of white, middle-class heterosexual women (Whalley and Hackett 2017: 457). To achieve its political objectives carceral feminism has increasingly been complicit with the more oppressive aspects of state power in (post)austerity Ireland. Funding cuts to voluntary organisations have forced mainstream feminist organisations into closer financially dependent relationships with the state. With regards to prostitution policy, ToRL's reliance on the criminal justice system to punish individual 'bad' men that purchase sex, while ignoring the myriad of social and economic structural disadvantages that force women and men into sex work was short-sighted.[6] Levy's (2015: 99–204) analysis of the sex purchase ban in Sweden, revealed how this carceral feminist approach contributed to the enforcement of migration policy, with police documents citing prostitution on migrant deportation papers, suggesting that not all women were protected by the legislation.

Secondly, ICI sought to provide advocacy leadership to support legislative change, commissioning research framed within a neo-abolitionist understanding. Their report, *Globalisation, Sex Trafficking and Prostitution*, published in 2009, rejected any distinction between prostitution and trafficking (ICI 2009: 1). Furthermore, it claimed that agency and choice were not relevant concepts and argued that one thousand women were working in prostitution each day in Ireland.

Thirdly, the ToRL campaign lobbied individual politicians and parties to bring independent motions for legislative change, upping the pressure on the government, which eventually forced it into a commitment to establish a review of prostitution policy (Ryan and Ward 2017: 52). The range of civil society organisations that had signed up to the ToRL campaign represented thousands of potential voters and increased political pressure on politicians more generally. Organisations and interested individuals received invitations to make written submissions to the Joint Committee on Justice, Defence and Equality (JCJDE). Subsequently, a number of them were asked to make presentations at an oral hearing. Ward has argued that even before the public consultation by the JCJDE had taken place, the political debate was in effect over. The main political parties accepted ToRL's definition of the problem and its preferred solution (Ward 2017: 87). This definition highlighted women's vulnerability to unscrupulous brothel owners, pimps, and traffickers. This rescue model was not extended beyond women 'victims'. In addition, men working in prostitution, even those working in brothels, were not included in the discourse of coercion and helplessness (Ryan 2019).

The dominance of the neo-abolitionist perspective led to an almost exclusive focus on the Nordic model of client criminalisation. Invitations were issued to civil servants from Sweden to give testimony before the JCJDE Committee. Policy alternatives such as the decriminalisation model favoured in New Zealand were neither presented nor discussed. Moreover, while the JCJDE embarked upon a fact-finding trip to Sweden the Committee choose not to visit or consult in any other European country or the wider world offering an alternative model of regulation of sex work (Ward 2017: 94). In the oral hearings, 13 out of the 15 groups that spoke supported the policy of client criminalisation, with organisations like the Irish Nurses and Midwives Organisation (INMO) conflating trafficking and voluntary economic migration in their presentation (FitzGerald and McGarry 2016: 299). Central to understanding how knowledge about the sex industry is constructed is the INMO assumption that no migrant woman from a developing country could give consent for her involvement in prostitution, in contradistinction to the 'voluntary' sex work of white, western women. Thus, the construction of gender knowledge, in this instance, is both classed and racialised. It is noteworthy that the INMO testimony and that of the Irish Medical Organisation (IMO) ran counter to the advice of global organisations like the World Health Organisation (WHO) and UNAIDS who advise member countries not to impose further criminalisation of sex work (FitzGerald and McGarry 2016: 296).

Unsurprisingly, the JCJDE recommended the introduction of client criminalisation, increased penalties for trafficking and making the act of accessing websites advertising prostitution illegal. The JCJDE specifically identified the testimony of prostitution survivors as persuasive evidence in constructing their final report. The passage of the *Criminal Law (Sexual Offences) Act 2017* saw the enactment of key JCJDE recommendations, including the criminalisation of the purchase of sex. The Act decriminalises the public solicitation of sex workers, but workers remain criminalised with increased penalties if they sell sex together under brothel-keeping laws and are also criminally liable under loitering laws.

FRAMING KNOWLEDGE ABOUT SEX WORK

Most testimony before the JCJDE Committee adapted a neo-abolitionist feminist frame, that is, a denial that prostitution can ever be a free choice (Barry 1995; O'Connor and Healy 2006). It is not suggested here that survivor testimonies of those coerced into prostitution should not be heard before parliamentary committees or in the wider public sphere. It is argued, however, that as social scientists we should be cognisant of the role power plays in how knowledge is produced; and how crucially 'the representation of people and problems' are used to legitimate certain types of knowledge (Doezema 2010: 10). The reliance on victimisation narratives may represent a convenient unitary truth to present to sympathetic policy makers about experiences within sex work; however, this approach conceals how individuals embody multiple identities that resist and negotiate experiences within wider structural contexts of labour migration, class, and family status. Such knowledge in turn supports specific constructions of women and ideas about male and female roles within the sex work industry.

Analysis of anti-trafficking campaigns in the United States suggests that the imperative to generate 'sympathetic visibility' for women also creates figures of pathos, to be identified, catalogued, and rescued (Hesford 2011:

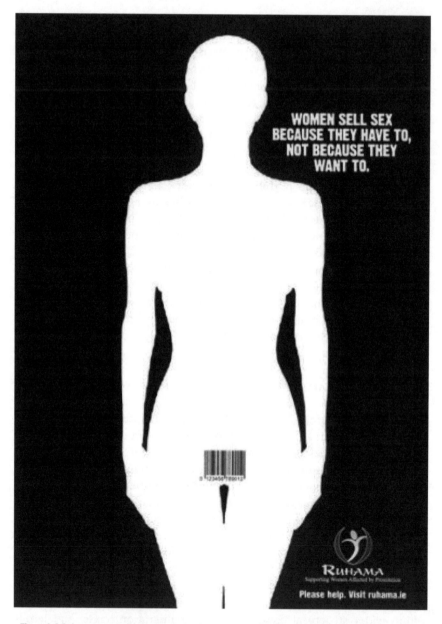

Figure 1.1 Ruhama's campaign poster of a faceless and speechless woman reduced to the barcode on her vagina denies the multiple other identities that sex workers carry throughout their lives.

130). The appeal of such campaigns centres on a unitary concept of *womanhood*. Regardless of whether consent has been given, prostitution diminishes *all* women to sexual objects. The testimonies of individual survivors reveal women to be dangerously naïve, passive victims of patriarchy who are susceptible to empty promises of a better life abroad (Hesford, 2011: 131). Anti-trafficking campaigns, particularly in the United States, are reminiscent of those conducted against 'white slavery' at the turn of the twentieth century when new waves of migration and accelerated urbanisation created fears for innocent young women duped into prostitution (Doezema 2010: 78). Stories of the sex industry reveal a distinction between forced and voluntary prostitution juxtaposing the passive, coerced migrant worker on the one hand, with the western sex worker, capable of exercising autonomy and agency, on the other (Doezema 1998: 40). These constructions also support specific forms of gender knowledge that 'other' sex workers as inevitably poor, vulnerable, and marginalised.

Andrijasevic and Mai (2016: 3) also suggest that the framing of the trafficking 'plot' never changes: deception, coercion into prostitution and then rescue by an NGO or the police. Such framing also legitimises criminalisation of both trafficked *and* non-trafficked people by a rescue industry aptly characterised as 'sexual humanitarianism' (2016: 2). Migrants working in prostitution are in turn forced to adopt these scripts of victimhood and exploitation to avoid imprisonment and deportation. While sex worker activists have attempted to re-negotiate these frames within a rights-based discourse about work, migration, and citizenship, the 'victim narrative' remains dominant (Jackson 2016).

INDIVIDUAL AND PUBLIC NARRATIVES OF SEX WORK

Individual and public narratives of sex work have gained increased visibility and importance as prostitution has become contested within parliaments and across wider society which serves to reminds us that storytelling 'becomes a creative political and symbolic strategy to bridge the macro and the micro'(Plummer 2017: 282). Narrative serves as a key conduit within which to construct new gender knowledge on sex work. Stories have a life cycle: they move from the solitude of the mind, to articulation to known others, to dissemination more widely into public discourse where they can coalesce with other stories that speak of a similar experience or event. Plummer's work on storytelling is adapted here to analyse the narrative power of stories about sex work. In particular, the intention is to problematise how we understand and represent prostitution in the political and public sphere. Plummer observed that a sexual confessional society has emerged in the late twentieth century, where there was both an innate need for the storyteller to tell their *truths* and an insatiable desire of media audiences to consume them. Gay and lesbian coming-out stories, rape and sexual abuse survivor stories and tales of sexual addiction, amongst others, represented a genre of recovery-tale narratives that demanded to be heard (Plummer 1995: 102). Three sets of actors are involved in this process: *storytellers* willing to share their lives and experiences, *coaxers* such as researchers, interviewers and documentary-makers who help to elicit them, and finally *consumers* who read, watch and interpret what is produced (ibid. 107). Stories are told within specific historical contexts that may encourage or impede their telling. The recovery-tale genre has adopted some habitual characteristics. The storyteller embarks upon a journey of self-discovery from often unspeakable suffering to finding an inner truth that enables a new *home* to be established, often alongside fellow survivors of the trauma endured (ibid. 107–08). There are parallels to the exposure of abuses and the campaign for justice for those incarcerated in Ireland's Magdalene laundries. Denied access to archival resources, religious orders and the state became gatekeepers of those experiences, making the survivor oral histories a powerful mechanism with which to seek redress (Yeager & Culleton 2016: 134–5; see also Crowe in the final chapter of this volume).

In more recent work, Plummer (2017) has incorporated the features of late modernity into his analysis of storytelling, arguing that the linear and unitary structure of the recovery-tale is of declining relevance in light of stories that will now be continually re-imagined and negotiated, where no essential truth is waiting to be discovered. The growing popularity of digital storytelling characterised by interactivity, non-linearity and flexible outcomes marks the advent of a new form of knowledge production (Barber 2016: 2). Digital storytelling, and the use of multi-media platforms to create and disseminate, has played a significant role in diversifying and democratising the voices in the public sphere (Poletti 2011: 73–4). Telling and listening to these digital stories creates the potential for wider engagement, because they have the potential to bring about the 'emancipation of large numbers of otherwise excluded (or neglected) . . . meaningfully challenging how knowledge is constituted, understood and disseminated through the media' (Poletti 2011: 80). While Plummer has alluded to a new digital future for late modern stories, he has not however provided clear examples of this emergent genre. To further explore, this chapter will now examine the transition to this new digital storytelling genre through the stories of two women who played high profile, opposing roles in the campaign to introduce a sex purchase ban in Ireland.

TWO SEX WORK STORIES: RACHEL MORAN AND KATE MCGREW

Rachel Moran was born in inner-city Dublin. Although she had written a blog on her experiences within the sex industry under a pseudonym between

2012–13[7] it was her appearance on the popular television chat show *The Late Late Show* to discuss her 2013 book, *Paid For*, that brought Moran into the public eye. The book told of Moran's personal experience, but it also told an explicitly political story. *Paid For* is a call to action for legislative change that claims to tell the universal experience of prostitution. Moran (2013: 292) directly asks the reader to respond indicating that she would 'take it as a personal favour if anyone reading this who wants to be supportive contacted their TDs and pressed their support for the "Turn Off The Red Light" campaign'. Moran's autobiography joined other evidence compiled by the ToRL campaign and proved influential in courting politicians and civil society leaders and organisations to support the campaign. Moran herself became a key spokesperson making many public appearances to lobby for the introduction of the sex purchase ban.

Moran's narrative identity hinged on the acquisition of a voice that had been denied. Moran writes (2013: 294) that she 'felt for the longest time like a woman screaming in a glass box where nobody can hear me. The book has been about shattering that box; it has been about giving voice to that scream'. Moran's story is very much in the tradition of the modernist recovery tale (Plummer 1995). It is a linear story. The subtitle – '*My Journey through Prostitution*' – presages a journey that moves from an abusive and neglectful childhood to sexual exploitation within the sex industry to a turning point that enables Moran to recast her identity as a prostitution survivor.[8] There are no steps backwards once the journey towards a new identity has begun. This is in direct contrast to the experience of many women in prostitution whose exit from sex work is likely to be discontinuous (NACD 2009: 133). Moran's journey starts with the 'realisation of urgent change' necessary for 'transitions (or recovery's) first step' (Moran 2013: 285). The book represents 'a journey where I do not want to go but must' (ibid.: 42); one motivated by the desire and imperative to speak the 'truth'. 'I *must* speak my truth,' she writes (ibid.: 275).

Moran is not the first woman to write about a life in prostitution in Ireland. Lyn Madden (Madden and Levine 1987) wrote her autobiography after testifying against her boyfriend and pimp, John Cullen. The latter murdered Dolores Lynch and two relatives by firebombing their house. Madden documents Dolores Lynch's life both in prostitution and her attempts to work with the Irish feminist movement in the late 1970s, which was divided on prostitution (1987: 27–30). Some wanted to abolish prostitution while others wanted to enact practical measures, like refuge centres, for women on the streets. The murder of Teresa Maguire in 1978 further galvanised the Irish feminist movement to protest violence against women and protect prostitutes. These campaign overtures of the 1970s, were incorporated into the recommendations of the Council for the Status of Women Report in 1993 (Ward 2010: 54).

It is both the timing and reception of *Paid For* that makes its contribution significant. Moran's story was published in the midst of a well-financed European wide political campaign for prostitution reform. There had been an increasingly transnational dimension to campaigns around prostitution policy; particularly since the mid-1990s. The UN Women's Conference in Beijing in 1995 and the UN anti-trafficking Palermo Protocol revealed extensive lobbying and contestation over terminology that set new normative frameworks. The European Parliament's Women's Rights and Gender and Equality Committee was also unequivocal in support for the neo-abolitionist framework as expressed in the findings of the Honeyball Report, which defined prostitution as a form of slavery and violence and recommended the Nordic model to all EU states). This recommendation came on foot of lobbying by both the Swedish Government and the European Women's Lobby (EWL) to Members of the European Parliament (MEPs) to support the eradication of prostitution as a perquisite to gender equality.

There was a receptive audience for Moran's story – conditions central to successful storytelling. It is a story that builds upon a long tradition of feminist autobiography. Feminist autobiography has brought a political dimension to storytelling in terms of what is remembered and what is forgotten, posing challenges to existing gender knowledge. Contributions range from feminist critiques of literary autobiography highlighting the absence of women's voices (Anderson and Broughton 1997) to demands for subjectivity to be built into research practice (Skeggs 1995). Central also is the extent of the credibility that is afforded the 'remembered'. As Cosslett et al. (2000: 5) point out 'the right to establish validity, authenticity or truth is never the storyteller's alone'. Moran's autobiography is written from authentic experience and from a specific second-wave feminist standpoint, articulated by women like Andrea Dworkin and Kathleen Barry (Harding 1986).

Moran (2013: 274) recognises that her story is located within the wider tradition of activism, writing that 'though certainly we were alone, there were non-prostituted others out there thinking of us and writing of us, I had no voice. I knew I had no voice; what I didn't know was there was a whole movement out there trying to speak *for* me'. Moran's story now takes a place within that very movement, forming in Plummer's (2017: 284) terms, a *narrative mobilisation and community-making*. This mobilisation is often political where individuals come together to find new communities of support, and new identities are reaffirmed. The collective intention of Moran's (2013: 9) book is clear as she states: 'I will detail my experience of it now, and you can believe that the stories of innumerable others are echoed within it.' Moran is a founding member of Space International (Survivors of Prostitution Abuse Calling for Enlightenment), an organisation that calls for the worldwide implementation of the Nordic sex purchase ban.[9] It has transformed Moran into an international expert on prostitution invited to speak at the United Nations and the European Parliament. Moran's gender expertise (see Hoard 2015: 21–2) and authoritative voice on prostitution policy is affirmed through both her personal testimony and her institutional links with bodies such as the European Women's Lobby.

Individual stories, like Moran's and her fellow survivors of prostitution now constitute what Plummer (2017: 284) describes as both *Public Narratives/ Private Narratives* that enter 'public arenas – governmental, digital – creating a culture of public problems'. The construction of those problems and their framing rests on the credibility of those making claims, and upon how media practices seek to portray them (Beckett 1996; Gamson and Modigliani 1989). The media portrayal of sex work is beyond the remit of this chapter. Suffice to say it has disproportionately used images of street work in the portrayal of sex work, although street work represents only about 10 percent of the commercial sex sector. The stories find new, louder voices in the world of celebrity humanitarianism where global bodies like the United Nations, the World Economic Forum, and national and international non-governmental organisations scramble to get endorsements for their campaigns (Repo and Yrjölä 2011: 45). Such campaigns often embody a 'white saviour complex' where privileged white protagonists seek to save hapless black or brown victims from misrule, tyranny, or environmental calamity, conveniently ignoring the normative assumptions and effects of neo-liberal global capitalism (2011: 53). Sex work, sex trafficking and the pathologisation of male clients within a neo-abolitionist framework have become popular celebrity causes.

Moran's story of prostitution was the focus of an RTÉ 2 documentary, *Paying for Sex: Reality Bites* in 2016, which followed Moran and sex worker Kate McGrew as both campaigned (on different sides) on the introduction of a sex purchase ban.[10] The documentary shows Moran's testimony in front of a committee of Northern Ireland (NI) Members of the Legislative Assembly (MLA) prior to the passage of the Democratic Unionist Party sponsored Morrow Bill that made NI the first part of the UK to outlaw the purchase of sex. Moran speaks of the abusive and disruptive childhood she suffered at the hands of her parents. They struggled to deal with mental health problems that would eventually lead to her father's suicide. This catalystic event forced Moran out of the family home and into homelessness and subsequently prostitution.

Government and parliamentary committees in Ireland relied heavily on personal testimonies as they mulled over the issue of prostitution law reform. It became clear which story about sex work carried the most credibility. In correspondence, the chairperson of the JCJDE David Stanton, states that the testimony of ex-sex workers was more compelling than that of current sex workers, because the former had no vested economic interest in the outcome (Ward 2017: 99). This suggests that the interests of the group most likely to be impacted by a change in the law were marginalised in the JCJDE considerations. Moran's story-telling – in the mass media and in the parliamentary hearings – was central therefore to the production of a particular gendered knowledge frame that relied heavily on a neo-abolitionist approach. This consolidation is the issue to which this chapter will now turn.

NARRATIVE HEGEMONY

Plummer (2017) writes that a *narrative hegemony and routinization* stage or moment of a life story occurs when the latter becomes routine and repetitive, and the key elements of the storyline are unchallenged. Readers are comfortable with such stories, knowing the genre and knowing how the story will end. They do not contain new evidence or plots that would cause the reader to re-evaluate key assumptions that underpin how the story is told. Moran's modernist story of prostitution survival is an example of testimony that has achieved unchallenged, hegemonic status. It is a testimony that has found resonance with an historic genre of survival and overcoming *and* a contemporary framing of prostitution as victimhood by national and transnational actors and institutions, from celebrities to parliaments. This consolidation was achieved and maintained through a campaign to de-legitimise or marginalise counter-narratives. Ward (2017: 87) argues that the power of the dominant narrative rested upon two strategies: firstly, the demonisation of alternative arguments as 'pimp thinking' and secondly, the power of 'victim scripts'. In terms of demonisation, I have previously written of the professional and personal costs to researchers of sex work and prostitution policy in communicating research findings that are counter to a neo-abolitionist approach (Ryan and Huschke 2017). Researchers who are committed to community-engaged research that reaches broader publics often struggle to communicate nuanced data findings. Moreover, they may experience exasperation or even hostility when they fail to produce *one* 'magic bullet' solution to the complex issue of prostitution or when they produce the 'wrong answer' (Ryan and Huschke 2017: 186–7). For instance, researchers investigating the extent and experience of prostitution for the Department of Justice in Northern Ireland were accused by MLAs during an oral evidence session in the Stormont Parliament of consorting with the 'pimp lobby' after they posted surveys on popular online escort sites (2017: 188).[11] Such experiences have a chilling effect on the research community and serve to dissuade engagement in the public sphere.

De-legitimising alternative stories of sex work served to bolster ToRL claims to be the sole authority that speaks the 'truth' of prostitution in Ireland. FitzGerald and McGarry (2016: 300) argue that de-legitimisation in the context of the JDCDE Committee extended to casting doubt on the testimony of sex workers opposed to client criminalisation. For instance, the ToRL campaign claimed that those providing such testimony could not be exercising choice and free will given their deprived backgrounds (2016: 301). In essence, *their* gender knowledge and testimony was called into question. Scientific 'expert' knowledge agents such as the INMO and IMO support client criminalisation and endorse the ToRL (FitzGerald and McGarry 2016: 296). The strategy of presenting individual stories of women within prostitution in a broader aspirational campaign focused on achieving greater gender equality was effective in unifying feminist activism around the ToRL campaign both in Ireland and in Europe. To oppose the campaign was coterminous with opposing gender equality itself. Moran (2013: 183) provides this contextualisation in her memoir:

> Prostitution clearly promotes the depersonalisation of sex, which can never be good news for women – any woman . . . When women tolerate prostitution, they are actually tolerating the dehumanisation of their own gender in a broader and more encompassing sense . . . If a woman tolerates this treatment of her fellow women, if she accepts it under the banner of 'liberalism' or anything else, then she must accept that she herself is only removed from prostitution by lack of the circumstances necessary to place her there . . . The acceptance of prostitution makes *all* women potential prostitutes in the public view

Finally, the dominant narrative excludes the perspective of male and trans sex workers from the client debate. Although accounting for 9 per cent of all sex work advertising in Ireland (Maginn and Ellison 2014) there was no place for stories that potentially could challenge the framing as one of men's entitlement to women's bodies. My own research on migrant sex male workers does indeed problematise this construction, particularly, the identification of victims and perpetrators. Men do not seek rescue from their involvement in commercial sex that they describe as transitory, ambiguous, and opportunistic (Ryan 2016; 2019). The lived realities and experiences of men engaged in sex work bears little resemblance to the accounts of survivors of prostitution that frame the legal and political debate.

NARRATIVE NEGOTIATION

Plummer (2017: 285) argues that out of well-rehearsed and routine stories, new ones emerge that challenge existing assumptions and understandings, forcing a re-negotiation. Stories have a life span – a birth, an institutional-isation and ultimately, a death. They are not therefore hegemonic but can be challenged, modified, and reinvented across time. The life and death of stories and the timing of when new dominant narratives emerge are intrin-sically linked to the framings offered by those who wield political and judicial power. In late modernity, digital communication presents an opportune power base for creating and disseminating alternative narratives. In the final section of this chapter it is argued that Kate McGrew's alternative story-telling represents such a re-negotiation of the dominant narrative surrounding sex work in Ireland. McGrew, born in Ohio, in the USA moved to Ireland in 2008. She has worked in the sex industry since she was 22 and has become the public face of *Sex Workers Alliance Ireland*: the group that campaigned to halt the introduction of the sex purchase ban. Like Moran, McGrew also takes an active role in the community-making that accompanies narrative mobilisation. She organises coffee mornings for sex workers and is a board member of the International Committee on the Rights of Sex Workers in Europe.[12]

McGrew has not written a book telling the story of her life. She tells her story to a wider public through a reality television show, TV and radio talk shows, and broadcast documentaries. Increasingly, she tells her story through her own content production using music and musical comedy performances. Here this content is drawn upon to explore McGrew's personal and political storytelling and the audience's reception.

Significantly, unlike Moran, McGrew grew up in a happy and stable family home, the daughter of a veterinarian and a gerontology professor. Her background enabled her to navigate through the sex industry in both New York and Ireland, exercising control over the conditions of her work; for example, the right to refuse certain clients. Given her relatively privileged background, McGrew faces the accusation that she is unrepresentative of workers within prostitution, and of promoting a myth of the 'happy and high-class hooker'. Moran (2013) dedicates an entire chapter to the refutation of the 'high-class hooker' thesis, claiming violence and degradation are also features of this element of the sex trade. McGrew responds stating that while violence may exist in any part of the industry, a sex purchase ban disproportionately affects the poorest and most vulnerable women in the industry who can exercise the least amount of control over their work. While her background affords her greater protection from stigma to speak openly, she is not immune to the risk of violence 'People consider us easy targets cause they know we are less likely to go the guards [Police].' she explains in the documentary *Paying for Sex*. Neither is McGrew insulated from the potential social opprobrium of 'coming-out' to her parents as a sex worker. In a scene from the reality television show *Connected* (RTÉ2 2014), McGrew nervously faces the camera and tells viewers:

> I am about to have a discussion with my mom telling her about the work that I do and I'm feeling really nervous. It makes me sad to think that she might be worried, and you don't want to upset your parents (*Connected*)

Figure 1.2 Sex worker Kate McGrew talking about telling her mother about her work on RTÉ2's *Connected* (2014)

In the documentary *Paying for Sex*, McGrew leaves the television studio after an appearance on the current affairs show *Claire Byrne Live* where she debated the sex purchase ban with Rachel Moran for the first time. She reads a SMS from her mother, who despite her misgivings about her daughter's life in sex work writes: 'I watched it live, I thought you did great in a really tough room, very proud of you.'

McGrew's middle-class background, and whether her story is representative or not, is important. The dominant framing of prostitution by neo-abolitionist campaigners has been to emphasise the deprivation, violence and control that push many women into the sex industry. Consent and choice are the prerogatives of a small minority they maintain. In fact, studies in the UK show that 25 per cent of students surveyed knew a student who had worked or was working in some aspect of the industry (Roberts et al., 2007). Similar findings in Australia (Lantz 2005) suggest that the social class profile of those within the sex industry is wider than traditionally thought. Changes in the funding of higher education that have shifted cost from the state to the family/individual has coincided with an increase in the number of university students working within the sex industry. In the UK, this increase is attributed to the debt burden now carried by students, but Sanders and Hardy (2015: 759) also argue that there has been a rise in the 'respectability' of sexual commerce. My own research with migrant male sex workers bears this out. Just over two-thirds of the 28 participants I interviewed were college-educated (Ryan 2016; 2019).

Irrespective of her background, McGrew is uncertain of a future outside of the sex work industry. In *Paying for Sex*, she said she would 'work as long as I have to, I mean what are the options . . . wait tables, go teach, write, knitting classes, I don't know. I really feel I have made the best choices for what I want in my life.' McGrew uses her work as a performing artist to communicate her reality as a sex worker. Moreover, she challenges audiences with *sex-positive feminism* that supports women's right to bodily autonomy while calling out forces of 'slut shaming' and 'whore' stigma in society. Her performances have a physicality beyond the spoken or sung word. She places the body centre stage – in both her work and her performances. Her rap *Hey Lady*, is an unapologetic call for solidarity among sex workers:

> In these meat-covered bones I'm a ghost and I drive it / hum and moan of our ghosts as they're colliding / my time imma sell it / take yours and do what /as long as you're happy I swear I couldn't give a fuck / abolitionists in this patriarchy go home / give women the power then leave us good and alone / cooperation has been forgotten lately / I'm a lady of the night / I don't need your saving (*Hey Lady*)

She calls upon patriarchal society and the rescue industry to relinquish control over women's bodies. McGrew believes that her writing and performances allow her a space to process her feelings, while providing a vehicle to challenge people's views around sexuality in a joyful and comedic way.[13] McGrew's lyrics provide a new form of 'presentational knowing' increasingly popular in the performing arts (Liamputtong & Rumbold 2008: 3). These new methodologies capture the diversity of experiences overlooked by the dominant, unitary narrative. This alternative and practical way of 'knowing' our research respondents, particularly in sex work research, holds the promise of, 'recasting the contents of experience into a form with the potential for challenging (sometimes deeply held) beliefs and values' (Barone 2001: 26). Sociologist and ethnographer Nick Mai has used film as a means to bring to life respondents' testimonies of trafficking and prostitution in films like

Samira (2013, 27 mins) and *Normal* (2012, 48 mins). Mai describes the process where he uses

> actors and ethno-fictional filmmaking to represent and reproduce both the process of knowledge production (research interviews and ethnographic observation) and the socio-anthropological truth of migrant sex workers' complex decisions and priorities, which deeply question humanitarian discourses (Mai 2016: 3).[14]

In the rap, *Sub Dentata,* McGrew confronts wider concerns about the treatment and surveillance of women's bodies, their life histories and slut shaming in rape trials. Her lyrics are visceral. McGrew appropriates a rights-based frame – the right to work and to work safely, but also to choose diverse work without having to publicly renounce sex work as inherently exploitative (Jackson 2016: 28). McGrew's anger mirrors campaigns against victim-blaming in sexual assaults trials (Stubbs Richardson et al. 2018) and feminist 'digilante' attempts to respond to the circulation of such allegations on social media (Jane 2017):

> Honour, one the night of April 3rd / she passed me by so delectable / you know what I thought she deserved? / I said oh no you can't have this priceless shit / I take back the night, I take back the day, I'll take your life while I'm at it / Pussy makes the world go round, order in court, we call a witness to the stand, exhibit A skirt so short / your honour as a man I'm a human animal . . . / I must have her, have her, have her / pussy makes the world go round . . . / kill your rapist the fucker is getting caught, kill your rapist your dick is getting tossed . . . kill your rapist / your honour let's look at this woman's history / objection your honour, what about her story / modern girl trips alone a long a twisted path / strength of character to carry on, now a lasting wrath / first second, then third wave feminism, nature v nurture, pop culture hypnotism (*Sub Dentata*)

McGrew presents rape not merely as an occupational hazard of sex work, but rather as a crime divorced from women's sexual histories. Moran (2013: 113) however, provides a diametrically opposite position, believing that every sexual encounter within her life in prostitution constituted rape, describing her work as 'being raped for a living'.

CONCLUSION

This chapter examined two competing genres of storytelling pertinent to the recent (successful) campaign to introduce a sex purchase ban in Ireland. The well-rehearsed, modernist genre of storytelling structured around suffering, turning point and redemption was most compelling to parliamentarians charged with regulating the sex industry. This 'gender knowledge' resonated closely with normative frames about sex work and prostitution policy at a transnational level in the European Union but also as filtered through key state actors within civil society. As a story, it is familiar to listeners, appeals to the notion of female sexual vulnerability, and promotes carceral solutions to protect, rescue and criminalise those who violate women. Rachel Moran's book is an exemplar of this type of storytelling. The almost exclusive focus on protection, rather than on wider contextual issues such as income distribution and migration reform, to deter women's entry into prostitution reflects the success of a gender knowledge frame that aligns closely with a patriarchal knowledge frame.

While stories have a 'life' – they also have a death. Moran's story has remained dominant within current debates about prostitution law reform, but it is a story that will be challenged, negotiated, and ultimately replaced. McGrew's story exemplifies the potential of narrative negotiation (Plummer 2017), to bring forward alternative stories that challenge the dominant narrative. The telling of this story is different. McGrew is part of a new wave of digital storytelling that uses a range of multi-media, by-passing traditional gatekeepers by providing accessible platforms to communicate stories previously denied an audience. These sex work stories are as nuanced and diverse as the means of communication. Migrants, mothers, trans, men, students, indoor/outdoor, online/real time, career, or opportunist – they all represent storytellers who increasingly defy both the definitions and genres imposed upon them. McGrew presents a version of herself as sex worker, but also a vision of herself as sex-positive feminist, a radically different casting from Moran's projection of victimhood and survival. McGrew ultimately rejects a carceral solution and calls on government to pursue a policy of decriminalisation that would provide both exit strategies and employment protections to women and men within the sex industry.

Notes

1   Carceral feminism relies on the criminalisation of perpetrators to end the violence against women but also with regards to prostitution, assuming the root causes are individual men rather than structural inequalities of income and race (Bernstein 2010 and Sweet 2016).

2   The so-called Swedish or Nordic model was first introduced in Sweden in 1999 and criminalised the purchase of sex while decriminalising sex workers. Advocates argue this 'end demand' approach has led to decreased violence against sex workers and lower levels of sex trafficking, claims that have been disputed by critics (Levy 2015). Norway, Iceland,

France, and Northern Ireland introduced similar legislation, before the Republic of Ireland followed in 2017.

3   RTÉ was forced to issue a statement justifying McGrew's inclusion in the show stating that 'the cast of *Connected* represent a diverse set of views on contemporary Irish life and the position and role of women in Ireland today . . . There is a strong public service argument for including Kate's story'. www.dailyedge.ie/everything-you-need-to-know-rte-2-connected-1684523-Sep2014

4   These acts concerned the 'protection of women and girls' and included laws against brothel keeping.

5   http://oireachtasdebates.oireachtas.ie/debates%20authoring/DebatesWebPack.nsf/takes/seanad1993062900006

6   It is worth noting that both Sweden and Norway recently stepped back from criminalising begging after international criticism. http://sverigesradio.se/sida/artikel.aspx?programid=2054&artikel=6155694

7   http://theprostitutionexperience.com

8   The concept of being a 'survivor' is a recurring theme in this genre e.g. Keogh, M. and J. Harrington, *Survivor: Memoirs of a Prostitute* (Gardners: Eastbourne, 2003).

9   http://www.spaceintl.org/

10   https://www.rte.ie/player/ie/show/paying-for-sex-reality-bites-30004286/10637341/?ap=1

11   https://www.justice-ni.gov.uk/sites/default/files/publications/doj/prostitution-report-nov-update.pdf

12   http://sexworkeurope.org

13   Personal communication.

14   https://vimeo.com/user3467382/about

REFERENCES

Anderson, L., and T. Broughton (eds), *Women's Lives/Women's Times: New Essays on Auto/Biography* (Prentice Hall: New York, 1997).

Andrijasevic, R. and N. Mai, '(2016) 'Editorial:Trafficking (in) representations'', special issue of the *Anti-Trafficking Review*, 7, 2016, pp 1–10.

Barber, J. F., 'Digital storytelling: New opportunities for humanities scholarship and pedagogy', in *Cogent Arts and Humanities*, 3(1), 2016, pp 1–14.

Barone, T., 'Science, art and the predisposition of educational researcher', in *Educational Researcher*, 30(7), 2001, pp 24–9.

Barry, K., *The Prostitution of Society* (NYU Press: New York, 1955).

Beckett, K., 'Culture and the politics of signification: The use of child sex abuse' in *Social Problems*, 43, 1996, pp 57 –76.

Bernstein, E., 'Militarized humanitarianism meets carceral feminism: The politics of sex, rights and freedom in contemporary anti-trafficking campaigns', in *Signs: Journal of Women in Culture and Society*, 36(1), 2001, pp 45–71.

Ibid., 'Carceral politics as gender justice?: The "traffic in women" and neo-liberal circuits of crime, sex and rights', in *Theory and Society*, 41(3), 2012, pp 233–59.

Connected 2013 [Reality Television] Dublin: RTÉ.

Cosslett, T., C. Lory and P. Summerfield (eds), *Feminism and Autobiography: Texts, Theories, Methods* (Routledge: London, 2000).

Doezema, J., *Sex Slaves and Discourse Masters: The Construction of Trafficking* (Zed: London, 2010).

FitzGerald S. and K. McGarry, 'Problematizing prostitution in law and polity in the Republic of Ireland: A case for reframing', in *Social and Legal Studies* 25(3), 2016, pp 289–309.

Gamson, W. and A. Modigliani, 'Media discourses and public opinion on nuclear power: A constructive approach', in *American Journal of Sociology*, 95, 1989, pp 1–37.

Harding, S., *The Science Question in Feminism* (Open University Press: Milton Keynes, 1986).

Hesford, W., *Spectacular Rhetorics: Human Rights Vision, Recognition and Feminism* (Duke University Press: Durham, 2011).

Hoard, S., *Gender Expertise in Public Policy: Towards a Theory of Policy Success* (Palgrave Macmillan: Houndsmill, 2015).

Immigrant Council of Ireland, *Globalisation, Sex Trafficking and Prostitution* (ICI: Dublin, 2009).

Jackson, C., 'Framing sex worker rights: How US sex worker rights activists perceive and respond to mainstream anti-sex trafficking advocacy', in *Sociological Perspectives*, 59(1), 2016, pp 27–45.

Jane, E. A., 'Feminist digilante responses to a slut-shaming on Facebook' in *Social Media and Society*, 3(2), 2017, pp 1–10.

King, R. and N. Mai, N., 'Love, sexuality and migration', in guest-edited special issue of *Mobilities*, 4(3), 2009, pp 1–10.

Lantz, S., 'Students working in the Melbourne sex industry: Education, human capital and the changing patterns of the youth labour market', in *Journal of Youth Studies*, 8(4), 2005, pp 385–401.

Levy, J., *Criminalising the Purchase of Sex: Lessons from Sweden* (Routledge: London, 2015).

Liamputtong, P. and J. Rumbold (eds), *Knowing Differently: Arts Based and Collaborative Research Methods* (Nova Science: New York, 2008).

Luddy Maria. *Prostitution and Irish Society 1800–1940* (CUP: Cambridge, 2007).

Madden, L. and J. Levine, *Lyn: A Story of Prostitution* (Attic Press: Cork, 1987).

Maginn, P. & G. Ellison, 'Male sex work in the Irish Republic and Northern Ireland', in V. Minichiello & J. Scott (eds), *Male Sex Work & Society* (Harrington Park Press: New York, 2014), pp 426–61.

Mai, N., '"Too much suffering": Understanding the interplay between migration, bounded exploitation and trafficking through Nigerian sex workers' experiences', in *Sociological Research Online* 21(4), 2016, p. 13.

Moran, R., *Paid For: My Journey Through Prostitution* (Gill and Macmillan: Dublin, 2013).

National Advisory Committee on Drugs, *Drug Use, Sex Work, and the Risk Environment* (NACD: Dublin, 2009).

O'Connor, Monica and Grainne Healy, *The Links between Prostitution and Sex Trafficking: A Briefing Handbook* (CATW/European Women's Lobby: Dublin, 2006).

Paying for Sex: Reality Bites 2016 [Documentary] RTÉ.

Plummer, K., 'Telling sexual stories in a late modern world', in *Studies in Symbolic Interactionism*, 18, 1995, pp 1,012–120.

Ibid., 'Narrative power, sexual stories and the politics of story telling' in I. Goodson (ed.), *The International Handbook on Life History and Narratives* (Routledge: Abingdon, 2017), pp 280–92.

Poletti, A., 'Coaxing an intimate sphere: Life narrative in digital story telling', in *Journal of Media & Cultural Studies*, 25(1), 2011, pp 73–83.

Repo, J. and Yrjölä, R. 'The Gender Politics of Celebrity Humanitarianism in Africa', in *International Feminist Journal of Politics*, Vol 13 (1) 2011: 44-62

Roberts, R., S. Bergstrom and D. La Rooy, 'Sex work and students: An exploratory study', in *Journal of Further and Higher Education*, 31(4), 2007, pp 323–34.

Ryan, P. 'Researching Irish gay male lives: Reflections on disclosure and intellectual autobiography in the production of personal narratives', in *Qualitative Research*, 6(2), 2006 pp 151–68.

Ibid., '#Follow: Exploring the role of social media in the online construction of male sex workers lives in Dublin, Ireland', in *Gender, Place and Culture*, 23(12), 2016, pp 1,713–24.

Ibid., *Male Sex Work in the Digital Age: Curated Lives* (Palgrave: London, 2019).

Ryan, P. and S. Huschke, 'Conducting sex work research in a politically contentious climate: Lessons from Ireland', in I. Crowhurst, A. King & A. C. Santos (eds), *Sexuality Research: Critical Interjections, Diverse Methodologies and Practical Applications* (Routledge: London, 2017), pp 182–95.

Ryan, P. and E. Ward, 'Ireland', in S. O. Jahnsen and H. Wagenaar (eds), *Assessing Prostitution Policies in Europe* (Routledge: London, 2017), pp 47–61.

Sanders, T., and K. Hardy, 'Students selling sex: Marketisation, higher education and consumption', in *British Journal of the Sociology of Education*, 36(5), 2013, pp 747–65.

Skeggs, B., *Feminist Cultural Theory: Process and Production* (Manchester University Press: Manchester, 1995).

Smith, J. M., *Ireland's Magdalen Laundries and the Nation's Architecture of Containment* (Manchester University Press: Manchester, 2007).

Stubbs Richardson, M., N. E. Rader, and A. G. Cosby, 'Tweeting rape culture: Examining portrayals of victim blaming of sexual assaults on Twitter', in *Feminism & Psychology*, 28(1), 2018, pp 90–108.

Ward, E., 'Prostitution and the Irish State: From prohibitionism to a globalised sex trade', in *Irish Political Studies*, 25(1), 2017, pp 47–66.

Ibid., 'The Irish parliament and prostitution law reform: A neo-abolitionist shoe-in?' in E. Ward and G. Wylie (eds), *Feminism, Prostitution, and the State: The Politics of Neo-Abolitionism* (Routledge: London, 2017), pp 86–102.

Whalley, E., and C. Hackett, 'Carceral feminisms: The abolitionist project and undoing dominant feminisms', in *Contemporary Justice Review*, 20(4), 2017, pp 456–73.

Yeager, J., and J. Culleton, 'Gendered violence and cultural forgetting: The case of the Irish Magdalenes', in *Radical History Review*, 126, 2016, pp 134–46.

EIGHT

Gendering Irish Homelessness: Policy Knowledge through Participatory Action Research

Rory Hearne and Mary P. Murphy

INTRODUCTION

Sometimes silence can be a tool of oppression; when you are silenced . . . it is not simply that you do not speak but that you are barred from participation in a conversation which nevertheless involves you (Ahmed 2010: xvi)

This chapter explores the gendered construction of social problems through the lens of a research project that sought to co-construct, with homeless lone parents, new gendered knowledge about family homelessness in Dublin city, Ireland. As such it genders a very salient contemporary social issue in Ireland and beyond. It draws on findings from research that was undertaken by the authors working directly with a group of homeless families in emergency accommodation in Dublin.[1] To gather data we used a Participatory Action Human Rights and Capability Approach (PAHRCA). This case study forms part of the H2020 funded ReInvest project, a multi-national study across 13 EU countries addressing the need to repair the social damage of the crisis through enhanced social investment. The research sought to strengthen arguments for social investment and the EU approach by adding human rights and capability dimensions to policy areas including labour market, early childhood care and education, financial services, housing, health and water policies. The specific case study addressed in this essay was undertaken in 2017.

At both EU and Irish levels, homelessness research and policy analysis continually fails to engage with the distinctly gendered experiences of homelessness and related issues (Mayock 2017). This is the case despite the growing efforts to develop gendered analysis by some researchers, and the existence of relatively long-standing demands for greater use of critical and feminist theory in homelessness research (Edwards et al. 1977; Milburn & D'Ercole 1991; Neale 1997; Savage 2016). Such an analysis is particularly necessary in the Irish context given that in the Dublin region, women comprise 47 per cent of the total adult homeless population, compared to 20 per cent –33 per cent amongst the homeless population across Europe (Mayock 2015; 2017).

Homelessness research has tended to treat structural economic and power inequalities as technical malfunctions of an otherwise unproblematic capitalism (Farrugia and Gerrard 2016; Flint 2003). We believe that any analysis of homelessness must take due cognisance of wider political economy and power structures. In the case study presented here, women's lived exper-ience and experiential knowledge of homelessness is explored. The focus is on creating new, bottom-up gendered understandings of the issue (Harding 2004). Nested within a political economy approach to housing markets and contextualised in a broader analysis of gender and the welfare state, these wider gendered forms of knowledge draw attention to structural gendered features of male breadwinner welfare systems (Crompton 1999; Lewis 2001). These prefigure deeply gendered systems of social reproduction which leave women more vulnerable to poverty, inequality and deprivation.

Ireland's strong male breadwinner regime sets the context for much of twenty-first century Irish social policy (Murphy 2003). Lynch (2009) refers to care 'less' states where gendered systems of social reproduction or welfare also intersect with wider gendered structural inequalities in markets parti-cularly, as relevant to this case, in housing markets and labour markets. Savage, writing about homelessness and gender in an Irish context, stresses the need to recognise 'the importance of the affective domain as a key site for understanding and analysing the multiple inequalities that shape women's experiences of homelessness' (2016: 43).

We understand gender knowledge as an analytical concept 'that can be used as a framework to identify explicit and implicit assumptions or concep-tions concerning gender and gender relations, and the norms which support them' (Cavaghan 2010: 18). Such knowledge bridges macro-level approaches to gender equality policy analysis and micro-level investigations of implemen-tation (Cavaghan 2010). Moreover, it can be operationalised at macropolitical economy levels as well as in more local site-specific research, and crucially can link these two levels.

In this chapter we explore the experience of a specific research process as a space for learning and action (Kemmis & Wilkinson 1998) which enabled academic researchers, peer researchers, NGOs, and people directly experiencing homelessness to co-construct new gendered knowledge about the experiences of homeless families. The study critically investigates the impact on women of new social housing and homeless policies predicated on the marketisation of social investment. In particular, we focus on private rental subsidies and new forms of emergency accommodation for homeless families, known as Family Hubs. We identify how a specific gendered construction of knowledge can illuminate policies and practices that produce distinctly gendered experiences (Lynch 1989).

The chapter is divided into five sections: Section 1 sets the policy context for the research by outlining the recent homelessness crisis. Section 2 provides a general discussion of Participatory Action Research and co-construction of gendered knowledge. Section 3 introduces the PAHRCA methodological approach and the research methods. In Section 4 the new gendered knowledge co-constructed in the PAHRCA process is presented and, finally, Section 5 provides a discussion of PAHRCA outcomes and limitations. In conclusion, the implications of this form of research for the gendering of knowledge about social problems and understandings of social vulnerability, as well as the experience of the research process itself are reflected on.

MARKETISATION AND AUSTERITY
THE GENDERED IMPACTS OF CONTEMPORARY IRISH HOUSING POLICY

The Irish State traditionally played a central role in the provision of state-supported, socialised home ownership with a 'protected' social complement to the general housing market. Recent decades saw a significant disinvestment from direct build social housing and a parallel shift towards the marketisation of social housing delivery. Over the period of austerity that followed the 2008 financial crash, reliance on the market led to a reliance on private rental subsidies to house families in housing need. This culminated in 2014 with the introduction of a means-tested rental subsidy paid to private landlords to house low-income social housing tenants, the Housing Assistance Payment (HAP). By 2016, HAP was the primary vehicle for the delivery of new social housing for people in need of a home in Ireland. These policy trends, combined with legacy issues related to the housing crash and the ease of evictions within the private rental sector in Ireland,[2] resulted in a new phase of the Irish housing crisis marked from 2014 by a dramatic increase in homelessness (particularly in Dublin).

The number of homeless individuals in emergency accommodation tripled nationally from 3,226 in July 2014 to over 9,000 by early 2018. In this same period in Dublin, where 78 per cent of homeless families are located, there was a four-fold increase in the number of homeless families living in commercial hotels and Bed and Breakfast (B&B) emergency accommodation (DRHE 2017). 67 per cent of these families are headed by lone parents (of which 86 per cent are women) while 65 per cent are Irish. The majority are made homeless from the private rental sector (Hearne and Murphy 2017). The high level of representation of lone parents within homeless families[3] reflects the wider gender bias implicit in many of the policies pursued during the period of austerity which followed the financial crash in 2008 (Barry and Conroy 2014). Lone parents suffered particularly harsh cuts to social supports and were the primary target of new workfare policies. The increase in the percentage of families suffering consistent poverty disproportionately affected female-headed households who also experienced significant material depriv-ation in the five-year period 2010–15.[4]

In early 2017, the government approved the creation of a new type of emergency accommodation for homeless families, the Family Hub. These Hubs, the Dublin Regional Housing Executive argued, would be a better alternative to hotels and Bed & Breakfast accommodation as they would offer 'family-focussed facilities to provide better short-term accommodation solutions for families' (DRHE 2017: 3). The Hubs were provided in a variety of refurbished buildings including former religious institutions such as Magdalene laundries, convents, warehouses, retail units and hotels. By February 2018 17 Family Hub facilities were operational in the Dublin region providing emergency accommodation for 437 families. One Hub housed 98 families, another 50, with others ranging from 40 to 12 families (Dublin City Council 2017). The Hubs not only provide an immediate practical solution, but also play an important role in legitimating government and market failure. The idea of a Family Hub emerged from the NGO sector who had initiated the first pilot Family Hub, and from collaboration between national state policy actors and regional and local authorities. The actual term 'Family Hub' has been deconstructed effectively by Mayock (2017), who highlights the intentional feminine imagery in the language of a 'family hub'. It is evoked as a positive, warm, central place in a home – revolving around the care of the mother. The name itself – family hub – is, therefore, a gendered construct that on one level is trying to de-stigmatise the centres, but may also be read as an attempt to hide its reality, to try and undermine and downplay the actual or potentially harmful nature of these emergency accommodation centres.

It is clear the policy was largely a pragmatic and practical response, and that it met an urgent need to address statutory child protection obligations. However, Family Hubs also appealed to underlying paternalistic assump-tions that homeless families need therapeutic supports. An underlying gendered assumption is that, even with increased housing supply, a minority of families, predominantly female-headed, will remain vulnerable to homelessness regardless of the housing market. This contradicts the parallel commitment of government to 'housing first' responses to homelessness.

Policy responses to homelessness systematically fail to meet women's needs and, as a consequence, trap them in circumstances that exacerbate their vulnerability and dependency, (Mayock 2017). Moreover, a gender-blind policy process masks the depth of inequality and affective injustices experienced by homeless women with children (Savage 2016). Over the period of devising, implementing, and reviewing the government's landmark housing plan *Rebuilding Ireland* (Government of Ireland 2016), there was no formal gendered analysis of homelessness policy, no gendered disaggregation of homeless data or social housing waiting lists, and no gender proofing of policy or practice (Murphy 2017). In addition, there was no response to the calls made by NGOs such as Women's Aid and Safe Ireland to include women in refuges within the official homelessness statistics, nor an effort made to more fully incorporate analysis of domestic violence as a cause of homelessness (IHREC 2017). Homeless policy in the Irish context remains ignorant of specific, gendered policy impacts. Yet it is not gender blind, as it is informed by deeply gendered and often implicit assumptions and biases about women. Our approach complements Savage's (2016) comprehensive examination of how official definitions and policy analysis of homelessness denies gendered experiences. We draw on experiences of homeless mothers, and in the process develop a more gender-sensitive knowledge of family homelessness.

PARTICIPATORY ACTION RESEARCH AND NEW KNOWLEDGE CREATION

Our methodology is based on Participatory Action Research (PAR), a social process whereby people actively engage in, examine, and interpret their own social world and shape their sense of identity as part of social science investigative work. As a process, in common with feminist methodology, it is closely related to experiential learning and to transformation (Byrne and Lentin 2000) and is concerned with an approach to knowledge production that promotes democratic social relations (Harding and Norberg 2005). While not explicitly focused on gender relations it is consistent with feminism in that it recognises that tackling gender oppression and promoting gender equality is at the heart of human rights. Like feminist standpoint theory PAR seeks to politicise research. From a qualitative research methods perspective, it goes beyond understanding to taking constructive action to ameliorate difficult, often oppressive, situations (Olshansky 2005). As an emancipatory process it seeks to enable people to both challenge and remove themselves from unjust social structures that limit their self-development and self-determination (Kemmis and Wilkinson 1998: 24).

PAR respects the universal right to participate in the production of knowledge and, while not necessarily feminist in approach, it is a method-ology particularly sympathetic to a feminist sensibility grounded in often chaotic and confusing lived experiences and realities (Harding 1997). Feminist critiques of conventional research emphasise the mining of data as an extrac-tive process and argue instead for more egalitarian and reciprocal meaning-making approaches that situate the researcher as a facilitator in an active relationship that leads to empowerment for participants (Oakley 1981). In PAR, researchers work collaboratively with the 'researched' in an effort to achieve social justice in the form of improved conditions. Rather than con-ducting a study 'on' a group of people, it is research 'with a group of people'. PAR 'commits to identifying and challenging unequal power relations within its process. It is rooted in dialogue attempting to work with, not on, people . . . it is committed to collective action for social change as its outcome' (Ledwith 2007: 599).

Feminist research methods offer guidance when understanding pro-cesses of gender knowledge production. Creswell (2013: 182) argues that researchers need to be self-aware about how all inquiry is laden with values. As Harding and Norberg (2005) and Smith (1990) also note social science research is not culture-free or value-free. Baker et al. (2004) advise of the gulf between predominantly middle-class academics and marginalised communities, and the requirement for researchers to be particularly reflective in this regard. A feminist approach locates the personal as political connecting the every-day lived reality to its profoundly structural and political contexts. But this in itself is not enough. In other words, researchers need to minimise the power differences between researchers and the disadvantaged groups that remain the objects of their study (Harding and Norberg 2005). The next section explores the Participatory Action Human Rights and Capability Approach (PAHRCA), the methodological frame-work used to guide the research discussed in this chapter.

THE PARTICIPATORY ACTION HUMAN RIGHTS AND CAPABILITY APPROACH

PAHRCA is a form of PAR which was used across the 13 countries in the ReInvest project to co-create new knowledge through mutual understanding and collaboration between vulnerable groups, researchers and policy makers. ReInvest is a H2020 funded research project focused on enhancing the European Social Investment Package through a human rights and capabilities approach. Our innovative methodological framework, PAHRCA, combined three theoretical approaches to enable a co-investigation of how austerity and marketisation policy impacted on the rights and capabilities of vulnerable groups. The PAHRCA methodology was primarily conceptualised through human rights and capability approaches using co-construction of knowledge to develop a particular model of PAR. While feminist principles did not explicitly inform its development, they did inform the implementation of PAHRCA in the Irish context. Capability approaches contribute to a PAR framework by providing a comprehensive and flexible theory of well-being and justice that captures the multiple, complex and dynamic aspects of poverty. Nussbaum (2011) defines a person's well-being in terms of 'what a person can do' to lead a life one values and has reason to value. She directly links human rights and capabilities through ten 'central capabilities'. Human Rights-Based Approaches promote principles of voice, accountability and participation. This approach has been developed in the Participation and Practice of Rights project based in Belfast and also implemented by Community Action Network in Dublin based projects (Hearne & Kenna 2014). The 'co-construction' of knowledge, as reflected in the Merging of Knowledge approach developed by the International Movement ATD Fourth World understands knowledge as constructed from three parts: scientific knowledge of academics and researchers; experiential knowledge of poverty and exclusion; and the knowledge of those who work among and with the vulnerable in places of poverty and social exclusion, (Godinot 2006).

PAHRCA revolved around five flexible steps involving an iterative and ongoing process of action, knowledge creation and reflection (Murphy & Hearne 2019). PAHRCA proved particularly useful for investigating the experiences of disadvantaged homeless women in Ireland. The co-construction of knowledge process offered an opportunity to understand better the gaps between women's experiences of specific forms of social exclusion, and the explicit and implicit knowledge about gender that informs policy responses. Drawing out implicit gendered assumptions illuminated reasons for policy contradictions and underlying tensions in policy discourses.

The Irish research was undertaken by the authors (one male and one female). We worked in a collaborative partnership with housing NGOs, three peer researchers (two female and one male who had experiential knowledge of homelessness and who are tenants of an Irish housing NGO), and with ten homeless families living in a Family Hub emergency accommodation in Dublin. Baker (et al 2004) challenges the researcher to be reflexive, while Harding (2004) insists we have to be aware of ourselves as oppressors. Gill

(2017) encourages us to be less silent about the conditions in which research is produced, our experiences as 'knowledge workers', and our labouring subjectivities. We are both middle-class academics with applied research backgrounds in community-based anti-poverty and housing campaigns. We work broadly within the 'scholar-activist'[5] tradition and are 'pracademics' who cross policy and academic worlds.[6] The research proved challenging for us as researchers, confronting our own biases and motivations, forcing us to re-examine notions of empowerment and to question the boundaries of our own commitment to this form of research. We found we had different levels of ambition for the contribution the research might, or could, make to empowerment, and had to adjust our different levels of expectations about what might be achieved. As middle-class academics we had to 'check our privilege' and we were challenged to do so by participants and peer researchers. Our own gender also influenced the process of research, as did the gender of the peer research team and research participants.

To protect the anonymity of our participants we are limited in our description of the particular Family Hub which served as the site for this research. Adapted from its previous institutional purpose, the Hub houses 29 families in small bedrooms. Families are required to share a kitchen, toilet and laundry facilities with up to four other families and can eat dinner daily in a large communal dining room. The research meetings took place in the mornings in the children's playroom in the Family Hub. The families stay in the Hub on a six month 'licence' with their stay contingent on them actively seeking HAP accommodation. They are supported in their search for this accommodation by key workers who, in this instance, are also responsible for the day-to-day management of the Hub. The ten participant families were all female-headed with the adult aged under 35 (nine were lone parents; seven were of Irish origin; and three were migrants). All were parents of young children ranging in age from six months to 13 years of age. The two female peer researchers played an important role in relationship-building with the families. Formerly homeless themselves, the peer researchers chatted informally with the families before and during the sessions. They explained to them the various aspects of the sessions in non-academic language, thus enabling the families to feel comfortable and to engage fully in the sessions. The peer researchers were involved in the analysis, drafting and dissemination stages of the research. The research team worked with the families over twelve weeks. Having met the partner NGO and having made a partnership agreement, we had preliminary 'meet ups' with the homeless family participants followed by trust building and then developmental work concerning human rights and capability approaches. We then began the inquiry and data gathering stage jointly identifying patterns and findings. The final stage was to undertake an action/outcome. A weekly group session was held on ten occasions. The approach was a pre-figurative form of developmental socialisation – where the capacity of both peer researchers and families was enhanced in a collaborative way using trust-building exercises information sessions, discussions, role play, and drawing. The final 'action' session constituted a 'dialogue' with senior policy makers, an elected member of the national parliament, and the Chief Commissioner of the Irish Human Rights and Equality Commission (IHREC).

NEW GENDERED KNOWLEDGE CO-CONSTRUCTED THROUGH PAHRCA

This section discusses new gendered knowledge co-constructed through the PAHRCA. Overall, our findings provide evidence for Mayock's (2017) argument that homeless policy and practice tends to infantilise homeless single women. The added-value of the research is in the additional knowledge that we generated (through co-investigation) of the lived experience of mothers and their families and how they are impacted by the two core policy initiatives: the Housing Assistant Payment (HAP) and Family Hubs. We detail six key findings below.

Marketisation, Structural Exclusion, Stigmatisation and Responsibilisation
A gendered analysis of the impacts of marketisation of social housing generated knowledge of how the HAP scheme transfers the responsibility from statutory local authorities onto individual families to source social housing through the private rental sector. The transfer of responsibility for policy and market failure on to families (who are already vulnerable) worsens their sense of shame and stigma leading to an internalisation (private trouble) of market failure (public issue), (Mills, 1959). The underlying assumptions of policy makers include a sense that success in achieving a HAP rental tenancy is the outcome of individual motivation. However, the research revealed that families experience *structural exclusion* from the private rental market in Dublin, which, regardless of their motivation, results in a denial of their capacity to action their right to access housing. In the quote below a mother describes her lived experience of competing in the tight rental market against professionals with work references. The mother describes double stigmatisation, or intersectional inequality, discriminated against both for being homeless *and* a single mother: She explained:

> I have been in the Family Hub for six months and I have had no replies to emails from landlords. The agencies and landlords keep asking for work references and past landlord references. But we don't have that. They say they don't take children

and they don't allow children in the house. When I tell them that I am a single mom – they say the viewing list is full.

Policy makers underestimate how inequalities inherent in the private market are operationalised in social housing through HAP. They also under-estimate the severe negative impacts on families' mental health arising from feelings of rejection and an implied 'failure' to secure HAP accommodation. Structural gender, class and racial inequalities weaken capabilities while the rental market reinforces gendered assumptions about the ideal tenant. Responsibilisation – the placing of responsibility and blame squarely on the individual – is a key feature of neo-liberalisation in social policy causing individuals to internalise market failures and inequalities (Brown 2015). While not an inherently gendered process there are gendered dimensions to how this process impacts the individual. In this case, it deeply affected the mothers, undermining their core identity as providers of fundamental needs for their children – most particularly a secure home. The experience also disempowers the affected group as it contributes to a reluctance to speak publicly about issues they have now internalised as their 'own fault'.

Marketisation and Insecurity of Tenure

The operation of the HAP scheme undermines the human right to housing by eroding the degree of 'security of tenure' traditionally associated with life-long tenancy within the social housing sector. Families used participa-tive art to describe key aspects of 'the right to a home' which centred on security, stability, safety and freedom and, in their view, these could only be provided through long-term, secure, accommodation. Our research generated insights into how ontological security and well-being is threatened by the prospect of continued housing loss, particularly for homeless female-headed families, who are determined to protect their children from the (re)trauma-tising impact of homelessness. Structural vulnerability is gendered. Women experience different thresholds of responsibility for dependents, and as such face greater challenges in adapting to the insecurity and turnover associated with the HAP-led policy prescription. The families' preference for traditional (local authority or housing association social housing) is understood as the only mechanism to provide a long-term secure home for their children. The absence of consideration of tenure insecurity in the conceptualisation and implementation of HAP by policy makers contrasts sharply to, and is in tension with, its centrality as a core concern of mothers wishing to provide adequate accommodation for their children.

Gendered Moral Rationality

Duncan (2003) discusses the 'moral economy' involved in reconciling parenting and paid work and warns of a 'rationality mistake' evident in policy rhetoric. Policy underestimates the degree to which people are emotional, affective beings, and policy makers underestimate the degree to which mothers' decisions are mediated primarily by childcare responsibilities: parental responsibility is prioritised over financial gain. Rationality mistakes can also be made in assumptions concerning how mothers negotiate housing and the reality of care means different financial, practical and emotional starting points. As the quote below demonstrates, the child's need for security is at the centre of the women's approach to housing:

> I don't want to keep moving my daughter around all the time . . . and then I'm afraid that I will end back up in the homeless services again after my lease is up . . . I would take HAP if I was guaranteed to be able to stay in the accommodation for a five-year lease or whatever, and that I would be guaranteed somewhere else after that lease was up . . . once it's not back to the homeless services. I will not keep putting my daughter through the same situation – it's not fair on her.

We see how the well-being of their children is the primary concern that determines women's decision-making processes in relation to housing and employment. To this end, female-headed families in the study prioritise living near vital existing family and community supports. If we understand decision making from this gendered knowledge standpoint, it challenges alternative explanations which suggest a more rational actor motivation for homelessness. Gendered moral rationales also explain some families' reluctance to take up HAP accommodation even if it means spending a longer time in emergency accommodation. Policy makers struggle to understand why families refuse HAP accommodation while waiting for a 'council house'. The data gathered in this research provides an explanation. Parents identify how they view housing appropriateness and adequacy through the eyes of their children's requirement for normality, stability, safety, security and connection. Some rationally determine that it is better to trade a longer wait in emergency homelessness against the likelihood of achieving longer-term security through the allocation of a traditional social housing unit. To reject HAP on the grounds that it does not offer the requisite security does not imply, as some policy makers and commentators have suggested, a pursuit of a strategy of 'gaming the system'. Rather, it demonstrates the degree to which people in vulnerable situations are emotional, affective beings and the extent to which a 'gendered morality' places parenting, care and children's needs at the centre of decision making.

Cumulative Disadvantage

Our research demonstrates how vulnerable women and their children are at the receiving end of multiple policy failures; job loss during the economic crisis; social welfare cuts as a result of austerity; the marketisation of social housing; housing precarity and homelessness. In the absence of holistic policy making, gender-proofing of policy, and the meaningful participation of lone parents (and other vulnerable groups) in the policy process, there is little regard paid to how housing policy is experienced in the context of wider gendered impacts of austerity. The social right to permanent 'housing for life' for low income households in Ireland has, in recent decades, shifted to social housing as a temporary 'support'. Current housing policy, rather than protecting families from market failure, further exposes them to the social violence and inequalities of both austerity and of the private market, both of which are experienced in a gendered way. One highly gendered experience is the exposure of homeless female-headed families to new versions of older (now discredited) policies of institutionalisation – emergency accommodation in Family Hubs: the subject of the next section.

Family Hubs as an Instance of 'Therapeutic Incarceration'

Family Hubs are promoted by policy makers and government as preferable to emergency accommodation in hotels and Bed & Breakfasts. The public image of the Family Hub as a positive one is actively reinforced through energetic public relations, including launches, press releases and promotional videos that seek to reassure that Family Hubs are a positive policy development. However, the PAHRCA methodology involving multiple visits with the families and the creation of a 'safe' space for families to express their views, enabled an alternative gendered knowledge to emerge beyond the superficial analysis garnered from site visits and guided tours. The gendered knowledge uncovered through the participatory research revealed the extremely difficult realities of day-to-day living in emergency accommodation. This, we argue, amounts to a new form of institutionalisation of poor mothers and their children, restricting their ability to live a normal life and producing developmental regression in children. The tensions posed by implementing child protection guidelines in the context of communal living require a range of restrictions which limit capacity to parent. Living conditions and parenting style and behaviour is monitored by staff. Strict curfews are in place; there is no accommodation of visitors in any part of the building; there are overnight leave rules; and there are restrictions on movement (a ban on being in others bedrooms) and parental rules (including a ban on holding and/or minding each other's children). This leads to mothers questioning their worth as parents – the core element of maternal identity. This is evident in the various quotes below as the mothers explained how the policies and rules in the homeless institutions created specific gendered experiences of homelessness which undermined and disempowered mothers. Gerstal et al. (1996) used the term 'therapeutic incarceration' to describe the move of voluntary homelessness agencies into service-intensive programmes with unintended consequences for the personal autonomy of homeless residents. At their worst, Family Hubs have the potential to replicate forms of 'therapeutic incarceration' operating akin to a prison-like regime that destroys personal autonomy. Issues of auton-omy, hidden conditionality and surveillance are common in analysis of various types of institutional care settings and welfare policy (activation, prisons, elder care and also homeless services).

Mothers described the undermining of their role and capacity to parent as a key factor leading to feelings of depression and low esteem. In keeping with Mayock's (2017) finding of the infantilisation of female residents in homeless shelters, mothers in the Family Hub where we conducted the research, reported feeling 'demeaned' and 'spoken down to', 'like a child', 'in school' and being 'in prison'.

> 'I got a warning, its feels like an institution instead of a home . . . .'
> 'We don't need our authority taken away from in front of our children . . .'
> 'They are taking the parenting role off the parent . . .'
> 'When someone speaks down to you like this you feel you are on the bottom'

The consequences for physical and mental health included increased use of anti-depressants and other prescription medications. The experiential knowledge helped researchers and participants to co-construct a new understanding of Family Hubs, one that linked them to the persistence of deeply held gendered beliefs about the supposed deficiencies of poor mothers, and to practices of policing women.

Co-Construction of Alternative Policy Solutions

Through the research process the families developed a number of concrete alternative policy proposals to realise the right to housing for homeless families. The families contrasted the significant budgets government spent building Family Hubs and renting hotels with the insufficient investment in building new social housing. Further, they believed that there was a bias on the part of government against social housing: 'because they see that's where all the social problems come from'; they also believed that government pursued policies that benefitted 'their landlord and developer friends'. They argued that vacant buildings – particularly vacant local authority buildings – should be used to house homeless families and that permanent social housing be constructed on a major scale. They also endorsed five or ten-year secure leases for HAP accommodation for homeless families and asserted that landlords should be restricted in their ability to evict tenants. Moreover, they contended that families who take up HAP should retain their priority on the social housing waiting lists and local authorities should be responsible for sourcing HAP accommodation for homeless families and for re-housing families who lose HAP accommodation. Finally, the families recommended a maximum limit of three months for families in emergency accommodation/ Hubs, and a 'sunset' clause, a legal time frame for closing Hubs to avoid permanent institutionalisation and societal hiding and blaming of homeless families.

PAHRCA AND CO-CONSTRUCTION OF KNOWLEDGE PROCESS, OUTCOMES AND IMPACT

We have outlined in this chapter how the participative PAHRCA process resulted in the co-construction of new and important gendered understandings related to the marketisation of social housing policy and new forms of institutionalised emergency accommodation. The transformative participatory methods involved in the weekly sessions enabled the co-construction of these insights. The focus on empowerment and participation of peer researchers and homeless families as equal co-researchers ensured that the research findings reflected their grounded realities while also enhancing their capacity to understand their own challenges in the wider policy context.

Importantly for policy-orientated research, the participatory human rights framework engaged the homeless female-headed families in a process of co-development of policy alternatives. Indeed, it was the explicit transformative aim within PAHRCA to influence and change policy that helped to engage the families in the research and motivated them to commit to the research process. In June 2016 five of the participant homeless families were involved in action to influence policy in the form of a dialogue with local authority officials, political representatives of the national parliament, and the Chief Commissioner of the IHREC. The dialogue sharply revealed the gendered nature of the homelessness landscape. The families – all female-headed – directly experiencing homelessness had the opportunity to exchange views with politicians and policy makers: all of whom were male. All participants were conscious of this gendered dynamic. The families communicated their issues effectively and asserted themselves to policy makers in the dialogue. The policy makers found the dialogue to be a powerful approach which gave them new insights and committed to bringing these back to inform policy development and practice within their institutions. For example, the knowledge generated by the research found an institutional home when IHREC subsequently took up the research recommendations which have since been used by advocacy groups to promote rights-based approaches to tackling family homelessness. The dialogical action was followed by the production and publication of a comprehensive policy brief to bring this new co-constructed knowledge and policy recommendations into the public sphere and seek to influence policy and practice (Hearne & Murphy 2017). The families, pleased to see the research published in the public domain, felt it was an accurate portrayal of their views and experiences.

We have shown that homelessness policy and practice is gendered from a number of perspectives. The three I's approach usefully allows us unpack three different variables in the policy process: institutions, ideas, and interests. While it is more obvious how interests and actors are gendered (the policy dialogue in particular highlighted this), policy institutions are also gendered in their cultures, norms and regulations. This is evidenced in assumptions of different forms of rationalities. Ideas and policies are also gendered, as highlighted in the contrast between formal housing policy and the altern-ative policy suggested when gender becomes a more explicit and central variable of analysis.

This process of pre-figurative politics with a sharp gender focus generated a genuine empowerment of this vulnerable group in the dialogue process. This happened through the education sessions, and in the experience of hearing their views expressed in the public sphere and in public policy documents. Achieving this level of empowerment within this case study was very challenging for both the researchers and the families as it required signifi-cant personal input, research resources, and time. The very short time frame of the research limited our ability to achieve a deeper level of participation and empowerment, and to sustain it beyond the immediate research. Furthermore, three of the ten women were migrants, two from Africa and one from Eastern Europe. This posed practical cultural and linguistic challenges and the research process did not provide sufficient opportunity to adequately explore or unpack their intersectional experiences.

Gender bias persists in policy and in the patriarchal state. A key issue is the lack of influence of new forms of gender knowledge produced and the resistance of the state to questioning the ways in which it reproduces specific knowledge(s) about gender.[7] The policy system continues to rationalise Family Hubs as an acceptable response to rising family homelessness. Gender and class-biased lens are employed to other female-headed homeless families and place responsibility for the crisis on to the victim. That said, gendered knowledge drawn from this participatory research project, at least in the short term, challenged dominant housing policy narratives in Ireland. The dialogue influenced IHREC's policy position, while the policy brief achieved significant public coverage and was debated in the national parliament. The lived experiences of this socially excluded group of female-headed homeless families were taken seriously within the national political and policy housing sphere. The perceived wisdom of Family Hubs as caring facilities disguises, sometimes intentionally, the reality of the impact of emergency accommodation on the well-being of lone parents and their children. The co-constructed knowledge of the gendered reality of Family Hubs now exists in the public sphere as a benchmark for assessing policy into the future and continues to be effectively drawn on by various political actors and civil society campaigns. At the more local level, the families reported that the Hub providers responded to some of the issues raised by the research. There is evidence to suggest that the research generated awareness of the potentially negative impacts and encouraged newly forming Hubs to examine how they might mitigate such impacts.

We hope that we have contributed to what Farrugia and Gerrard call an unruly, critical or 'an alternative politics of homelessness research' (2016: 277): one that challenges gendered and other assumptions underpinning hegemonic or orthodox homelessness research. We have also tried to be sensitive about what disadvantaged groups want to know and to be accountable to the women with whom we worked (Harding and Norberg 2005). The PAHRCA research co-creation of new knowledge is, therefore, at least a 'potential' power (Gaventa and Cornwall 2003) and a more democratic and inclusive form of knowledge (Harding 1997). A strength of the research is how the families' lived experience is discussed and understood in the context of the political economy of housing markets. Gowan (2010) has described the political contestation of homelessness in terms of 'sin talk', 'sick talk' and 'system talk' where discourses lay the causes for homelessness at the feet of moral culpability, pathological incapacity, or structural inequality respectively (cited in Farrugia and Gerrard 2016: 270). This research situated experiences clearly within 'system talk', with the added value of bringing a gendered analysis of the impacts of that system. The value and usefulness of this approach lies not just in the 'new knowledge' it creates but also in its more inclusive way of generating knowledge and breaking silences. In reflecting more closely on the lived experience it offers possibilities to re-position 'the researched' from being simply a 'social problem' to become 'a community of valorised and normatively legitimate subjectivities' (Farrugia and Gerrard 2016: 267). This form of new gendered knowledge disrupts embedded, and often implicit, knowledge or deep assumptions about gender employed in homelessness and housing policy.

Notes

1 The research was part of the Re-InVEST H2020 funded project which aims to strengthen social investment through a human rights and capability lens.

2 Private landlords can terminate leases relatively easily by declaring that the property is to be sold or is needed for a family member, thus making private rental accommodation very insecure.

3 Female-headed lone-parent families represent 20 per cent or 1 in 5 of all families with children in Ireland. In contrast, female-headed lone-parent families represent 58 per cent of homeless families with children in Dublin.

4 Female-headed consistent poverty increased from 13 per cent in 2010 to 26 per cent in 2015, this compares to the general increase from 6.3 per cent to 8.7 per cent in the same period (CSO, 2016).

5 Scholar-activists, for the purposes of this article, are academics working as both teachers and researchers in third-level institutions, while also being activists striving for progressive or more radical social change (Murphy, 2016).

6 'Pracademic' describes scholars who have professionally bridged the academic and practical world, particularly those who go into academia having already embarked on a career as a practitioner (Volpe & Chandler, 2001).

7 Farrugia and Gerrard (2016) argue critical research is invariably steeped in the politics of power and privilege whereas Bourdieu (1991) finds – given its capacity to represent and to name social experience – research carries significant symbolic power, particularly when authorised by the academy. Unsurprisingly given the academy's long-standing interest in marginality, disadvantage and 'the other', academic knowledge has been subject to challenge and critique from a range of standpoints in the attempt to unveil and upend the taken-for-granted assumptions and authorial positions on which research narratives are based.

REFERENCES

Ahmed, S. 'Foreword , in R. Flood and R. Gill (eds), *Secrecy and Silence in the Research Process: Feminist Reflections* (Routledge: London, 2010), pp xvi–xxii.

Baker, J., K. Lynch, S. Cantillon, and J. Walsh, *Equality from Theory to Action* (Sage: London, 2004).

Barry, U., and P. Conroy, 'Ireland in crisis 2008–2012: Women, austerity and inequality', in H. Rubery and M. Karamessini (eds), *Women and Austerity: The Economic Crisis and the Future for Gender Equality* (Routledge: London, 2014), pp 186–206.

Brown, W., 'Feminism unbound: Revolution, mourning, politics', in *Edgework: Critical Essays on Knowledge and Politics* (Princeton University Press: Princeton, 2005), pp 98–115.

Byrne, A. and R. Lentin, *Researching Women: Feminist Research Methodologies in the Social Sciences in Ireland* (IPA: Dublin, 2000).

Cavaghan, R., 'Gender knowledge: A review of theory and practice', in B. Young and C. Scherrer (eds), *Gender Knowledge and Knowledge Networks in International Political Economy* (Nomos Verlagsgesellschaft: Baden-Baden, 2010), pp 18–35.

Creswell, J. W., *Research Design: Qualitative, Quantitative, and Mixed Methods Approaches*, 2nd edn (Sage: California, 2003).

Crompton, R., *Restructuring Gender Relations and Employment: The Decline of the Male Breadwinner* (Oxford University Press: Oxford/New York, 1999).

Croteau, D., 'Which side are you on? The tension between movement activism and scholarship', in D. Croteau, W. Hoynes & C. Ryan (eds), *Rhyming Hope and History: Activists, academics and Social Movement Scholarship* (University of Minnesota Press: Minneapolis, 2005), pp 20–40.

CSO (Central Statistics Office), *SILC 2016* (CSO: Dublin, 2016).

Dublin Regional Homeless Executive, *March 2017 Homelessness Data* (DRHE: Dublin, 2017).

Duncan, S., 'Mother knows best: Social division and work and childcare', WP 31, in *Families, Life Course and Generational Research Centre Working Paper Series* (Leeds University: Leeds, 2003).

Edwards, J., Y. Zammit, H. Hakendorf, et al., *A Study of Homeless Women in Melbourne* (University of Melbourne: Melbourne, 1977).

Farrugia, D. and J. Gerrard, 'Academic knowledge and contemporary poverty: The politics of homelessness research', in *Sociology*, 2016, 50(2), pp 267–84.

Flint, J., 'Housing and ethopolitics: Constructing identities of active consumption and responsible community', in *Economy and Society*, 32(4), 2003, pp 611–29.

Freire, P., *Education: The Practice of Freedom* (Writers & Readers Publishing Cooperative: London, 1974).

Gaventa, J. and A. Cornwall, 'Power and knowledge', in P. Reason and H. Bradbury (eds), *Handbook of Action Research: Participative Inquiry and Practice* (Sage: London, 2001).

Gerstal, N., J. Cynthia, J. Bogard, J. McConnell and M. Schwartz, 'The therapeutic incarceration of homeless families', in *Social Service Review*, 70(4), 1986, pp 543–72.

Gill, R., 'Beyond individualism: The psychosocial life of the neoliberal university', in M. Spooner (ed.), *A Critical Guide to Higher Education & the Politics of Evidence: Resisting Colonialism, Neoliberalism, & Audit Culture* (University of Regina Press: Regina, Canada, 2017), pp 1–21.

Godinot, X. and Q. Wodon, *Participatory Approaches to Attacking Extreme Poverty: Cases Studies Led by the International Movement ATD Fourth World* (World Bank: New York, 2006).

Government of Ireland, *Rebuilding Ireland* (Stationery Office: Dublin, 2016).

Gowan, T., *Hobos, Hustlers and Backsliders: Homeless in San Francisco* (UMP: Minneapolis, MN, 2010).

Harding, S., *The Feminist Standpoint Theory Reader: Intellectual and Political Controversies* (Routledge: New York, 2004).

Harding, S. and K. Norberg, 'New feminist approaches to social science methodologies: An introduction', in *Signs*, 30(4), 2005, pp 2,009–15.

Hearne, R. and M. Murphy, *Investing in the Right to a Home: Houses HAP and Hubs* (Maynooth University: Maynooth, 2017).

IHREC, *CEDAW Submission* (IHREC: Dublin, 2017).

Kemmis, S. and M. Wilkinson, 'Participatory action research and the study of practice', in B. Atweh, S. Kemmis and P. Weeks (eds), *Action Research in Practice: Partnerships for Social Justice in Education* (Routledge: London, 1998), pp 21–36.

Kindon, S., R. Pain and M. Kesby, *Participatory Action Research Approaches and Methods: Connecting People, Participation and Place* (Routledge: London, 2007).

Ledwith, M., 'On being critical: Uniting theory and practice through emancipatory action research', in *Educational Action Research*, 15:4, 2007, pp 597–611.

Lewis, J., 'The decline of the male breadwinner model: Implications for work and care', in *Social Politics: International Studies in Gender, State & Society*, 8(2), 2001, pp 152–69.

Lynch, K., *The Hidden Curriculum: Reproduction in Education, A Reappraisal* (Falmer Press: London, 1989).

Mayock, P., S. Sheridan and S. Parker, *The Dynamics of Long-Term Homelessness among Women in Ireland* (Dublin Regional Homeless Executive: Dublin, 2015).

Mayock, P. and J. Bretherton, *Women's Homelessness in Europe* (Palgrave MacMillan: Basingstoke, 2017).

Milburn, N. and A. D'Ercole, 'Homeless women: Moving toward a comprehensive model' in *American Psychologist*, 46(11), 1991, pp 1,161–9.

Murphy, M., 'Advancing human rights and equality proofing in Ireland', in *Administration*, 65(3), 2017, pp 59–80.

Ibid., 'Reflections of an Irish pracademic: Mixing public advocacy, teaching and research?', in *Studies in Social Justice*, 9(2), Jan. 2015, pp 215–30.

Ibid., *A Woman's Model of Social Welfare Reform* (NWCI: Dublin, 2003).

Mills, C. Wright (1959) *The Sociological Imagination*. New York: Oxford University Press.

Murphy, M. and R. Hearne, *Participatory Action Capability and Human Rights Approach Draft Methodological Toolkit* (Reinvest: Maynooth, 2016).

Neale, J., 'Homelessness and theory revisited', in *Housing Studies*, 12(1), 1997, pp 47–61.

Neuman, W., *Social Research Methods: Qualitative and Quantitative Approaches*, 7th edn (Pearson: Boston, 2011).

Nussbaum, M. C., 'Capabilities, entitlements, rights: Supplementation and critique', in *Journal of Human Development and Capabilities: A Multi-Disciplinary Journal for People-Centred Development*, 12:1, 2011, pp 23–37.

Oakley, A. 'Interviewing women: A contradiction in terms', in H. Roberts, *Doing Feminist Research* (Routledge: London, 1981), pp 30–61.

Olshansky, E. et al., 'Participatory action research to understand and reduce health disparities', in *Nursing Outlook*, 53, 2005, pp 121–6.

Reason, P. and H. Bradbury (eds), *The SAGE Handbook of Action Research: Participative Inquiry and Practice*, 2nd edn (Sage: London, 2008).

Savage, M., 'Gendering women's homelessness', in *Irish Journal of Applied Social Studies*, 16(2), 2016, pp 43–64.

Smith, D. E., *The Conceptual Practices of Power: A Feminist Sociology of Knowledge* (Northeastern University Press: Boston, 1990).

Volpe, M. and D. Chandler, 'Resolving and managing conflicts in academic communities: The emerging role of the "pracademic"', in *Negotiation Journal*, 17(3), 2001, pp 245–55.

PART III

Gender, Knowledge and Public Culture

NINE

Gender and Knowledge Production in the Teaching Professions

Delma Byrne and Clíona Murray

INTRODUCTION

In this chapter, we cast light on the gendered nature of knowledge production in the teaching professions in Ireland. Elsewhere in this volume, the gendered structure and organisation of higher education institutions is critically interrogated (O'Connor and O'Hagan). In contrast, this chapter focuses on teachers – those working outside the higher education sector to include the early childhood care and education, primary, secondary and further education sectors. The profession of teaching represents a largely neglected area of research in the sociology of knowledge production in the Irish context. Yet, as we will demonstrate, teaching – like other professions explored in this volume (information technology, financial services and sex workers for instance) – powerfully represents (and reproduces) symbolic conflicts over the nature of gender codes: the mechanisms through which unequal gender relationships are generated, maintained and challenged (Arnot 2002). We argue that within the teaching profession, gender inequality is routinely reproduced in its structure, practices and pedagogic mission. We highlight that the formation of teachers through undergraduate programmes at higher education must be understood within the context of the production and control of gendered knowledge more generally in society. In the existing literature, these gendered structures remain largely unaddressed, and to some degree therefore, become naturalised within the profession and the academy.

As a starting point, we first address the macro-level, highlighting the statistical patterns of students by field of study in higher education institutions in Ireland, which themselves constitute and convey gender codes and the deeply embedded gender order in education. We then delve into an examination of the work of teachers as a specific site of knowledge production. Here, we describe the historical context of the profession, and address a considerable gap in the literature on the work of teachers as a site of knowledge production. In doing so, we outline the meaning that knowledge production takes on in the context of the teaching profession, and the gendered structures that are produced.

Our arguments rely on quantitative data analysis to illustrate gender representation across entrants to teaching courses, and across the range of education sectors. Specifically, we use anonymised micro-level population data derived from the Central Applications Office (CAO) on applicants to publicly funded Higher Education Institutions (HEIs) in the Republic of Ireland for 2010 and 2017. We consider change over time in the gender composition of admission to teaching courses over that period. We critically interrogate gender inequalities between sectors within education, and consider the operation of gendered structures pertaining to education as a site of knowledge production. Moreover, the patterns of students taking teaching courses at undergraduate level constitute and convey gender codes and the gender order.

GENDER, FIELD OF STUDY AT HIGHER EDUCATION AND PATTERNS OF DE-SEGREGATION

In Ireland, as in other institutional contexts, there is a strong relationship between gender and educational outcomes. Here, females have made significant gains in the education system, particularly in higher education. Indeed, since the mid-1990s, Ireland has experienced the closure and reversal of the gender gap in rates of entry to college, and the expansion of higher education has had very considerable consequences for the gender composition of higher education entrants (Byrne & McCoy 2017; McCoy & Smyth 2011; O'Connor 2007). Females have made substantial gains and now generally outperform males on several key educational attainment benchmarks. For example, since 2012/13, females have bypassed males as the dominant group among new entrants to the academically selective university sector.[1] While the composition of the new entrant group to Institutes of Technology continues to be predominately male – reflecting a historical orientation of vocational subject offerings – the composition of female entrants has increased from 38 per cent in 2011/12 to 44 per cent in 2016/17 (HEA 2018). Furthermore, recent statistics published by the Higher Education Authority (HEA) on the types of higher education qualifications that graduates hold, shows that females generally outnumber males in receipt of both graduate and postgraduate rewards.

Yet, despite the gains that females have made overall at higher education, it is paradoxical that the trends in gender segregation within and between fields of study have followed a very different trajectory. In the Irish context, the education system has been shown to be deeply stratified, in both gender and social class terms (Byrne & McCoy 2017; Russell, Smyth & O'Connell 2010). To illustrate these gender patterns, Table 1 compares female representation in fields of study between 2010 and 2016, and clearly illustrates that the broad gendering of field of study has remained remarkably stable during the 2000s. As argued by Walby (2011), females are increasingly maintaining advantage in the HE system by acquiring substantial forms of human capital, but not necessarily those requiring the specific technical skills that are most relevant to science, technology, engineering and mathematics (STEM), and high technology, knowledge economy jobs. Thus, despite the existence of a higher education system that produces a relatively high share of science, technology and mathematics graduates in European terms, females are greatly under-represented in the STEM workforce in Ireland. For example, based on Census of Population data from 2011, it is estimated that less than 25 per cent of employees working in jobs that utilise STEM skills are female (Accenture 2014; STEM Education Review Group 2016).

Table 1: *Number of Graduates and Percentage Share of Females, by Field of Study, 2010 and 2016 Graduates (Undergraduate Only)*

	2010 Graduates		2016 Graduates	
	Total	% Female	Total	% Female
Education	1,693	78.0	1,897	74.3
Arts & Humanities	5,018	63.5	6,310	60.9
Social Sciences, Journalism, Business & Law	8,126	57.2	7,989	50.5
Natural Sciences, Mathematics & Statistics	3,283	45.6	3,313	52.3
Information & Communication Technologies	*	*	1,709	17.4
Engineering, Manufacturing & Construction	3,137	18.4	2,758	17.4
Agriculture, Forestry, Fisheries & Veterinary	274	50.7	561	43.9
Health & Welfare	4,687	81.9	5,968	77.6
Services	580	57.2	1,004	45.3
Total	26,798	58.0	31,510	54.4

Note: *Figures not available for 2010 graduates

Source: HEA online sources, various years

These patterns of sex segregation come as little surprise, as sociologists have identified the relationship between the structure of the school/higher education curriculum and power structures in society. For example, in 1971 Young argued that knowledge is stratified, reflecting the power structure of society both in terms of differential access to forms of knowledge for different groups in society, and resistance to the de-stratification or re-stratification of knowledge. As a result, distinct forms of knowledge contribute to the normative ordering of society. Almost 50 years later, the argument made by Young maintains its relevance, as the gendering of fields of study remains deeply embedded.

These patterns hold because of the persistence of the logic of gender essentialism – the notion that males and females are innately and fundamentally different from each other in interests and skills, coupled with the encouragement of traditional gender choices in the home and in the education system, and an unwillingness to undo gender differentiation for its own sake (England 2010). While gender egalitarianism can be demonstrated in the fact that women are now entering and outperforming men in HE; gender essentialism is evidenced in the disciplinary segregation of men and women. Thus, a tension exists between with the contemporaneous logics of gender essentialism and gender egalitarianism in Irish society, with the implication that the rate of de-segregation is slow in young people's choice of field of study.

To illustrate, Table 1 suggests that there is some evidence of what England (2010) refers to as 'de-segregation' of fields of study in the recent period during the 2000s, but little radical change. That is, Table 1 shows some evidence of a progressive process of de-segregation over the 2000s, evidenced by males increasing their participation in fields of study dominated by females, rather than females increasing their participation in fields dominated by males. For example, we find a small declining share of female representation in traditionally 'female' fields of study; as males are slowly increasingly participation in the fields of education (teaching); arts and humanities; social sciences, business and law; and health and services. At the same time, we observe a mixed picture when it comes to females entering male-dominated fields of study. Here, Table 1 shows a declining share of female representation in engineering, but some increase in the female share in natural sciences, mathematics and statistics – each traditionally male-dominated fields – most likely because of efforts to encourage STEM among female students, as we discuss later in the chapter.

However, longer-term processes of de-segregation in the Irish context, as evidence by time-series data covering the period since the 1990s (not shown here), have largely taken the form of females entering male-dominated field of study, rather than males moving into female-dominated fields (O'Connor 2007; Russell, McGinnity, Callan, & Keane 2009; Russell, McGinnity &

O'Connell 2017). For example, Russell et al. (2009) found that with increased female participation in the labour market, women had made significant inroads into some traditionally male managerial/executive and business/commercial occupations between 1996 and 2006, while also observing a decreasing share of women in computer software occupations. While an increase in female labour force participation has been associated with some decline in occupational segregation, the Irish labour market remains strongly gender segregated by international standards (Russell et al. 2017). England (2010) argues that this longer-term trend of females entering male-dominated field of study rather than males moving into female-dominated fields is not surprising given the devaluation of and underpayment within female dominated occupations. As a result, upward mobility is difficult for females, and given the degree of gender essentialism, depends on mechanisms such as other females moving out of upwardly mobile occupations, or alternatively on structural changes in the labour market which would advantage women over men.

We now attempt to delve further into a case study of a field that is both knowledge-intensive and dominated by females – education, or what is more commonly known in the Irish context as 'teaching'. It is well documented that the majority of entrants to the teaching professions in Ireland are indeed female (Drudy 2006; Drudy, Martin, Woods & O'Flynn 2005; Heinz 2008, 2013; Moane & Quilty 2011; Moloney 2010; Moran 2008). This is reinforced by the evidence presented in Table 1 which shows that over three-quarters of education graduates are female (78 per cent in 2010, 74 per cent in 2016). This pattern is not unique to Ireland, as the overrepresentation of females as teaching staff is a widespread phenomenon in Europe and internationally, particularly in the developed countries (Eurostat 2015; Feistritzer 2005). To illustrate, in 2013, of the 8.3 million persons working as teaching staff across all education sectors (from pre-primary to tertiary level) in the European Union; 70 per cent (5.8 million) were female. In all European Union member states, the teaching staff was predominately female, with shares ranging from more than 80 per cent in Estonia, Latvia and Lithuania, to less than 65 per cent in Greece and Spain.

GENDER AND TEACHING

The operation of gender codes in teaching in Ireland proves an interesting case study given the emergence of Ireland from colonialism, the historical centrality of the role of the church and the state in educational matters, and associated patriarchy in the selection, training, recruitment and management of teachers and schools. That is, the origins and nature of gender differences in the contemporary education system cannot be disassociated from the existence of male, bourgeois, hegemonic and dominant ideologies that have historically controlled gender relations in education (O'Donoghue, Harford, & O'Doherty 2017; Lynch, Grummell, & Devine 2012). Here, we emphasise the economic and social structures that have governed women's work in teaching. Of particular interest to us, is how the gender of teachers is part and parcel of the whole range of knowledge constructions and transmissions in education.

A prime example of this in the Irish context is the marriage bar, driven by an economic rationale as well as ideological assumptions about women's rightful place in society (Oram 1996). The ban on married women remaining in or occupying jobs in the public sector was extended in 1932 from the civil service to primary school teachers. The marriage bar came at a time when 58 per cent of primary school teachers were female (increasing to 85 per cent in 2017/18). At the time, teaching as an occupation represented a symbol of upward mobility for many women, particularly middle-class women, but was also considered an extension of the nurturing role of women, and the productive and reproductive work that women engaged in at home. The marriage bar had the effect of terminating the employment and career prospects of higher-earning older women and reinforcing the familial ideology of the 1937 Constitution of Ireland.

Primary school teachers were targeted for the marriage ban because primary school education was compulsory and state-funded while the secondary sector was fee-paying at the time. Teachers in the secondary school sector were not therefore considered public servants in the state in the same way primary teachers were (Redmond & Harford 2010). However, a special dispensation introduced in 1958 allowed women to remain as primary school teachers after marriage, even though most women in the public service were still forced to resign their public service jobs on marriage, until 1973, the year Ireland joined the EEC. Although the original ban only applied to primary school teachers, it also had implications for the market for secondary school teachers. It was only in the mid-1990s (fully two decades after the introduction of equality legislation) that secondary teachers became predominately female, rising to 69 per cent of second level teachers in 2016/17 (O'Connor 2007).

Separate and higher pay scales in teaching existed for married men, compared to women and single men, as well as differential tax and social welfare benefits (O'Connor 1999). Thus, although women outnumbered their male colleagues in primary school teaching, historically the salaries they were paid were significantly lower. Males who worked in primary school teaching tended to be found in higher-status and higher-paying jobs. As the formalisation of the education system and the curriculum got underway and proceeded during the 1930s, 1940s and later in the 1970s and increased efforts were made to enhance teacher accountability, males left the primary school classroom and teaching more generally. While equal pay was achieved in legislation in 1977, these historic dualisms continue to inform the construction of the modern teacher and to create a market for a particular 'type' of teacher.

In the Irish context, more recent work has emerged exposing the gender hierarchies and gender dualisms that shape the experience of women teachers and highlighting their subordinate status. Such studies have typically highlighted the gender division of labour in the profession, most notably the under-representation of women in principal and senior management positions across sectors and in trade union management (Lynch et al. 2012; O'Connor 2007; Pillinger 2010; Lynch 1999). As education became increasingly formalized over time, the advent of new managerial positions moved responsibility for managerial concerns out of the (largely female) classroom and into (largely male) senior management positions. Subsequently, case law revealed that gender had been used by schools in a discriminatory manner with regards to appointments, conditions of employment and promotion (Glendenning 1999). A gender imbalance still holds today. In 2017/18 while two thirds of principals of primary schools are female, just 6.4 per cent of female teachers occupy principal posts compared to 17.9 per cent of male teachers. In the second-level sector, just over half (53 per cent) of principals are male, but only 1.6 per cent of female teachers occupy principal posts compared to 4 per cent of male teachers (DES 2019).

Research also highlights a sexual division of labour by gender differences in caring relations within and outside teaching work. In the more feminised organisational school culture of the primary school sector, caring work is a barrier to applying for senior positions (Devine, Grummell & Lynch 2011). While the findings of the OECD Teaching and Learning International Survey (TALIS) revealed few gender differences in the study of teachers practices, females were more likely than males to participate in the invisible work of attending workshops and participating in networks of teachers or being involved in mentoring, exchange and co-ordination (Gilleece et al. 2009).

GENDER, TEACHING AND THE POLITICS OF KNOWLEDGE PRODUCTION

Many of the arguments pertaining to the gendered politics of knowledge and knowledge production in education in Irish and European research are illustrated by focusing on academics working in teacher education in higher education institutions (Acker & Dillabough 2007; Acker & Feuerverger 1996; Brooks 1997; Dillabough & Acker 2002; Dillabough 2005; Maguire

2000; Reay 2004; Ball & Reay 2000) or academics working in HE (O'Connor 2014 in Ireland). These studies have offered important contributions to the knowledge production literature and highlight the forms of inequality that diverse groups of women face in largely male- dominated labour structures and masculinised organisational cultures, despite increasing female visibility. Less examined, however in the Irish context, are debates about teachers as knowledge workers, or the gendered nature of knowledge production about the teaching profession. The argument we make is that while academics are firmly placed as knowledge workers and key actors in the process of knowledge production, this is generally not the case in relation to teachers and the politics of gender and knowledge production. To this end, the concept of knowledge production takes on a number of particularly interesting meanings when applied to teachers, including the production of knowledge about *what counts as a professional teacher*. We also interrogate the production of knowledge *about the profession* more generally and the status of teachers as knowledge workers. The ambiguous status of the teaching – which is often referred to as a 'quasi-profession' – is both a function and an effect of the perception of teaching as a feminised profession (Braun 2015). The status, structural position, and job content of teaching are all predicated on a gender dimension.

Here, we argue that the occupation of teacher has a much more ambiguous professional status than that of a university lecturer/professor. That is, the status of teachers as knowledge workers, or as actors involved in knowledge production is under threat, whereas for those teaching at tertiary level, their knowledge worker status is considerably more secure. The ambiguous status of teachers derives from the dominant framing discourse around teaching and knowledge production in which teachers have been re-positioned in national and supranational policy terms as *facilitators* or *managers* of knowledge, rather than as active agents themselves in the production of knowledge (Biesta 2015; Bonal & Rambla 2003).

This status ambiguity is also highlighted by Francis and Paechter (2015; 2008) when they observe that the feminisation of the profession is characterised as a 'crisis of male absence' – a discourse which has also been evident in the Irish context. They argue that the continuing ambiguity of status of a profession in which there is an overrepresentation of females serves to further embed gender inequalities in broad terms. Applying this perspective to the gendered structures within the teaching profession, Braun (2015) questions whether the devaluing of pastoral roles and the reduced space for affect and emotion contribute to the continuing pathologisation of the feminine within the profession.

While the historical dimension has relevance for our understanding of gender hierarchies in teaching, so too has a number of contemporary developments dating from the 2000s, the period under investigation in the empirical section of this chapter. Here, we pay attention to the production of knowledge about *what counts as a professional teacher*. Firstly, while subject specialisation has always been part of second-level teaching, in the past decade the scale of the production of 'expert' knowledge for teaching has intensified. Increasingly, there is specialisation and diversification. For instance, there has been an unprecedented growth of undergraduate second-level teacher education denominated degree courses, particularly in the areas of science, technology, mathematics and engineering (STEM) in the period 2010–16. A focus on gender, and the drive to increase the number of girls in STEM, has been evident for some time in national STEM policy. This drive has been accompanied by an emphasis on the need for continuing professional development for STEM teachers across sectors (Government of Ireland 2015; RIA 2014), while provision of continuing professional development for teachers outside the STEM disciplines has waned. Secondly, concern has been expressed within the education community that teacher autonomy is diminishing (Gleeson & O'Donnabháin 2009; Gleeson 2012). In 2006, the teaching profession became self-regulated, with the formal establishment of the Teaching Council. The Teaching Council is the statutory body that sets the standards of academic achievement and professional training required of primary, secondary and further education teachers. As a result, the work of teachers in Ireland is now increasingly experienced through the construction of a self-regulated enhanced system of professionalism, accountability, inspection and monitoring of performance, steering teachers and schools towards targets and goals established by the state, framed in the language of audit culture and public sector reform.

These shifts regarding what counts as a professional teacher followed a politically sensitive decline in the 2010 Programme for International Student Assessment (PISA) reading and math scores among 15 year olds in Ireland. A Literacy and Numeracy Strategy was published in 2011 with increased emphasis on the quality and relevance of initial teacher education and 'teaching skills'. This reconstitution of teachers' work and an imperative towards teacher professionalism it has been argued has resulted in complex and uneven transformations in teachers' identities, roles and working lives in other jurisdictions. For example, in the UK, Ozga (1988) has argued that increased regulation represented a shift from 'autonomy' to 'licenced autonomy', while Ball (2003) argues that such reforms result in the opposite of the intended effects – corroding quality of work and working lives - with implications for the effectiveness of teaching and the professional practice of teachers.

From a British perspective, Dillabough (1999) adds a gender dimension to these concerns, critiquing how policy (both national and supranational) frames 'the modern teacher', making the case alongside Apple that 'women's work is very often the target of both rationalisation and attempts to gain control over it' (Apple 1985: 455). England (2010) points to the devaluation of and underpayment within female dominated occupations. Dillabough problematises 'the relationship between male power and the construction of the modern rational teacher, where teachers behave in the name of student achievement and social and economic change as agents of educational reform' (1999: 375). Furthermore, she argues that the concept of 'teacher professionalism' is gendered, and that women teachers are still constrained by what Arnot (1982) identified as 'dominated gender codes' that are embedded in human interaction in educational organisations. It is argued that the construction of the rational, professional teacher in pursuit of academic standards and as agents of change is formed from a traditional masculine perspective. In this model, care and other kinds of invisible work that occurs in teaching, and which is mostly the domain of female teachers, is left to one side.

These processes are also being accompanied by changes to the employment conditions of teachers across education sectors in Ireland. There are considerable disparities in the salary expectations and conditions of employment for teachers in each of the sectors. In particular, the salary career structure is less developed in the largely female early childhood sector, with considerable difference in the salary associated with being an Early Childhood Care and Education (ECCE) practitioner, relative to all other teaching professions. While the primary, secondary and to some extent further education sectors are supported strongly by unionisation, such representation is not evident among ECCE educators. The latter therefore are not in as powerful a position to advance their case in relation to pay entitlements and employment rights. Furthermore, teacher autonomy is diminishing precisely at a time when the pay of teachers is being deflated through recession era wage controls, austerity politics and casualisation of the workforce (see Gilleece et al. 2009; Clarke & Kileavy 2012). The effects of the recession are evident in reports of the casualisation of the teaching profession (Ward 2014), coupled with a decision taken by the government during the austerity years to introduce lower pay scales for new entrants, thus creating pay inequalities among teachers. Growing unease of 'over-supply' of teachers has also come to the fore (O'Donoghue et al. 2017). These changes have come at a time when teachers are now required to provide additional hours of work as part of wider public sector reforms.

We now use quantitative data on entrants to undergraduate teaching courses in Ireland to consider the internal hierarchies on teaching: how gender representation is distributed across the education sectors, and how the cultural production of forms of expert professional knowledge is gendered.

We approach this issue from a quantitative perspective, using population data on applicants to publicly funded Higher Education Institutions (HEIs) in the Republic of Ireland in 2010 and 2017, derived from the Central Applications Office (CAO). The data represents those who have applied to and accepted an offer made by the CAO on behalf of the HE sector. That is, the data represents those who applied and accepted a course, but does not include those who applied and were not offered/did not accept a course. The main objective is to highlight sectoral differentiation in the gendering of courses at undergraduate level leading to a teaching qualification in both 2010 and 2017.

Importantly, the data allows us to distinguish applicants according to gender and field of study. The main dependent variables relate to the type of HE course that applicants have been offered and accepted, conditional on application. Our analytic strategy has been devised to better understand the gendered structures that are inherent in the production of educational practitioners at undergraduate level. In doing so, a distinction is made between courses leading to each of the education sectors (early childhood care and education; primary education; second level education; and further education) and all other fields of study. This is because little attention has been paid to the characteristics of the collective undergraduate body of higher education students pursuing careers aimed at educational practitioners more broadly, and issues pertaining to gender and knowledge production in the profession. A further distinction is made between those pursing STEM and non-STEM second-level teacher education courses. While it is well established that females are much less likely than males to choose science, technology, engineering or mathematics (STEM) as a field of study at graduate level (OECD 2011), much less attention has been paid to the gendered patterns underpinning entry to STEM undergraduate teaching courses, despite the recent policy initiatives in relation to both gender and STEM, and national support for STEM teachers.

CAO data allows us to take into account the complexity of the decision-making process that results in females and males ending up in pathways leading to different sectors of education. Importantly, the data allows us to observe two key aspects of decision-making processes – both the individual's choice, and the institutional response (offer of admission). Entry into higher education is the result of a competitive process so our data analysis provides insights on the larger set of preferences and constraints at play. To this end, an advantage of using this data is that it allows us to capture *the gendered basis of choice processes*. That is, it captures both the actual course and field of study that students were offered by the CAO, as well as the first-choice course and field of study that students opted for, allowing an observation of the student's process of ranking and choosing from among candidate fields. The data also allows an observation of the type of track (academic/pre-vocational) pursued when completing the Leaving Certificate, LC attainment, and school attended – differentiating by gender mix and social class intake. The gender mix of the school attended by the CAO applicant is included given that gender norms and cultural beliefs about gender are likely to shape the field of study preferences of both males and females.

Analyses were conducted using bivariate and multivariate methods. CAO data represents cross-sectional census data – meaning that it captures all those who applied to higher education at a single point in time. The full working sample comprises of over 46,000 CAO applicants for each year, almost 23,000 of whom accepted a Level 8 offer.[2] To highlight the gendered

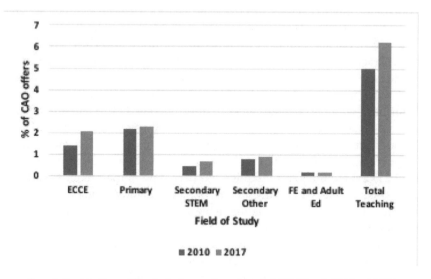

Figure 1: Teaching Course Offers by Sector, as a Percentage of all CAO Offers in 2010 and 2017

pattern of course choices on entry to HE, the distribution of males and females are presented graphically. Econometric modelling (using multinomial models) then allows an examination of the probability of accepting a teaching course on offer at undergraduate level, conditional on applying.

FINDINGS

Changes in Entry to Undergraduate Teaching Courses 2010–17
Figure 1 provides a description of the distribution of CAO offers made for teaching courses at undergraduate level in both years, at all levels (including Levels 6, 7 and 8). Between 2010 and 2017 the share of CAO offers made for teaching courses increased from 5.1 per cent to 6.2 per cent, representing an increase of 5.3 per cent. This growth was more evident in some sectors of the education system than others and reflects increasing specialisation in the production of knowledge for teaching. In response to government concern regarding STEM, the number of offers to second-level STEM courses rose by 63 per cent from 213 in 2010 to 347 in 2017. In response to policy developments and universal provision of early childhood care and education, the number of offers to ECCE courses rose by 59 per cent from 648 offers in 2010 to 1,030 by 2017. Numbers of offers to all other teaching courses remained relatively stable over the period.

Gender and CAO Offers to Teaching Courses 2010–17
The gender distribution of CAO offers made is presented in Figure 2. While in both years, 49 per cent of all HE applicants who secured an offer from the CAO were female, as expected females were considerably over-represented in the vast majority of teaching courses relative to all other fields of study. Furthermore, there is considerable differentiation across education sectors, and over the time period investigated here, these gender patterns have largely been maintained. In 2017, 96 per cent of offers to ECCE courses and 80 per cent of offers to primary teaching courses were made to females. For non-STEM second-level teaching courses, 63 per cent and 68 per cent of offers were made to females in 2010, and 2017, respectively. Female representation among offers for FE and adult education courses increased over the period from almost 62 per cent in 2010 to 72 per cent by 2017. The patterns relating to second-level STEM teaching courses are of particular interest. Here we find that STEM teaching courses reach greater gender parity: in 2010 almost 55 per cent of offers for these courses were made to females. However, by 2017 this had dropped considerably to just under 42

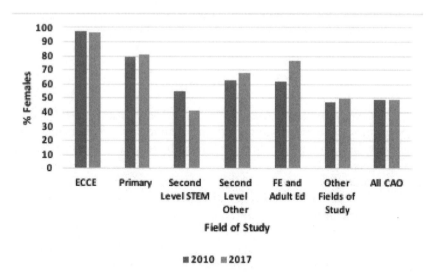

Figure 2: Gender Distribution of Education Practitioner Course Offers by Sector in 2010 and 2017 (% Female)

per cent, indicating that the female share of CAO offers to second-level STEM teaching courses actually fell over the period. *Thus, males are increasing their participation in teaching, but in selective areas of teaching that reflect broader gendered STEM patterns.*

Multivariate Analyses were conducted to determine if the gender pattern remains persistent when controlling for the range of factors that are known to influence entry to higher education including choice preference, attainment in the Leaving Certificate (GPA), age, track pursued, and characteristics of the school attended including average social class mix and gender mix of the school. A summary of the results which highlight the gender patterns are presented in Table 2 in the form of regression coefficients. A positive and significant regression coefficient (indicated by the use of stars) means that females are more likely than males to be selected for a particular type of teaching course. A negative and significant regression coefficient means that females are less likely than males to be selected for a particular type of teaching course. If the coefficient is not significant (indicated by the non-presence of stars) then there is no gender difference.

The multivariate models indicate that all else being equal, in 2017 females were 3.7 times more likely than males to gain entry to a ECCE course; 1.8 times more likely to gain entry to a primary teaching course; and 1.3 times more likely to gain entry to a second-level teaching course. Clearly,

Table 2: *Binary Logistic Regression Coefficients for Gender, 2010 and 2017*

	ECCE		Primary		STEM		Second Level Other		FE & Adult	
	2010	2017	2010	2017	2010	2017	2010	2017	2010	2017
Female	1.27***	1.30***	0.42***	0.56***	0.02	-0.25***	0.15**	0.27***	0.01	0.49***
Ref: Male										
N	29304	35830	29304	35830	29304	35830	29304	35830	29304	35830
R²	.162	.171	.197	.120	.057	.050	.027	.028	.067	.094

Standard errors in parentheses

$^* p < 0.05,\ ^{**} p < 0.01,\ ^{***} p < 0.001$

Model also contains age, track pursed at senior cycle, school sector (public/private), school composition (concentration of students from disadvantaged background), school sector (vocational, comm/comp, secondary) and previous educational attainment.

females are more likely than males to gain entry to the majority of teaching courses. There is, however, some deviation from this pattern when it comes to second-level STEM and FE/Adult education courses. Our findings show that, in 2010, there was no clear gender effect with regards to entry to these teaching courses; but there were clear gender effects by 2017. In the case of second-level STEM, an increase in the number of places on STEM teaching courses had the effect of introducing gender inequity: that is, by 2017 females were now less likely to gain entry to a second-level STEM teaching course than males, when we compare like-with-like. By 2017 males became 1.3 times more likely to gain access to a STEM teaching course than females. In the case of Further Education, while the number of offers made by CAO for FE teaching courses remained stable between 2010 and 2017, by 2017 females were more likely to gain entry to the FE teaching sector than males (indicating that the sector is becoming more female-dominated). These patterns suggest that far from creating greater gender equality across the sector, there is a reinforcement of women in 'female-type' teaching fields, and a concomitant increase in men in more 'male-type' teaching fields (STEM).

CONCLUSION

This chapter began by casting light on the paradoxical sex segregation in fields of study at Higher Education, despite high levels of participation in Higher Education among females. As the broad gendering of fields of study has remained remarkably stable during the 2000s, females remain under represented in key knowledge economy sectors (including STEM), with little evidence of de-segregation at play, particularly of the progressive type. Thus, despite the spread of egalitarian norms and a female advantage in Higher Education academic achievement, the logic of gender essentialism seems to be winning over the logic of gender egalitarianism.

Attention was focused on education graduates in particular – a group that is predominately female, and holds comparatively high graduate employment rates; strong graduate salaries and career prospects; as well as positive subjective feelings about the relevance of their education for current employment relative to graduates of other fields of study (HEA 2018). Yet the profession of teaching has largely been neglected in the sociology of knowledge production in the Irish context, despite the fact that teaching as a profession has traditionally attracted an increasing share of the female labour force over time – up from 3 per cent in 1926 to 7.2 per cent in 2016 (own calculations based on Census of Population 1926; 2016). Furthermore, how teaching as a profession has changed over time (the labour process of the job), and the changing economic and gender conditions surrounding it, have attracted relatively little attention.

We have cast light on a profession that is both knowledge intensive and dominated by females – drawing on the conceptualisation of teachers work as 'women's work' (Apple 1985), and work that is often the target of rationalisatisation and control. We have discussed the work of teachers and the associated teaching professions, highlighting the manner in which gender inequality is routinely reproduced in its structure, practices and pedagogic mission. We argue that there is a strong relationship between the entry of large numbers of women into an occupation and the slow transformation of the job . . . as pay is lowered and the job is regarded as 'low-skilled' so that 'control' is needed from the outside. That is, as the profession is feminised it has come under ever tighter conditions of control, with some loss of paths of upwards mobility and reduction in wages.

While previous research has highlighted inequalities in the gender composition of the teaching workforce, here, we brought to light issues of knowledge production about teaching in terms of (i) the ambiguous status of teaching as a profession and of teachers as knowledge workers and (ii) the production of knowledge about *what counts as a professional teacher*. Processes of rationalisation and control are clearly at play in the Irish context as teachers are increasingly accountable as professionals through the establishment of the Teaching Council and to the demands of the curriculum, as evidenced by the Literacy and Numeracy Strategy. Such changes in teachers' work is viewed as attempts to de-skill them, in a political context that attributes responsibility to teachers for national decline in educational standards.

Furthermore, teachers and new entrants to the profession were subject to (and continue to be subject to) austerity measures despite resistances from the profession.

Our empirical findings illustrate the highly visible gender codes that emerge in the patterns of admission to undergraduate teacher courses in Irish higher education, and the persistence of vertical occupational sex segregation (across the education sectors). The human capital that under-pins the knowledge economy in the field of non-HE education is gendered, as females dominate undergraduate teaching courses. Yet, the gender effect is more pronounced among teachers of ECCE, the most insecure and precarious of the teaching professions. The relationship between gender and types of teaching is unsurprising given that single-sex schooling is a common model in Ireland and that the range of subjects on offer to students in those schools is often affected by traditional assumptions around gender (Doris, O'Neill and Sweetman 2013). Furthermore, this points to a possible reluc-tance on the part of male entrants to apply for primary teaching or courses in Early Childhood Care and Education (ECCE), and less cultural permission for male students who wish to pursue a profession that is traditionally understood as being dominated by females. Yet, exceptionally, males are more likely to be selected for STEM second-level teaching courses, all else being equal. While this is not so surprising, it is somewhat of a paradox. In a context of increasing awareness about a gender bias in STEM subjects, and drives to improve female participation in STEM, new entrants to STEM teaching courses are in fact more likely to be male. We argue that contrary to stated policy objectives, processes of expansion and specialisation in formation of teachers at undergraduate level in reality uphold the persis-tence of gender inequality and occupational sex segregation. This suggests deeply embedded gender inequality not only in STEMS practices, cultures and institutions (see Kerr and Savage in this volume), but also in educational policy more broadly. These findings are important given that in 2018 the Minister for Education and Skills announced an expansion of the number of places on post-primary teacher education courses for STEM teachers.

Finally, it is worth noting that while there is a distinct policy emphasis on increasing the number of girls entering STEM courses, there is not a corresponding drive to increase the number of boys taking ECCE courses. This discrepancy points to a continued devaluing of roles in the affective and caring domains. In this context then, bringing about equality cannot be merely a numbers game, as our analysis has shown. Rather, it must be about emphasising gender deconstruction (Francis & Paechter 2015) and valuing equally those domains traditionally perceived as 'feminine'. This area merits further research on the processes and experiences involved in students' choices around further and higher education.

Notes

1 In the academic year 2016/17, over 700 more females than males entered HE (22, 177 compared to 21,392 (HEA, 2018).
2 The data represents 46,283 applicants in 2010 and 47,997 applicants in 2017.

REFERENCES

Accenture, *Powering Economic Growth: Attracting More Young Women into Science and Technology* (Accenture: Dublin, 2014).

Acker, Sandra and Jo-Anne Dillabough, 'Women "learning to labour" in the "male emporium": exploring gendered work in teacher education', in *Gender and Education*, 19(3), 2007, pp 297–316.

Acker, Sandra and Grace Feuerverger, 'Doing good and feeling bad: The work of women university teachers', in *Cambridge Journal of Education*, 26, 1996, pp 401–22.

Apple, Michael W., 'Teaching and "women's work": A comparative and historical analysis', in *Teachers College Record*, 86(3), 1985, pp 455–73.

Arnot, Madeline, 'Male hegemony, social class and women's education', in *Journal of Education*, 164(1), 1982, pp 64–89.

Ibid., *Reproducing Gender: Critical Essays on Educational Theory and Feminist Politics* (Routledge: London, 2002).

Ball, Stephen J., 'The teacher's soul and the terrors of performativity', in *Journal of Education Policy*, 18(2), 2003, pp 215–28.

Ball, Stephen J., and Diane Reay, 'Essentials of female management: Women's ways of working in the education marketplace', in *Educational Management & Administration*, 28(2), 2000, pp 145–59.

Biesta, Gert, 'What is education for? On good education, teacher judgement, and educational professionalism', in *European Journal of Education*, 50(1), 2015, pp 75–87.

Bonal, Xavier and Xavier Rambla, 'Captured by the totally pedagogised society: Teachers and teaching in knowledge economies', in *Globalisation, Societies & Education*, 1(2), 2003, pp 131–49.

Braun, Annette, 'The politics of teaching as an occupation in the professional borderlands: The interplay of gender, class and professional status in a biographical study of trainee teachers in England', in *Journal of Education Policy*, 30(2), 2015, pp 258–74.

Brooks, Ann, *Academic Women* (Buckingham: SRHE & Open University Press, 1997).

Byrne, Delma and Selina McCoy, 'Effectively maintained inequality in educational transitions in the Republic of Ireland', in *American Behavioral Scientist*, 61(1), 2017, pp 49–73.

Clarke, Marie and Maureen Killeavy, 'Charting teacher education policy in the Republic of Ireland with particular reference to the impact of economic recession', in *Educational Research*, 54(2), 2012, pp 125–36.

Devine, Dympna, Bernie Grummell and Kathleen Lynch, 'Crafting the elastic self? Gender and identities in senior appointments in Irish education', in *Gender, Work & Organisation*, 18(6), 2011, pp 631–49.

Dillabough, Jo-Anne, 'Gender, "symbolic domination", and female work: The case of teacher education', in *Discourse: Studies in the Cultural Politics of Education*, 26(2), 2005, pp 27–148.

Dillabough, Jo-Anne and Sandra Acker, 'Globalisation, women's work and teacher education: A cross-national analysis', in *International Studies in Sociology of Education*, 12(3), 2002, pp 227–60.

Doris, Aedín, Donal O'Neill, and Olive Sweetman, 'Gender, single-sex schooling and maths achievement', in *Economics of Education*, 35, 2013, pp 104–19.

Drudy, Sheelagh, 'Gender differences in entrance patterns and awards in initial tteacher education', in *Irish Educational Studies*, 25(3), 2006, pp 259–73.

Drudy, Sheelagh, Maeve Martin, Máiríde Woods, and John O'Flynn (eds), *Men and the Classroom: Gender Imbalances in Today's Schools* (Routledge Falmer: London and New York, 2005).

England, Paula, 'The gender revolution: Uneven and stalled', in *Gender & Society*, 24(2), 2010, pp 149–66.

Eurostat, 'Women teachers over-represented at early stages of education in the EU'. Eurostat news release 2015, Source http://ec.europa.eu/eurostat/documents/2995521/7017572/3-02102015-BP-EN.pdf/5a7b5406-4a0d-445b-8fa3-3558a8495020

Feistritzer, C. Emily, *Profile of Alternate Route Teachers in the US* (National Center for Education Information: Washington, DC, 2005).

Francis, Becky and Carrie F. Paechter, 'The problem of gender categorization: Addressing dilemmas past and present in gender and education research', in *Gender and Education*, 27(7), 2015, pp 776–90.

Gilleece, Lorraine, Gerry Shiel, Rachel Perkins, and Maeve Proctor, *Teaching and Learning International Survey (2008), National Report for Ireland* (Dublin: Education Research Centre, 2009).

Gleeson, Jim, 'The professional knowledge base and practice of Irish post-primary teachers: What is the research evidence telling us?', in *Irish Educational Studies*, 31(1), 2012, pp 1–17.

Gleeson, Jim and Diarmaid O'Donnabháin, 'Strategic planning and accountability in Irish education', in *Irish Educational Studies*, 28(1), 2009, pp 27–46.

Glendenning, Dympna, *Education and the Law* (Butterworths: Dublin, 1999).

Government of Ireland, *Innovation 2020* Source, https://dbei.gov.ie/en/Publications/Publication-files/Innovation-2020.pdf

HEA, *Key Facts and Figures: Higher Education 2016/17* (Higher Education Authority: Dublin, 2018).

Heinz, Manuela, 'The composition of applicants and entrants to teacher education programmes in Ireland: Trends and patterns', in *Irish Educational Studies*, 27, 2008, pp 223–40.

Ibid., 'The next generation of teachers: An investigation of second-level student teachers' backgrounds in the Republic of Ireland', in *Irish Educational Studies*, 32, 2013, pp 139–56.

Lynch, Kathleen, *Equality in Education* (Gill and Macmillan: Dublin, 1999).

Lynch, Kathleen, Bernie Grummell, and Dympna Devine, *New Managerialism in Education: Commercialization, Carelessness and Gender* (Palgrave Macmillan: Basingstoke, 2012).

Lynch, Kathleen and Marie Moran, 'Markets, schools and the convertibility of economic capital: The complex dynamics of class choice', in *British Journal of Sociology of Education*, 27(2), 2006, pp 221–35.

McCoy, Selina and Emer Smyth, 'Higher education expansion and differentiation in the Republic of Ireland', in *Higher Education*, 61, 2011, pp 243–60.

Maguire, Meg, 'Inside/outside the ivory tower: Teacher education in the English academy', in *Teaching in Higher Education*, 5(2), 2000, pp 149–65.

Moane, Geraldine and Aideen Quilty, 'Feminist education and feminist community psychology: Experiences from an Irish context', in *Journal of Community Psychology*, 40(1), 2011, pp 145–58.

Moloney, Mary, 'Professional identity in early childhood care and education: Perspectives of pre-school and infant teachers', in *Irish Educational Studies*, 29(2), 2010, pp 167–87.

Moran, Anne, 'Challenges surrounding widening participation and fair access to initial teacher education: Can it be achieved?', in *Journal of Education for Teaching: International Research and Pedagogy*, 34, 2008, pp 63–77.

O'Connor, Muiris, *Sé Sí: Gender in Irish Education* (Department of Education and Science with Brunswick Press: Dublin, 2007).

O'Connor, Pat, *Emerging Voices: Women in Contemporary Irish Society* (Institute of Public Administration: Dublin, 1999).

Ibid., *Management and Gender in Higher Education* (Manchester University Press: Manchester, 2014).

O'Donoghue, Tom, Judith Harford, and Teresa O'Doherty, *Teacher Preparation in Ireland: History, Policy and Future Directions* (Emerald Publishing: Bingley, UK, 2017).

OECD, *Report on the Gender Initiative: Gender Equality in Education, Employment and Entrepreneurship* (OECD: Paris, 2011).

Oram. Alison, *Women Teachers and Feminist Politics, 1900–1939* (Manchester University Press: Manchester and New York, 1996).

Ozga, Jenny, *Schoolwork: Approaches to the Labour Process of Teaching* (Open University Press: Milton Keynes, 1988).

Pillinger, Jane, *Improving the Representation of Women on the TUI Executive Committee* (TUI: Dublin, 2010).

Reay, Diane, 'Gendering Bourdieu's concepts of capitals? Emotional capital, women and social class', in *The Sociological Review*, 52, 2004, pp 57–74.

Redmond, Jennifer and Judith Harford, '"One man, one job": The marriage ban and the employment of women teachers in Irish primary schools', in *Pedagogica Historica*, 46(5), 2010, pp 639–54.

Royal Irish Academy, *The Royal Irish Academy's Submission to the STEM Education Review Group*, Advice Paper no 3/2014 Source https://www.ria.ie/sites/default/files/academy-advice-paper-3-submission-to-the-national-stem-review-group_0.pdf

Russell, Helen, Frances McGinnity, Tim Callan and Claire Keane, *A Woman's Place? Female Participation in the Irish Labour Market* (Equality Authority in association with The Economic and Social Research Institute: Dublin, 2009).

Russell, Helen, Emer Smyth, and Philip J. O'Connell, 'Gender differences in pay among recent graduates: Private sector employees in Ireland', in *Journal of Youth Studies*, 13(2), 2010, pp 212–33.

Russell, Helen, Frances McGinnity, and Philip J. O'Connell, 'Gender equality in the labour market 1966–2016: Unfinished business?', in *The Economic and Social Review*, 48(4), 2017, pp 393–418.

STEM Education Review Group, *STEM Education in the Irish School System* (Department of Education and Skills: Dublin, 2016).

Walby, Sylvia, 'Is the knowledge society gendered?', in *Gender, Work & Organisation*, 18(1), 2011, pp 1–29.

Ward, Peter, *Report to the Minister for Education and Skills of the Chairperson of the Expert Group on Fixed-Term and Part-Time Employment in Primary and Second Level Education in Ireland* 2014, Source https://www.ictu.ie/download/pdf/ward_report.pdf

Young, Michael, F. D., *Knowledge and Control: New Directions for the Sociology of Education* (Collier: Macmillan; London, 1971).

TEN

Hacking at the Techno-Feminist Frontier: Gendered Exclusion and Inclusion in Informal Technology Events

Aphra Kerr and Joshua D. Savage

The knowledge economy developed in the late 1960s in the United States when academics began to notice that the value of knowledge-based occupations and industries to the overall economy had overtaken that of manufacturing and the extractive industries (Kerr and Ó Riain 2009). Ireland's knowledge economy developed somewhat later but has become highly salient. Information and communication technologies (ICTs) are a core enabler of knowledge-based industries, and in many ICT companies today the most highly sought after (and highly paid) roles are often in programming. Computer programmers produce formal and professionally certified forms of knowledge in technical languages to deliver services. Other forms of knowledge are often less valued in financial and social terms. So-called 'soft skills', design skills and contextual knowledge are often constructed as feminine, even if they are critical to the ultimate success of many technical and creative projects (Preston et al. 2009). Two key features of computer programmers stand out: their status in contemporary society, and their gender.

As Walby (2011) points out, the gender composition of the knowledge economy varies depending on which sector you focus on. However, the more the industry is based on technology, the more gendered masculine it is. This pattern is replicated in Ireland: the female share of employment in the computer software industries in Ireland fell between 1991 and 2006 (Russell et al. 2017). This occurred during a period in which women's participation in the labour force more generally grew, women's educational attainment at third level exceeded that of men, and the share of women's employment in some previously male-dominated occupations like commerce and science increased. Further, in 2015 less than 16 per cent of professors in STEM-related positions in higher education institutions in Ireland were women (O'Connor and O'Hagan in this volume). This poses key questions for policy makers and researchers: Why is computer programming as an occupation and as an object of study dominated by men? What are the implications of this pattern for technical knowledge and the design and use of technology in the knowledge society?

For almost two decades, state and industry-funded education and media initiatives in Ireland have attempted to increase the number of young people entering Science, Technology, Engineering and Maths (STEM). The approach taken mostly involves a range of promotion and awareness-raising activities aimed at children, parents and teachers. Science and technology competitions abound, and television programmes partly funded by Science Foundation Ireland have proliferated, e.g. RTÉ's 'the Science Squad'. A number of these activities have specifically targeted girls and women. For example, the annual I-Wish conferences in Cork and Dublin are fronted by high-profile female scientists and engineers. Their aim is to influence the subject choices of 14–17-year-old teenage girls. Another set of promotional initiatives have mobilised digital games as a means of attracting young people to events where attendees learn to programme. CoderDojo, for example, involves volunteers from the IT industry teaching children as young as seven years old how to programme simple applications, often games. These events take place at weekends in a variety of settings, from companies to universities. The volunteers organise the events and often share what is produced online. While these events are open to everyone, their role, efficacy and social impact is rarely critically examined, especially from a gender perspective.

In this chapter we examine how informal education events, like gamejams, contribute to the gendered structure of the knowledge economy in Ireland. We identify how communication, temporal and spatial structure, hierarch-ies of knowledge and unpaid labour contribute to gendered knowledge hierarchies, and to gendered pathways into ICT-related occupations. Game making and game playing events may reinforce a relationship between codified and abstract forms of knowledge, certain forms of masculinity, and computers, ultimately undermining the assumption that digital games provide an equal pathway into STEM for all. Even if the focus of these events is on learning technical skills, we would suggest that a range of 'informal' and 'incidental' social learning is taking place that may serve to reinforce wider patterns of social inequality. We first place our work in the context of historical and feminist research into the gender/technology/know-ledge relationship in production and consumption cultures. We then present our findings from research at two day-long gamejam events in Ireland in

2016 to identify who attends these events and the ways in which these events are gendered. Finally, we discuss how academics and civil society organisations have collaborated to organise inclusive female-friendly informal learning events. These events are inspired by the techno-feminist approach of Judy Wajcman (2010; 2004). They aim to challenge the association between hegemonic masculinity, men and technology which is often found (implicitly or explicitly) in informal and formal educational settings. They explicitly seek to promote knowledge diversity, gender equality and inclusion in the digital games community in Ireland.

THE MUTUAL SHAPING OF GENDER AND TECHNOLOGY

Promotional activities aimed at diversifying the workforce within the computing and games industries often fail to take account of the long history of women's systematic marginalisation from technologies, and to examine how existing structures and cultures may discourage diversity. Histories of technology have identified that the marginalisation of women in the technical sciences and industries has had a profound impact on the design of technologies, which in turn has contributed to the gendering of the everyday cultures of use surrounding these technologies. Histories of the design of fridges, ovens, televisions and telephones have identified the implicit and explicit gendered assumptions embedded in the technologies, and the impact these assumptions have on cultures of use (Cowan 1987; Grint and Gill 1995). In many instances domestic technologies were designed by men to be used by women in the home. The sale and marketing of white (kitchen) goods versus black (entertainment) goods, as well as cultures of maintenance and repair, often reproduced existing gendered stereotypes and relations of power in the home.

The development of the personal computer, the internet and a range of associated information and communication technologies (ICTs) held out the promise that the association of masculinity, mastery and expertise with technology might be broken. Here was a technology that did not require strength to operate. The first computer programmer was a woman: Ada Lovelace. Women dominated in the early history of computers when computing was seen as an extension of typing and secretarial work, and female human computers could be legally paid less than men for the same work. Some early feminist writing on women and technology saw technology as in opposition to femininity and sought to reject it (see Wajcman 2004 for a discussion). Cyberfeminists in the 1990s lauded the potential for gender fluidity in online spaces and for new forms of socio-technical and hybrid human/machines. Yet the optimism was short lived and challenged by empirical studies. Gendered patterns of design, marketing and use have continued with media technologies and increasingly with children's leisure technologies. Gendered social and cultural practices continue to shape educational and occupational choices, including pathways into computing and software programming. The knowledge economy and the gender composition of technology-based occupations has become dominated by men.

Years of public and private initiatives in Western countries to promote computing and technology as a career to young people have resulted in static, and in some cases declining, numbers of women studying STEM subjects, particularly computer science (Kafai et al. 2016: 5). Occupational segregation based on sex persists in computer programming and related jobs in the West, as evidenced by the data on Ireland (Russell et al. 2017). Those women who do work in high technology industries are likely to leave mid-career citing workplace culture, work/life balance issues and sexism as factors. Following Wajcman (2004), we can identify this as a liberal approach. We suggest that this approach is insufficient to tackle diversity issues in technological industries, workplaces and cultures. The liberal approach leaves existing structures in the workplace, entertainment cultures and wider event culture intact and rarely questions the design of technologies. As Sandra Harding (1986: 18) has noted, there is a relationship between gendered occupational structures, gender symbolism and gender identity: things that are gendered female are often attributed lower status and lower pay.

An alternative to the liberal approach can be found in techno-feminism. Wajcman (2010) notes that techno-feminism is concerned with both understanding gender power relations and intervening to change the cultures and practices surrounding the design of technological artefacts (including technological knowledge). Inspired by socialist feminism, techno-feminism combines insights from within science and technology studies (STS) and one strand within feminism to argue that gender and technology are mutually shaping: technology is both a source and a consequence of gender relations. A key insight is that while technology is not fixed, neither is gender: both are subject to, and part of, a wider set of contingent and changeable social relations. An additional consideration is that the construction and design of technologies requires a range of knowledge, skills and expertise. Lay or 'vernacular' knowledge is increasingly acknowledged as a key source of innovation in technology cultures. Yet differences in technical expertise are often perceived as gendered (Jenson and de Castell 2008). In the IT industries expert, codified and statistical forms of knowledge bring more reputational status and financial advantages. Thus, the production of both technical knowledge and material technologies is deeply entwined with gender, race and class distinctions in contemporary technological cultures. Techno-feminism provides a useful approach from which to question the relationship between gender and technical knowledge and prompts us to explore how social codes shape computer code, and vice versa. It also argues that there is scope for intervention and change.

Current research has found that the digital games industry, game content, and online and offline gaming cultures are highly gendered. The industry in the US, the UK and Ireland has one of the lowest percentage rates of female employment of all media and ICT industries (hovering around 10 per cent), and in programming occupations it is even lower (Kerr 2017). The percentage of workers from non-white racial and ethnic backgrounds is lower still. Research on the digital games industry in Ireland has found the highest paying programming jobs dominated by men; women more commonly occupy business operations and 'below the line' community management jobs (Kerr and Cawley 2012; Kerr and Kelleher 2015). Working conditions are often poor with 'crunch' working hours of 60–80 hours not uncommon in the run up to deadlines (Consalvo 2011). Recruitment into the industry is highly reliant on informal networks and a mix of cultural and social capital.

The association between games and heteronormative masculinity is often reinforced by the industry in its marketing, advertising and content, which can be highly stereotyped and explicitly targets boys, teens and young men. Attempts in the 1980s to target women with pink boxes and Barbie-related games are emblematic of a highly essentialised approach to gender (Cassell and Jenkins 1998). Research has critiqued the colour stereotyping of game packaging, highly sexualised female avatars in games, and a range of gendered practices in the increasingly professionalised e-sports field that associates heteronormative masculinity with excellence in competitive gameplay (Taylor et al. 2009). Core to the 'gamer identity' is knowledge of the history of games, who makes games, and of the particular techniques and language of games. Those without this knowledge are called 'newbies', and this lack of insider knowledge is often associated with women (Shaw 2012). However, when digital game play is studied empirically over time, gendered patterns of game play, gender preferences and expertise are less marked by sex than often assumed (Kerr 2003). There are female-identified high-level players and some women enjoy violent and fast-paced action games. Public gaming events, from gaming parties to game nights in internet cafes, are primarily attended by men and increasingly adopt the language of highly masculine sporting events. Women, when present, are largely in supportive or decorative roles. Recent work on gender and digital games has attempted to incorporate a more intersectional approach, exploring race, class and different forms of masculinity in digital game play (Kafai et al. 2016).

Professional games industry associations largely adopt a liberal approach to addressing this lack of diversity, establishing special committees for 'Women in Games' which showcase women already working in the industry and running conferences and seminars for networking. The underlying assumption is that if women and girls have more knowledge of the industry and what it does, they will want to work in it. The problem is often conceptualised as a 'pipeline problem' that can be solved by increasing the numbers of women entering the industry. However, Quality of Life surveys of the industry have identified persistent sexism in the workplace, and research indicates that there is a 'leaky pipeline' when it comes to women and ethnic minorities. Such initiatives have succeeded in raising awareness of gender issues, but they have done little to change the numbers of women studying or making digital games, or to move discussions of gender in a more intersectional direction. As critiques of gendered and misogynistic representations, structures and cultures by activist and feminist game designers and researchers over the past 20 years grew, a significant backlash has emerged. This is most apparent in the US.

Indeed, 'backlash' as a word understates the persistent online and offline harassment and threats made to some women who question the dominant culture and the representation of women and minorities in the industry and in its products (Chess and Shaw 2015). The ire focused partly on attempts to make game characters and stories more representative; to make game characters less sexualised; and to introduce community management stand-ards into online cultures and codes of conduct to public events. If game cultures were seen as inaccessible to many women before the online event that became known as #gamergate,[1] they were seen as downright hostile to their presence in the aftermath (Mortensen 2016). Gender is therefore a significant and fraught issue in digital games, and it is a marker of inequality in terms of access, status and content that operates at numerous levels. Given that some surveys state that almost 50 per cent of 'people who play games' are women (ESA 2015), it is likely that many female gamers have encountered hostility as part of their online cultural experience. The differential gaming and technology experiences of many women must be the starting point for any interventions attempting to tackle persistent gender inequalities in accessing highly paid computer, games or programming jobs. This is even more important given that some of the digital services developed by these companies produce, control and shape our access to knowledge.

GAMEJAMS AS INFORMAL TECHNOLOGY LEARNING EVENTS

Little attention has been paid to exploring the role that informal learning events play in relation to reproducing gendered structures in knowledge economies. Informal learning events are ephemeral by their nature and much of the organisational work and promotion takes place online. They are organised through websites and social media and take place in a range of borrowed spaces – from rooms in pubs to university computer labs and innovation spaces. They usually take place in the evenings or at weekends. Hackathons and gamejams are two types of informal learning events that focus on computer and game programming. Both are predicated on the belief that everyone can programme, and that collaborative coding can be empowering. They have their origins in the emancipatory politics of hacking and in the open software movement. Game jams, in particular, have their origins in the independent music scene (i.e. jamming), and the culture of hacking into computers. Game jams are promoted as spaces for social networking and do-it-yourself (DIY) game-making events. However, histories of hacking and gaming cultures have also found that they are dominated by men and are often hostile to women (Jordan and Taylor 2004). Studies of hackathons in the US have found that they replicate the individualist, competitive, temporally intense, and deadline-driven workplace cultures of the software and technology industries. Many 'hackathons' are underpinned by an explicit neo-liberal belief that everyone can be a technology entrepreneur (Irani 2015), and a more implicit belief that the perfect neo-liberal subject is continually striving to upgrade their technical knowledge and skills. Hackathons and gamejams are marketed as ostensibly 'open to all.' This ignores the existence of gendered economic, social and cultural barriers to access, and the ways in which the design of these events may be exclusionary.

Game jams are defined as 'accelerated' and 'constrained' forms of collaborative game-making (Kultima 2015). Attendees must design a game in a pre-defined length of time on a theme that is announced at the start of the day. Research on gamejams would suggest that they are a useful way to motivate people to learn content, technical and collaborative skills (Kultima 2015; Locke et al. 2015). Game jams are initiated by a range of organisations including the games and technology industry, universities and schools, and small-scale independent developers. At the same time, gender dynamics and gendered knowledge systems may come into conflict in mixed informal learning environments like after-school clubs and gamejams (Jenson et al. 2011). Diane Carr (2005) researched an after-school club in London. She noted how game preferences and competencies developed over time for both girls and boys, but that boys and girls coming from different socio-economic backgrounds often have a broader range of pre-existing skills and competencies. Informal experience with computer technologies provides some children with a greater advantage when entering both formal and informal education, and digital games may provide not only computing experience but also confidence with problem solving, managing failure, and basic programming. It may also contribute to the early formation of a computing or IT identity, and an interest in related occupations (Hayes 2011). Game jams, then, are one type of informal learning event where learning, gender and technology are mutually shaped, but where prior knowledge and social capital play an important role.

Dublin is home to a flourishing scene of informal technology learning events, from meet ups and hackathons to gamejams. They are usually organised by volunteers from academia or the IT industry, but increasingly they are used by research centres, technology festivals and companies for public engagement. They promote the 'coolness' of technology work, encourage technological upskilling, and are an important informal marketing and recruitment tool. They are intrinsically linked to online and offline social networks, with many organised through websites. On the website 'meetup. com' there were almost 250 registered 'tech' interest groups for the Dublin area, and five of these groups had over 1,000 members. Other social networks for technology and games related events include Facebook and designated channels on sites like 'Discord'. These groups are less formalised than traditional clubs, rarely requiring paid membership or other forms of commitment. It is sufficient to sign up online, paying with your data. Some are international associations with an Irish 'chapter', while others are Dublin-based only. Some of these events explicitly target women or girls (e.g., PyLadies, Girl Geeks, Women Who Code Dublin, Ladies who UX), but most are promoted as events that are open to all. A recent study of a female coding event in Ireland found that it had a range of competing goals and frictions involving commercialism, entrepreneurialism, recruitment, knowledge hierarchies and gender differences (Maalsen and Perng 2018; Perng et al. 2017).

GameCraft is a bottom up, 'independent', Irish only, volunteer-run gamejam with the tagline: 'Connect, Create, Collaborate' (see https://www. GameCraft.it/). It was established in 2012 by a female programmer and is still predominantly organised by a (different) woman. It is a registered not-for-profit organisation and runs 4–8 events on average each year. Its website states:

> GameCraft is a games jam event designed around building the gaming community. We aim to create events which allow game-makers to meet, share ideas, have fun, compete for prizes and most importantly make games!

The goal of GameCraft is to design a playable game in 10–12 hours. Our knowledge of GameCraft goes back to 2013, and one of the authors has observed their events over a number of years. Attendees form small teams with others who have complementary skills and then work together all day to develop a game. These teams may be composed of individuals who knew one another before starting the event; individuals who just met at the event itself; or some combination of the two. GameCraft events often charge little or no admission fee (often <€10 to cover lunch and soft drinks) and attendees must be 18 years of age or older. Attendance can range from 20–120 people and the website states that no prior game design experience is required. In addition to digital games, GameCraft also encourages the design and development of non-digital games, such as board games or card games, and provides materials for producing them. GameCraft has been invited to organise events in London, New York, Paris and Vienna, but over the past six years most of their events have taken place in Dublin, Cork, Galway and Limerick.

In 2016 the authors formally started to conduct research on GameCraft. Our project sought to explore how independently organised gamejams might contribute to, or challenge, the gendering of the wider games industry and culture. This research was conducted within the auspices of the 'Refiguring Innovation in Digital Games' [ReFiG] project funded by the Social Sciences and Humanities Research Council of Canada (see http://www.refig.ca/). The starting premise of that project is that game cultures and the games industry are highly gendered. It advocates mapping these gendering processes and encouraging interventions for change in the industry, in formal and informal education, and in online communities. Our methodology was mixed-method and, in this chapter, we largely draw upon surveys of attendees at two GameCraft events and on our observational field notes. We also provide some initial insights into three game design workshops that we designed as interventions; but these interventions were still ongoing at the time of writing.

Between January and March of 2016, one GameCraft event was held in the Dublin Institute of Technology (now Technological University Dublin) in Dublin, and another in the University of Limerick, Limerick. Both were held on Saturdays from 9 am to 9 pm. We were given permission to survey participants at both events, and given access to the organisers' documentation, including their code of conduct. Both authors attended. The Dublin event was held in a refurbished church on a university campus, while the Limerick event was held in a social area of a university building. People brought along their own computers and shared communal desks. Snacks and lunch were provided, with pizza and soft drinks furnished at the end of the day. Each event culminated in a play session. Attendees were asked to judge the games and were awarded small prizes. Of the total attendees at the two events (n=53), 27 individuals, or 51 per cent, completed the online survey. The survey had four sections: Gamejam Experience; Game Making Knowledge and Experience; Diversity and Discrimination; and Demographics. Our results largely confirmed our observations: most respondents at the GameCraft events identified as male (77 per cent in Dublin; and 93 per cent in Limerick), white (92 per cent in Dublin; and 93 per cent in Limerick), and straight (77 per cent in Dublin; and 93 per cent in Limerick). Respondents in Dublin were fairly evenly distributed between different age groups, while attendees in Limerick were primarily aged 18–24. 38 per cent of attendees at Dublin were studying at least part-time, while 43 per cent of attendees at Limerick were doing so. Of those that were not, most were working at least part time, and most were already working in some part of the IT industry.

So, this 'open to all' event, which had sought to attract males and females with no game design experience, attracted mostly males who were already studying or working in programming and the IT industry. Indeed, a majority of attendees at both events were programmers (85 per cent in Dublin; 57 per cent in Limerick), and when asked most respondents said they were attending in order to improve game-making skills (92 per cent in Dublin; and 93 per cent in Limerick) and to meet others in the Irish games-making community (92 per cent in Dublin; and 64 per cent in Limerick). The results are consistent with findings from similar events, such as the international Global Game Jam (GGJ). A 2013 survey of GGJ participants found that participants were 86 per cent male, 56.5 per cent were aged 21–29 years, and 60 per cent had a college or degree level qualification (Fowler et al. 2013). GameCraft attracted those with existing programming and IT skills enabling them to further develop their skills and to build a social network that may be useful in future in terms of hearing about employment and other opportunities. They primarily attracted and benefited young males with pre-existing IT knowledge, and social and cultural capital. How did GameCraft manage to attract such a narrow set of attendees with such a singular set of skills? In the next section we explore four findings in more depth: communication and recruitment for the events; the temporal and spatial structure of the events; the hierarchies of knowledge and identities that are validated throughout the day; and the invisible labour that people invest in such events.

EXPLORING THE REPRODUCTION OF GENDERED FORMS OF EXCLUSION AND KNOWLEDGE HIERARCHIES

GameCrafts are advertised on the GameCraft website, other gaming websites, and social media. One might think that such open advertising would attract a diverse set of attendees. However, our survey found that the most effective form of communication about the event (for almost 60 per cent) was 'word of mouth', followed by gaming accounts on Twitter and some gaming websites. This sharing on gaming-related online media restricted the range of people reached, and the word-of-mouth sharing of information meant that many people were arriving with friends and pre-established teams. This suggests that the communication channels and messages employed by GameCraft were very successful at attracting young males who specialise in programming and are already interested in games, but were not so successful in attracting or reaching outside gaming communities and pre-existing social networks. The forms of communication used to recruit also impacted team formation at the events. While collaboration in teams is at the core of the event, there seemed to be little attempt by attendees or organisers to diversify the range of skills in teams. Some teams were already working on college projects together or were in college together. Later in the year we attended another GameCraft and, on this occasion, only two of the 52 participants were without a team at the start of the day.

Other temporal elements in the structure of GameCraft are noteworthy and influence who can attend. One of the events we attended took place on Valentine's Day. This provoked much joking that attendees must all be single if they were free to attend on that day. Regardless of this fact, a 12-hour event presupposes that participants have 12 hours of free time at the weekend to participate in this type of event. They are free from caring and other responsibilities. The following figure gives the running order of one of the events we attended. While 12 hours might seem long to some readers, this was a short gamejam compared to others. The annual Global Game Jam for example runs over a 48-hour period and attendees often sleep at the venues, or not at all. These events are designed for those who can sit at a table for up to 12 or 48 hours. The events often represent a very long working day at the end of a working week or study week for most attendees. Such events replicate the intense working conditions experienced in deadline-driven creative, gaming or IT projects.

Breakdown of the day

08:30 Registration
09:00 Introduction
09:10 Game jam starts
13:00 lunch
19:00 Game jam ends, start playing games, voting
20:45 Award winners
21:00 End

Here's how it works:

- You have twelve hours to make a game. Starting at 9am
- The theme will be advertised during breakfast
- Work on your own or with a team. You can form a team on the day if you like
- Use whatever platform or framework you like
- Judges review and vote on the games
- Prizes.

Figure 1: Schedule of a GameCraft. Source: https://www.gamecraft.it/

Organisers announce a theme in the morning and all projects should relate in some way to that theme. It is usually an abstract concept such as 'borders' or 'love'. At GameCraft, once 10 hours of development is over a bell sounds and everyone plays each other's games and eats pizza. Attendees vote on the best games and small prizes are awarded. Most prizes are sponsored by companies. While the competition was low key at the events we attended, voting appeared to be influenced by the pre-existing social networks and friendships of those attending.

The event website states that no game-making experience is required to attend and according to our survey learning new skills is a key motivation for attendees. However, we observed that the pre-existing knowledge of attendees is important and those who attended had very good levels of computer, game and IT literacy. In a 12-hour period there is not sufficient time to learn new software and to develop complex graphics, animations or interaction for a game. While the goals of the event are to include everyone, and all skillsets, the strict deadline meant that access to programming knowledge was key to finishing a game, or at least getting a game to work. The pleasure of getting a game 'to work' was evident. Getting things to 'work' is often a euphemism for programming something to move and respond to the player on screen. The two events were dominated by those with programming and computing skills, and those who were already embedded in the educational or occupation culture of computing and IT. This was reinforced by holding events on university or college campuses with the support of computing and games lecturing staff. Many attendees self-identified as gamers on our survey and were interested in making and releasing a digital game. Indeed, three participants had already developed and launched a game on an online application store. The requirement to get things to work in a 'constrained' 12-hour period on an unannounced theme reinforces the need for programming skills and introduces a semi-public competitive aspect to these events.

Participants bring along their own laptops, ancillary hardware and in some cases virtual reality headsets. It should be noted that gaming computers are among the most expensive computers (costing up to €4,000), given their need for high end graphics cards and computing power. Some participants showed off their new laptops, or a piece of open source software that others might not know about. Others sat with large headphones on. These technology requirements (in terms of cost and knowledge) were clearly a barrier to participation. GameCraft organisers provide crafting materials to make non-digital games but we observed little engagement with these. Only one person designed a non-digital game over the two events we observed.

Finally, we wish to reflect on the forms of labour involved in running and attending GameCraft. These gamejams relied upon significant unpaid labour by female volunteers, with support from mostly male, full-time academics and industry representatives. The (largely unseen) organisational and communication work of the events relies heavily on volunteer labour. While the advisory board for GameCraft involves both men and women, the current key organiser is a long-time unpaid organiser of GameCrafts and female-friendly programming events. Her educational background is in programming and, with an MA-level qualification, she is highly qualified in IT, gaming and event organisation. She takes care of the technical, catering and organisational structure of the events as well as taking care of the well-being of attendees on the day. She is also the person to whom people report any misconduct. This role involves a large degree of face-to-face affective labour, a core element of many contemporary service industries (Kennedy 2018). More free labour and technical knowledge are embodied in the free and open source software used to advertise the event, run the sign-up process and post the games after the event.

Another aspect of the free labour embodied in these events is the 'aspirational' labour (Duffy 2017) of the attendees. Many of the attendees are students or working in IT who hope to enter the games industry and have given up their leisure time to learn new skills and build their social networks. The rise of unpaid labour is widespread in the contemporary knowledge economy and reveals additional gendered knowledge patterns. In the online world of beauty bloggers and YouTube celebrities, we find the aspirational labour of primarily female content creators who believe that their 'unpaid work, motivated by passion and the infectious rhetoric of entrepreneurialism, will eventually yield respectable income and rewarding careers' (Duffy 2017: 15). We find another version of this entanglement of aspiration and gender in the 'passionate labour' of mostly male gamers keen to enter the games industry (Kerr and Kelleher 2009). GameCraft and similar types of informal technology learning events enable those with the social and cultural capital, and the free time, to invest in upgrading their technical knowledge. It trains them to work in an intense deadline-driven culture. Most participants are willing to sit for 12 hours powered by copious amounts of tea, coffee, soft drinks and cigarettes. In the large open-plan spaces participants circulate to survey the work of others. Everyone can observe the performance of technical expertise, or its absence, in such a space, seeing who produced a working game in these 12-hour marathons. GameCraft makes visible and public the aspirational labour and passion of mostly men, while making less visible the organisational labour of mostly women behind the event.

Despite the best efforts of community volunteers, these events demon-strate how the association between games, IT knowledge, and masculinity, gets reinforced and reproduced. Wider gender and knowledge hierarchies are actively shaping who has the time and resources to attend these events, and these intersect with class, race and ethnicity. Locating the events in universities, technology companies or innovation hubs provides informal knowledge of these venues and companies. Locating events at HEIs means that the attendance is skewed by those already attending university technology courses, which are themselves already heavily male-dominated.

We returned to observe a third GameCraft in Dublin in December 2017, and a fourth in Cork in March 2019. Little had changed in terms of participation. These events further reinforce social networks and social capital for those who can attend, giving attendees a 'head start' in game-related recruitment as part of the insider culture. Sponsors provide free t-shirts, stickers, company information and, in some cases, information on jobs. While GameCraft succeeds in providing social networking and collaborative learning opportunities for attendees, the design of these types of informal learning events, and the necessity for them to partner with others to find suitable venues, means that they are shaped by pre-existing gendered structures of production and reproduction. These types of events implicitly exclude those with caring responsibilities or atypical work schedules, and those without IT skills, hardware and gaming knowledge. Furthermore, the time intensity of these events places abstract coding and programming knowledge at the top of the knowledge hierarchy. Further work is required to establish if our findings hold for other information technology events and if 'open to everyone' events are in fact reinforcing rather than reducing the gendered digital divide in the wider IT industries.

GENDER-BASED DISCRIMINATION AND TECHNO-FEMINIST INTERVENTIONS FOR CHANGE

In the course of our field research the issue of diversity moved centre stage in public discourse in Ireland through the 2015 same-sex referendum; the 2015 #WakingTheFeminists movement in Irish theatre; and the 2017 international #MeToo movement. These events were preceded by the #gamergate controversy. It is within this context that we situate our discussion of the findings from our survey on diversity, experiences of discrimination, and our own interventions in local game culture.

Our survey asked participants about diversity at local game events. Overwhelmingly respondents felt that events were not diverse, and of those who answered the follow up question many felt that women, people over 30, and 'non-Irish' people were missing. Despite this finding many respondents were unconvinced that local game events should explicitly address diversity issues. We also asked whether attendees had observed, or experienced, discrimination in game cultures: 44 per cent responded that they had. While the survey population here is small, and our attendees were primarily male and young, the level of observed discrimination is quite high. This result may be partly explained by response bias, as the participants may have been primed to think about discrimination, but the discrepancy is notable not only for the amount of reported discrimination but also for its type. While in national surveys the most common grounds for discrimination are age and race/ethnicity (CSO 2014), in our survey of GameCraft participants it was gender. This level of gender-based discrimination is in line with international studies of the prevalence of gender-based discrimination in online and offline game cultures.

While some attendees were ambivalent about addressing discrimination, the ReFiG project sought not only to identify gendered structures and practices, but also to design interventions to change local gaming and IT cultures. Many of our research partners were running female-only after-school clubs, female-only incubation centres, and female-only gamejams (Kennedy 2018). The New York based 'alterconf' ran an inclusive technology conference in Dublin in 2016 (see https://www.alterconf.com/). Their approach sought to run technology events for all marginalised people. Such an approach goes beyond codes of conduct and embraces a policy on bathrooms, venues, and event content. Our local collaborator already ran 'female-friendly' events, which encouraged heterosexual, queer and trans individuals, couples, and allies to attend. In our planning discussions for our intervention we felt that female-friendly events would be more open to genderqueer, trans and non-cis individuals than women only.

We wanted to embrace a feminist and intersectional pedagogy with the aim of creating safe spaces for alternative forms of knowledge and marginalised groups. In collaboration with local partners we designed three half-day workshops which sought to address the exclusion mechanisms we identified in GameCraft in terms of: communication and recruitment, access to hardware and software, cost, duration of events, venues, knowledge diversity and free organisational labour. We publicised these workshops across a range of creative and non-gaming websites, networks, and organisations in an attempt to reach beyond existing game networks and to attract a range of artistic, creative, and non-technical skills and knowledge. To promote accessibility to all groups, we did not charge an admission fee, and we provided all materials and computers. We highlighted our Code of Conduct in the application process, emphasising standards of behaviour that would be expected of all attendees and providing clear avenues for reporting problematic experiences (see also http://www.refig.ca/safer-space-policy/ and www.gamedevelopers.ie/diversity). Any complaints were only acted on if the attendees wished for action to be taken, a provision intended to allow attendees to feel that they maintained control over the process.

In the summer of 2016 we ran three beginner and female-friendly free workshops on successive weekends in Dublin city, with 30 attendees. Our attendees were predominantly female (100 per cent of attendees at the first event; 70 per cent at the second; and 64 per cent at the third). The 18–24 age group that was dominant at GameCraft made up only a marginal percentage of attendees at the Network in Play workshops (0 per cent at the first session; 10 per cent at the second; 14 per cent at the third). The 25–34 age group was the most common at our events, followed by those in the 45–64 age group. Some who attended were unemployed. However, people of colour were notably absent. Feedback on the exit surveys from our first three workshops was very positive.

Advertising our event on non-gaming channels was very successful: many who attended had first learned of the event through its advertisement on mailing lists for visual and creative artists. This was reflected in the skill mix of attendees, which was more diverse than at GameCraft. Attendees included jewellery makers, painters, animators, and graphic designers, in addition to those with programming skills. Positive word of mouth meant that the numbers of attendees increased over the three workshops. Our attention to using inclusive language in recruitment also appeared to be successful. The code of conduct and the language used during the workshops were positively evaluated. Many expressed an interest in attending more events.

We purposely designed a half-day rather than a full-day event to address time commitment issues. Some attendees had to leave early, while others asked for longer sessions. Access challenges remained, however: potential attendees identified childcare, parking, and the locations of the event space as significant barriers. In terms of pre-existing knowledge, we worked closely with our tutors to ensure they were aware of our goals and we included a range of commercial and non-commercial, digital, and non-digital games as examples, which also included a diverse range of representations and avatars. Collaboration was encouraged; competition was not: there were no prizes, deadlines or ticking clocks. Finally, the tutors, organisers and research assistants were paid for their time and expertise.

Our workshops focused on the fundamentals of game design, game narratives and game programming. The workshops that we designed moved from non-technical in the first workshop to the use of computer hardware and software in the second and third. The more technical workshops introduced significant material challenges in terms of hardware, software, and knowledge requirements. Partnering with educational institutions to gain access to computer labs inevitably means that the technologies that they provide are high-end computers and may have non-standard software. This introduced challenges for our tutors and attendees in one of our 2016 workshops. However, by far the most complex challenge involved designing an introduction to game coding for beginners. Attendees at this workshop were 50:50 male and female with a majority working full time. The feedback from attendees was very positive: attendees commented on the 'friendly tutors' and that the events were 'an absolute pleasure to be part of'. At the same time this workshop required two tutors rather than one, more supports from the organisers, and introduced a technological barrier – people needed their own laptops. We had a much higher demand from males to attend the third workshop, and we had to turn away some of them in order to keep a mixture of attendees.

In 2018 we brought our three beginner and female-friendly game-making workshops to another Irish city. We recruited 33 people and a majority of females to our workshops over three weekends. A majority of attendees were already either working or in full-time study, and two were following game-related courses. In an attempt to overcome the necessity for attendees to have a computer for our coding workshop we used a technology training centre. Unfortunately, this was not entirely successful. The computer laboratories were arranged to facilitate individualised rather than collaborative learning, and most of the computers were locked down to prevent their being moved. The computers were not fast enough to run even the basic games tutorials and the projector was not of sufficient quality to display the software. Our tutor was an experienced developer but struggled to design an introductory session for beginners. Despite the best efforts of tutors and organisers, significant techno-spatial hurdles prevailed. Feedback was mixed – with non-beginners frustrated with the slow speed of the computers and session, and beginners frustrated with the fast pace. Some beginners wanted paper handouts to supplement the online material.

On reflection we, as organisers, learned a lot from this final game-coding workshop. While we succeeded in diversifying participants at our workshops, and created inclusive teaching resources, we realised that this is only the first step in challenging gendered pathways. The hardware, software, and venues we used restricted our pedagogical freedom – challenges faced by many students entering formal computing or gaming education. Training software is pre-coded with significant assumptions about prior IT knowledge and an unsettling requirement for our workshop to sign up for an account with the key industry software provider in order to download their educational software. This experience raised some important questions about where and how to teach game coding to beginners – and the ways in which software can co-opt our learning experiences into the wider knowledge economy.

CRAFTING INCLUSIVE LEARNING SPACES AND CHALLENGING EXCLUSION MECHANISMS

Game jams are just one type of informal technology event which are being used to promote STEM occupations and educational choices. We need to question the assumptions that these events are 'open to all'. We have mapped some of the gendered structures which operate to exclude many from attending. These events rely on narrow communication and social networks for promotion; their temporal and spatial structure presuppose able-bodied participants and available leisure time; and they require access to computing resources. Consequently, attendance is dominated by young males and by those already studying and working in IT-related industries. Furthermore, the semi-public performance of technical knowledge at these gamejams often comes at the expense of other forms of knowledge needed to innovate creatively. We also need to highlight these events' reliance on volunteer and aspirational labour. This practice risks further entrenching the feminisation of behind-the-scenes, invisible and unrewarded labour while foregrounding a competitive, masculinist, deadline-driven technology identity and working culture. Attendance at these events further reinforces the social and cultural capital required to get a head start in the IT industries and may be contributing to the reproduction of wider gendered structures and hierarchies in our knowledge economy.

Many of our surveyed attendees were aware of the lack of diversity at game events. While one solution might be to organise women-only events, these too can be problematic, depending on one's goals. Maalsen and Perng (2018) found that women only events encounter resistance from the broader computing community, who argue that they are discriminatory. Some of respondents perceived the problem of diversity as being with those who do not turn up.

Our experience organising our female-friendly workshops indicates that we can remove some of the exclusionary and masculinist elements and create events that are attractive to a more diverse range of people (while acknowledging that there were still some groups that we were not able to reach, such as non-white and non-straight individuals). We can produce safe, informal spaces of learning aimed at opening up the range of skills needed to produce a digital game. Our project highlights the importance of organisational innovation to create inclusive learning spaces, and the importance of having supportive intermediaries (researchers, tutors and technologies, etc) to foster an inclusive pedagogy.

At the same time, technology barriers persisted. We found that we needed to decode the affordances built into our computer laboratories, our hardware, and our software tools if we are truly to hack the technology/ gender relationship. The lessons of techno-feminism are that while 'technology affords or inhibits the doing of particular gender power relations, the relationship is not "immutably fixed"' (Wajcman 2010: 150). Gender and artefacts that seem obdurate can be reprogrammed. Our biggest challenge was access to a space and computer resources that did not presuppose pre-existing computing, gaming, and IT knowledge. Some computing technologies are unsuitable for beginners. Some formal educational spaces come with a built-in expert-centred pedagogy. Many presuppose fully abled bodies. Our focus remains on the potential of informal learning, supportive networks and both digital and non-digital technologies to rethink the mutual shaping of gender, technology, and games. Our project's goal is not to 'attract' more marginalised people into the technology pipeline. We do not wish to bring more women and marginalised groups into companies whose cultural and workplace norms are based on highly gendered values and practices. As in other domains the simple presence of more women will not in itself change gendered norms and structures. The goal must be to empower women and other marginalised groups to re-code gender power relations and challenge the relationship between masculinity, knowledge, and technology. This is imperative given the ubiquity of computing technologies, and the status and power of those working in the IT industries in contemporary Irish society.

Notes

1 #Gamergate started in 2014 and saw a number of American and European academics and female game designers subject to an online backlash from game players and some industry spokespersons. The backlash sought to 'protect' digital games from attempts to increase diversity, especially in relation to gender and sexuality.

Acknowledgements

The authors would like to thank Ms Vicky Twomey-Lee for her support throughout the Network in Play project and acknowledge the financial support of the Social Sciences and Humanities Research Council of Canada.

REFERENCES

Carr, Diane. 'Contexts, gaming pleasures, and gendered preferences', in *Simulation & Gaming*, 36(4), 2005, pp 464–82.
Cassell, Justine and Henry Jenkins (eds), *From Barbie to Mortal Kombat: Gender and Computer Games* (MIT Press: Cambridge, Massachusetts, 1998).

Chess, Shira and Adrienne Shaw, 'A conspiracy of fishes, or, how we learned to stop worrying about #Gamergate and embrace hegemonic masculinity', in *Journal of Broadcasting & Electronic Media*, 59, 2015, pp 208–20, a9h.

Consalvo, Mia, 'Crunched by passion: Women game developers and workplace challenges', in Yasmin B. Kafai et al. (eds), *Beyond Barbie and Mortal Kombat: New Perspectives on Gender and Gaming* (MIT Press: Cambridge, Massachusetts, 2011), pp 177–90.

Cowan, Ruth, 'The consumption junction: A proposal for research strategies in the sociology of technology', in W. Bijker et al. (eds), *The Social Construction of Technological Systems* (MIT Press: Cambridge, Massachusetts, 1987), pp 261–78.

CSO, 'Quarterly National Household Survey, Equality Module', Central Statistics Office, 2014. http://www.cso.ie/en/releasesandpublications/er/q-eq/qnhsequalitymodulequarter32014/

Duffy, Brooke Erin, *(Not) Getting Paid to Do What You Love: Gender, Social Media and Aspirational Work* (Yale University Press: New Haven, Connecticut, 2017).

ESA, 'Essential facts about the computer and video game industry', Entertainment Software Association, 2015. http://www.theesa.com/wp-content/uploads/2015/04/ESA-Essential-Facts-2015.pdf

Fowler, Allan et al., 'The global game jam for technology and learning', in *Computing and Information Technology Research and Education New Zealand (CITRENZ2013)* edited by Mike Lopez and Michael Verhaart, 2013.

Grint, Keith and Rosalind Gill (eds), *The Gender-Technology Relation: Contemporary Theory and Research* (Taylor and Francis: London, 1995).

Harding, Sandra, *The Science Question in Feminism* (Cornell University: NY, 1986).

Hayes, Elisabeth, 'Girls, gaming and trajectories of it expertise', in Yasmin B. Kafai et al. (eds), *Beyond Barbie and Mortal Kombat* (MIT Press: Cambridge, Massachusetts, 2011), pp 217–30.

Irani, Lilly, 'Hackathons and the making of entrepreneurial citizenship', in *Science, Technology & Human Values*, 40(5), 2015, pp 1–26.

Jenson, Jennifer and Suzanne de Castell, 'Theorizing gender and digital gameplay: Oversights, accidents and surprises', in *Eludamos. Journal for Computer Game Culture*, 2(1), 2008, pp 15–25.

Jenson, Jennifer et al., 'Disrupting the gender order: Leveling up and claiming space in an after-school gaming club', in *International Journal of Gender, Science and Technology* 3(1), 2011, p. 149.

Jordan, Tim and Paul Taylor, *Hacktivism and Cyberwars: Rebels with a Cause?* (Routledge: London, 2004).

Kafai, Yasmin B. et al., *Diversifying Barbie and Moral Kombat: Intersectional Perspectives and Inclisve Designs in Gaming* (Carnegie Mellon University ETC Press: Pittsburgh, PA, 2016).

Kennedy, Helen W., 'Game jam as feminist methodology: The affective labors of intervention in the ludic economy', in *Games and Culture*, 2018.

Kerr, Aphra, 'Girls just want to have fun!', in *Strategies of Inclusion: Gender in the Information Society 3: Surveys of Women's Experience*, edited by Nelly Oudshoorn, Els Rommes, Irma van Sloten (Edward Elgar: Trondheim, Cheltenham, UK, 2003), pp 211–32.

Ibid., *Global Games: Production, Circulation and Policy in the Networked Age* (Routledge: London, 2017).

Kerr, Aphra and Anthony Cawley, 'The spatialisation of the digital games industry: Lessons from Ireland', in *International Journal of Cultural Policy*, vol 18(4), 2012, pp 398–418.

Kerr, Aphra and John D. Kelleher, 'The recruitment of passion and community in the service of capital: Community managers in the digital games industry', in *Critical Studies in Media Communication*, 32(3), 2015, pp 177–92.

Kerr, Aphra and Seán Ó Riain, 'Knowledge economy', in *International Encyclopedia of Human Geography*, R. Kitchin and N. Thrift, Elsevier (eds), 2009, pp 31–6.

Kultima, Annakaisa, 'Defining game jam', in *10th International Conference on the Foundations of Digital Games* (FDG: US, 2015).

Locke, Ryan et al., 'The game jam movement: Disruption, performance and artwork' in *Proceedings of the 10th International Conference on the Foundations of Digital Games* June 22–25, 2015 (FDG: Pacific Grove, CA, 2015).

Maalsen, Sophia and Sung-Yueh Perng, 'Crafting code: Gender, coding and spatial hybridity in the events of pyladies Dublin', in *Craft Economies: Cultural Economies of the Handmade*, S. Luckman and N. Thomas (eds) (Bloomsbury: London and New York, 2018).

Mortensen, Torill Elvira, 'Anger, fear, and games: The long event of #Gamergate' in *Games and Culture*, 13(8), 2016, pp 787–806.

O'Connor, Pat et al., 'Micro-political practices in higher education: A challenge to excellence as a rationalising myth?', in *Critical Studies in Education*, 2017, pp 1–17.

Perng, Sung-Yueh et al., 'Hackathons, entrepreneurship and the passionate making of smart cities', in *The Programmable City Project* (Maynooth University: Maynooth, 31 Mar. 2017).

Preston, Paschal et al., 'Digital media sector innovation in the knowledge economy: Rethinking knowledge inputs and policies', in *Information, Communication and Society*, 12(7), 2009, pp 994–1,014.

Russell, Helen et al., 'Gender equality in the Irish labour market 1966–2016: Unfinished business?', in *The Economic and Social Review*, 48(4), 2017, pp 393–418.

Shaw, Adrienne, 'Do you identify as a gamer? Gender, race, sexuality, and gamer identity', in *New Media & Society*, 14(1), 2012, pp 28–44.

Taylor, Nicholas et al., 'Cheerleaders/booth babes/*Halo* hoes: Pro-gaming, gender and jobs for the boys', in *Digital Creativity*, 20(4), 2009, pp 239–52.

Wajcman, Judy, 'Feminist theories of technology', in *Cambridge Journal of Economics*, 34(1), 2010, pp 143–52.

Ibid., *Techno Feminism* (Polity Press: Cambridge, UK, 2004).

Walby, Sylvia, 'Is the knowledge society gendered?', in *Gender, Work and Organisation*, 18(1), 2011, pp 1–29.

ELEVEN

Marking Your Cards: Gender Distinction in the Broadsheet Book Review

Mary P. Corcoran

INTRODUCTION

This chapter assesses women's opportunity to contribute to discursive public space in twenty-first century Ireland. The analysis is set against the recent emergence of a powerful feminist voice challenging the under-representation of women as knowledge producers and disseminators within the public (and primarily cultural) sphere. The broadsheet book review is a core element of cultural knowledge production, yet it has been largely overlooked by academics and movement activists in Ireland, although not elsewhere (CWILA 2015; Vida 2016; Harvey and Lamond 2016). I apply a gendered analytical framework to interrogate women's contributions to, and visibility in, the broadsheet book review.

The findings suggest that while a broadsheet newspaper may adapt a largely benign stance on gender issues (through for instance, its socially liberal ideology and provision of space to feminist columnists), it may simultaneously reproduce and legitimate forms of male gendered expertise. In the Book Review Section, women are marginalised both as authors and as reviewers; books by and about men are privileged over those by and about women, and a high degree of gendered segregation of book genres prevails. There is, in other words, a clear disjuncture between a tacit commitment to gender equity in liberal broadsheet print media and the practice of gender equal representation. This case study illuminates the durability of the gender knowledge regime arising from the unreflective reproduction of gendered institutional practices.

SILENCING IN THE CULTURAL KNOWLEDGE PRODUCTION SPHERE

A truly democratic society creates spaces and opportunities for people to express themselves not just as economic actors, but as cultural, social and public actors as well. It is one that values diversity and the idea of public citizenship, and of public intellectuals (Corcoran and Lalor 2012). Public intellectuals can spring from a broad church: academia, journalism, literature, law, theatre, visual arts, and so on. What they have in common is a concern 'with creating new agendas and raising issues that those in power currently would wish to avoid; they can also be seen as concerned with transforming what Wright Mills (1970) called "private troubles" into "public issues"' (O'Connor 2012: p 56). It follows that public intellectuals – as knowledge producers – require access to the public sphere.

History teaches us that the public sphere is a problematic space for women's voices (Fraser 1990; Young 1997). According to the classicist Mary Beard (2014) an integral part of growing up as a man in the Greek Homeric tradition was learning to take control of public utterance and to silence the female of the species. Authoritative public speech was 'men's business'. What interests Beard is how that classical moment of woman silencing is refracted in contemporary culture. She traces a long line to Greek and Roman antiquity where the prerogative of men was 'not only to exclude women from public speech but also to parade that exclusion' (2014: 11). She suggests that there are two main exceptions in which women may claim the right to public speech: when they are speaking out as victims or martyrs; or when they are defending their own sectional interests (and not advocating on behalf of the community or the public as a whole). This legacy – of writing women out of public discourse – remains with us today and 'underlies some of our own assumptions about, and awkwardness with, the female voice in public' (2014: 14). The persistence of such (unexamined) assumptions has recently been brought into sharp relief in the Irish context, and is explored in the body of this chapter.

In June 2018, headlines were made in the Irish media when the co-leaders of the Social Democrats, a left of centre political party, threatened to withdraw from the MacGill Summer School[1] unless the organisers addressed significant gender imbalance in the programme (*The Irish Times*, 22 June 2018). Year on year, the issues *du jour* are debated at the School and widely reported in the national newspapers, largely because of the unrivalled professional connections of the School's Director, Joe Mulholland. Poor gender balance in deliberations largely went under the radar. However, the recent global sensitisation on gender issues (including gender representation) meant that a showdown with Joe Mulholland was inevitable. The question is, why had it taken so long? And how is it possible to organise a public, deliberative event in 2018 about 'The future of Ireland in the new Europe' without any regard to the gender and diversity of panel participants? The controversy about MacGill resulted in a contrite Joe Mulholland revising the programme at the last minute and promising to address the imbalance in 2019.

This controversy mirrored an earlier showdown that erupted after the Abbey Theatre launched its *Waking the Nation* programme to mark the 2016 Centenary of the Easter Rising. Questions were raised by women across the sector as to how it was possible for Fiach Mac Conghail, then Director of Ireland's national theatre – which receives the bulk of Arts Council funding for theatre in Ireland every year – to curate a programme of plays that almost wholly excluded women. In the aftermath Mac Conghail regretted his failure to attend to gender balance and to check his privilege (*Irish Independent*, 15 Nov. 2015). His *faux pas* catalysed #WakingTheFeminists, a social movement that has since become a significant advocate for the inclusion of gender equality policies in Irish theatre organisations. To provide context to the testimonials of hundreds of women in the theatre sector, an independent analysis of gender in Irish theatre 2006–2015 was undertaken (Donohue et al. 2017). This research focused on a sample of ten publically funded theatre organisations, and examined the gender distribution across seven occupational categories. The picture painted was one of systematic gender exclusion. Women were poorly represented in six of the seven cultural production roles examined. Just over one third of directors and one quarter of authors were women. Theatre on the margins (and therefore more precarious and contingent) was most gender balanced while elite theatre (in receipt of highest state funding) was lowest in terms of gender representation.

Both the MacGill Summer School and *Waking the Nation* controversies effectively exposed the subtle ways in which women may come to be 'written out' of public discourse. This happens because, as the various contributions to this volume have shown, deep-structured gender divisions and forms of gendered power continue to frame many of our institutions, processes, and practices. Men in power mirror and filter social reality in their own image. These get inscribed into subjective identities, institutional practices, and the wider interpretative frameworks that shape our culture. The problem does not end with the introduction of equality policies in Irish theatre, or greater gender balance in Summer School panel selection. As this volume shows there are many neglected sites of knowledge production where forensic examination illuminates the myriad of means – overt and covert – through which gender inequality continues to be reproduced.

GENDERED KNOWLEDGE AND EXCLUSION IN THE MEDIA AND CULTURAL SPHERES

The media have been shown to be particularly effective at constructing meanings, and offering those constructs in a systematic way to audiences where they are likely to be incorporated to one degree or another, into personal meaning structures (Gamson and Modigliani 1989) that are highly gendered (Gill 2006). Media scholarship has consistently shown that while the conversion effect of media is limited, it has an important reinforcing effect (Schudson 1989). So, it matters whose voices feature in the media and the cultural spheres because it is those voices that help to frame wider public discourse.

In the Irish context, O'Brien (2014) has demonstrated how the Irish national broadcaster RTÉ's flagship current affairs series *Prime Time* in the lead up to the 2011 General Election, was structured on highly gendered terms (2014: 505). In the eleven episodes of dedicated election coverage men and women occupied distinctly different spaces. Women's engagement with politics was gendered through processes of numeric underrepresentation, gendered visual practices, use of predominantly male sources and casting the discussion in such a way that women were dominant on 'soft' or caring issues and made interventions less frequently on 'hard' issues such as economics and politics (2014: 506). In the same vein, Rafter (2014) found that there was 'a near-total absence of female voices' broadcast across two flagship radio programmes tasked with covering the financial crisis of 2008 and its aftermath. Commentators were mostly drawn from an elite pool of authoritative figures selected by programme makers. He concludes that selection practices amount to a significant failure on the part of editorial decision makers because 'a narrow range of voices limits alternative perspectives in public debate' (2014: 1).

The arrival of the internet held out considerable hope for more egalitarian and democratic access to channels of communication. Castells (2007) places considerable emphasis on the transformative interplay between communication and power relationships in the technological context presaged by the network society. He contends that the development of interactive, horizontal networks of communication (across social media) produces a new form of mass self-communication. Potentially, he argues this should make it easier for alternative voices, dissenters, insurgents, and social movements more generally to access and intervene much more decisively in the newly emerged communication space of social media. In reality, Castells vision appears to have been overly optimistic, particularly when we consider the issue of gender and technology. Herring, et al. (1995) found that utopian predictions about the potential of computer-mediated communication to create transgressive and radically new non-gendered subjectivities were widely off the mark (cited in Cameron 1998). Rather, they suggest that social relations in the virtual world are almost identical to those in the real one. Indeed, there is now a wealth of empirical evidence to show that:

> Gendered social and cultural practices continue to shape educational and occupational choices, including pathways into computing and software programming. The knowledge economy, and technology-based occupations in particular, are dominated by men (Kerr and Savage in this volume).

Even in less formal information technology platforms the evidence supports a gender divide. Herring et al. (2004) studied the first-generation blogs that emerged in the wake of discussion forums and chat rooms as 'democratic' spaces that could represent diverse demographic groups. Paradoxically, blogs tended to be age and gender representative, but *discourses* about blogs in the mainstream media, in scholarly communication and in the blogsphere itself, principally highlighted the blogs of adult males. Clearly, this indicates a process of selection, interpretation and remediation that effectively filters out women's voices. Who does the filtering? Herring et al. (2004) identified a focus on 'a particular blog type, the so-called 'filter' blog, which is produced mostly by adult males' (2014, no page given). The authors argue that privileging filter blogs implicitly valorises the activities of adult men who are automatically deemed to be more interesting, important and/or newsworthy than other blog authors. Blogging in its early iteration came to be seen as the preserve (and prerogative) of adult men 'thereby indirectly reproducing societal sexism and ageism, and misrepresenting the fundamental nature of the weblog phenomenon' (2014, no page given).

Kerr and Savage (in this volume) explore informal learning spaces and technological cultures and demonstrate that while both are ostensibly open to all, in reality they reinforce a gendered digital divide. Events are dominated by those with higher, prior skill levels, unlimited time and access to pre-existing tech networks. Collaborative practice in so far as it occurs, is among pre-existing, (mostly male) colleagues and friends. This produces a form of social closure that not only limits women's access to informal learning spaces, but crucially may impact on their opportunities to pursue tech culture jobs in the future.

REVIEWING THE BOOK REVIEW: RATIONALE AND METHODOLOGY

The mass media continues to play a role in promoting and mediating the arts and culture to the wider public. Yet there is very little scholarly research (and none that I could find in the Irish context) on the representation of women in media coverage of the arts and culture more generally, and book and literary review outlets, in particular. Book reviews are of interest because like other forms of media and culture they exercise a symbolic power. Reviews are important vehicles for enabling a population to speak to itself, to hold up a mirror to the wider culture and mediate that to audiences through the interpretive actions of those who are tasked with the reviewing. In other words, 'reviewers play an important role in setting the agenda in terms of the way an individual text is engaged with and understood' (Harvey and Lamond 2016: 87). But books also embody a form of both cultural and economic capital. There are many more books published than will ever receive a review, and the strictures of space and time mean that any given book has a very small arc of possibility of coming to wider public attention. In the face of this competition, to receive a book review is a bonus and is a measure of prestige. Clearly, the longer the review the more prestigious the reader understands the book to be. A review potentially has a longer shelf life than its single appearance in a digital or print edition: reviews will frequently pop up online (especially if searching a title or theme); reviews can be used to market the book; reviews can be recapitulated in end-of-year book specials or summer reading recommendations.

Books pages are significant because they direct us to what is published, and effectively promote the titles that will be purchased by individuals (discerning readers) and institutions (public libraries); chosen by book clubs (mainly women); selected and assigned by academics seeking ways to engage students. Book reviewing therefore plays a significant role in the political economy of the publishing industry specifically, and cultural production more generally. Yet, 'book reviewing is an under-studied sector of the literary field, despite the fact that it has an influence on authors' careers, book sales and publishers' commissions as well as on the determinations of literary value' (Harvey and Lamond 2016: 84). One UK-based study carried out in the 1980s examined 28 publications across high culture and popular culture. The study concluded that regardless of political orientation or type of outlet their book sections are concerned mainly with reviewing books by men (Women in Publishing, 1987). Vida – a New York-based, feminist organisation for Women in Literary Arts – has been compiling data on women writers annually since 2009. Their 1,000 data points are selected from 'Tier 1' journals, publications and press outlets from around the world by which the literary community defines and rewards its most valued arts workers (www.vidaweb.org). The data consistently shows that the authors and the critics who are evaluating those authors, are about two thirds men. Moreover, the more prestigious the outlet, the less equitable it is (Guest 2017). A McGill University student survey of over 10,000 reviews in *The New York Times* Book Review, that tracked both gender and genre, also found that two thirds of reviewed books were written by men, and that reviewed books tended to reflect gender stereotypes, an effect the researchers called 'topic bias' (Hu 2017). Similarly, the Canadian Women in the Literary Arts (CWILA) 2015 count on gender representation, found that 59 percent of reviewed non-fiction books were by male authors (ibid). Harvey and Lamond's (2016) comparative study of reviewing in Australia across genre and across time, reaches a similar conclusion: male authors were more likely than their female counterparts to have their work featured in published reviews. Despite the fact that two thirds of published authors in Australia are women, two thirds of the books being reviewed are by men; a ratio that remained largely unchanged between 1987 and 2013. Finally, a study that explored whose poetry is reviewed and whose reviews are commissioned and published (based on data from outlets that publish poetry and poetry criticism over a six year period across the UK and Ireland), revealed similar levels of gender bias. Though female critics were roughly as likely to review female poets as not, male critics reviewed male poets 66.9 per cent of the time, compared with just 28.9 per cent female poets. In ten of the 39 magazines surveyed, less than 40 per cent of contributors were female or non-binary (*The State of Poetry and Poetry Criticism in the UK and Ireland*, 2012–18).

According to Fraser the public sphere 'is an institutionalised arena of discursive interaction – a theatre for debating and deliberation rather than buying and selling' (1990: 57). I argue that the book review section of broadsheet newspapers and periodicals constitutes an important element of the symbolic public sphere. Book Review sections are intended to engage the wider public, and they simultaneously confer status on the newspaper itself, the featured authors and the reviewers. Arts & Books pages create visibility for arts and culture events as well as books, and thus have a degree of influence. Your status and work (whether as author or reviewer) is validated by your presence in these pages. The assignation of space to reviews (although they garner a lot less space than that which is assigned to sport, property or business) allows the newspaper or periodical to continue to enjoy prestige status because 'it recognises that cultural objects remain significant and are powerful in shaping human action' (Schudson 1989: 155). Moreover, book 'knowledge' (what's in and out) and book reading (or listening) remains a core part of cultural capital, particularly of elites in society.

Over the decades that I have perused *The Irish Times* Book Review Weekend section I had frequently been struck by a sense that an implicit gender bias operated in its structure and organisation. So I set out to interrogate the way in which the Book Review Section as a knowledge producing and dissemination platform is framed; the extent to which the interpretive frameworks produced are diverse or hegemonic; and the consequences of such framing for men and women, authors and reviewers.

Polletta and Chen argue that among the key factors that matter for creating a truly public and participatory public sphere are the social norms defining topics that are appropriate and *the people whose opinions are authoritative* (2013: 291). They seek to locate the gendered character of the institutional settings in which public talk takes place' (2013: 292). The focus of the next section is to assess the extent to which a broadsheet Book Review Section may 'communicate different messages about the *appropriate gender of authoritative speakers, topics and styles of talk*' (2013: 293).

My overall research question is: 'To what extent does a gender regime operate in the Book Review Section of *The Irish Times*?' By gender regime I mean a particular set of institutional practices underpinning structure and organisation in a given sphere *and* contributing to a broader gender order (Connell 1987). I operationalise the research question through a number of sub-questions:

1. To what extent are men and women equally represented as contributors (authors and reviewers) to the Book Review Section of *The Irish Times*?
2. Are men more likely to review books by men, and women more likely to review books by women, i.e. is there gender segregation built into the reviewing process?
3. To what extent is the pool of contributors relatively open or relatively closed?
4. Is there evidence of a gendering of genres in the selection and framing of books in the Book Review Section?

Founded in 1859, *The Irish Times* sees itself as representing a left-of-centre political ideology and historically has strong links with the Protestant community (Brady 2005). It prints a morning paper, has no evening edition, and publishes six days a week excluding Sunday. The newspaper operates in an increasingly crowded media market and nowadays has a strong online presence and publishes dedicated sections catering to special interests such as travel, fashion, health, property, and sports. It is widely viewed as a 'serious' newspaper, or a newspaper of 'repute'. My decision to analyse *The Irish Times* was deliberate – it is a national quality broadsheet newspaper with combined average daily sales of 79,406 for the print and ePaper editions (Audit Bureau of Circulation, 2019), and has all-island distribution. Although its circulation (like all print journalism) has been declining it maintains 90,000 subscribers across print and online platforms. Readership is wider, with the Joint National Readership Survey reporting a daily readership for *The Irish Times* and irishtimes.com of 427,000 in 2015. Moreover, some 80 per cent of the readership of *The Irish Times* belongs to the ABC1 social group which are the most educated and must affluent classes, and includes opinion formers across government, civil society, business and culture. *The Irish Times* is owned by a Trust that guarantees its independence 'free from any form of personal or party political, commercial, religious or other sectional control' (www.irishtimes.com). The paper is governed by progressive principles and has employed high profile literary editors over the years including Fintan O'Toole and John Banville.

I chose a content analysis methodology which allowed me to explore the issue of framing of communicated text focusing on the twin issues of selection and salience. Specifically, I wanted to focus on what kinds of books (authors) are selected for review; who is selected to do the reviewing; and whether or not gender is salient to these processes. The framing device allows us to identify both the selection of subject matter and the way in which that selection results in a highlighting of some features of reality and omitting others (that do not make the selection cut) (Entman 1993). I collected and retained 50 paper editions of *The Irish Times* Book Review Section beginning in November 2015 and ending in November 2016. The choice of time period was somewhat serendipitous. In November 2015 #WakingTheFeminists shone a light on marginalisation of women within the arts more generally. In November 2015 we were heading into the centenary year of 1916, when there would be lots of focus on the aspirations of the Proclamation and opportunities to reflect on that legacy. It seemed opportune to begin systematically analysing the profile of women in a flagship Book Review that constitutes a significant player in the Irish public sphere.

The Book Review section was contained in the Weekend Review supplement issued with the paper every Saturday and typically ran to 4–5 pages in length.[2] The mainstay and most prominently featured content on the pages are the book reviews, which are generally illustrated by images of authors and book covers. Each of the 50 editions over the time period was read closely and for every headlined book review, the date published; book title; author gender; book reviewer gender; genre; and short synopsis of book content were recorded. The sampling frame (for this analysis) was confined to book reviews only (i.e. I excluded essays, eBook columns, poems, and the browser column from the analysis). This yielded an excel file of 581 entries. In the case of five of those entries, the reviewer had written a 'group review', i.e. more than one book was discussed in the review. For simplicity, I excluded the titles included in those five reviews from the author analysis as they are trickier to classify. However, it is worth noting that across the five 'group reviews', eleven of the featured books were by men whereas 5 were authored by women, a ratio of 2:1 which closely mirrors the gender ratio in the overall analysis.

FINDINGS

Publishing is an industry dominated by women, and women are more likely to read than men, (*Publishers' Weekly* 2010). The *Publishers' Weekly* survey found that 85 per cent of publishing employees with less than three years of experience are women. Hesmondhalgh and Baker (2015: 24) note that book publishing (61 per cent female) is the only subsector of the cultural industries where female employment is above 50 per cent. Publishing is then a feminised occupation. In stark contrast, the public space that constitutes the Book Review Section of *The Irish Times* is overwhelmingly dominated by men.

The first question examined is the relative representation of men and women as authors and reviewers. As Table 1 shows, in terms of authors selected for review there is a clear preponderance of men over women. Fully two thirds of books reviewed have been authored by men. In the case of the reviewers, the gender balance is more equitable but reviewers who are men are still in the majority at 54 per cent. We are not privy to the selection criteria for books but it is managed by a book editor and is presumably the outcome of a number of factors such as profile of the author; currency or topicality of the title; influence of publisher; membership of literary networks; ability and connections of the literary agent/publicist, and so on. What is clear is that male authorship has significantly higher visibility than female authorship in the newspaper.[3] This is entirely consistent with the findings of Vida and CWILA counts, and with the Australia study by Harvey and Lamond (2016), and confirms the durability of gender imbalance first demonstrated in the Women in Publishing study more than 30 years ago.

Table 1: *Featured books by author's and reviewer's gender in The Irish Times Book Review Section, 2016*

Gender of author	Number of titles	Percentage	Gender of reviewer	%
Men	241	64%	207	54%
Women	131	35%	174	46%
Authors/editors of book are both men and women	4	1%	–	
	N=376* Excludes titles group reviewed	100%	N=381** one reviewer recorded for each book review included	100%

The second question pertains to the possibility of gender segregation being built into the book reviewing process itself. We have noted from Table 1 that male reviewers are in a slight majority. But are men more likely to review books by men and women more likely to review books by women? Table 2 demonstrates that a considerable degree of gender segregation is at work in the Book Review Section. Most books written by men are reviewed by other men (68 per cent), and most books written by women are reviewed by other women (72.5 per cent). If reviewers were randomly distributed we would expect to see much greater equality in terms of who reviews whom. As it is, the reviewing process itself appears to be organised (whether deliberately or unthinkingly) on gender differentiated lines. Harvey and Lamond also found that in *The Australian* broadsheet paper, 74 per cent of all book reviews written by men were of books by men in 1985, a statistic that remained unchanged in 2013 (2016: 97). However, they found that women tended to review books by both men and women, whereas in the case of *The Irish Times* women are much more likely to be reviewing books by other women.

Table 2: *Gender match between author and reviewer 2016*

Gender author x gender reviewer	N	%
Books authored by men and reviewed by men	164	164/241=68%
Books authored by men and reviewed by women	77	77/241= 32%
Books authored by women and reviewed by women	95	95/131=72.5%
Books authored by women and reviewed by men	36	36/131=27.5%
Books authored/edited by both men & women reviewed by men	4	4/4=100%
Books authored/edited by both men & women reviewed by women	0	0%
'group review' by men	3	3/5=60%
'group review' by women	2	2/5=40%
	N=381	

Qualification to review is usually associated with being a published author oneself and/or an academic, or a journalist, or a commentator, or someone who has made a particular contribution in their chosen field of specialism. In this sense, reviewers broadly speaking might be loosely categorised as public intellectuals: 'people who have an authoritative voice.' What is instructive about Table 3 below is the degree to which the pool of women reviewers is far narrower in scope than the pool of men who contribute to critical review. This is partly a structural effect of the way the Book Review pages are organised. In the case of reviews by women, 56 per cent of all contributions are made by just two *Irish Times* journalists, Sarah Gilmartin who reviews new fiction, and (the late) Eileen Battersby, who had a featured literary fiction review each week. Since only a finite number of books are reviewed, and these two reviewers occupy dominant roles, opportunities for other women to contribute (to popular and literary fiction reviews) is foreclosed. Eighteen women have contributed two or more reviews in the time period studied, and 23 others have contributed one review each.

Table 3: *The gendered field of reviewing: Women, men and the number of reviews they contributed in 2016*

Reviews by women	No.	Reviews by men	No.	Reviews by men	No.
Sarah Gilmartin	50	Eoin McNamee	10	Paddy Agnew	2
Eileen Battersby	47	Houman Barekat	9	John Banville	2
Éilís Ní Dhuibhne	7	Diarmaid Ferriter	9	Colin Barrett	2
Anna Carey	5	John Boyne	8	Declan Burke	2
Martina Evans	5	Rob Doyle	7	Clifford Coonan	2
Patricia Craig	4	Brian Boyd	6	Laurence Douglas	2
Molly McCluskey	4	Eamon Maher	6	Bryce Evans	2
Sarah Baume	3	Mathew Adams	4	Gerry Hassan	2
Sinead Gleeson	3	Carlo Gebler	4	Andrew Hatfield	2
Catriona Crowe	2	Robert Gerwarth	4	Neil Hegarty	2
Elizabeth Day	2	Chris Kissane	4	Tom Hennigan	2
Anne Enright	2	Chris Mullin	4	Patrick Honohan	2
Tara Flynn	2	Peter Murphy	4	John Horne	2
Selina Guinness	2	Michael O'Loughlin	4	Declan Hughes	2
Anne Haverty	2	Tony Clayton-Lea	3	Ian Maleney	2
Claire Hennessy	2	Brian Dillon	3	Brian Maye	2
Linda Hogan	2	Denis Donoghue	3	Paraic O'Donnell	2
Sarah Keating	2	Roy Foster	3	Joseph O'Connor	2
Catriona H. Mahoney	2	Kevin Gildea	3	Bernard O'Donoghue	2
Katherine A. Powers	2	Terence Killeen	3	Michael O' Flaherty	2
One-time reviewer	23	Brian Lynch	3	Fintan O'Toole	2
		Johnny Rogan	3	Charles Townshend	2
		Geoffrey Roberts	3	Eibhear Walshe	2
				One-time reviewer	53

The distribution of reviewing is far wider when it comes to men. No single reviewer dominates; only 5 reviewers were tasked with reviewing 7 or more titles in the time period studied. Moreover, 41 contributed between 2 and 6 reviews over the course of the year, and a further 53 men contributed a single review. The distribution of reviewing among men allows for a significant number of male voices to be written into the reviewing discourse, and to extend across a wider range of genres. Overall, *The Irish Times* book pages feature reviews by 42 different women, and 98 different men. This dovetails precisely with the findings of Harvey and Lamond who note that on *The Australian* (in both 1985 *and* 2013) the pool of male reviewers was more than twice the size of that of female reviewers (2016: 97). What these findings suggest is that social closure works against women's inclusion in the reviewing space, because of (a) their absolute numerical disadvantage when compared to men in terms of the invitation to review and (b) the gendered organisational structure of the reviewing process that somehow manages to select from a much wider pool of male than female reviewers. Women are perhaps not as much 'in the network' or 'in the know' to be selected to review a book.[4]

For Walby (2011) networks are not just about connecting and sharing, they are also deeply implicated in structures of power and the distribution of resources. As she notes 'the concept of social capital is predicated upon networks collectively providing access to resource to those who are in the network and not to those who are not' (2011: 9). It is possible to view the field of book reviewers as constituting a network but one in which there is gendered closure at work in a variety of ways. There is privileged access for male reviewers in terms of their preponderance as reviewers, but more importantly, the resource (of reviewing for a prestigious newspaper) is much more evenly distributed among men than it is among women. Men, therefore, have much greater access to the opportunity structure than women. Moreover, there is clear evidence of preferment in that men who review, tend to review more serious and more prestigious works, categories that are highly gendered and impact on what is considered relevant and important for public sphere discussion and debate. For instance, books by men in the fields of history, biography, memoir, world and political affairs are mostly reviewed by other men. Women (with the exception of Eileen Battersby's literary reviews) are confined to more sex-stereotyped subject areas, particularly within the fiction genre. It is noteworthy that Battersby's reviews of *literary novels* (which number 41 see Table 4) in the sample period, are heavily oriented towards literary novels by men (see below). Although it is beyond the scope of this chapter to analyse visual as well as textual messaging, almost every review of a literary text by a male author is accompanied by a relatively large scale, portrait photograph of the author, generally staring with gravitas into the middle distance. In contrast, Sarah Gilmartin who is the most prolific reviewer in *The Irish Times* (50 reviews in the sample period) focuses more on popular new fiction. In the selection of books for review, the preponderance (64 per cent) are the work of women authors. While there are photographic accompaniments to featured reviews, these are generally in the form of passport-size images of authors and or their book cover. Both reviewers are working in different genres which are gendered both in terms of the authors selected for review, and in terms of the key thematics that are explored, reinforcing a gendered regime where subject matter, position, and visual representation combine to reinforce differential status.

The next question is to do with the gendering of genres in *The Irish Times*. In Table 4 I have classified book reviews on the basis of the genre into which they fit, based on my own reading of the review. The categories are broadly based and below I have represented the main categories that emerged from the analysis of the reviews. I have not included all of the categorisations as some have only a couple of entries. There are a number of observations that can be made. First, fiction is by far the most popular category of book reviewed. Table 4 divides fiction into three separate sub-sections. In terms of general fiction books, there are almost an equal number of titles by men and women appearing in the Book Pages.[5] However, if we look more closely at two further sub-categories we can identify a clear gender trend. Literary fiction (international writing that often comes in translation) was primarily reviewed by Eileen Battersby. Two thirds of the books she reviewed were authored by men. In contrast, new fiction (generally more popular in content) is regularly reviewed by Sarah Gilmartin. Here the ratio is reversed: two thirds of the books reviewed are authored by women. So while fiction writers are equitably represented overall, within the pages of the Book Review, a distinction is made which frames 'highbrow' fiction as the preserve largely of men, while 'popular' fiction is primarily the preserve of women.

History books are the second most featured works in the Book Review Section. Clearly, a strong gender bias is at work here with the majority of titles presented to the reader authored by men, even though this was the centenary year of the 1916 Easter Rising, and considerable emphasis was placed by government agencies and civil society groups on commemorative inclusivity. Anne Enright's wry observation that 'In Ireland the question of ownership is overwhelmingly about who owns the past, a place that remains unstable or unfinished, and one from which women have tended to disappear', is more than apt in the context of the Book Review Section (2017: 34). A gender bias is also discernible in the combined category of world affairs, politics and economics, as well as for philosophy and studies of religion. Sociology barely gets a look in. Women authors *and* women reviewers are simply not represented equitably across a range of genres. Finally, it is noteworthy that the biography/autobiography category is heavily weighted towards male subject matter. 37 books can be classified as either autobiography or biography. The subjects of female biography are confined to a handful of women: three books discussed in a single review relate to the Gore-Booth family; another focuses on Constance and Casimir Markievicz. This focus probably reflects interest garnered by the centenary year and the exceptional role that Constance Markievicz played in Irish history as one of the leading female rebels and politicians. Other books in this category include studies of Wilhemina Geddes, Beatrix Potter, Maeve Brennan, Angela Carter, the Australian writer Helen Garner, and Kathleen 'Kick' Kennedy. In contrast, works on and about men are more expansive including: Elvis Costello, Johnny Marr, Erza Pound, Big Jim Larkin, Arthur Griffith, Laurence of Arabia, William F Buckley, Norman Mailer, Handel, Pope Francis, David Bowie, Jeremy Paxman, Mark Twain. Accomplishment in a wide range of creative and leadership activities is recognised in the selection of (male) biographical subjects for review. This contrasts with the much narrower range of female biographical subjects, most of whom are fiction writers.

Table 4: *Selected genres featuring in The Irish Times Book Review Section 2016*

Selected genres	Total	Authored by men	Authored by women
History including (cultural, art, urban, literary)	76	56	20
Fiction general including historical, gothic, fantasy)	83	43	40
New fiction reviewed by Sarah Gilmartin	50	18	32
Literary fiction reviewed by Eileen Battersby	41[6]	29	12
Biography/autobiography	37	27	10
Memoir	28	16	12
Politics, political satire, Economics & World Affairs	16	15	1
Poetry	11	9	2
Philosophy	7	5	2
Religion/Spirituality	5	4	1
Cultural/literary criticism	5	5	0
Sociology	2	1	1

So far it is evident that a gender regime operates in *The Irish Times* Book Review Section. Access and visibility are differentially distributed and remain unequal, for both women authors and women reviewers, across all genres except for fiction. But even within the fiction genre we see evidence of gendered knowledge production in terms of the key themes explored.

Table 5 below is based on a qualitative assessment of each book review paying attention to the key words, characterisations, and plot summaries in the reviews. It provides an interesting insight into the gendered nature of the 'fictional' voice.

Table 5: *Dominant themes in general/new/literary fiction*

General fiction authored by women	General fiction authored by men
Coming of age	Exploration of sexuality and identity
Family drama	Explorations of estrangement
Love, sex, relationships	Primarily male protagonist
Primarily female protagonist	
New fiction authored by women	**New fiction authored by men**
Coming of age	War and conflict
Love, sex, relationships	Search for meaning
Overcoming personal adversity	Primarily male protagonist
Primarily female protagonist	
Literary fiction authored by women	**Literary fiction authored by men**
Dystopian world	War and conflict
Tragedy	Existential crises
Human condition	Father/son relationships
Primarily male protagonist	Primarily male protagonist

Overall, there are three sub-categories of fiction explored in *The Irish Times* Book Review Section. General fiction by men and women reviewed by a range of people is the most gender balanced of the three sub-genres. As we see from Table 5, woman authors tend to write about a female protagonist whereas men tend to write about a male protagonist. This pattern is replicated for new fiction titles, reviewed on a weekly basis, by Sarah Gilmartin. Most of the titles reviewed by Gilmartin are authored by women. In contrast, literary fiction is heavily dominated by male authors, and both the men and women whose work is reviewed here, primarily configure their fiction around a male protagonist or male 'authorial voice'. The literary/ international fiction novel is reframed within the Review pages as a prestigious genre featuring mainly male novelists whose work is privileged in terms of the attention it is paid [word length]; the frequently hagiographic approach [including portraiture] taken to the authors under review; and the article-headings [for the reviews] which generally speak to a broad thematic. Literary fiction is categorised as a masculinised genre whereas mainstream fiction is a largely feminised genre.

There is some thematic convergence and variation across the three sub-genres. Women's fiction tends to focus on interpersonal relationships, overcoming personal challenges and doing so against the backdrop of a domestic or bounded context. In contrast, men's fiction tends to be more concerned with larger existential questions about meaning and identity, and tends to be set against more public world backdrops such as war, conflict, extreme zones. All fiction to some degree or another, of course, deals with the human condition. In the selection of titles for review in *The Irish Times* explorations of 'private troubles' seem to dominate women's fiction, while explorations of 'public issues' are more the prerogative of selected authors who are men. These selections create a gender regime in the book pages that reinforces the notion of gendered private and public spheres more broadly in society.

This distinction becomes more pernicious when we take into account the dominance of men as authors in other genres such as history, biography, memoir and politics/world affairs. In the pages of *The Irish Times* separate spheres are identifiable: women's worlds are represented mostly through fiction and a focus on relationships, domesticity and interiority. Men's worlds, in contrast, are well represented through fiction that explores existential questions. But their capacity to explore a world beyond private troubles is evidenced in the significant number of male-authored titles reviewed that interpret history, the state, the nation, the global world, war and conflict, and so on. Women occupy niches within the Book Pages, whilst men occupy a more broad-based platform of public intellectualism.

Why does this matter? According to Ridgeway 'the use of sex or gender as a primary cultural frame for defining self and other drives the content of gender stereotypes to focus on presumed gender differences' (2009: 149). Unwittingly or not, there is a gender regime at work in the Book Review Section and it does ultimately stereotype men and women, and limits women's opportunity to contribute as equal players. The gendered division of labour has the same impact as in any work segregated arena: 'it limits the autonomy, freedom and recognition of individual woman and men . . . limits collective flourishing, and militates against the achievement of the common good' (Hesmondhalgh and Baker 2015: 25).

CONCLUSION

Beard (2014) writes about how historically idiomatic presuppositions about men and women privatise women; and resist their move into traditional male discursive territory. My starting point was to deconstruct how the voice of authorial authority is constructed and framed within a single broadsheet newspaper's Book Review Section. I believe this is important because the very existence of these pages makes a strong statement about what is deemed to have literary and discursive value in our public culture. Published reviews constitute what Meyer-Lee calls 'acts of valuing' (2015: 88). Despite its progressive principles alluded to earlier, *The Irish Times* Book Review is framed by a highly gendered worldview in which women are marginalised both as authors and as reviewers, and women's opportunities to contribute to this public space are far more restricted than those of men, numerically and in terms of the subject matters they write on. Indeed, a high degree of gendered segregation of book genres prevails. The voices of men are clearly valorised at the expense of those of women.

It is important to understand both the practice of gender stereotyping and its consequences, because 'unless we take into account how gender frames social relations, we cannot understand how the gendered structure of contemporary society both changes and resists changing' (Ridgeway 2009: 145). How can we interrupt the discursive construction of gender in this particular field of cultural practice? Beard (2014) argues for some old-fashioned conscious raising about what we mean by the voice of authority and how we have come to construct it. As we have seen through the recent examples of Irish theatre and the MacGill Summer School, it is possible to become much more politicised about gender representation and gender equity in our engagements in the public sphere, and to bring about change. In theory, there are no barriers to including more women as authors and reviewers in a periodical such as *The Irish Times*. A talent pool exists of women as well as men, and the selection criteria currently employed to identify male reviewers can easily be adapted to include a much wider group of women reviewers. Awareness raising about the breadth and range of women's scholarship must be a priority for any newspaper that falls so far short in terms of reflecting upon its own institutional biases that directly and indirectly marginalise women's voices. As Cameron (1998) notes what counts as a reality – and in this case a representation of reality – is not self-evident, but is in fact constructed and contingent. As such, it is open to change and to doing things differently in the future.

Notes

1 An annual two-week forum for intellectual and political debate that has been running in the village of Glenties, County Donegal for 40 years.

2 In 2017, *The Irish Times* changed its format and now publishes the Book Review Section in a magazine type format that appears on Saturday with the main newspaper.

3 In an essay for *The London Review of Books* (21 Sept. 2017) author Anne Enright alluded to a similar study which she had undertaken. She reported that in 2016, 39 per

cent of books reviewed were written by women. Her enumeration system may have been different to mine, as I chose to narrow the focus of my study to exclude eBook reviews.

4   Interestingly, *The Australian* broadsheet has adapted a similar template to *The Irish Times*. Harvey and Lamond note that of the 639 books reviewed in *The Australian* in 1985, 468 were capsule reviews written by two women: Sandra Hall, then literary editor of *The Australian*, and Vicki Wright, who was responsible for the regular 'Paperbacks Worth Having' column in the paper (2016: 96).

5   Anne Enright reports in her *The London Review of Books* essay that nearly 40 per cent of fiction is currently written by women (*LRB*, 21 Sept. 2017).

6   Excludes six other reviews contributed by Eileen Battersby in other genres.

REFERENCES

Beard, Mary, 'The public voice of women', in *The London Review of Books*, 36(6), Mar. 2014, pp 11–14.

Brady, Conor, *Up with the Times* (Gill and MacMillan: Dublin, 2005).

Cameron, D, 'Gender, language, and discourse: A review essay', in *Signs*, 23(4), (Summer) 1998, pp 945–73.

Canadian Women in Literary Arts (CWILA), *CWILA Count Methods and Results*. Source: http://www.cwila.com Accessed 24 Oct. 2018.

Castells, Manuel, 'Communication, power and counter power in the network society', in *International Journal of Communication*, 1, 2007, pp 238–66.

Centre for New and International Writing, *The State of Poetry and Poetry Criticism in the UK and Ireland, 2012–2018* (University of Liverpool: Liverpool, 2018).

Connell, R. W., *Gender and Power: Society, the Person and Sexual Politics* (Allen & Unwin: Sydney, 1987).

Corcoran, Mary P., and Kevin Lalor (eds), *Reflections on Crisis: The Role of the Public Intellectual* (Royal Irish Academy: Dublin, 2012).

Donohue, B., C. O'Dowd, T. Dean, C. Murphy, K. Cawley and K. Harris, *Gender Counts: An Analysis of Gender in Irish Theatre* 2006–2015 (Dublin: The Arts Council, 2017).

Enright, Anne, 'Diary', in *The London Review of Books*, 21 Sept. 2017, pp 33–5.

Entman, Robert M., 'Framing: Toward clarification of a fractured paradigm', in *Journal of Communication*, 43(4), Autumn, 1993, pp 51–8.

Fraser, Nancy, 'Rethinking the public sphere: A contribution to the critique of actually existing democracy', in *Social Text*, 25/26, 1990, pp 56–80.

Gamson William A and Andre Modigliani, 'Media discourse and public opinion on nuclear power: A constructionist approach', in *American Journal of Sociology*, 95(1), July 1989, pp 1–37.

Gill, R., *Gender and the Media* (Polity Press: Cambridge, 2006).

Guest, Katy. 'Male writers still dominate book reviews and critic jobs: Vida study finds', in *The Guardian*, 19 Oct. 2017.

Harvey, M., and J. Lamond, 'Taking the measure of gender disparity in Australian book reviewing as a field, 1985 and 2013', in *Australian Humanities Review*, 60, 2016, pp 84–107.

Herring, Susan, Deborah A. Johnson, and Tamra diBenedetto, 'This is going too far!: Male resistance to female participation on the internet', in Kira Hall and Mary Bucholtz (eds), *Gender Articulated: Language and Socially Constructed Self* (Routledge: Abingdon, Oxon, 1995), pp 67–96.

Herring, Susan, Inna Kouper, Lois Ann Scheidt, and Elijah L. Wright, 'Women and children last: The discursive construction of weblogs', in L. Gurak, S. Antonijevic, L. Johnson, C. Ratliff, and J. Reyman (eds), *Into the Blogosphere: Rhetoric, Community, and Culture of Weblogs*, 2004. Source: http://blog.lib.umn.edu/blogosphere/ Accessed 11 Oct. 2018.

Hesmondhalgh, David and Sarah Baker, 'Sex, gender and work segregation in the cultural industries', in *The Sociological Review*, 63(1), 2016, pp 23–36.

Hu, Jane C., 'The overwhelming gender bias in *New York Times* book reviews', in *Pacific Standard*, 28 Aug. 2017.

Kerr, Aphra and Joshua Savage, 'Hacking at the techno-feminist frontier: Gendered exclusion and inclusion in technology cultures', in Pauline Cullen and Mary P. Corcoran (eds), *Producing Knowledge, Reproducing Gender: Power, Production and Practice in Contemporary Ireland* (UCD Press: Dublin, 2020).

Meyer-Lee, Robert J., 'Toward a theory and practice of literary valuing', in *New Literary History*, 46(2), 2015, pp 335–55.

O'Brien, Anne, 'It's a man's world: A qualitative study of the (non) mediation of women and politics on *Prime Time* during the 2011 General Election', in *Irish Political Studies*, 29(4), 2014, pp 505–21.

O'Connor, Pat, 'Reflections on a public intellectual's role in a gendered society', in Mary P. Corcoran and Kevin Lalor (eds), *Reflections on crisis: The Role of the Public Intellectual* (Royal Irish Academy: Dublin, 2012), pp 55–76.

Polletta, F and P C B Chen, 'Gender and Public Talk: Accounting for Women's Variable Participation in the Public Sphere' in *Sociological Theory*, Vol. 13, Issue 4, 2013: 291-317

'Where the boys are not', in *Publishers' Weekly*, 20 Sept., 2010.

Rafter, Kevin, 'Voices in the crisis: The role of media elites in interpreting Ireland's banking collapse', in *European Journal of Communication*, 29(5), 2014, pp 598–607.

Ridgeway, Cecilia, 'Framed before we know it: How gender shapes social relations', in *Gender and Society*, 23(2), Apr. 2009, pp 145–60.

Schudson, Michael, 'How culture works: Perspectives from media studies on the efficacy of symbols', in *Theory and Society*, 18(2), Mar. 1989, pp 153–80.

Walby, Sylvia, 'Is the knowledge society gendered?', in *Gender, Work and Organization*, 18(1), Jan. 2011, pp 1–29.

Women in Publishing, *Reviewing the Reviews: A Woman's Place on the Book Page* (Journeyman Press: London, 1987).

Young, Iris Marion, 'Feminism and the public sphere', in *Constellations*, 3(3), 1997, pp 340–63.

TWELVE

Guilt, Shame, Acknowledgement, and Redress: A Personal Reflection on Ireland's Institutional Treatment of Women and Children

Catriona Crowe

In Jimmy McGovern's extraordinary TV series, *Broken*, which aired in spring 2017 on the BBC, and was later broadcast on RTÉ, one of the afflicted characters, Roz Demichelis, a woman addicted to slot machine gambling who has been found out stealing from her workplace to fund her habit, responds to Michael Kerrigan, the local parish priest who is trying to help her, with the statement: 'Guilt is when you know you have done something wrong; shame is when everyone else knows too.' Roz cannot bear the toxic mixture of guilt and shame resulting from her addiction, and despite having children who love her, she tragically takes her own life.

This chapter examines Ireland's recent history of unprecedented disclosures relating to the country's treatment of vulnerable women and children, across a unique archipelago of institutions, run by the Catholic Church and the Church of Ireland, with the full blessing of the State. Disclosures in the public sphere about the treatment received by inmates were shocking: physical, emotional, and sexual abuse, and severe neglect, were found to be common, with consequential life-changing results for the victims. Acknowledgment and redress have been partially achieved, as I outline below. The only way to provide a full picture of what happened in these places, and thus to achieve redress as fully as possible, is to have full access to the archives relating to them. These are largely in the custody of the religious orders who ran the institutions, with some in the custody of the State. While the State is subject to statutory obligations regarding access to their records, the religious orders are not. This situation has to change, for the sake of survivors who need personal information; for the sake of scholarship which can help us to make sense of this troubling story; and to speak truth to the institutionalised-power structures that produced and reproduced a culture of gender repression in Irish society. Although my focus is primarily on archives, I raise broader questions about the historical and contemporary nature of institutional knowledge creation, retention, and control.

The history of women in Ireland has been occluded until relatively recently, when historians began to chart the story of (the other) half of the population. Sources for women's history have to be excavated from general archives, as record keeping in the nineteenth and twentieth centuries took no account of gender, and certainly did not highlight women where they turned up in the records. An extensive process of discovery and recuperation, including the Women's History Project and the *Field Day Anthology of Women's Writings and Traditions* (2002), has unearthed myriad archival and other sources relating to women, which have been used by scholars to produce a body of work on Irish women's history.

The records under discussion in this chapter form an essential part of that process. My professional life has been concerned with the collection, preservation, and dissemination of individual and community memory in accessible formats such as radio, television, and the internet. A large part of my role as senior archivist and head of special projects at the National Archives of Ireland, was to bring primary sources to the attention of individuals and communities. The Irish Census Online Project which I managed, made available the 1901 and 1911 Censuses of Ireland online and free-of-charge to the general public, enabling ordinary people to trace and learn about their families. Public history, I believe, engages people of all ages and classes to reflect upon the past; to think about consequences for the present; and, in some cases, to change public policy. No individual or group should be excluded from access to their own history and to knowledge about the circumstances of their own birth.

KNOWLEDGE DEFICIT AND HISTORICAL CHILD ABUSE

Ireland has been convulsed over the last 30 years by revelations of abuse of women and children in institutions allegedly dedicated to their welfare. These institutions existed in Ireland long after they had vanished elsewhere in Europe. They were run mainly, but not exclusively, by the Catholic Church, with the grateful blessing of the State. The institutions in question were industrial schools and reformatories; Magdalen refuges; and Mother

and Baby Homes. Industrial schools and reformatories dealt disproportionately with boys, and male children were born and sometimes reared in
Mother and Baby homes, but the inhabitants of those homes were overwhelmingly female, and exclusively so in the case of Magdalen asylums. On
foot of initially disbelieved revelations of terrible abuse by brave survivors,
aided by pioneering investigative journalism, independent research, and
survivor activism, three inquiries were established by the State.

The Ryan Commission (2009) investigated nine congregations: the
Christian Brothers; the Sisters of Mercy; the Oblates; the Rosminians; the
Presentation Brothers; the Brothers of Charity; the Sisters of Charity; the
Dominican Nuns; and the Daughters of Liege. Some of these congregations
did not run industrial schools, for example, the Dominican Nuns ran a
school for deaf girls, and not all congregations who ran industrial schools
were investigated, for example the order of Our Lady of Charity of Refuge,
which ran an industrial school in Dublin. The criterion for investigation was
the receipt of more than 20 complaints in respect of one institution.

The McAleese Committee (2013) investigated four congregations which
ran Magdalen laundries: the Sisters of Our Lady of Charity of Refuge; the
Sisters of Charity; the Sisters of Mercy; and the Sisters of the Good Shepherd.

The Commission to Investigate the Mother and Baby Homes and
Certain Related Matters is investigating the Sacred Heart Sisters; the
Daughters of Charity; the Sisters of the Good Shepherd; the Bons Secours
Sisters; and the Sisters of Mercy. The Commission is also investigating
homes run by lay Catholics such as the Regina Coeli Hostel and St Gerard's
Home, Mountjoy Square, and the Bethany Home, the only Protestant Mother
and Baby Home. The religious congregations under investigation, and the
State, were obliged to pass all relevant archives to the Ryan Commission and
were asked to voluntarily pass their records to the McAleese Committee.
After they had been examined, they were returned to the religious orders, who
are not subject to the provisions of the National Archives Act in terms of
preservation of and access to their records. The State's records are,
however, subject to those provisions. It is a central value of most civilised
societies that citizens have access to the records of their history: administrative; political; social; economic; and personal. The National Archives Act
of 1986 largely achieved this objective in Ireland.

Many of the records of Mother and Baby Homes have now been deposited
with the nearest Tusla[1] office to the location of the Home. A list of the
records of various institutions and their locations is to be found on the Tusla
website. Paradoxically, the Church in many instances kept much better
records than the State relating to this cohort of people. But these records are

unavailable which makes the challenge of uncovering stories of abuse all the more difficult. Like Mary Raftery[2] before her, Catherine Corless's hard work tracking the deaths of children in the Tuam Mother and Bay Home led to the establishment of a Commission of Investigation. The records of the Tuam Mother and Baby Home are now with the Tusla Adoption Services in Galway city.

Tusla is co-operating with the Commissioners of Investigation and is digitising records relating to the homes under review. All of this is good news. What is not is the fact that some of the religious congregations are not being co-operative with the Commission. Tusla holds only records relating to individuals who resided in the homes. The Commission naturally wants to see the administrative material from the congregations which ought to shed light on the organisational systems which underlay the running of the homes. We will not fully understand why these institutions functioned as they did without access to the records of their objectives, policies, and operations.

Most people read these reports of institutional abuse with mounting horror and sadness. But just to remind ourselves of what happened in institutions established for the care of vulnerable people, here are three testimonies from survivors. The first comes from a witness at the Ryan Commission, speaking of his experiences in Artane industrial school, one of the largest in the country:

> John was a very slow learner, but the Brother teaching Irish was not aware of this. He kept asking him questions, and persisted until he got the right answers, even though the boy had no idea what the questions meant. We started tittering laughing. I think Br Laurent thought we were laughing at him. He asked him again. Poor John kept guessing and always getting the wrong one. Eventually Br Laurent just blew his top. He hit that lad and got his head and smashed it . . . on the bench. The ink wells went up, he was covered in ink, snots, blood, everything. He spent the entire half an hour, three quarters of an hour beating this lad until John eventually had a run of luck and picked out [the right answer] three times in a row. With that when the bell went. . ., Br Laurent just slumped down exhausted from beating this lad. While we were, in the beginning, tittering, though some of the lads were crying, we were frightened that he was going to kill him. We made way for him at the door. It was ghastly. The Brother at the other end, one class faced that way and the other faced that way, never intervened once to come down.

The second testimony includes contributions gathered by the McAleese Committee on Magdalen laundries from former residents. One woman spoke of her family background as being unkindly referred to – she testified that 'the nuns looked down on me because I had no father.' Another woman in that same laundry said 'we were never happy. You were lonely.' She described how, on the journey to the laundry, 'in the car the nuns were saying I had the devil in me, shaking holy water and saying the rosary in the car.' She had been raised in an industrial school with no known family, and she also described how on her induction to the laundry, a Sister – in front of all the other women – said 'tell them where you were brought up and reared.'

And the last testimony is the undertaking that Philomena Lee had to sign after the birth of her child in Sean Ross Abbey Mother and Baby Home in Tipperary in 1952:

> I relinquish full claim for ever to my child and surrender him to Sister Barbara, Superioress of Sean Ross Abbey. The purpose is to enable Sister Barbara to make my child available for adoption to any person she considers fit and proper, inside or outside the state. I further undertake never to attempt to see, interfere with or make any claim to the said child at any future time.

The fact that the reports of the Ryan Commission and the McAleese Committee are freely available online testifies to changing attitudes regarding the secret inviolability of church activities. The internet offers methods of dissemination which make information widely and democratically available, and in these cases, has revealed important testimonies and facts about these institutions. I have provided these testimonies as a prelude to an examination of how the religious orders and the State are *currently* dealing with access to the precious archives they hold on these institutions, and whether the situation can be improved, and if so, how? While all change involves confronting powerful institutions, and none has been more powerful in twentieth-century Ireland than the Catholic Church, a great deal of change in relation to gender has already taken place, most of it spurred by the second wave of feminism from the late 1960s to the mid-1980s. The task now is to insist on behaviour on the part of the Church which matches what civil society demands from the State with regards to access to information.

PUBLIC INQUIRIES AND THE BREAKING OF SILENCE

I am interested in the way the three public inquiries came about, and how they changed, or did not change, the balance of guilt and shame in our society in relation to proven mistreatment of women and children. Personal testimonies – mediated through autobiographical publication and through broadcast media – created a powerful impetus for public investigation which continue to the present day. (In this volume, Ryan notes that the role of personal testimonies continues to influence legislators, though not all testimony put forward at Oireachtas Committees and in published or mediated form is afforded equal status.)

The victims of abuse, and a number of journalists and activists who believed them, were the people who broke the silence and began the long journey towards proper investigation of these matters. In 1983, *Nothing to Say*, a fictionalised account of a terrible childhood in an industrial school, was published by Mannix Flynn, who was drawing on his experiences in Letterfrack.[3] Flynn went on to become a serious advocate for those who suffered in these schools. In 1988, Paddy Doyle's *The God Squad* appeared, revealing serious abuse in Cappoquin industrial school, and culpable neglect of a disability which left the author in a wheelchair. Another fearless advocate, Doyle still maintains a website on institutional abuse and has worked with victims and with fellow disability sufferers.

These two ground-breaking accounts of life in Ireland's industrial schools were followed by many more, including Patrick Touher's *Fear of the Collar* (1991) about Artane, and *Founded on Fear* (2008) by Peter Tyrrell, discovered and published by Diarmaid Whelan, about Letterfrack. On other institutions, we had June Goulding's *A Light in the Window* (1998): a midwife's account of a year in Bessborough Mother and Baby Home; Bernadette Fahy's *Freedom of Angels* (1999): a survivor's account of Goldenbridge orphanage; and *The Lost Child of Philomena Lee*, by Martin Sixsmith (2009), later made into a film about a mother's search for the child whom she was forced to give up for adoption. Dr James Deeny's *To Cure and to Care* (1989) gave us the memoirs of a Chief Medical Officer who found appalling levels of infant infection and death at Bessborough in the late 1940s, and despite concerted clerical opposition, closed the place down until it was disinfected, and sacked the matron and medical officer. These works demonstrate the power of compelling narratives to break silence and capture the public imagination (see Ryan in this volume). All of these books opened up a world known intimately to those who had inhabited it, but unknown (allegedly) to those of us who had not.

Broadcasting always has a wider reach than books, and Louis Lentin's *Dear Daughter*, broadcast in 1996, began a public debate about industrial schools. It told the story of Christine Buckley, who had been savagely abused at Goldenbridge Industrial School as a child. But the programme which did most to open up the discussion and led directly to the establishment of the Commission to Inquire into Child Abuse was *States of Fear*, broadcast in 1999; a series of three documentaries impeccably researched by Mary Raftery and Sheila Ahern and directed by Raftery. *States of Fear*, foregrounded by interviews with survivors, covered the whole country and a large number of schools. Raftery and Ahern got access to the records of the Department of Education relating to the schools, and they were able to evaluate the State's relationship with the religious orders who ran them, in terms of funding and inspection, if it happened. The religious orders did not grant access to their records. Eoin O'Sullivan worked with them on the history and policies of the system and went on to co-author, with Raftery, the book *Suffer the Little Children*, published in 1999.

States of Fear caused a furore. The overwhelming testimonies of so many survivors, combined with well-sourced research on the State's involvement in the schools, created a public demand for inquiry and redress. On 1 May 1999, while Raftery and Ahern were working on the third programme, the then Taoiseach Bertie Ahern, called a press conference. On the national broadcaster RTÉ's *Six O'Clock* news, he made a fulsome apology on behalf of the State and the citizens of the state. Within a year the Commission of Inquiry was established.

Change always involves confronting deeply held and embedded cultural values and policy frames that have long been supported by institutions and powerful advocacy coalitions. Crucial to bringing about such change is the capacity to use the means of knowledge production to make visible that which had heretofore remained invisible. Here we see a direct link between survivors' memoirs, high-quality broadcasting, and a change in public and political opinion leading to first, acknowledgment of the reality of the survivors' accounts; second, investigation of the background and extent of these accounts; and third, redress for survivors. Another crucial factor in this trajectory was the fact that a number of survivors had begun to take civil actions in the courts against the State and the religious orders, and some had won. The Commission provided a redress scheme but prohibited those who availed of it from taking civil actions thereafter. So had guilt and shame moved from the survivors, on whom they had been imposed, and taken their rightful place with those who had done the imposing? State apologies are not to be discounted; the evidence is that they mean a lot to survivors.

In fact, the State apology had been preceded by an apology in 1998 from the Christian Brothers, who ran the Artane Industrial School among dozens of others, and whose apology appeared as a half-page advertisement in all of the national newspapers. The Christian Brothers' example, whether absolutely sincerely meant or part of a strategic move in the context of the many court cases facing them, or a mixture of both, at least offered no excuses for the Order's behaviour. The Sisters of Mercy had apologised in 1996, after seeing *Dear Daughter*, which had a serious impact on them. But their apology was hedged with qualifications, bearing the pusillanimous hallmarks which have become familiar from other scandals since, including those of powerful male American media figures who have fallen foul of investigative journalism that has exposed their wrongdoings towards women: 'they were different times'; acknowledgment of 'mistakes' in a broader context of good works; in this case, the offer of counselling for victims to be provided by the very institution which carried out the abuse. It took until 2004 for the order to apologise unreservedly, as public outrage grew towards the Church as both an institutional and diocesan abuser. This move towards an unreserved apology to replace the earlier conditional apology seems to indicate a dawning awareness of the growing power of public opinion in support of appropriate redress for those who have had their lives scarred by institutional child abuse. The strength of that public opinion has not waned and was on display again during the visit of Pope Francis to Ireland in the summer of 2018.

The Christian Brothers and the Sisters of Mercy were the orders by far most involved in the industrial school system, running most of the schools during the period under investigation by the Ryan Commission. Not all of the schools under their control were investigated: seven in the case of the Christian Brothers, including Artane and Letterfrack, and five in the case of the Sisters of Mercy, including Goldenbridge and Cappoquin. Because of the large numbers of children who passed through their institutions, their public apologies assumed great importance. However, as time went on, The Sisters of Mercy's consistent denials of harsh corporal punishment on their part, as well as constant legal action by the Christian Brothers, mostly to prevent access to records, devalued these apologies.

The then Taoiseach Enda Kenny's very long apology to Magdalen survivors in 2013 was well received by them, but as time went on and as the rights they thought had been granted to them seemed to evaporate, they began to question the State's sincerity regarding recognition of what they had suffered. The Magdalen asylums were particularly egregious examples of gender persecution, with the 'fallen woman' myth to the fore, and little prospect of escape for inmates, who were often there as a result of court cases. Many were also there as a result of placement by their families, as they threatened family respectability. As regards the history of gender politics, the Irish family has played a significant, and still not fully uncovered, role (see Gray et al. 2017; Connolly 2015).

LEARNING FROM THE PAST THE POWER OF ARCHIVES

How do we find out what happened in the past? Some people think there is a master narrative somewhere which tells the story of Ireland. I had a query once from someone looking for the piece of that narrative on Michael Collins. They assumed that it was all written down somewhere. I had to explain that there were numerous biographies of Collins, often differing in their conclusions, and what we had in the National Archives were documents by or about him, which would have to be interrogated and understood as part of Collins's life story, and that other repositories would have different documents, also part of the jigsaw. This did not go down well with my caller. Indeed, the discovery that our record of the past is incomplete, sometimes difficult to read, often contradictory, often fragile, suffused with the biases of its creators, and alas, in the Irish case, largely blown to bits in 1922, is dismaying, to say the least.[4]

I want to recount two archival stories with a bearing on these institutions, because they highlight the precariousness of vital records and how difficult it can be to ensure their survival. Poor record keeping and conservation of documents leaves us with partial or no accounts of our past. The silencing of voices from the past impacts on our capacity to understand that past and its impact on the present; and also, it mitigates against holding responsible individuals and institutions accountable for wrongdoing.

In 1983, before we had a National Archives Act to safeguard and make accessible official records, I was surveying the basements of the Department of Education in Marlborough Street, logging details of the various records to be found there, in some disarray. I came upon a room within the basement and within it were the records of the Irish industrial school system, from its inception in the 1860s to the late twentieth century. There were shelves of ledgers, bound in calfskin, each marked with the name of a school; Artane; Cappoquin; Goldenbridge; Letterfrack; Tralee; and so on – giving details of the children who resided in them, and case files, giving much more detail, on individual children. I realised that these were really important records, both for those recorded in them and for social history, and I had no idea how to safeguard them. We had no space in the Public Record Office – as it was then –, and in any case the Department already had a shocking record of destruction of its records, including its entire nineteenth-century corres-pondence archive.

The person in charge of my visit to Marlborough Street was Paddy Hickey, a paperkeeper, a grade which no longer exists, but which then meant someone who retrieved and returned files from and to storage. I showed Paddy this room full of serious history and asked him what we could do to ensure its survival. Paddy said: 'there is only one key to this door, and I have it, I won't be giving it up to anyone who means harm to these records.' And he thus saved a cohort of records of inestimable value. In 1986, the National Archives Act was passed, which threatened imprisonment or a stiff fine on anyone who destroyed official records without permission. (Up to that point, Ireland, in this as in many other sectors, operated under nineteenth-century legislation which the State was slow to change. Change always has cost implications.)

Some years later, I told Mary Raftery about these records, and she managed, as only she could, to get access to the administrative records which underpinned the industrial school system. The Department set up a special section to deal with queries from survivors who wanted personal information regarding their stays in the schools. These records, and those held by the religious orders who ran the schools, are the main sources for survivors and their relatives seeking such information. Something useful that the Department of Education could do now would be to transfer to the National Archives the administrative files relating to the industrial schools. These would be of immense value to scholars, in the present and the future, as they were to Mary Raftery and Eoin O'Sullivan.

The second story concerns the records of the adoption of Irish children in the United States, from Mother and Baby homes in Ireland. In late 1995, I heard a woman called Maggie Butler on the radio describing her search for her birth mother, having been adopted in the US in the 1950s. She was having no luck, and it appeared that her birth certificate had been falsified. I had never really thought about the identity needs of adopted people before, but she was so eloquent that her predicament stuck in my mind. On Christmas Eve 1995, I was looking through the files from the Irish Embassy in Washington, which had just arrived and would be released to the public on 2 January 1996. I found a file dealing with Irish children adopted in America, which contained the names of some such children, and noted it as of possible use to people like Maggie Butler. Then I forgot about it, but remembered in February 1996, when I heard Maggie Butler on the radio again, still having no luck with her search. I got out the Washington file and searched it for a reference number to a headquarters file, which might at least give more information on how the system operated. I found such a number, went down to the third floor of the repository to where the relevant file should be, and found 1,700 case files, each referring to one child, dealing with the adoption of Irish children in the US between 1948 and 1972. You might wonder why records relating to adoption ended up in the Department of Foreign Affairs; it was because each child had to have a passport in order to travel to America.

Two things occurred to me on this discovery: first, that these files could help people like Maggie Butler who were searching for their birth mothers; second, that those same birth mothers might be living in mortal fear of someone turning up on their doorstep about whom they had told nobody. Herein lies the dilemma of competing rights which underlies the whole adoption issue from a certain period. The Department of Foreign Affairs announced the existence of the records, with some prodding, and it became a worldwide story. I had my first experience of taking to the airwaves (the *Gay Byrne Radio Show*), and in the course of a long interview, called on the State to establish a contact register, with proper counselling resources, to facilitate reunions between mothers and children, with the maximum possible success for both parties. The records have been digitised by the Department of Foreign Affairs, and they respond to queries from both sides with as much information as they can give. The administrative files have been available to researchers in the National Archives since 1996.

The stories of mothers separated from their children, sometimes successfully reunited, sometimes not, some still searching to this day, are a living legacy of a state and church which stigmatised and degraded women pregnant outside marriage, and their children. One of the crucial ways both church and state can atone for this is to give all parties every possible assistance, particularly through access to all records affecting their lives. These stories illustrate how carelessly, up to recently, we treated records of huge importance to the people about whom they held vital information. That is no longer the situation as regards the State's records, but there is still cause to wonder about the religious orders.

CONGREGATIONAL GATE KEEPING

The various religious orders investigated by both the Ryan Commission and the McAleese Committee hold the records of their congregations, and the institutions under their care, as private records which are not subject to preservation and access rules as laid down in the National Archives Act, 1986. The Act decrees that official records may not be destroyed without the permission of the National Archives, and that all records with a few exceptions must be opened to the public 30 years after their creation. Data Protection legislation insists on the closure of personal records until after death, except in the case of individuals seeking their own records, which may be accessed under Freedom of Information provision.

A full audit of all of the congregations investigated by these commissions would take a lot of time. Here I look at three congregations investigated by the Ryan Commission and the McAleese Committee: the Christian Brothers and the Sisters of Mercy, who ran the majority of the industrial schools in Ireland and the Sisters of Our Lady of Charity of Refuge, who ran the two largest Magdalen Laundries in Ireland. An interesting fact about all the congregations under investigation is that only one of them – the Sisters of Mercy – has a website dedicated to its archives; some others have single pages as part of the order's website, giving a contact number, but with very little information about records in their custody. Some have no online presence with regards to archives at all.

Complaints against the Christian Brothers to the Commission exceeded complaints received against all of the other congregations combined. I had a challenging time trying to locate the Christian Brothers' Archive. There is no online mention of them, telephone numbers which used to operate are now disconnected. I eventually got help from the historian of the order, Professor Daire Keogh, who told me the records are centralised in the Order's Provincialate in Marino, Dublin. He gave me the name of the archivist. I found the address online, but still with no mention of archives. I called the number of the Provincialate in Marino and left a message. The archivist called me back. She told me that the order's archives are now centralised in Marino, that they have a small reading room which is, however, not open to the public. Email and written queries from former residents of industrial schools are responded to by sending copies of entries from the school registers, as are queries from relatives, who are asked to provide a copy of the death certificate for the inmate they wish to research. Survival of the registers is good, with only a few missing. A database index of names has been created to the registers.

The administrative archive does not appear to be open to scholars. The Brothers themselves apparently research the history of the members of the order, and information on them is copied and sent to proven relatives. Requests for research projects are vetted by the Order, and if the project is small scale, access may be granted to a small cohort of non-institutional records. There is no intention to create a website with catalogues and other useful information. Because the order has two professional part-time archivists, standard protocols relating to preservation are observed. Two reputable services for industrial school survivors told me that since the Christian Brothers appointed a professional archivist, in the aftermath of the Ryan Report, they have had no difficulty accessing personal records when requested.

The Sisters of Mercy have a dedicated website relating to their archives which contains a history of the congregational archives by their archivist, who has been with them since the late 1990s. She responded very quickly to my query and explained how the service works. They have a reading room in central Dublin, to which access is granted by appointment during normal opening hours. Industrial school registers are open when 100 years old. Copies from later ones, relating to their own time in the school, can be seen by survivors or relatives, on provision of proof of identity. The records of the congregation, including the annals of the order, are open after 40 years. Academic research is actively encouraged. The archivist told me that they are revamping their website. I urged putting their catalogues online so that potential researchers can see what they have in their custody. She neither agreed nor disagreed. Because the order has a professional archivist, standard protocols relating to preservation and access are observed. Once again, services for industrial school survivors told me that since the Redress scheme was established, they have had no difficulty accessing personal records from the order when requested.

The Sisters of Our Lady of Charity of Refuge's records are a treasure trove of information about the congregation from its arrival from France in the 1850s, and their establishment of Magdalen laundries, an industrial school, and a reformatory. Their records of the industrial school they ran seem to contain very detailed information about the children who resided there, better than a lot of other orders. When I say: 'seem to contain', that is because these wonderful records are closed to the public. We know that they exist, and a great deal about their contents, because of a published history of the congregation, *The Monasteries, Magdalen Asylums and Reformatory Schools of Our Lady of Charity in Ireland, 1853–1973* (Dublin: Columba Press, 2017) by Jacinta Prunty, a meticulously detailed study of the women who joined the order; their families and social networks; class distinctions among the nuns; their spiritual formation; their connections and battles with the diocesan hierarchy; and of course the women and children who passed through their institutions. Yet there is no public access to the records of this congregation. A spokesperson for Justice for Magdalenes Research told me that they are not at all happy with access to records for the women in contact with them. Repeated requests to meet with the congregation to discuss access to records and issues affecting Magdalene survivors have met with refusal. The congregation is prepared to meet with individual survivors, but not *bona fide* groups acting on their behalf. As can be imagined, such individual meetings can be extremely difficult for survivors.

The three examples display differing approaches to congregational archives: severe limits on access; reasonable access; and no access at all. Is this really satisfactory given all that we have learned from the McAleese Committee and the Commissions of Inquiry that have reported, and all we have left to learn from the Commission still sitting? Has it not been more or less proven that the Catholic Church was operating as a quasi-state, with the full approval of the actual State, with its control over education, health, and institutional care? Does that conclusion, in turn, not require the orders and the State to reconsider the status of the precious records which should really be seen, not as private records with which the orders can do as they wish, but as public records which should be available to anyone who wishes to see them, as official records are?[5]

At this point it may be useful to reflect on Catholic Diocesan Archives, which have a varied set of practices as regards their records. The most important records in the custody of the diocesan Catholic Church are parish records, some of which go back to the eighteenth century. They are schematic records, providing, at a minimum, names of parents and children, names of marrying couples, sponsors, and witnesses, but they can often provide more, such as addresses, occupations and birth status if illegitimate. Probably the greatest loss to the fire in the Public Record Office in 1922 was the census records for 1821–51, which contained details for almost all households in

Ireland for the pre-Famine and Famine periods, and were an unparalleled source of information about the population of the country. Civil registration of births, deaths, and most marriages did not commence until 1864. The records of the two major property valuations of the early-to-mid-nineteenth century, the Tithe Applotment Books, 1823–37, and Griffith's Primary Valuation, 1846–65, only give the names of occupiers of land and houses, with no details of other family members, and in the case of the Tithe Applotment Books, give nothing at all for most urban areas.

In these circumstances, the records of the churches are the only surviving nation-wide source of detailed information on individuals and families for the period prior to the beginning of civil registration in 1864. The records of the Catholic Church are by far the most important, as the majority of the population was Catholic; but the records of the main Protestant denominations are also essential genealogical sources. The loss of the census records makes church records a unique and hugely important part of our cultural and historic heritage, which needs to be preserved and made accessible in the best possible way and to the widest possible readership.

While the church records are of greatest interest to genealogists and family historians, they are also a major source for social, economic, demographic, and religious historians. The work of these historians suffers from the lack of easy access to these records, which are the only surviving micro-demographic material for the whole of the country in the pre-Famine period. Connolly (1982, reissued 2001) shows what can be done with this material as part of a scholarly exploration of religious and social practice in the late eighteenth/early nineteenth century, although his book was itself limited by constraints on access.

Some original parish records have been deposited in diocesan archives and local heritage centres. However, a great many remain in local custody, under the care of hard-pressed parish priests with no training in archival preservation. There are anecdotal tales of valuable records being destroyed or damaged as a result of storage in unsuitable conditions, frequent handling, or accidental catastrophe. It is vital that an island-wide survey of Catholic parish records is carried out; and that those no longer in use in the parishes are deposited in an archivally acceptable environment. In the event that historic records are needed in parishes, copies should be made and issued to those parishes. The majority, but not all, of the Catholic parish records up to 1880 are available on microfilm in the National Library of Ireland. The quality of the microfilms varies considerably, and some of the records need to be re-filmed or digitised to provide the best possible surrogates of these valuable records. Digital copies of the microfilms have been made and have proved very popular with users. This digitisation initiative was resisted by some members of the episcopate; some, but not all of whom retain a proprietorial and conservative attitude towards 'their' records. Records not already microfilmed; records in physical danger; and records after 1880 urgently need to be rescued and processed.

Catholic and Church of Ireland parish records for the dioceses of Dublin, Carlow, Kerry and Cork and Ross are available free to access on the government-funded website: irishgenealogy.ie, and the indexes on that website link to images of the physical records, which is optimum archival practice with regard to digital access. Apart from Catholic parish records, there are the archives of the various bishops and archbishops, which have a huge bearing on the development of state social policy both before and after independence. They are an essential resource also for the social history of the country in myriad ways. Although the bishops meet once a year, they are not bound to agree on policies to be followed nation-wide (although they did agree on child protection guidelines in 1996). CORI, the Conference of Religious of Ireland, is the umbrella organisation for the congregations, and it does not appear to have any kind of a policy on archival access. Each bishop and congregation can act autonomously in relation to archives.

CONCLUSION

It is my view that the religious orders, the diocesan authorities and the Irish State should consider establishing a religious records repository – under State control – with input from all stakeholders, including the Church itself, in which all of the archives of the Catholic Church can be deposited. The registers and case files relating to institutions should be digitised so that survivors, many now in old age, can see their records and be sure everything that survives about them is in their possession. Those databases could be copied and anonymised so that scholars do not have to wait for years before analysing patterns of entry, exit, and treatment in these institutions. The fascinating records of the congregations themselves could be mined by academic researchers to uncover a huge part of the social history of nineteenth and twentieth-century Ireland. So many families had a member who was a nun or a priest until relatively recently. They are a big part of the story of every Irish family, as well as that of the church and the state. Such a repository could be staffed by some of the professional archivists employed by the congregations and dioceses, many of whom have done extremely valuable work already, but are hampered by the small-scale and limited staffing of their archives. Economies of scale would really work in such a repository, with shared access to reading room, cataloguing, conservation, digitisation, and outreach facilities. A comprehensive website could be established giving access to digitised records and using some of the already existing histories of the orders and the dioceses. Such a repository could be an international example of how to deal with church records in the aftermath of an abuse scandal.

It is clear that the religious orders are wounded by the exacting work of the Commissions that have investigated them. Some may feel that most members did not behave in the way the worst did. But they did nothing to stop the worst of them, and vulnerable children and women were severely damaged by that inaction. That must give pause for thought to people who have dedicated their lives to an ideal of helping others. The gesture proposed here could be deemed part of the Church's payment to the redress schemes which exist to compensate survivors. Moreover, it could go some way towards restoring public trust in an institution which has suffered terrible reputational damage over the last 30 years, and to contribute to the process of redress.

At this stage, it is likely that most of those who require information regarding their stays in industrial schools have had their needs met. Those who remain deserve speedy help. It is likely that the Mother and Baby Homes Commission will lead to another large group of people seeking access to records of their past, and hopefully they will be facilitated. The history of the Catholic Church in Ireland is intensely bound up with the social, economic, and political history of the country. It needs to be integrated into that general history so that we have the fullest picture possible of what happened, in the dioceses; the religious congregations; and the institutions, which they oversaw and ran.

Most of us take for granted information which is not available to some of us: who our parents are; who our siblings are; what medical conditions we might inherit; what the hinterland of our family history entails. Most of the adults (at the time of their incarceration) who inhabited these institutions were women. Society has generally recognised that patriarchy, and particularly religious patriarchy, did great damage to women in Ireland. Continued restrictions on access to vital records only serve to perpetuate that damage. Scholarship is denied important sources for the social history of nineteenth and twentieth-century Ireland. This information constitutes a public good that should belong to us all and cease to be the private property of organisations who have an obligation to help those whom they hurt in the past.

Notes

1 Tusla: The Child and Family Agency was established on the 1 January 2014 and is now the dedicated State agency responsible for improving wellbeing and outcomes for children, including child protection and welfare and adoption services.

2 Mary Raftery was an investigative journalist whose television documentaries exposed decades of abuse of children in state-sponsored, church-run schools in Ireland prompting

an apology by the Taoiseach and the establishment of the Commission to Inquire into Child Abuse in 1999.

3   St Joseph's Industrial School was an industrial school for young boys in Letterfrack, County Galway. The school was opened in 1887 and run by the Congregation of Christian Brothers.

4   At the beginning of the Irish Civil War in June 1922, the Public Record Office of Ireland was blown up, containing 800 years of Irish archives, including nineteenth-century census records, ecclesiastical records from the 12th century on, and the official history of the British administration in Ireland.

5   The small number of institutions run by the Church of Ireland, among them the Bethany House in Dublin, present serious problems in terms of survivor and scholarly access to their records.

REFERENCES

Bourke, Angela, *Field Day Anthology of Women's Writings and Traditions* (NYU Press: New York, 2002).

Commission to Inquire into Child Abuse (the Ryan Commission) (Stationery Office: Dublin, 2009).

Commission of Investigation into Mother and Baby Homes and Certain Related Matter, ongoing, Five Interim Reports published (Department of Youth and Children's Affairs: Dublin, 2015).

Connolly, Linda (ed.), *The 'Irish' Family* (Routledge: London, 2015).

Connolly, Seán, *Priests and People in Pre-famine Ireland 1780–1845* (Four Courts Press: Dublin, 1982; Reissued 2001).

Deeney, James, *To Cure and to Care: Memoirs of a Chief Medical Officer* (Glendale Press: Dublin, 1989).

Doyle, Paddy, *The God Squad: A Remarkable True Story* (Raven Arts Press: Dublin, 1988).

Fahy, Bernadette, *Freedom of Angels* (O'Brien Press: Dublin, 1999).

Flynn, Mannix, *Nothing to Say* (Ward River Press: Dublin, 1983).

Goulding, June, *A Light in the Window* ((Poolbeg Press: Dublin, 1998).

Gray, Jane, Ruth Geraghty and David Ralph, *Family Rhythms: The changing Texture of Family life in Ireland* (Manchester University Press: Manchester, 2016).

Irish Association for Research in Women's History, *The Women's History Project* (Dublin, est. 1997).

Lentin, Louis, *Dear Daughter*, Television documentary (RTÉ Television: Dublin, 1996).

McAleese Committee, The, *Report of the Inter-Departmental Committee to Establish the Facts of State Involvement with the Magdalen Laundries* (Department of Justice and Equality: Dublin, 2013).

McGovern, Jimmy, *Broken*, British Television series (BBC: London, 2017).

Prunty, Jacinta, *The Monasteries, Magadalen Asylums and Reformatory Schools of Our Lady of Charity in Ireland, 1853–1973* (Columba Press: Dublin, 2017).

Raferty, Mary and Eoin O'Sullivan, *Suffer the Little Children* (Bloomsbury: London, 2002).

Sixsmith, Martin, *The Lost Child of Philomena Lee* (Penguin: London, 2009).

BIBLIOGRAPHY

Accenture, *Powering Economic Growth: Attracting More Young Women into Science and Technology* (Accenture: Dublin, 2014).

Acker, Joan, 'Hierarchies, jobs, bodies: A theory of gendered organizations', in *Gender and Society*, 4(2), 1990, pp 139–58. Retrieved from http://www.jstor.org/stable/189609.

Acker, Sandra and Jo-Anne Dillabough, 'Women "learning to labour" in the "male emporium": Exploring gendered work in teacher education', in *Gender and Education*, 19(3), 2007, pp 297–316.

Acker, Sandra and Grace Feuerverger, 'Doing good and feeling bad: The work of women university teachers', in *Cambridge Journal of Education*, 26, 1996, pp 401–22.

Adcroft, Andy and David Taylor, 'Support for new career academics: An integrated model for research intensive university business and management schools', in *Studies in Higher Education*, 38(6), 2013, pp 827–40.

Adshead, Maura and Jonathan Tonge, 'Politics in Ireland', in *Convergence and Divergence in a Two-Polity Island* (Palgrave Macmillan: New York, 2009).

Adshead, Maura, 'An advocacy coalition framework approach to the rise and fall of social partnership', in *Irish Political Studies*, 26(1), 2011 pp 73–93.

Ahmed, S., 'Secrets and silences in feminist research', in R. Flood, and R. Gill (eds), *Secrecy and Silence in the Research Process: Feminist Reflections* (Routledge: London, 2010).

Aiken, Abigail, 'Opening statement to the Joint Oireachtas Committee on the Eighth Amendment to the Constitution', 11 Oct. 2017 http://www.oireachtas.ie/parliament/media/committees/eighthamendmentoftheconstiution/Opening-Statement-by-Professor-Abigail-Aiken,-University-of-Texas.pdf Accessed 27 July 2018.

Aiken, Abigail, Rebecca Gomperts and J. Trussell, 'Experiences and characteristics of women seeking and completing at-home medical termination of pregnancy through online telemedicine in Ireland and Northern Ireland: A population-based analysis' in *British Journal of Obstetrics Gynaecology*, 124(8), 2017, pp 1,208–15.

Aitchison, C., 'She's not one of the boys', in *The Independent*, 16 Feb. 1995.

Allvin, Michael, 'New rules of work: Exploring the boundaryless job', in Katharina Naswall, Johnny Hellgren and Magnus Sverke (eds), *The Individual in the Changing Working Life* (Cambridge University Press: Cambridge, 2008).

Anderson, G., *Cityboy: Beer and Loathing in the Square Mile* (Headline: London, 2009).

Anderson, L. and T. Broughton (eds), *Women's Lives/Women's Times: New Essays on Auto/ Biography* (Prentice Hall: New York, 1997).

Andresen, Sünne and Irene Dölling, 'Umbau des geschlechter-wissens von reformakteurInnen durch gender mainstreaming', in Ute Behning and Birgit Sauer (hrsg), *Was Bewirkt Gender Main-Streaming* (Evaluierung durch Policy-Analysen Ebook: Campus Verla, 2005).

Andrijasevic, R. and N. Mai, 'Trafficking (in) representations', special issue of *the Anti-Trafficking Review*, 7, 2016.

Apple, Michael W., 'Teaching and "women's work": A comparative and historical analysis', in *Teachers College Record*, 86(3), 1985, pp 455–73.

Arnot, Madeline, 'Male hegemony, social class and women's education', in *Journal of Education*, 164(1), 1982, pp 64–89.

Ibid., *Reproducing Gender: Critical Essays on Educational Theory and Feminist Politics* (Routledge: London, 2002).

Ashley, L., '"They're not all bastards': Prospects for gender equality in the UK's elite law firms', in *Cass Centre for Professional Service Firms* Working Paper, 23 Dec. 2010.

Atwood, Margaret, *The Handmaid's Tale* (Vintage: London, 1996).

Avdelidou-Fischer, Nicole., and Gail Kirton, 'Beyond burned bras and purple dungarees: Feminist orientations within working women's networks', in *European Journal of Women's Studies*, 23(2), 2016, pp 124–39.

Azocar, Maria J. and Myra Marx-Ferree, 'Gendered expertise ', in *Gender & Society*, 29(6), 2015, pp 841–86.

Bacik, Ivana, 'Legislating for Article 40.3.3°', in *Irish Journal of Legal Studies*, 3(3), 2013, pp 18–35.

Bagilhole, Barbara, 'Survivors in a male preserve: A study of British women academics experiences and perceptions of discrimination in a UK university', in *Higher Education* 26(4), 1993, pp 431–47.

Bagilhole, Barbara and Jackie Goode, 'The contradiction of the myth of individual merit, and the reality of a patriarchal support system in academic careers: A feminist investigation', in *European Journal of Women's Studies*, 8, 2001, pp 161–80.

Bagilhole, Barbara and Kate White (eds), *Gender, Power and Management: A Cross Cultural Analysis of Higher Education* (Palgrave Macmillan: Basingstoke, 2011).

Baker, J., L. Lynch, S. Cantillon and J. Walsh, *Equality from Theory to Action* (Sage: London, 2004).

Ball, Stephen J., 'The teacher's soul and the terrors of performativity', in *Journal of Education Policy*, 18(2), 2003, pp 215–28.

Ball, Stephen J. and Diane Reay, 'Essentials of female management: Women's ways of working in the education market place', in *Educational Management & Administration*, 28(2), 2000, pp 145–59.

Barber, J. F., 'Digital storytelling: New opportunities for humanities scholarship and pedagogy', in *Cogent Arts and Humanities*, 3, 2016.

Barker, James R, 'Tightening the iron cage: Concertive control in self-managing teams', in *Administrative Science Quarterly*, 38(3), 1993, pp 408–37.

Barone, T., 'Science, art and the predisposition of educational researcher', in *Educational Researcher*, 30(7), 2001, pp 24–9.

Barry, K., *The Prostitution of Society* (NYU Press: New York, 1955).

Barry, Michael, 'Censorship board bans book for the first time since 1998' in *The Irish Times*, 12 Mar 2016. https://www.irishtimes.com/news/ireland/irish-news/censorship-board-bans-book-for-the-first-time-since-1998-1.2571029 Accessed 27 July 2018.

Barry, Ursula, 'Gender perspective on the economic crisis: Ireland in an EU context', in *Gender, Sexuality & Feminism*, 1(2), 2014, pp 82–103.

Barry, U., and P. Conroy, 'Ireland in crisis 2008–2012: Women, austerity and inequality', in H. Rubery and M. Karamessini (eds), *Women and Austerity: The Economic Crisis and the Future for Gender Equality* (Routledge: London, 2014).

Barton, Sarah, 'HSE: Tackling rogue pregnancy agencies is constant battle', *The Irish Times* 17 Nov. 2017. https://www.irishtimes.com/news/politics/hse-tackling-rogue-pregnancy-agencies-is-constant-battle-1.3293342 Accessed 30 July 2018.

Bassel, Leah and Akwugo Emejulu, *The Politics of Survival: Minority Women, Activism and Austerity in France and Britain* (Policy Press: Bristol, 2017).

Beard, Mary, 'The public voice of women', in *The London Review of Books*, 36(6), March 2014, pp 11–14.

Ibid., *Women & Power: A Manifesto* (Profile Books: London, 2017).

Beckett, K. 'Culture and the politics of signification: The use of child sex abuse' in *Social Problems*, 43, 1996, pp 57–76.

Beech, Nic, 'Liminality and the practices of identity reconstruction', in *Human Relations*, 64(2), 2011, pp 285–302.

Benner, Chris, *Work in the New Economy: Flexible Labor Markets in Silicon Valley* (Blackwell Publishers Ltd.; Oxford, 2002).

Benson, John and Michelle Brown, 'Knowledge workers: What keeps them committed; what turns them away', in *Work, Employment & Society*, 21(1), 2007, pp 121–41.

Berardi, Franco, *The soul at work: From alienation to autonomy* (Semiotext(e): California, 2009).

Beraud, Andre, 'Women in the rat race: Women's careers in technological higher education', in Anke Lipinsky (ed.), *Encouragement to Advance: Supporting Women in European Science Careers* (Kleine Verlag: Bielefield, Germany, 2009), pp 154–83.

Bernstein, E. 'Militarized humanitarianism meets carceral feminism: The politics of sex, rights and freedom in contemporary anti-trafficking campaigns', in *Signs: Journal of Women in Culture and Society*, 36(1), 2001, pp 45–71.

Ibid., 'Carceral politics as gender justice? The "traffic in women2 and neo-liberal circuits of crime, sex and rights', in *Theory and Society*, 41(3), 2012, pp 233–59.

Bevan, V. and M. Learmonth, '"I wouldn't say it's sexism, except that … it's all these little subtle things": Healthcare scientists' accounts of gender in healthcare science laboratories', in *Social Studies of Science*, 43(1), 2013, pp 136–58.

Biesta, Gert, 'What is education for? On good education, teacher judgement, and educational professionalism', in *European Journal of Education*, 50(1), 2015, pp 75–87.

Blackmore, Jill., Pat Thomson and Karin Barty, 'Principal selection: Homosociability, the search for security and the production of normalised principal identities', in *Educational Management, Administration and Leadership*, 34(3), 2006, pp 297–317.

Blair, Helen, '"You're only as good as your last job": The labour process and labour market in the British film industry', in *Work, Employment and Society*, 15(1), 2001, pp 149–69.

Blauner, Robert, *Alienation and Freedom: The Factory Worker and His Industry* (University of Chicago Press: Chicago, 1964).

Bolton, S. C. and D. Muzio, '"Can't live with 'em: Can't live without 'em": Gendered segmentation in the legal profession', in *Sociology*, 41(1), 2007, pp 47–64.

Bonal, Xavier and Xavier Rambla, 'Captured by the totally pedagogised society: Teachers and teaching in knowledge economies', in *Globalisation, Societies & Education*, 1(2), 2003, pp 131–49.

Borg, Elisabeth and Jonas Söderlund, 'Liminality competence: An interpretative study of mobile project workers' conception of liminality at work', in *Management Learning*, 46, 2014, pp 260–79.

Bourke, Angela, *Field Day Anthology of Women's Writings and Traditions* (NYU Press: New York, 2002).

Bracken, Claire, *Irish Feminist Futures* (Routledge: London, 2016).

Brady, Conor, *Up with the Times* (Gill and MacMillan: Dublin, 2005).

Braun, Annette, 'The politics of teaching as an occupation in the professional borderlands: The interplay of gender, class and professional status in a biographical study of trainee teachers in England', in *Journal of Education Policy*, 30(2), 2015, pp 258–74.

Braverman, Harry, *Labor and Monopoly Capital: The Degradation of Work in the Twentieth Century* (Monthly Review Press: New York, 1974).

Britton, Dana M., 'Beyond the chilly climate: The salience of gender in women's academic careers', in *Gender and Society*, 31(1), 2017, pp 5–27.

Broadbridge, A. M., '"Window dressing?": Women, careers and retail management', DPhil thesis, University of Stirling: Stirling, 2010).

Brooks, Ann, *Academic Women* (SRHE & Open University Press: Buckingham, 1997).

Brown, W., 'Feminism unbound: Revolution, mourning, politics' in *Edgework: Critical Essays on Knowledge and Politics* (Princeton University Press: Princeton, 2005).

Ibid., 'Undoing the demos: Neoliberalism's stealth revolution', in *European Journal of Cultural and Political Sociology*, 3(1), 2015, pp 129–37.

Buckley, Fiona, and Yvonne Galligan, 'Politics and gender on the island of Ireland: The quest for political agency', in *Irish Political Studies*, 28(3), 2013, pp 315–21.

Burke, W. W., *Organisation Change: Theory and Practice* (Sage: Columbia, 2017).

Bustelo, Maria, Lisa Ferguson and Maxine Forest (eds), *The Politics of Feminist Knowledge Transfer: Gender Training and Gender Expertise* (Palgrave Macmillan: Basingstoke, 2016).

Butler, J., *Gender Trouble: Feminism and the Subversion of Identity* (Routledge: New York, 1990).

Byrne, John-Paul, 'The antinomies of autonomy: The social structure of stressors in Ireland and Denmark (Maynooth University ethesis repository: Maynooth, 2016). Source, http://eprints.maynoothuniversity.ie/8149/)

Byrne, A. and Lentin, R. *Researching Women: Feminist Research Methodologies in the Social Sciences in Ireland* (IPA: Dublin, 2000).

Byrne, Delma and Selina McCoy, 'Effectively maintained inequality in educational transitions in the Republic of Ireland', in *American Behavioral Scientist*, 61(1), 2017, pp 49–73.

Cameron, D., 'Gender, language, and discourse: A review essay', in *Signs*, 23(4), summer 1998, pp 945–73.

Canadian Women in Literary Arts (CWILA), 'CWILA count methods and results', 2018 Source: http://www.cwila.com Accessed 24 Oct., 2018.

Canty, Katherine, 'Evolving a patient filmmaking practice', 2017. Source http://www.directedbywomen.com Accessed September 2017.

Carr, Diane, 'Contexts, gaming pleasures, and gendered preferences', in *Simulation & Gaming*, 36(4), 2005, pp 464–82.

Carson, Julie (ed.), *Banned in Ireland: Censorship and the Irish Writer* (Routledge: London, 1990).

Cassell, Justine and Henry Jenkins (eds), *From Barbie to Mortal Kombat: Gender and Computer Games* (MIT Press: Cambridge, Massachusetts, 1998).

Castells, Manuel, 'Communication, power and counter power in the network society', in *International Journal of Communication*, 1, 2007, pp 238–66.

Cavaghan, Rosalind, 'Gender knowledge: A review of theory and practice', in Christoph Scherrer, Brigitte Young (hrsg), *Gender Knowledge and Knowledge Networks in International Political Economy*, Seite 2010, pp 18–35.

Ibid., 'Gender mainstreaming in the DGR as a knowledge process: Epistemic barriers to eradicating gender bias', in *Critical Policy Studies*, 7(4), 2013, pp 407–21.

Ibid., *Making Gender Equality Happen: Knowledge, Change and Resistance in EU Gender Mainstreaming* (Routledge: London, 2017).

Central Statistics Office, *Women and Men in Ireland 2016* (CSO: Cork, 2017). Source: https://www.cso.ie/en/releasesandpublications/ep/pwamii/womenandmeninireland2016/

Centre for New and International Writing, *The State of Poetry and Poetry Criticism in the UK and Ireland, 2011–2018* (University of Liverpool: Liverpool, 2019).

Chang, S. A. 2010, 'Outsiders and outperformers: Women in fund management", *Finance Professionals Post* [online], available from: http://post.nyssa.org/nyssa-news/2010/04/outsiders-and-outperformers-women-in-fund-management.html Accessed 31 Oct. 2018.

Charmaz, Kathy, *Constructing Grounded Theory* (Sage: London, 2006).

Chess, Shira and Adrienne Shaw, 'A conspiracy of fishes, or, how we learned to stop worrying about #Gamergate and embrace hegemonic masculinity, in *Journal of Broadcasting & Electronic Media*, 59, 2015, pp 208–20, a9h.

Childs, Sarah and Mona Lena Krook, 'Critical mass theory and women's political representation', in *Political Studies*, 56(3), 2018, pp 725–36.

Chivers, G., 'Supporting informal learning by traders in investment banks', in *Journal of European Industrial Training*, 35, 2011, pp 154–75.

Chreim, Samia, 'Influencing organisational identification during a major change: A communication-based perspective', in *Human Relations*, 55(9), 2002, pp 1,117–37.

Chung, Heejung, *Work Autonomy, Flexibility, and Work–Life Balance* (University of Kent Work Autonomy and Flexibility Project: Kent, 2017).

Ciccia, Rossella and Mieke Verloo, 'Parental leave regulations and the persistence of the male breadwinner model: Using fuzzy-set ideal type analysis to assess gender equality in an enlarged Europe', in *Journal of European Social Policy*, 22(5), 2012, pp 507–28.

Clarke, Marie and Maureen Killeavy, 'Charting teacher education policy in the Republic of Ireland with particular reference to the impact of economic recession', in *Educational Research*, 54(2), 2012, pp 125–36.

Coakley, John, 'Society and political culture', in John Coakley and Michael Gallagher (eds), *Politics in the Republic of Ireland* 5th edn (Routledge: New York, 2010).

Coalition to Repeal the Eighth, 'Trapped in time 1983–2017: Round table discussion with '83 anti-amendment campaigners – 5 Oct. 2017 (Dublin, .2017) Source https://www.repealeight.ie/1983-2017-trapped-in-time/

Coalition to Repeal the Eighth, 'Campaign Launch Statement' (Dublin, 2017).

Coate, Kelly and Camille Kandiko Howson, 'Indicators of esteem: Gender prestige in academic work', in *British Journal of Sociology of Education*, 37(4), 2016, pp 567–85.

Coliver, Sandra. 'Ireland' in Article 19, International Centre Against Censorship, *The Right to Know: Human Rights and Access to Reproductive Health Information* (University of Pennsylvania Press: Philadelphia, 1995), pp 159–80.

Collins, Barry & Patrick Hanafin, 'Mothers, maidens and the myth of origins in the Irish Constitution', in *Law and Critique*, 12, 2001, pp 53–73.

Collins, Michael and Mary P. Murphy, '"Activation for what?" Employment or a low pay economy', in Mary P. Murphy and F. Dukelow (eds), *The Irish Welfare State in the 21st Century: Challenges and Changes* (Palgrave: Basingstoke, 2016), pp 67–92.

Collins-Hill, Patricia and Sirma Bilge, *Intersectionality: Key Concepts* (Polity: Cambridge, 2016).

Connected [Reality Television] (RTÉ: Dublin, 2013).

Connell, Raewyn W., *Gender and Power: Society, the Person and Sexual Politics* (Allen & Unwin: Sydney, 1987).

Ibid., *Gender, Power and Society* (Polity Press: Cambridge, 1987).

Ibid., *Gender* (John Wiley & Sons: UK, 2002).

Ibid., *Masculinities*, 2nd edn (Polity Press: Cambridge, 2005).

Ibid., *Confronting Equality: Gender, Knowledge and Global Change* (Polity Press: Cambridge, 2011)

Connolly, Eileen, 'Parliaments as gendered institutions: The Irish Oireachtas', in *Irish Political Studies*, 28(3), 2013, pp 360–79.

Connolly, Linda, 'Symphysiotomy report begets more questions', in *The Irish Examiner*, 29 Nov. 2016 https://www.irishexaminer.com/viewpoints/analysis/symphysiotomy-report-begets-more-questions-432728.html Accessed 27 July 2018.

Ibid. (ed.), *The 'Irish' Family* (Routledge: London and New York, 2015).

Ibid., *The Irish Women's Movement: From Revolution to Devolution* (MacMillan/Palgrave: London and New York, 2003).

Connolly Linda and Tina O'Toole, *Documenting Irish Feminisms: The Second Wave* (Wood Field Press: Dublin, 2005).

Connolly, Seán, *Priests and People in Pre-Famine Ireland 1780–1845* (Four Courts Press: Dublin, 1982; Reissued 2001).

Conor, Bridget, Rosalind Gill and Stephanie Taylor, *Gender and Creative Labour* (Wiley Blackwell: Malden MA & Oxford, 2015).

Conrad, Kathryn, *Locked in the Family Cell: Gender, Sexuality, and Political Agency in Irish National Discourse* (University of Wisconsin Press: Madison, 2004).

Consalvo, Mia, 'Crunched by passion: Women, game developers and workplace Challenges', in *Beyond Barbie and Mortal Kombat: New Perspectives on Gender and Gaming*, edited by Yasmin B. Kafai et al. (MIT Press: Cambridge, Massachusetts, 2011), pp 177–90.

Corcoran, Mary P. and Kevin Lalor (eds), *Reflections on Crisis: The Role of the Public Intellectual* (Royal Irish Academy: Dublin, 2012).

Cosslett, T. C., Lury and P. Summerfield (eds), *Feminism and Autobiography: Texts, Theories, Methods* (Routledge: London, 2000).

Costen, W. M., C. E. Hardigree and M. A. Testagrossa, '"Glass ceiling or Saran Wrap™?" Women in gaming management', in *UNLV Gaming Research and Review Journal*, 7(2), 2012, pp 1–12.

Courtois, A., *Elite Schooling and Social Inequality* (Palgrave Macmillan: London, 2018).

Cowan, Ruth, 'The consumption junction: A proposal for research strategies in the sociology of technology', in *The Social Construction of Technological Systems*, edited by W. Bijker et al. (MIT Press: Cambridge, Massachusetts, 1987), pp 261–78.

Crenshaw, Kimberle, 'Mapping the margins: Intersectionality, identity politics, and violence against women of color', in *Stanford Law Review*, 43(6), 1991, pp 1,241–99.

Creswell, J. W., *Research Design: Qualitative, Quantitative, and Mixed Methods Approaches*, 2nd edn (Sage: California, 2003).

Crompton, R., *Restructuring Gender Relations and Employment: The Decline of the Male Breadwinner* (Oxford University Press: Oxford New York, 1999).

Cronin, Michael, *Impure Thoughts: Sexuality, Catholicism and Literature in Twentieth Century* (Manchester University Press: Manchester, 2012).

Croteau, D. '"Which side are you on?" The tension between movement activism and scholarship', in D. Croteau, W. Hoynes & C. Ryan (eds), *Rhyming Hope and History: Activists, Academics and Social Movement Scholarship* (University of Minnesota Press: Minneapolis, 2005).

Crowley, Martha, 'Gender, the labor process and dignity at work', in *Social Forces*, 91(4), 2013, pp 1,209–38.

Cruz-Castro Laura and Luis Sanz-Menéndez, 'Mobility versus job stability: Assessing tenure and productivity outcomes', in *Research Policy*, 39(1), 2010, pp 27–38.

CSO (Central Statistics Office), *SILC 2016* (CSO: Dublin, 2016).

Ibid., 'Quarterly National Household Survey, Equality Module', in Central Statistics Office, 2014. Source http://www.cso.ie/en/releasesandpublications/er/q-eq/qnhsequalitymodule quarter32014/

Cullen, Paul, 'Symphysiotomy: The whitewash that never was', in *The Irish Times*, 23 Nov. 2016. Source https://www.irishtimes.com/opinion/symphysiotomy-the-whitewash-that-never-was-1.2878271 Accessed 27 July 2018.

Cullen, Pauline, 'Irish women's organizations in an enlarged Europe', in S. Roth (ed.), *Gender Issues and Women's Movements in the Expanding European Union* (Berghahn Press: Oslo, 2008).

Cullen, Pauline and Clara Fischer, 'Conceptualising generational dynamics in feminist movements: Political generations, waves and affective economies', in *Sociology Compass*, 8(3), 2014, pp 282–93.

Cullen, Pauline and Mary P. Murphy, 'Gendered mobilizations against austerity in Ireland' in *Gender, Work and Organization*, 24(1), 2016, pp 83–97.

Ibid., 'Leading the debate for the business case for gender equality: Perilous for whom?', in *Gender, Work and Organization*, 25(2), 2018, pp 110–26.

Cullen, Pauline, Myra Marx Ferree and Mieke Verloo, 'Introduction to Special Issue: Gender, knowledge production and dissemination', in *Gender Work and Organization*, 26(6), pp 765–71.

Cushen, Jean, and Paul Thompson, 'Doing the right thing? HRM and the angry knowledge worker', in *New Technology, Work and Employment*, 27(2), 2012, pp 79–92.

Danowitz-Sagaria, Mary Ann and L. J. Agans, 'Gender equality in US higher education: Inter/National framing and institutional realities', in K. Yokoyama (ed.), *Gender and Higher Education: Australia, Japan, the UK and USA* (Higher Education Institute Press: Hiroshima, 2006), pp 47–68.

Davey, Kate Mackenzie, 'Women's accounts of organizational politics as a gendering process', in *Gender, Work & Organization*, 15(6), 2008, pp 650–71.

David, Miriam E., 'Overview of researching global higher education: Challenge, change or crisis?', in *Contemporary Social Science*, 2011, p. 6; pp 147–63.

Deeney, James, *To Cure and to Care: Memoirs of a Chief Medical Officer* (Glendale Press: Dublin, 1989).

De Jong, Sara, and Sara Kimm, 'The co-optation of feminisms: A research agenda', in *International Feminist Journal of Politics*, 19(2), 2017, pp 185–200.

De Londras Fiona and Mairead Enright, *Repealing the 8th: Reforming Abortion Law in Ireland* (Policy Press: Bristol, 2018).

Denzin, Norman. K. and Yvonna S. Lincoln, 'Introduction: The discipline and practice of qualitative research', in Norman K. Denzin and Yvonna S. Lincoln (eds), *The Landscape of Qualitative Research* 4th edn (Sage: California, 2013), pp 1–42.

Devine, Dympna, Bernie Grummell, and Kathleen Lynch, 'Crafting the elastic self? Gender and identities in senior appointments in Irish education', in *Gender Work and Organization*, 18, 2011, pp 631–49.

DeWan, Jennifer K., 'The practice of politics: Feminism, activism and social change in Ireland', in J. Hogan, P. F. Donnelly and B. K. O'Rourke (eds), *Irish Business and Society: Governing, Participating and Transforming in the 21st Century* (Gill & MacMillan: Dublin, 2010), pp 520–36.

Dillabough, Jo-Anne, 'Gender, "symbolic domination", and female work: The case of teacher education', in *Discourse: Studies in the Cultural Politics of Education*, 26(2), 2005, pp 27–148.

Dillabough, Jo-Anne and Sandra Acker, 'Globalisation, women's work and teacher education: A cross-national analysis', in *International Studies in Sociology of Education*, 12(3), 2002, pp 227–60.

Doezema, J., *Sex Slaves and Discourse Masters: The Construction of Trafficking* (Zed: London, 2010).

Donohue, B., C. O'Dowd, T. Dean, C. Murphy, K. Cawley and K. Harris, *Gender Counts: An Analysis of Gender in Irish Theatre 2006–2015* (The Arts Council: Dublin, 2017).

Doris, Aedín, Donal O'Neill, and Olive Sweetman, 'Gender, single-sex schooling and maths achievement', in *Economics of Education*, 35, 2013, pp 104–19.

Doyle, Paddy, *The God Squad: A Remarkable True Story* (Raven Arts Press: Dublin, 1988).

Drudy, Sheelagh, 'Gender differences in entrance patterns and awards in initial teacher education', in *Irish Educational Studies*, 25(3), 2006, pp 259–73.

Drudy, Sheelagh, Maeve Martin, Máiríde Woods, and John O'Flynn (eds), *Men and the Classroom: Gender Imbalances in Today's Schools* (Routledge/Falmer: London and New York, 2005).

Dublin Regional Homeless Executive, *March 2017 Homelessness Data* (DRHE: Dublin, 2017).

Duffy, Brooke Erin, *(Not) Getting Paid to Do What You Love: Gender, Social Media and Aspirational Work* (Yale University Press: Yale, 2017).

Duncan, S. '"Mother knows best": Social division and work and childcare', in *WP 31: Families, Life Course and Generational Research Centre Working Paper Series* (Leeds University: Leeds, 2003).

Eagly, Alice H. and Linda L. Carli, 'Women and the labyrinth of leadership', in *Harvard Business Review*, Sept. 2007 Source: https://hbr.org/2007/09/women-and-the-labyrinth-of-leadership

Edwards, J., Y. Zammit, H. Hakendorf et al., *A Study of Homeless Women in Melbourne* (University of Melbourne: Melbourne, 1977).

Edwards, Richard, *Contested Terrain: The Transformation of the Workplace in the Twentieth Century* (Basic Books: New York, 1979).

Elomäki, Ana, 'Gender quotas for corporate boards: Depoliticizing gender and the economy', in *Nora: Nordic Journal of Feminist and Gender Research*, 26(1) 2018, pp 53–68.

Emejulu, Akwugo, 'Crisis politics and the challenge of intersectional solidarity', in *London School of Economics and Political Science (LSE)*, 2018 https://www.youtube.com/watch?v=tVL_8497-co

England, Paula, 'The gender revolution: Uneven and stalled', in *Gender & Society*, 24(2), 2010, pp 149–66.

Enright, Anne, 'Diary', in *The London Review of Books*, 21 Sept. 2017, pp 33–5.

Enright, Mairéad, 'Notes on Judge Harding-Clark's report on the symphysiotomy payment scheme', in *Human Rights in Ireland Blog* http://humanrights.ie/*law-culture-and-religion/notes-on-judge-harding- clarks-report-on-the-symphysiotomy-payment- scheme*/ Accessed 30 Mar. 2018.

Entman, Robert M. 'Framing: toward clarification of a fractured paradigm', in *Journal of Communication*, 43(4), autumn 1993, pp 51–8.

Equality and Human Rights Commission, *Financial Services Inquiry: Sex Discrimination and Gender Pay Gap Report of the Equality and Human Rights Commission*, (Equality and Human Rights Commission: Manchester, 2009).

ESA, 'Essential facts about the computer and video game industry', Entertainment Software Association, 2015. Source: http://www.theesa.com/wp-content/uploads/2015/04/ESA-Essential-Facts-2015.pdf

Eschle, Catherine, and Bice Maiguashca, 'Theorising feminist organising in and against neoliberalism: Beyond co-optation and resistance?', in *European Journal of Politics and Gender*, 1(2), 2018, pp 223–39.

Esping Andersen, Gøsta, *The Three Worlds of Welfare Capitalism* (Princeton University Press: Princeton, 1990).

Etzkowitz Henry, S. Fuchs, N. Gupta, et al. (2007), 'The coming revolution in science', in E. J. Hackett, O. Amsterdamska, M. Lynch et al. (eds), *The Handbook of Science and Technology Studies* 3rd edn (MA: Society for Social Studies of Science: Cambridge, 2007), pp 403–29.

Eurofound, *First Findings from the 6th European Working Conditions Survey* (European Foundation for the Improvement of Living and Working Conditions: Dublin, 2015).

Ibid,, *Occupational Change and Wage Inequality: European Jobs Monitor 2017* (Publications Office of the European Union: Luxembourg, 2017).

European Commission (2019), *She Figures 2018*. Available at *https://publications.europa.eu/en/ publication-detail/-/publication/954off a1-4478-11e9-a8ed-01aa75ed71a1/language-en*

European Institute for Gender Equality, *Gender Equality Index 2017: Measuring Gender Equality in the European Union 2005–2015* (Publications Office of the European Union: Luxembourg, 2017).

Eurostat, 'Women teachers over-represented at early stages of education in the EU', in Eurostat news release 2015, Source http://ec.europa.eu/eurostat/documents/2995521/ 7017572/3-02102015-BP-EN.pdf/5a7b5406-4a0d-445b-8fa3-3558a8495020

Fahy, Bernadette, *Freedom of Angels* (O'Brien Press: Dublin, 1999).

Fanning, Bryan, *Migration and the Making of Ireland* (UCD Press: Dublin, 2018).

Farrell, Elaine, *A Most Diabolical Deed: Infanticide and Irish Society, 1850–1900* (Manchester University Press: Manchester, 2013).

Farrugia, D., and J. Gerrard, 'Academic knowledge and contemporary poverty: The politics of homelessness research', in *Sociology*, 50(2), 2016, pp 267–84.

Faulkner, Wendy, *Genders in/of Engineering* (University of Edinburgh, Research report: Edinburgh, 2006) http://www.sps.ed.ac.uk/__data/assets/pdf_file/0020/4862/Faulkner GendersinEngineeringreport.pdf

Fegan, Joyce, 'Imperfect system and cruel barriers still stopping women accessing abortion' in *The Irish Examiner*, 3 June 2019. https://www.irishexaminer.com/breakingnews/special reports/imperfect-system-and-cruel-barriers-still-stopping-women-access-abortion- 928382. html Accessed 20 June 2019.

Feistritzer, C. Emily, *Profile of Alternate Route Teachers in the US* (National Center for Education Information: Washington, DC, 2005).

Ferguson, Lisa, *Gender Training: A Transformative Tool for Gender Equality* (Palgrave Macmillan: Basingstoke, 2018).

Ferree, Marx Myra, '"Theories don't grow on trees': Contextualizing gender knowledge', in J. W. Messerschmidt and Patricia Yancey Martin, Michael A. Messner and Raewyn Connell (eds), *Gender Reckonings New Social Theory and Research* (NYU Press: NY, 2018).

Ferree, Marx Myra, and Kathrin Zippel, 'Gender equality in the age of academic capitalism: Cassandra and Pollyanna interpret university restructuring', in *Social Politics: International Studies in Gender, State, and Society*, 22(4), 2015, pp 561–84.

Ferriter, Diarmaid, *The Transformation of Ireland 1900–2000* (Profile Books: London, 2005).

Fine-Davis, Margret, *Gender Role Attitudes in Ireland: Three Decades of Change* (Routledge: London, 2016).

Fischer, Clara and Mary McAuliffe (eds), *Irish Feminisms: Past, Present, and Future* (Arlen House/Syracuse University Press: Syracuse, 2015).

Fisher, V. and S. Kinsey, 'Behind closed doors! Homosocial desire and the academic boys club', in *Gender in Management: An International Journal*, 29(1), 2014, pp 44–64.

FitzGerald S. and K. McGarry, 'Problematizing prostitution in law and polity in the Republic of Ireland: A case for reframing', in *Social and Legal Studies* 25(3) 2016, pp 289–309.

Fletcher, Ruth, 'Reproducing Irishness: Race, gender, and abortion law', in *Canadian Journal of Women and Law*, 17(2), 2005, pp 356–404.

Flint, J., 'Housing and ethopolitics: Constructing identities of active consumption and responsible community', in *Economy and Society*, 32(4), 2003, pp 611–29.

Flood, Michael and Bob Pease, 'Undoing men's privilege and advancing gender equality in public sector institutions', in *Policy and Society* Special Issue, 24(4), 2005, pp 119–38.

Flynn, Mannix, *Nothing to Say* (Ward River Press: Dublin, 1983).

Forfás, *Assessing the Demand for Big Data and Analytics Skills, 2013–2020*, Report of the Expert Group on Future Skills Needs (Forfás: Dublin, Aprr. 2014).

Forfás, *Future Skills and Research Needs of the International Financial Services Industry*, Report of the Expert Group on Future Skills Needs (Forfás: Dublin, Dec. 2007)

Foucault, Michel, *The History of Sexuality: Volume 1* (Penguin: London 1998).

Fowler, Allan et al., 'The global game jam for technology and learning', in *Computing and Information Technology Research and Education New Zealand (CITRENZ2013)* edited by Mike Lopez and Michael Verhaart, 2013.

Francis, Becky and Carrie F. Paechter, 'The problem of gender categorization: Addressing dilemmas past and present in gender and education research', in *Gender and Education*, 27(7), 2015, pp 776–90.

Fraser, Nancy, 'Rethinking the public sphere: A contribution to the critique of actually existing democracy', in *Social Text*, 25/26, 1990, pp 56–80.

Ibid., *Adding Insult to Injury: Nancy Fraser Debates her Critics*, in K. Olson (ed.) (Verso: London, 2008).

Ibid., 'Progressive neoliberalism versus reactionary populism: A choice that feminists Should refuse', in *NORA: Nordic Journal of Feminist and Gender Research*, 24:4, 2016, pp 281–4.

Freedman, Lynn P., 'Censorship and manipulation of reproductive health information: An issue of human rights and women's health', in Article 19, International Centre Against Censorship, *The Right to Know: Human Rights and Access to Reproductive Health Information* (University of Pennsylvania Press: Philadelphia, 1995), pp 1–37.

Freedman, Lynn P. & Stephen L. Isaacs, 'Human rights and reproductive choice', in *Studies in Family Planning*, 24(1), 1993, pp. 18–30.

Freire, P., *Education: The Practice of Freedom* (Writers & Readers Publishing Cooperative: London, 1974).

Friedman, Andrew L., *Industry and Labour* (Macmillan: London, 1977).

Fuchs Epstein, Cynthia, 'Great divides: The cultural, cognitive, and social bases of the global subordination of women', in *American Sociological Review*, 2007.

Gamson, William A., and Andre Modigliani, 'Media discourse and public opinion on Nuclear power: A constructionist approach', in *American Journal of Sociology*, 95(1), July 1989, pp 1–37.

Garsten, Christina, 'Betwixt and between: Temporary employees as liminal subjects in flexible organisations', in *Organisation Studies*, 20(4), 1999, pp 601–17.

Gaventa, J. and A. Cornwall, 'Power and knowledge', in P. Reason and H. Bradbury (eds), *Handbook of Action Research: Participative Inquiry and Practice* (Sage: London, 2001).

Gerstal, N., J. Cynthia, J. Bogard, J. McConnell and M. Schwartz, 'The therapeutic incarceration of homeless families,' in *Social Service Review*, 70(4), 1986 pp 543–72.

Gherardi, S., 'Feminist theory and organisation theory; A dialogue on new bases', in *The Oxford Handbook of Organisation Theory* (Oxford University Press: Oxford, 2005).

Gill, Rosalind, 'Cool, creative and egalitarian? Exploring gender in project-based new media work in Europe' in *Information, Communication & Society*, 5(1), 2002, pp 70–89.

Ibid., *Gender and the Media* (Polity Press: Cambridge, 2006).

Ibid., '"Life is a pitch": Managing the self in new media work', in Mark Deuze (ed.), *Managing Media Work* (Sage: California, London, New Delhi & Singapore, 2011), pp 249–62.

Ibid., 'Post-feminism? New feminist visibilities in postfeminist times', in *Feminist Media Studies*, 16(4), 2016, pp 610–30.

Ibid., 'Beyond individualism: The psychosocial life of the neoliberal university', in M. Spooner (ed.), *A Critical Guide to Higher Education & the Politics of Evidence: Resisting Colonialism, Neoliberalism, & Audit Culture* (University of Regina Press: Regina, Canada, 2017).

Gill, Rosalind, and Christina Scharff, *New Femininities: Post-feminism, Neoliberalism and Subjectivity* (Palgrave Macmillan: Basingstoke, 2011).

Gilleece, Lorraine, Gerry Shiel, Rachel Perkins and Maeve Proctor, *Teaching and Learning International Survey (2008): National Report for Ireland* (Education Research Centre: Dublin, 2009).

Gilmartin, Mary, *Ireland and Migration in the 21st Century* (Manchester University Press: Manchester, 2015).

Gilmartin Mary and Bettina Migge, 'Migrant mothers and the geographies of belonging', in *Gender, Place, and Culture*, 23(2), 2016, pp 47–161.

Gleeson, Jim, 'The professional knowledge base and practice of Irish post-primary teachers: What is the research evidence telling us?', in *Irish Educational Studies*, 31(1), 2012, pp 1–17.

Gleeson, Jim and Diarmaid O'Donnabháin, 'Strategic planning and accountability in Irish education', in *Irish Educational Studies*, 28(1), 2009, pp 27–46.

Glendenning, Dympna, *Education and the Law* (Butterworths: Dublin, 1999).

Godinot, X., and Q. Wodon, *Participatory Approaches to Attacking Extreme Poverty: Cases Studies Led by the International Movement ATD Fourth World* (World Bank: New York, 2006).

Goulding, June, *A Light in the Window* (Ebury: London, 2005).

Government of Ireland, *Rebuilding Ireland* (Stationery Office: Dublin, 2016).

Ibid., *Innovation 2020* https://dbei.gov.ie/en/Publications/Publication-files/Innovation-2020.pdf

Gowan, T. *Hobos, Hustlers and Backsliders: Homeless in San Francisco* (UMP: Minneapolis, MN, 2010).

Graff, Agnieszka, Ratna Kapur and Suzanna Danuta Walters, 'Introduction: Gender and the frise of the global right', in *Signs: Journal of Women in Culture and Society*, 44(3), 2019, pp 541–60.

Granleese, J., 'Occupational pressures in banking: Gender differences', in *Women in Management Review*, 19(4), 2004, pp 219–26.

Gray, Jane, Ruth Geraghty, David Ralph, *Family rhythms: The Changing Texture of Family Life in Ireland* (Manchester University Press: Manchester, 2016).

Greenfield, S., J. Peters, N. Lane, T. Rees, and G. Samuels, *Set Fair: A Report on Women in Science, Engineering, and Technology from the Baroness Greenfield CBE to the Secretary of State for Trade and Industry* (Greenfield Report) (Department of Trade and Industry: London, 2002).

Gregory, M. R., *The Face of the Firm: Corporate Hegemonic Masculinity at Work* (Routledge: London, 2016).

Griffin Penny 'Crisis, austerity and gendered governance: A feminist perspective', in *Feminist Review*, 10(9), 2015, pp 49–72.

Grint, Keith and Rosalind Gill (eds), *The Gender–Technology Relation: Contemporary Theory and Research* (Taylor and Francis: Bristol, 1995).

Grosen, Sidsel Lond, Holt, Helle, and Henrik Lambrecht Lund, 'The naturalization of gender segregation in a Danish bank', in *Nordic Journal of Working Life Studies*, 2(1), 2012, pp 61–79.

Groysberg, B., 'How star women build portable skills', in *Harvard Business Review*, Feb. 2008.

Grummell, Bernie, Dympna Devine and Kathleen Lynch, 'The care-less manager: Gender, care and new managerialism in higher education', in *Gender and Education*, 21, 2009, pp 191–208.

Guerrier, Yvonne, Christina Evans, Judith Glover, and Cornelia Wilson, '"Technical, but not very…": Constructing gendered identities in IT-related employment', in *Work, Employment and Society*, 23:3, 2009, pp 494–511.

Guerrina, Roberta, *Gender and the Economic Crisis*, in J. Kantola and E. Lombardo (eds), *Gender and the Economic Crisis in Europe: Politics, Institutions and Intersectionality* (Palgrave MacMillan: Basingstoke, 2013) pp 95–115.

Guest, Katy. 'Male writers still dominate book reviews and critic jobs, Vida study finds', in *The Guardian*, 19 Oct. 2017.

Hall, Douglas T., *Careers in Organisations* (Scott Foresman and Co.: Santa Monica, CA, 1976).

Halley, Janet, Prabha Kotiswaran, Rachel Rebouché, and Hila Shamir, *Governance Feminism: An Introduction* (Minnesota University Press: Minnesota, 2018).

Halpin, Brian W., and Vicki Smith, 'Employment management work: A case study and theoretical framework', in *Work and Occupations*, 44(4), 2017, pp 339–75.

Harding, S. *The Science Question in Feminism* (Open University Press: Milton Keynes, 1986).

Ibid., *The Feminist Standpoint Theory Reader: Intellectual and Political Controversies* (Routledge: New York, 2004).

Harding, S. and K. Norberg, 'New feminist approaches to social science methodologies: An introduction', in *Signs*, 30(4), 2005, pp 2,009–15.

Hari, Amrita, 'Who gets to "work hard, play hard"?: Gendering the work–life balance rhetoric in Canadian tech companies', in *Gender, Work & Organisation*, 24(2), 2017, pp 99–114.

Harris, Patricia, Bev Thiele and Jan Currie, 'Success, gender and academic voices: Consuming passion or selling the soul?', in *Gender and Education*, 10, 1998, pp. 133–48.

Harvey, Brian, 'Are we paying for that', in *Government Funding and Social Justice Advocacy* (Dublin: The Advocacy Initiative 2014)

Harvey, M. and J. Lamond, 'Taking the measure of gender disparity in Australian book reviewing as a field, 1985 and 2013', in *Australian Humanities Review*, 60, 2016, pp 84–107.

Hayes, A. and M. Meagher (eds), A *Century of Progress? Irish Women Reflect* (Arlen House/ Syracuse University Press; Dublin/Syracuse, 2016).

Hayes, Elisabeth, 'Girls, gaming and trajectories of it expertise', in *Beyond Barbie and Mortal Kombat*, edited by Yasmin B. Kafai et al. (MIT Press: Cambridge, Massachusetts, 2011), pp 217–30.

HEA, *Key Facts and Figures: Higher Education 2016/17* (Higher Education Authority: Dublin, 2018).

Hearit, L. B., 'Women on Wall Street', in *The Handbook of Financial Communication and Investor Relations*, 2017, pp 137–44.

Hearne, R. and M. Murphy, *Investing in the Right to a Home: Houses HAP and Hubs* (Maynooth University: Maynooth, 2017).

Heffernan, Elisabeth, 'Poverty and risk the impact of austerity on vulnerable females in Dublin's inner city', in E. Henderson, J. McHale and N. Moore Cherry (eds), *Debating Austerity in Ireland: Crisis Experience and Recovery* (Royal Irish Academy: Dublin, 2017).

Heinz, Manuela, 'The next generation of teachers: An investigation of second-level student teachers' backgrounds in the Republic of Ireland', in *Irish Educational Studies*, 32, 2013, pp 139–56.

Hekman, Susanne, 'Truth and method: Feminist standpoint revised', in Sandra Harding (ed.), *Feminist Standpoint Theory and Reader: Intellectual and Political Controversies* (Routledge: London, 2004), pp 225–42.

Hemmings, Clare, 'Affective solidarity: Feminist reflexivity and political transformation', Special Issue: 'Affecting feminism: Questions of feeling in feminist theory', in *Feminist Theory*, 13(2), 2012, pp 147–61.

Herman, Clem, Suzan Lewis and Anne Laurie Humbert, 'Women scientists and engineers in European companies: Putting motherhood under the microscope', in *Gender, Work and Organization*, 20(5), 2013, pp 116–31.

Herring, Susan, Deborah A. Johnson, and Tamra diBenedetto, '"This is going too far!": Male resistance to female participation on the internet', in Kira Hall and Mary Bucholtz (eds), *Gender Articulated: Language and Socially Constructed Self* (Routledge: Abingdon, Oxon, 1995), pp 67–96.

Herring, Susan, Inna Kouper, Lois Ann Scheidt, and Elijah L. Wright, 'Women and children last: The discursive construction of weblogs', in L. Gurak, S. Antonijevic, L. Johnson, C. Ratliff, & J. Reyman (eds), *Into the Blogosphere: Rhetoric, Community, and Culture of Weblogs*, 2004. Source: http://blog.lib.umn.edu/blogosphere/ Accessed 11 Oct. 2018.

Hesford, W., *Spectacular Rhetorics: Human Rights Vision, Recognition and Feminism* (Duke University Press: Durham, 2011).

Hesmondhalgh, David and Sarah Baker, 'Sex, gender and work segregation in the cultural industries', in *The Sociological Review*, 63(1), 2016, pp 23–36.

Hey, Valerie, 'Affective asymmetries: academics, austerity and the mis/recognition of emotion' *Contemporary Social Science*, 6, 2011, pp 207–22.

Hoard, S., *Gender Expertise in Public Policy: Towards a Theory of Policy Success* (Palgrave Macmillan: Houndsmill, 2015).

Hobson, Barbara (ed.), *Work-Life Balance: The Agency & Capabilities Gap* (Oxford University Press: Oxford, 2014).

Hochschild, Arlie, *The Managed Heart* (University of California Press: Berkeley, 1983).

Hochschild, Arlie and Anne Machung, *The Second Shift: Working Families and the Revolution at Home* (Penguin: New York, 1989).

Holland, Kitty, *Savita: A Tragedy that Shook a Nation* (Transworld: Dublin, 2013).

Ibid., 'Timeline of Ms Y Case', in *The Irish Times*, 04 Oct. 2014. Source: www.irishtimes.com/news/ social-affairs/timeline-of-ms-y-case-1.1951699 Accessed 6 June 2018.

Holt, Helle and Suzan Lewis, '"You can stand on your head and still end up with lower pay": Gliding segregation and gendered work practices in Danish "family-friendly" workplaces', in *Gender, Work & Organization*, 18, 2011, pp e202–21.

Holton, Judith A., 'The coding process and its challenges' in Anthony Bryant and Kathy Charmaz (eds), *The Sage Handbook of Grounded Theory* (Sage: London, 2007), pp 265–89.

Hoskyns, Catherine and Shirin M. Rai, 'Recasting the global political economy: Counting women's unpaid work', in *New Political Economy*, 12(3), 2007.

Hozić, Aida and Jacqui True, *Scandalous Economics: The Politics of Gender and Financial Crises* (Oxford University Press: NY, 2016).

Hu, Jane C., 'The overwhelming gender bias in *New York Times* book reviews', in *Pacific Standard*, 28 Aug. 2017.

Hug, Chrystel, *The Politics of Sexual Morality in Ireland* (Macmillan: London, 1999).

Hughes, C. and C. Sheerin, 'Reflections on the relationship between mentoring, female development and career progression: Investment management versus human resource management', in *International Journal of HRD Practice Policy and Research*, 1(2), 2016, pp 41–54.

Husu, Liisa, 'Gender discrimination in the promised land of gender equality', in *Higher Education in Europe*, 25, 2000, pp 221–8.

Ibid., 'Gate-keeping, gender equality and scientific Eexcellence', in Margo Brouns and Elizabetta Addis (eds), *Gender and Excellence in the Making* (European Commission: Brussels, 2004), pp 69–76.

Ibid., 'Recognize hidden roadblocks. Laboratory life: Scientists of the world speak up for equality', in *Nature*, 495, 2013, pp 35–8.

Hvid, Helge, Henrik Lambrecht Lund and Jan Pejtersen, 'Control, flexibility and rhythms', in *Scandinavian Journal of Work, Environment and Health*, 6, 2008, pp 83–90.

Immigrant Council of Ireland, *Globalisation, Sex Trafficking and Prostitution* (ICI: Dublin, 2009).

Inglis, Tom, 'Origins and legacies of Irish prudery: Sexuality and social control in modern Ireland', in *Éire Ireland*, 40(3–4), (2005), pp 9–37.

Irani, Lilly, 'Hackathons and the making of entrepreneurial citizenship', in *Science, Technology & Human Values*, 2015.

Irish Association for Research in Women's History, *The Women's History Project* (Dublin, est. 1997).

Irish Family Planning Association, *The Irish Journey: Women's Stories of Abortion* (IFPA: Dublin, 2000).

Irish Funds, 'Why Ireland?', 2017. Source: https://files.irishfunds.ie/1489525513-IF_WhyIreland_Brochure_euro_03-2017.pdf, accessed 31 Oct.2018.

Irish Human Rights and Equality Commission, *IHREC CEDAW Submission* (IHREC: Dublin, (2017) Source: www.ihrec.ie/documents/ireland-convention-elimination-forms-discrimination- women/

Jackson, C., 'Framing sex work rights: How US sex worker rights' activists perceive and respond to mainstream anti-sex trafficking advocacy', in *Sociological Perspectives*, 59(1), 2016, pp 27–45.

Jane, E. A., 'Feminist digilante responses to a slut-shaming on Facebook' in *Social Media and Society*, 3(2), 2017, pp 1–10.

Jenkins, Richard, *Being Danish: Paradoxes of Identity in Everyday Life* (Museum Tusculanum Press: Copenhagen, 2012).

Jones, S. A., A. Dy, and N. Vershinia, '"We were fighting for our place": Resisting gender knowledge regimes through feminist knowledge network formation', in *Gender, Work and Organisation*, 26(6), 2019 pp 789–804.

Kafai, Yasmin B. et al., *Diversifying Barbie and Moral Kombat: Intersectional Perspectives and Inclisve Designs in Gaming* (ETC Press: Pittsburgh, PA, 2016).

Kamp, Annette, Henrik Lambrecht Lund, and Helge Søndergaard Hvid, 'Negotiating time, meaning and identity in boundaryless work', in *Journal of Workplace Learning*, 23(4), 2011, pp 229–42.

Kanter, Rosabeth Moss, *Men and Women of the Corporation* (Basic Books: New York, 1977).

Kantola, Johanna and Judith Squires, 'From state feminism to market feminism?', in *International Political Science Review*, 33(4), 2012, pp 382–400.

Kantola, Johanna and Emanuela Lombardo (eds), *Gender and the Economic Crisis in Europe: Politics, Institutions and Intersectionality* (Palgrave MacMillan: Basingstoke, 2017).

Kelan, E., *Performing Gender at Work* (Palgrave: Basingstoke, 2009).

Kemmis, S., and M. Wilkinson, 'Participatory action research and the study of practice', in B. Atweh, S. Kemmis and P. Weeks (eds), *Action Research in Practice: Partnerships for Social Justice in Education* (Routledge: London, 1998).

Kennedy, Helen W., 'Game jam as feminist methodology: The affective labors of intervention in the ludic economy', in *Games and Culture* (Brighton, 2018).

Kennedy, M. and M. J. Power, 'The smokescreen of meritocracy: Elite education in Ireland and the reproduction of class privilege', in *Journal for Critical Education Policy Studies*, 8(2), 2010, pp 222–48.

Kerr, Aphra, '"Girls just want to have fun": Strategies of inclusion: Gender in the information society, 2010, edited by Nelly Oudshoorn et al., *Surveys of Women's Experience* (Centre for Technology and Society NTNU, 2003), pp 211–32.

Ibid., *Global Games: Production, Circulation and Policy in the Networked Age* (Routledge: NY, 2017).

Kerr, Aphra and Anthony Cawley, 'The spatialisation of the digital games industry: Lessons from Ireland', in *International Journal of Cultural Policy*, 2011, pp 1–21.

Kerr, Aphra and John D. Kelleher, 'The recruitment of passion and community in the service of capital: Community managers in the digital games industry', in *Critical Studies in Media Communication*, 32(3), 2015, pp 177–92.

Kerr, Aphra and Seán Ó Riain, 'Knowledge economy', in *International Encyclopedia of Human Geography*, edited by R. Kitchin and N. Thrift (Elsevier: Amsterdam, 2009), pp 31–6.

Kindon, S., R. Pain, and M. Kesby, *Participatory Action Research Approaches and Methods: Connecting People, Participation and Place* (Routledge: London, 2007).

King, R. and N. Mai (eds), 'Love, sexuality and migration', in guest-edited special issue of *Mobilities*, 4(3), 2009, pp 1–10.

Kirby Peadar, and Mary Murphy, *Towards A Second Republic Ireland Politics After the Celtic Tiger* (Pluto Press: London, 2011).

Kohn, Melvin L., 'Occupational structure and alienation', in *American Journal of Sociology*, 82(1), 1976, pp 111–30.

Kossek, E. E., R. Su, and L. Wu, '"Opting out" or "pushed out"? Integrating perspectives on women's career equality for gender inclusion and interventions', in *Journal of Management*, 43(1), 2017, pp 228–54.

Kovats Eszter, 'Questioning consensus: Right-wing populism, anti-populism and the threat of "gender ideology"', in *Sociological Research Online*, 23(2), 2018, pp 528–38.

Krippendorff, Klaus, *Content Analysis: An Introduction to its Methodology* (Sage: California, 1980).

Kuhar, Roman and David Paternotte, *Anti-Gender Campaigns in Europe: Mobilizing Against Equality* (Rowman & Littlefield: London, 2017).

Kultima, Annakaisa, 'Defining game jam', in*10th International Conference on the Foundations of Digital Games* (FDG: California, 2015).

Kumra, S. and S. Vinnicombe, 'Impressing for success: A gendered analysis of a key social capital accumulation strategy', in *Gender, Work & Organisation*, 17(5), 2010, pp 521–46.

Kunda, Gideon, *Engineering Culture: Control and Commitment in a High-Tech Corporation* (Philadelphia: Temple University Press, 2006).

Lantz, S., 'Students working in the Melbourne sex industry: Education, human capital and the changing patterns of the youth labour market', in *Journal of Youth Studies*, 8(4), 2005, pp 385–401.

Leahy, Pat, 'Yes campaign's outreach to middle ground delivered the landslide: Undecideds swung in huge numbers to Yes, as politicians struggled to keep up with pace of change', in *The Irish Times*, Sunday, 27 May 2018.

Ledwith, M., 'On being critical: Uniting theory and practice through emancipatory action research', in *Educational Action Research*, 15(4), 2007, pp 597–611.

Lefevre, J. H., M. Roupret, S. Kerneis, and L. Karila, 'Career choices of medical students: A national survey of 1780 students', in *Medical Education*, 44(6), 2010, pp 603–12.

Lentin, Louis, *Dear Daughter*, television documentary (RTÉ Television: Dublin, 1996).

Lentin, Ronit, 'A woman died: Abortion and the politics of birth in Ireland', in *Feminist Review*, 105, 2013, pp 130–6.

Levy, J., *Criminalising the Purchase of Sex: Lessons from Sweden* (Routledge: London, 2015).

Lewchuk, D. K., 'Collateral consequences: The effects of decriminalizing prostitution on women's equality in business', in *Appeal*, 18(1), 2013, pp 105–63.

Lewis, J., 'The decline of the male breadwinner model: Implications for work and care', in *Social Politics: International Studies in Gender, State & Society*, 8(2), 2001, pp 152–69.

Ibid., 'Gender and the development of welfare regimes', in *Journal of European Social Policy*, 2(3), 1992, pp 159–73.

Lewis, Suzan and Janet Smithson, 'Sense of entitlement for the reconciliation of employment and family life', in *Human Relations*, 54(11), 2001, pp 1,455–81.

Liamputtong, P. and J. Rumbold, (eds), *Knowing Differently: Arts based and Collaborative Research Methods* (Nova Science: New York, 2008).

Lincoln, Y. S. and E. G. Guba, *Naturalistic Inquiry* (Sage: Newbury Park, CA, 1985).

Locke, Ryan et al., 'The game jam movement: Disruption, performance and artwork, in *Proceedings of the 10th International Conference on the Foundations of Digital Games*, 22–25 June 2015 (FDG: California, 2015).

Lombardo, Emanuela, Pietra Meier, and Mieke Verloo, 'Discursive dynamics in gender equality politics: What about "feminist taboos"?' in *European Journal of Women's Studies*, 17(2), 2010, pp 105–23.

Lorey, Isabelle, *State of Insecurity: Government of the Precarious* (Verso Futures: London & New York, 2015).

Luddy, Maria, *Prostitution and Irish Society 1800–1940* (CUP: Cambridge, 2007).

Luibhéid, Eithne, *Pregnant on Arrival: Making the Illegal Immigrant* (University of Minnesota Press: London & Minneapolis, 2013).

Lund, Henrik Lambrecht, Helge Hvid and Annette Kamp, 'Perceived time, temporal order and control in boundaryless work', in Peter Vink and Jussi Kantola (eds), *Advances in Occupational, Social, and Organizational Ergonomics* (Taylor and Francis: Boca Raton, Florida, 2011).

Lutter, M., 'Do women suffer from network closure?: The moderating effect of social capital on gender inequality in a project-based labor market, 1929 to 2010', in *American Sociological Review*, 80(2), 2015, pp 329–58.

Lynch, Kathleen, *The Hidden Curriculum: Reproduction in Education, A Reappraisal* (Falmer Press: London, 1989).

Ibid., *Equality in Education* (Gill and Macmillan: Dublin, 1999).

Lynch, Kathleen, Sara Cantillon and Margaret Crean, 'Inequality', in W. K. Roche, P. J. O'Connell and A. Prohtero (eds), *Austerity and Recovery in Ireland Europe's Poster Child in Recession* (Oxford University Press: Oxford, 2016), pp 252–71.

Lynch, Kathleen, Bernie Grummell, and Dympna Devine, *New Managerialism in Education: Commercialization, Carelessness and Gender* (Palgrave Macmillan: Basingstoke, 2012).

Lynch, Kathleen and Mariya Ivancheva, 'Academic freedom and commercialisation of universities: A critical ethical analysis', in *Ethics in Science and Environmental Politics*, 15, 2015, pp 71–85.

Lynch, Kathleen and Marie Moran, 'Markets, schools and the convertibility of economic capital: The complex dynamics of class choice', in *British Journal of Sociology of Education*, 27(2), 2006, pp 221–35.

Maalsen, Sophia, and Sung-Yueh Perng, 'Crafting code: Gender, coding and spatial hybridity in the events of Pyladies Dublin', in *Craft Economies: Cultural Economies of the Handmade*, edited by S. Luckman and N. Thomas (Bloomsbury: London, 2018).

Madden, L. and J. Levine, *Lyn: A Story of Prostitution* (Attic Press: Cork, 1987).

Maginn, P. and G. Ellison, 'Male sex work in the Irish Republic and Northern Ireland', in V. Minichiello & J. Scott (eds), *Male Sex Work & Society* (Harrington Park Press: New York, 2014).

Maguire, Meg, 'Inside/Outside the Ivory Tower: Teacher education in the English Academy', in *Teaching in Higher Education*, 5(2), 2000, pp 149–65.

Mai, N., '"Too much suffering": Understanding the interplay between migration, bounded exploitation and trafficking through Nigerian sex workers' experiences', in *Sociological Research Online*, 21(4), 2016, p. 13.

Martin, Patricia Yancey, '"Mobilizing masculinities": Women's experiences of men at work', in *Organization*, 8(4), 2001, pp 587–618.

Ibid., '"Said and done" versus "saying and doing": Gendering practices, practicing gender at work', in *Gender and Society*, 17, 2003, pp 342–66.

Ibid., 'Practicing gender at work: Further thoughts on reflexivity', in *Gender Work and Organization*, 13(3), 2006, pp 254–76.

Mayer, Vicki, *Below the Line: Producers and Production Studies in the New Television Economy* (Duke University Press: Durham, 2011).

Mayock, P. and J. Bretherton, *Women's Homelessness in Europe* (Palgrave MacMillan: Basingstoke, 2017).

Mayock, P., S. Sheridan, and S. Parker, *The Dynamics of Long-Term Homelessness among Women in Ireland* (Dublin Regional Homeless Executive: Dublin, 2015).

Mac Cormaic, Ruadhán, *The Supreme Court* (Penguin: Dublin, 2017).

McCoy, Selina and Emer Smyth, 'Higher education expansion and differentiation in the Republic of Ireland', in *Higher Education*, 61, 2011, pp 243–60.

McCracken, Douglas, 'Winning the talent war for women: Sometimes it takes a revolution', in *Harvard Business Review*, 78(6), 2000, pp 159–60, 162, 164–7.

McDowell, L., 'Capital culture revisited: Sex, testosterone and the city', in *International Journal of Urban and Regional Research*, 34(3), 2010, pp 652–8.

Ibid., *Capital Culture: Gender at Work in the City* (Wiley-Blackwell: Oxford, 2011).

McGing, Claire, 'The single transferable vote and women's representation in Ireland', in *Irish Political Studies*, 28(3), 2013, pp 322–40.

McGoey, Linsey, 'The logic of strategic ignorance', in *British Journal of Sociology*, 63(3), 2012, pp 533–76.

McGovern, Jimmy, *Broken*, British television series (BBC: London, 2017).

McKay, Lorraine, and Sue Monk, 'Early career academics learning the game in Whackademia', in *Higher Education Research and Development*, 36(6), 2017, pp 1,251–63.

McKay, Susan, 'Ireland's feminists lost the abortion argument in '83: This time we can win', in *The New York Times*, 5 May 2018.

Maclean, K., 'Gender, risk and the Wall Street alpha male', in *Journal of Gender Studies*, 25(4), 2016, pp 427–44.

McRobbie, Angela, *The Aftermath of Feminism: Gender, Culture and Social Change* (Sage: London, 2008).

MERJ Migrants and Ethnic-minorities for Reproductive Justice 2018 https://www.togetherforyes.ie/together-for-yes-supports-migrants-rights-groups-calling-for-the-removal-of-the-8th-amendment/

Meyer-Lee, Robert J., 'Toward a theory and practice of literary valuing,' in *New Literary History*, 46(2), 2015, pp 335–55.

Miles, M. B. and A. M. Huberman, *Qualitative Data Analysis: An Expanded Sourcebook*, (Sage: Thousand Oaks, CA/London, 1994).

Mills, E., 'Sisterhood costs us jobs', in *The Sunday Times*, 7 Feb. 2010.

Moane, Geraldine and Aideen Quilty, 'Feminist education and feminist community psychology: Experiences from an Irish context', in *Journal of Community Psychology*, 40(1), 2011, pp 145–58.

Moloney, Mary, 'Professional identity in early childhood care and education: Perspectives of pre-school and infant teachers', in *Irish Educational Studies*, 29(2), 2010, pp 167–87.

Montes Lopez, Estrella and Pat O'Connor, 'Micropolitics and meritocracy: Improbable bedfellows?', in *Educational Management Administration and Leadership*, 2018, DOI: 10.1177/1741143218759090.

Moran, Anne, 'Challenges surrounding widening participation and fair access to initial teacher education: Can it be achieved?', in *Journal of Education for Teaching: International Research and Pedagogy*, 34, 2008, pp 63–77.

Moran, R., *Paid For: My Journey through Prostitution* (Gill and Macmillan: Dublin, 2013).

Morley, Louise, *Exploring Professionalism* (Bedford Way Papers: London, 2008).

Ibid., 'Misogyny posing as measurement: Disrupting the feminisation crisis discourse', in *Contemporary Social Science*, 6, 2011, pp 223–35.

Ibid., 'The rules of the game: Women and the leaderist turn in higher education', in *Gender and Education*, 25(1), 2013a, pp 116–31.

Ibid., *Women and Higher Education Leadership: Absences and Aspirations* (Leadership Foundation for Higher Education: London, 2013b).

Ibid., 'Education and neo-liberal globalization', in *British Journal of Sociology of Education*, 3, 2014, pp 457–68.

Morningstar, 2015, 'Morningstar: Fund Managers by Gender', [online] June 2015. Available from: https://corporate.morningstar.com/US/documents/ResearchPapers/Fund-Managers-by-Gender.pdf. Accessed 31 Oct. 2018.

Mortensen, Torill Elvira, 'Anger, fear, and games: The long event of #Gamergate', in *Games and Culture*, 2016.

Messerschmidt J. W. and Patricia Yancey Martin, Michael A. Messner and Raewyn Connell (eds), *Gender Reckonings New Social Theory and Research* (NYU Press: NY, 2018).

Milburn, N. and A. D'Ercole, 'Homeless women: Moving toward a comprehensive model', in *American Psychologist*, 46(11), 1991, pp 1,161–9.

Moen, Phyllis, Jack Lam, Samantha Ammons, and Erin L. Kelly, 'Time work by overworked professionals: Strategies in response to the stress of higher status', in *Work and Occupations*, 40(2), 2013, pp 79–114.

Moen, Phyllis, Anne Kaduk, Ellen Ernst Kossek, Leslie Hammer, Orfeu M. Buxton, Emily O'Donnell, David Almeida, Kimberly Fox, Eric Tranby, J. Michael Oakes and Casper Lynne, 'Is work-family conflict a multilevel stressor linking job conditions to mental health?: Evidence from the work, family and health network', in Samantha K. Ammons and Erin L. Kelly (eds), *Research in the Sociology of Work: Work and Family in the New Economy*, 26, 2015, pp 177–217.

Morfoot, Addie, 'Oscars: Examining gender bias in the documentary categories.' Source: http://variety.com/2016/film/news/gender-bias-documentary-industry-1201708404/

Moss-Racusin, A. Corinne, John F. Dovidio, Victoria L. Brescoll, Mark J. Graham, and Jo Handelsman, 'Science faculty's subtle gender biases favour male students', in *PNAS* 9 Oct. 2012, 109(41), pp 16,474–9.

Mullaly, Siobhan, 'Migrant women destabilising borders: Citizenship debates in Ireland', in *Intersectionality and Beyond: Law, Power and the Politics of Location* (London: Routledge: London, 2008).

Mundy, Liza, 'Why is Silicon Valley so awful to women' in *The Atlantic*, 319(3), 2017, pp 37–61.

Murphy, Mary P., *A Woman's Model of Social Welfare Reform* (NWCI: Dublin, 2003).

Ibid., 'Civil society in the shadow of the Irish State', in *Irish Journal of Sociology*, 19(2), 2011, pp 170–87.

Ibid., 'Gendering the narrative of the Irish crisis', in *Irish Political Studies*, 30(2), 2015, pp 220–37.

Ibid., 'Reflections of an Irish pracademic: Mixing public advocacy, teaching and research?' in *Studies in Social Justice*, 9(1–2), 2016.

Ibid., 'Advancing human rights and equality proofing in Ireland', in *Administration*, 65(3), 2017, pp 59–80.

Ibid. '"Irish flex-insecurity: The reality for low paid workers in Ireland": Women, migrants and young people. Special Issue, Changes in labour markets – impact on welfare states', in *Social Policy & Administration*, 52(2) 2017.

Murphy, Mary P. and Pauline Cullen, *Feminist Response to Austerity in Ireland: Country Case Study* (Rosa Luxembourg Foundation: Brussels, 2018).

Murphy, Mary P. and Rory Hearne, *Participatory Action Capability and Human Rights Approach Draft Methodological Toolkit* (Reinvest: Maynooth, 2016).

National Advisory Committee on Drugs, *Drug Use, Sex Work, and the Risk Environment* (NACD: Dublin, 2009).

National Women's Council of Ireland (NWCI), 'Affordable, accessible healthcare options for women and girls in Ireland', in *Every Woman* (Dublin, Nov. 2018).

Neale, J. 'Homelessness and theory revisited', in *Housing Studies*, 12(1), 1997, pp 47–61.

Negra, Diane and Yvonne Tasker, *Gendering the Recession: Media and Culture in an Age of Austerity* (Duke University Press: Durham, 2014).

Neuman, W., *Social Research Methods: Qualitative and Quantitative Approaches, 7th edn* (Pearson: Boston, 2011).

Newman, Janet, 'Spaces of power: Feminism, neoliberalism and gendered labor', in *Social Politics Social Politics: International Studies in Gender, State & Society*, 20(2). 2013, pp 200–21.

Nielsen, Mathias Wullum, 'Limits to meritocracy?: Gender in academic recruitment and promotion processes', in *Science and Public Policy*, 43(3), 2016, pp 386–99.

North-Samardzic, A. and L. Taksa, 'The impact of gender culture on women's career trajectories: An Australian case study', in *Equality, Diversity and Inclusion: An International Journal*, 30(3), 2011, pp 196–216.

Nussbaum, M. C., 'Capabilities, entitlements, rights: Supplementation and critique', in *Journal of Human Development and Capabilities: A Multi-Disciplinary Journal for People-Centered Development*, 12(1), 2011, pp 23-37.

Oakley, A., 'Interviewing women: A contradiction in terms', in H. Roberts, *Doing Feminist Research* (Routledge: London & New York, 1981).

Oaks, Laury, 'Irishness, Eurocitizens, and reproductive rights', in *Reproducing Reproduction* (University of Pennsylvania Press: Philadelphia, 1997).

O'Brien, Anne, '"Men own television": why women leave media work', in *Media, Culture & Society*, 36(8), 2014, pp 1,207–18.

Ibid., '"It's a man's world": A qualitative study of the (non) mediation of women and politics on *Prime Time* during the 2011 General Election', in *Irish Political Studies*, 29(4), 2014, pp 505–21.

Ibid., 'Producing television and reproducing gender', in *Television & New Media* 16(3), 2015, pp 259–74.

Ibid., '(Not) getting the credit: Women, liminal subjectivity and resisting neoliberalism in documentary production', in *Media, Culture & Society*, 40(5), 2018, pp 673–88.

Ibid., *Women, Inequality and Media Work* (Routledge; London & New York, 2019).

O'Carroll, Aileen, *Working Time, Knowledge Work and Post-Industrial Society: Unpredictable Work* (Palgrave MacMillan: New York, 2015).

O'Connor, Monica and Grainne Healy, *The Links between Prostitution and Sex Trafficking: A Briefing Handbook* (CATW/European Women's Lobby: Dublin, 2006).

O'Connor, Muiris, *Sé Sí: Gender in Irish Education* (Department of Education and Science with Brunswick Press: Dublin, 2007).

O'Connor, Pat, *Emerging Voices: Women in Contemporary Irish Society* (Institute of Public Administration: Dublin, 1999).

Ibid., 'Reflections on a public intellectual's role in a gendered society', in Mary P. Corcoran and Kevin Lalor (eds), *Reflections on Crisis: The Role of the Public Intellectual* (Royal Irish Academy: Dublin, 2012), pp 55–76.

Ibid., *Management and Gender in Higher Education* (Manchester University Press: Manchester, 2014).

Ibid., 'Understanding success: A case study of gendered change in the professoriate', in *Journal of Higher Education Policy and Management*, 36(2), 2014, pp 212–24.

Ibid., 'Good jobs – but places for women?', in *Gender and Education*, 2015, p. 27; pp 304–19.

O'Connor, Pat and Anita Goransson, 'Constructing or rejecting the notion of the Other in university management: The cases of Ireland and Sweden', in *Educational Management Administration and Leadership*, 43(2), 2015, pp 323–40.

O'Connor, Pat, Clare O'Hagan and Julia Brannen, 'Exploration of masculinities in academic organisations: A tentative typology using career and relationship commitment', *Current Sociology*, 63(4), 2015, pp 528–46.

O'Connor, Pat and Clare O'Hagan, 'Excellence in university academic staff evaluation: A problematic reality?', in *Studies in Higher Education*, 41(11), 2016, pp 1,943–57.

O'Connor, Pat et al., 'Micro-political practices in Higher Education: A challenge to excellence as a rationalising Myth?', in *Critical Studies in Education*, 2017, pp 1–17.

O'Donoghue, Tom, Judith Harford, and Teresa O'Doherty, *Teacher Preparation in Ireland: History, Policy and Future Directions* (Emerald Publishing: Bingley, UK, 2017).

OECD, *Report on the Gender Initiative: Gender Equality in Education, Employment and Entrepreneurship* (OECD: Paris, 2011).

Ó Fátharta, Conall, 'Bessborough death record concerns were raised in 2012', in *The Irish Examiner*, 2 June 2015.

O'Hagan, Clare, *Complex Inequality and Working Mothers* (Cork University Press: UCC Cork, 2015).

O'Hagan, Clare, Pat O'Connor, Eva Sophia Myers et al., 'Perpetuating academic capitalism and maintaining gender orders through career practices in STEM in Universities', in *Critical Studies in Education*, 2016, DOI 10.1080/17508487.2016.1238403.

Oireachtas Bill to establish the referendum on the Eighth Amendment https://www.oireachtas.ie/en/debates/debate/dail/2018-03-20/10/ (2017)

O'Keefe, Theresa, *Feminist Identity Development and Activism in Revolutionary Movements* (Palgrave Macmillan: London, 2013).

Olshansky, E. et al., 'Participatory action research to understand and reduce health disparities', in *Nursing Outlook*, 53, 2005, pp 121–6.

Oram, Alison, *Women Teachers and Feminist Politics, 1900–1939* (Manchester University Press: Manchester, 1996).

O'Reilly, Emily, *Masterminds of the Right* (Attic Press: Cork, 1992).

Ó Riain, Seán, 'Time space intensification: Karl Polanyi, the double movement and global informational capitalism', in *Theory and Society*, 35, 2006, pp 507–28.

Ibid., 'The missing customer and the ever-present market: Software work in the service economy', in *Work and Occupations*, 37, 2010, pp 320–48.

O' Sullivan, Sara, '"All Changed, Changed Utterly"?: Gender role attitudes and the feminisation of the Irish labour force', in *Women's Studies International Forum*, 35(4), 2012, pp 223–32.

Ozga, Jenny, *Schoolwork: Approaches to the Labour Process of Teaching* (Open University Press: Milton Keynes, 1988).

Padgett, Deborah K., *Qualitative Methods in Social Work* 2nd edn (Sage: New York, 2008).

Palmer, C., '"A job, old boy?" The school ties that still bind', in *The Observer* [online], 11 June 2000. Available from: www.guardian.co.uk/money/2000/jun/11/workandcareers. madeleinebunting2> Accessed 31 Oct. 2018.

Parkin, F., *The Social Analysis of Class Structure* (Routledge: London, 1974).

Paternotte, David and Roman Kuhar, 'Disentangling and locating the "global right": Anti-gender campaigns in Europe' in *Politics and Governance*, 6(3), 2018, pp 6–19.

Paying for Sex: Reality Bites, television documentary (RTÉ: Dublin, 2016).

Pereira, Maria do Mar, *Power, Knowledge and Feminist Scholarship: An Ethnography of Academia* (Routledge, 2017).

Perlow, Leslie A., 'The time famine: Toward a Sociology of work time', in *Administrative Science Quarterly*, 44(1), 1999, pp 57–81.

Perng, Sung-Yueh et al., 'Hackathons, entrepreneurship and the passionate making of smart cities', The Programmable City Project (Maynooth University: Maynooth, 31 Mar. 2017).

Petchesky, Rosalind Pollack, *Abortion and Woman's Choice: The State, Sexuality, and Reproductive Freedom* (Northeastern University Press: Boston, 1990).

Peterson, Helen and Birgitta Jordansson, 'Gender equality as a core academic value: Undoing gender in a "non-traditional" Swedish university', in Kate White and Pat O'Connor (eds), *Gendered Success in Higher Education: Global Perspectives* (Palgrave Macmillan: London, 2017), pp 27–48.

Pillinger, Jane, *Improving the Representation of Women on the TUI Executive Committee* (TUI: Dublin, 2010).

Plummer, K., 'Telling sexual stories in a late modern world' in *Studies in Symbolic Interactionism*, 18, 1995, pp 1,012–120.

Ibid., 'Narrative power, sexual stories and the politics of story telling', in I. Goodson (ed.), *The International Handbook on Life History and Narratives* (Routledge: Abingdon, 2017).

Poletti, A. 'Coaxing an intimate sphere: Life narrative in digital story telling', in *Journal of Media & Cultural Studies*, 25(1), 2011, pp 73–83.

Polletta, F. and P. C. B. Chen, 'Gender and public talk: Accounting for women's variable participation in the public sphere', in *Sociological Theory*, 13(4), 2013, pp 291–317.

Powell, A. and K. J. Sang, 'Everyday experiences of sexism in male-dominated professions: A Bourdieusian perspective', in *Sociology*, 49(5), 2015, pp 919–36.

Prentice, Susan, 'The conceptual politics of chilly climate controversies', in *Gender and Education*, 12(2), 2000, pp 195–207.

Preston, Paschal et al., 'Digital media sector innovation in the knowledge economy: Rethinking knowledge inputs and policies', in *Information, Communication and Society*, 12(7), 2009, pp 994–1,014.

Prügl, Elisabeth, '"If Lehman Brothers had been Lehman Sisters…": Gender and myth in the aftermath of the financial crisis.', in *International Political Sociology*, 6(1), 2012, pp 21–35.

Ibid., 'Neoliberalising feminism', in *New Political Economy*, 20(4), 2015, pp 614–31.

Ibid., 'Neoliberalism with a feminist face: Crafting a new hegemony at the World Bank', in *Feminist Economics*, 23(1), 2017, pp 30–53.

Prunty, Jacinta, *The Monasteries, Magdalen Asylums and Reformatory Schools of Our Lady of Charity in Ireland, 1853–1973* (Columba Press: Dublin, 2017).

Pryce, P. and R. Sealy, 'Promoting women to MD in investment banking: Multi-level influences', in *Gender in Management: An International Journal*, 28(8), 2013, pp 448–67.

Publishers' Weekly, 'Where the boys are not' 20 Sept., 2010.

Pullen, A., C. Rhodes, and T. Thanem, 'Affective politics in gendered organisations: Affirmative notes on becoming-woman', in *Organisation*, 24(1), 2017, pp 105–23.

PwC, 2017, 'Global assets under management set to rise to $145.4 trillion by 2025', available from: <https://press.pwc.com/News-releases/global-assets-under-management-set-to-rise-to--145.4-trillion-by-2025/s/e236a113-5115-4421-9c75-77191733f15f>, accessed 31 Oct. 2018

Quilty, Aideen, Sinéad Kennedy, and Catherine Conlon (eds), *The Abortion Papers Ireland: Volume II* (Cork University Press: Cork, 2015).

Raddon, Arwen, 'Mothers in the academy: Positioned and positioning within discourses of the "successful academic" and the "good mother"', in *Studies in Higher Education*, 27(4), 2002, pp 387–403.

Raferty, Mary and Eoin O'Sullivan, *Suffer the Little Children* (Bloomsbury: London, 2002).

Rafnsdóttir, Gudbjörg Linda and Thamar M. Heijstra, 'Balancing work-family life in academia: The power of time', in *Gender, Work and Organization*, 20(3), 2011, pp 283–96.

Rafter, Kevin, 'Voices in the crisis: The role of media elites in interpreting Ireland's banking collapse', in *European Journal of Communication*, 29(5), 2014, pp 598–607.

Ramaswami, A., N. M. Carter, and G. F. Dreher, 'Expatriation and career success: A human capital perspective', in *Human Relations*, 69, 2016, pp 1,959–87.

Ranson, Gillian, ' No longer one of the boys"': Negotiations with motherhood as prospect or reality among women in engineering', in *Canadian Review of Sociology*, 42(2), 2005, pp 45–66.

Reason, P. and H. Bradbury (eds), *The SAGE Handbook of Action Research: Participative Inquiry and Practice* 2nd edn (SAGE: London, 2008).

Reay, Diane, 'Gendering Bourdieu's concepts of capitals? Emotional capital, women and social class', in *The Sociological Review*, 52, 2004, pp 57–74.

Redmond, Jennifer and Judith Harford, '"One man, one job": The marriage ban and the employment of women teachers in Irish primary schools', in *Pedagogica Historica*, 46(5), 2010, pp 639–54.

Repeal the Eighth, Oct. 2017 https://www.repealeight.ie/1983-2017-trapped-in-time/

Repo, J. and R. Yrjölä, 'The gender politics of celebrity humanitarianism in Africa', in *International Feminist Journal of Politics*, 13(1), 2011, pp 44–62.

Report of the Inter-Departmental Committee to Establish the Facts of State Involvement with the Magdalen Laundries (the McAleese Committee), (Department of Justice and Equality: Dublin, 2013).

Rhoton, Laura A., 'Distancing as a gendered barrier: Understanding women scientists gender practices', in *Gender and Society*, 25(6), 2011, pp 696–716.

Richardson, Diane, 'Conceptualising gender', in V. Robinson and D. Richardson (eds), *Introducing Gender and Women's Studies* (Palgrave Macmillan: Basingstoke, 2015), pp 3–22.

Richardson, Ita, 'Gender audit of Science, Engineering and Technology staff and researchers at the University of Limerick', Final Report (UL: Limerick, 2008).

Ridgeway, Cecilia, 'Framed before we know it: How gender shapes social relations', in *Gender and Society*, 23(2), Apr. 2009, pp 145–60.

Ibid., *Framed By Gender: How Gender Inequality Persists in the Modern World* (Oxford University Press: Oxford, 2011).

Rivera, L. A., *Pedigree: How Elite Students Get Elite Jobs* (Princeton University Press: Princeton, 2016).

Roberts, Adrienne, The political economy of 'transnational business feminism', in *International Feminist Journal of Politics*, 17(2), 2015, pp 209–31.

Roberts, R., S. Bergstrom, and D. La Rooy, 'Sex work and students: An exploratory study', in *Journal of Further and Higher Education*, 31(4), 2007, pp 323–34.

Rossiter, Ann, *Ireland's Hidden Diaspora: The 'Abortion Trail' and the Making of the London-Irish Underground, 1980–2000* (Iasc Publishing: London, 2009).

Roth, L. M., *Selling Women Short: Gender and Money on Wall Street* (Princeton University Press: Princeton, NJ, 2006).

Rottenberg, Catherine, 'Women who work: The limits of the neoliberal feminist paradigm', in *Gender Work and Organization*, 2018, pp 1–10.

Rowe, T. and A. Crafford, 'A study of barriers to career advancement for professional women in investment banking', in *South African Journal of Human Resource Management*, 1(2), 2003, pp 21–7.

Royal Irish Academy, 'The Royal Irish Academy's submission to the STEM Education Review Group', Advice Paper no 3/2014 Source https://www.ria.ie/sites/default/files/academy-advice-paper-3-submission-to-the-national-stem-review-group_0.pdf

RTÉ Archives, 'Newspaper Pulled Over Abortion Services Ad 1992' Source: https://www. rte.ie/archives/2017/0518/876228-guardian-newspaper-withheld-from-sale/ Accessed 24 Jun. 2019.

RTE & Behaviour & Attitudes Exit Poll, 'Thirty-Sixth Amendment to the Constitution Exit Poll 25th May 2018'. Available at https://static.rasset.ie/documents/news/2018/05/rte-exit-poll-final-11pm.pdf Accessed 17 Oct. 2018.

Ruiz Ben, Esther, 'Defining expertise in software development while doing gender', in *Gender, Work & Organization*, 14(4), 2007, pp 312–32.

Russell, Helen, Frances McGinnity, Tim Callan, and Claire Keane, *A Woman's Place?: Female Participation in the Irish Labour Market* (Equality Authority in association with The Economic and Social Research Institute: Dublin, 2009).

Russell, Helen, Emer Smyth, and Philip J. O'Connell, 'Gender differences in pay among recent graduates: Private sector employees in Ireland', in *Journal of Youth Studies*, 13(2), 2010, pp 212–33.

Russell, Helen., , Frances McGinnity, and Gillian Kingston, *Gender and the Quality of Work: From Boom to Recession* (ESRI and The Equality Authority: Dublin, 2014).

Russell, Helen, Frances McGinnity, and Philip J. O'Connell, 'Gender equality in the labour market 1966–2016: Unfinished Business?', in *The Economic and Social Review*, 48(4), 2017, pp 393–418.

Rutherford, Sarah, 'Are you going home already?: The long hours culture, women managers and patriarchal closure', in *Time and Society*, 10(2–3), 2001, pp 259–76.

Ibid., 'Gendered organisational cultures, structures and processes: The cultural exclusion of women in organisations', in *Gender in Organisations: Are Men Allies or Adversaries to Women's Career Advancement* (Edward Elgar: Cheltenham, 2014), pp 193–216.

Ryan, Mary, 'A feminism of their own?: Irish women's history and contemporary Irish women's writing', in *Estudios Irlandeses*, 5, 2010, pp 92–101.

Ryan, Paul, 'Researching Irish gay male lives: Reflections on disclosure and intellectual autobiography in the production of personal narratives', in *Qualitative Research*, 6(2), 2006, pp 151–68.

Ibid., '#Follow: Exploring the role of social media in the online construction of male sex workers' lives in Dublin, Ireland', in *Gender, Place and Culture*, 23(12), 2016, pp 1,713–24.

Ibid., *Male Sex Work in the Digital Age: Curated Lives* (Palgrave: London, 2019).

Ryan, P., and S. Huschke, 'Conducting sex work research in a politically contentious climate: Lessons from Ireland', in I. Crowhurst, A. King and A. C. Santos (eds), *Sexuality Research: Critical Interjections, Diverse Methodologies and Practical Applications* (Routledge: London, 2017).

Ryan, P., and E. Ward, 'Ireland', in S. O. Jahnsen, and H. Wagenaar (eds), *Assessing Prostitution Policies in Europe* (Routledge: London, 2017).

Ryan, Richard M., and Edward L. Deci, 'Self-regulation and the problem of human autonomy: Does psychology need choice, self-determination, and will?', in *Journal of Personality*, 74(6), 2006, pp 1,557–85.

Ryan Commission, The,*Commission to Inquire into Child Abuse* (Stationery Office: Dublin, 2009).

Sandberg, S., *Lean In: Women, Work, and the Will to Lead* (Random House: NY, 2013).

Sanders, T. and K. Hardy, 'Students selling sex: Marketisation, higher education and consumption', in *British Journal of the Sociology of Education*, 36(5), 2013, pp 747–65.

Sanger, Carol, *About Abortion: Terminating Pregnancy in Twenty-First Century America* (Harvard University Press: Cambridge Mass., 2017).

Savage, M. 'Gendering women's homelessness', in *Irish Journal of Applied Social Studies*, 16(2), 2016.

Scally, Gabriel, 'Scoping inquiry into the CervicalCheck Screening Programme', Final Report Sept. 2018. Available at http://scallyreview.ie/wp-content/uploads/2018/09/Scoping-Inquiry-into-CervicalCheck-Final-Report.pdf Accessed 18 Oct. 2018.

Scharff, Christina, 'The psychic life of neoliberalism: Mapping the contours of entrepreneurial subjectivity', in *Theory, Culture and Society*, 33(6), 2016, pp 107–22.

Schatzki, Theodore R, 'Introduction: Practice theory', in Theodore R. Schatzki, Karin Knorr Cetina and Eike Von Savigny (eds), *The Practice Turn in Contemporary Theory* (Routledge: New York, 2001), pp 10–23.

Schieman, Scott, Melissa A. Milkie, and Paul Glavin, 'When work interferes with life: Work-Nonwork interference and the influence of work-related demands and resources', in *American Sociological Review*, 74(6), 2009, pp 966–88.

Schilt, K., and C. Connell, 'Do workplace gender transitions make gender trouble?', in *Gender, Work, & Organisation*, 14(6), 2007, pp 596–618.

Schudson, Michael, 'How culture works: Perspectives from media studies on the efficacy of symbols', in *Theory and Society*, 18(2), Mar. 1989, pp 153–80.

Schweppe, Jennifer, 'Introduction', in J. Schweppe (ed.), *The Unborn child, Article 40.3.3 and Abortion in Ireland: 25 Years of Protection?* (Liffey Press: Dublin, 2008).

Ibid., *Article 40.3.3° and Abortion in Ireland* (Liffey Press: Dublin, 2015).

Sealy, R., 'A qualitative examination of the importance of female role models in investment banks', PhD thesis (Cranfield University: Bedford, 2009).

Ibid., 'Changing perceptions of meritocracy in senior women's careers', in *Gender in Management: An International Journal*, 25(3), 2010, pp 184–97.

Sen, Amartya, *Development as Freedom* (Alfred A. Knopf Inc.: New York, 1999).

Sennett, Richard, *The Corrosion of Character: The Personal Consequences of Work in the New Capitalism* (W. W. Norton & Co.: New York, 1998).

Shaw, Adrienne, 'Do you identify as a gamer? Gender, race, sexuality, and gamer identity', in *New Media & Society*, 14(1), 2012, pp 28–44..

Shih, Johanna, 'Circumventing discrimination: Gender and ethnic strategies in Silicon Valley', in *Gender and Society*, 20(2), 2004, pp 177–206.

Ibid., 'Project time in Silicon Valley', in *Qualitative Sociology*, 27(2), 2004, pp 223–45.

Siegrist, Johannes, 'Adverse health effects of high-effort/low-reward conditions', in *Journal of Occupational Health Psychology*, 1(1), 1996, pp 27–41.

Siggins, Lorna, 'RTÉ told us our abortion film lacked balance', in The *Irish Times*, 11 Apr. 2016. Source: https://www.irishtimes.com/life-and-style/people/rté-told-us-our-abortion-film- lacked-balance-1.2602308 Accessed 27 July 2018

Sixsmith, Martin, *The Lost Child of Philomena Lee* (Penguin: London, 2009).

Skeggs, B., *Feminist Cultural Theory: Process and Production* (Manchester University Press: Manchester, 1995).

Smith, D. E., *The Conceptual Practices of Power: A Feminist Sociology of Knowledge* (Northeastern University Press: Boston, 1990).

Smith, J. M., *Ireland's Magdalen Laundries and the Nation's Architecture of Containment* (Manchester University Press: Manchester, 2007).

Smith, Vicki, 'New forms of work organization', in *Annual Review of Sociology*, 23, 1997, pp 315–39.

Smith, Chris, and Alan McKinlay, *Creative Labour: Working in the Creative Industries* (Palgrave Macmillan: Basingstoke, 2009).

Social Justice Ireland, 'Time to stop paying lip service to notions of gender equality, and start investing', Source: www.socialjustice.ie/content/policy-issues/time-stop-paying-lip-service-notions-gender-equality-and-start-investing Accessed 2019.

Soe, Louise and Elaine Yakura, 'What's wrong with the pipeline?: Assumptions about gender and culture in IT work', in *Women's Studies*, 37(3), 2008, pp 176–201.

Stachowitsch, Saskia, 'Beyond "market" and "state" feminism: Gender knowledge at the intersections of marketization and securitization', in *Politics & Gender*, 15(1) 2019, pp 151–73.

Statistics Denmark, *Statistical Yearbook 2017* (Statistics Denmark: Copenhagen, 2017).

Steiner, Linda, 'Glassy architectures in journalism', in Cynthia Carter (ed.), *The Routledge Companion to Media and Gender* (Routledge: London & New York, 2015), pp 620–31.

STEM Education Review Group, *STEM Education in the Irish School System* (Department of Education and Skills: Dublin, 2016).

Stubbs Richardson, M., N. E. Rader and A. G. Cosby, 'Tweeting rape culture: Examining portrayals of victim blaming of sexual assaults on Twitter', in *Feminism & Psychology*, 28(1), 2018, pp 90–108.

Sturdy, Andrew, Timothy Clark, Robin Fincham, and Karen Handley, 'Between innovation and legitimation-boundaries and knowledge flow in management consultancy', in *Organisation*, 16(5), 2009, pp 627–53.

Sweeney, Brendan, 'Producing liminal space: Gender, age and class in Northern Ontario's tree planting industry', in *Gender, Pace and Culture*, 16(5), 2009, pp 569–86.

Tajlili, M. H., 'A framework for promoting women's career intentionality and work–life integration', in *The Career Development Quarterly*, 62(3), 2014, pp 254–67.

Tannen, D., 'The double bind', in S. Morrison (ed.), *Thirty Ways of Looking at Hillary* (Harper Collins: New York, NY, 2008), pp 126–39.

Taylor, Nicholas et al., 'Cheerleaders/booth babes/*halo* hoes: Pro-gaming, gender and jobs for the boys', in *Digital Creativity*, 20(4), 2009, pp 239–52.

Teljeur, C. and T. O'Dowd, 'The feminisation of general practice: Crisis or business as usual', in *The Lancet*, 374(9,696), 2009, p. 1,147.

The 30% Club National Women's Strategy Submission, 2017a.

The 30% Club Gender Pay Gap Submission, 2017b.

The 30% Club Information Booklet, 2018.

Thompson, Paul, 'Disconnected capitalism: Or why employers can't keep their side of the bargain', in *Work, Employment and Society*, 17(2), 2003, pp 359–78.

Thornton, Margaret, 'The mirage of merit', in *Australian Feminist Studies*, 28, 2013, pp 127–43.

Time Magazine, 2018.

Together for Yes, 'The National campaign to remove the Eighth Amendment', Source: www.togetherforyes.ie/about-us/who-we-are/, 2018.

Trowler, Paul, and Roni Bamber, 'Compulsory higher education teacher training: Joined up policies, institutional architectures and enhancement cultures', in *International Journal for Academic Development*, 10(2), 2005, pp 79–93.

Truss, Catherine, Edel Conway, Alessia d'Amato, Gráinne Kelly, Kathy Monks, Enda Hannon, and Patrick C. Flood, 'Knowledge work: Gender-blind or gender-biased?', in *Work, Employment & Society*, 26(5), 2012, pp 735–54.

Turner, Victor W., *From Ritual to Theatre: The Human Seriousness at Play* (Performing Arts Journal: New York, 1982).

United Nations Human Rights Committee, 'Concluding observations on the Fourth Periodic Report of Ireland', CCPR//C/IRL/CO/4, para 11, 19 Aug. 2014.

Urry, John, 'Small worlds and the new "social physics"', in *Global Networks*, 4, 2004, pp 109–30.

Ursell, Gillian, 'Television production: Issues of exploitation, commodification and subjectivity in UK television labour markets', in *Media, Culture & Society*, 22(6), 2000, pp 805–25.

Van den Brink, Marieke and Yvonne Benschop, 'Slaying the seven-headed dragon: The quest for gender change in academia', in *Gender, Work & Organization*, 19, 2012, pp 71–92.

Ibid., 'Gender in academic networking: The role of gatekeepers in professorial recruitment', in *Journal of Management Studies*, 51(3), 2014, pp 460–92.

Valian, Virginia, 'Beyond gender schemas: Improving the advancement of women in academia', *Hypatia*, 20(3), 2005, pp 198–213.

Valilius, Maryann Gialanella, 'Defining their role in the new State: Irishwomen's protest against the Juries Act of 1927', in *Canadian Journal of Irish Studies*, 18(1), 1992, pp 43–60.

Van Gennep, Arnold, *The Rites of Passage* (University of Chicago Press: Chicago, 1960).

Vázquez-Cupeiro, Susana, and Mary Ann Elston, 'Gender and academic career trajectories in Spain: From gendered passion to consecration in a sistema endogámico?', in *Employee Relations*, 28(6), 2006, pp 588–603.

Verloo, M., *Varieties of Opposition to Gender Equality in Europe* (Routledge: London, 2018).

Volpe, M., and D. Chandler, 'Resolving and managing conflicts in academic communities: The emerging role of the "pracademic"', in *Negotiation Journal*, 17(3), 2001, pp 245–55.

Wade, Lisa, and Myra Marx Ferree, *'Gender Ideas, Interactions, Institutions* (W. W. Norton Publishing: NY, 2018).

Wajcman, Judith, *Managing Like a Man: Women and Men in Corporate Management* (Polity Press in association with Blackwell Publishers Ltd.: Cambridge, 1998).

Ibid., *Techno Feminism* (Polity: Cambridge, 2004).

Ibid., 'Feminist theories of technology', in *Cambridge Journal of Economics*, 34(1), 2010, pp 143–52.

Ibid., *Pressed for Time: The Acceleration of Life in Digital Capitalism* (University of Chicago Press: Chicago: 2015).

Walby, Sylvia, 'Is the knowledge society gendered', in *Gender, Work & Organization*, 18(1), 2011, pp 1–29.

Walker, Judith, 'Time as the fourth dimension in the globalization of higher education', in *The Journal of Higher Education*, 80, 2009, pp 483–509.

Walton, Richard E., 'From control to commitment in the workplace', in *Harvard Business Review*, 63(2), 1986, pp 76–84.

Ward, Margaret, *Unmanageable Revolutionaries: Women and Irish Nationalism* (Pluto Press: London, 1996).

Ward, E., 'Prostitution and the Irish State: From prohibitionism to a globalised sex trade', in *Irish Political Studies*, 25(1), 2017, pp 47–66.

Ibid., 'The Irish Parliament and prostitution law reform: A neo-abolitionist shoe-in?', in E. Ward and G. Wylie (eds), *Feminism, Prostitution and the State: The Politics of Neo-Abolitionism* (Routledge: London, 2017).

Ward, Peter, 'Report to the Minister for Education and Skills of the Chairperson of the Expert Group on fixed-term and part-time employment in Primary and Second-Level Education in Ireland', 2014, Source: www.ictu.ie/download/pdf/ward_report.pdf

Weber, L., 'Go ahead, hit the snooze button', in *Wall Street Journal* [online], 23 Jan,. 2013. Source: www.wsj.com/articles/SB10001424127887323301104578257894191502654> Accessed 31 Oct. 2018.

Weber, Robert Philip, *Basic Content Analysis* 2nd edn (Sage: Newbury Park, CA, 1990).

West, C., and D. H. Zimmerman, 'Doing gender', in *Gender & Society*, 1(2), 1987, pp 125–51.

Whalley, E., and C. Hackett, 'Carceral feminisms: The abolitionist project and undoing dominant feminisms', in *Contemporary Justice Review*, 20(4), 2017, pp 456–73.

White, Kate, *Keeping Women in Science* (Melbourne University Press: Melbourne, 2014).

Williams, Christine, 'The glass escalator, revisited: Gender inequality in neoliberal times', in *Gender & Society*, 27(5), 2013, pp 609–29.

Wilson, F. M., *Organisational Behaviour and Gender* (Routledge: London, 2017).

Women's Budget Group Intersecting Inequalities, 2017.

Women Help Women, 'In solidarity with Repeal the 8th! Referendum in Ireland on May 25th!', in *Women Help Women Blog*. 10 Apr. (2018), Source: https://womenhelp.org/en/page/900/in-solidarity-with-repeal-the-8th-referendum-in-ireland-on-may-25th Accessed 27 July 2018.

Women in Publishing, *Reviewing the Reviews: A Woman's Place on the Book Page* (Journeyman Press: London, 1987).

Yeager, J. and J. Culleton, 'Gendered violence and cultural forgetting: The case of the Irish Madgalenes', in *Radical History Review*, 126, 2016, pp 134–46.

Young, Iris Marion, 'Feminism and the public sphere', in *Constellations*, 3(3), 1997, pp 340–63.

Young, B. and C. Scherrer (eds), *Gender Knowledge and Knowledge Networks in International Political Economy* (Nomos: Baden-Baden, 2010).

Young, Michael F. D., *Knowledge and Control: New Directions for the Sociology of Education* (Collier: Macmillan: London, 1971).

Youth and Children's Affairs, Department of, 'Commission of Investigation into Mother and Baby Homes and Certain Related Matter', ongoing, five interim reports published (Dublin, 2015).

Index